COMMERCIALIZING NEW TECHNOLOGIES

COMMERCIALIZING NEW TECHNOLOGIES

Getting from Mind to Market

Vijay K. Jolly

HARVARD BUSINESS SCHOOL PRESS

Boston, Massachusetts

Library of Congress Cataloging-in-Publication Data

Jolly, Vijay K.
    Commercializing new technologies : getting from mind to market /
  Vijay K. Jolly.
      p. cm.
    Includes index.
    ISBN 0-87584-760-9 (alk. paper)
    1. Inventions—Marketing.   I. Title.
  T339.J58   1997
  658.5'75—DC21   96-48032
                                                  CIP

Contents

Acknowledgments

"STAND UP AND LIVE BEFORE YOU SIT DOWN AND WRITE!" IS AN ADMONITION that applies to many fields—particularly to technology commercialization. What we know about this field comes mostly from the experience of innovators—from their joy and anguish in discovering something new and their frustrations and rewards in commercializing it. Straddling the rational world of technology and the complex socioeconomic forces at work in the market, technology commercialization does not easily lend itself to elegant generalizations. Indeed, when asked to draw some general lessons from their experience in bringing a new technology to the market, most people are at a loss themselves. "My case was unique," they are likely to say. They recall the uncertainties they encountered all along, the accidents, the fortuitous combination of events, the intransigence of colleagues, and the solutions that had to be found, often in extremis, which they doubt have parallels elsewhere. None of this lends confidence to building a post facto theory.

The elusive nature of the process, combined with its economic importance, has captivated many to research it. My own interest in bringing new technologies to market goes back some fifteen years, when I launched a seminar on the marketing of technology at the International Management Institute (IMI) in Geneva. During this time I was fortunate enough to observe from close up about a dozen cases of companies formulating and trying to implement strategies to exploit a new technological capability. The variety was enormous. Some were start-up companies, others new ventures within large companies. They covered a broad spectrum of technologies and represented varying degrees of market readiness.

The uniqueness of each case challenged comprehension. The published literature on the subject helped, but it consisted mainly of *how* things should be done generally, not *what* should be done in a particular case. Wanting to know more about the *what,* I widened the net, collecting more cursory information on another twenty cases by interviewing managers who had been involved in them and following press reports. Gradually, some generalizable concepts began to form that I found useful. I hope others will too.

Through it all, others took the risk while I learned. It is these inventors and executives to whom I would like to acknowledge my biggest debt. To give credit to all of them would make for an inconveniently long list. I would, however, like to single out the following:

John Benjamin and his colleagues at Alcoa; Greg Smith, Clifford Ballard, James Yardley, and Krish Rao at AlliedSignal, Inc., for encouragements and updates over a five-year period; Gordon Binder and his colleagues at Amgen, Inc., for an introduction to the biotechnology industry in 1989; Masaru Ozaki of Asahi Chemical; Anthony Pottage, Håkan Björklund, Christer Carling, and several others at Astra AB; Robert Kerwin of AT&T Bell Laboratories; Roland Belz and Roman Kainz of Belland AG for giving me a ringside seat on their work; Linda Capuano of Conductus, Inc.; Tom Cross and Brian Cronin of Diamond Shamrock Technologies SA; Norman D'Allura at DuPont; Bruce Godfrey of the Australian Energy Research and Development Corporation for many insightful comments; Norman Haber of Haber, Inc.; Teruo Hiruma and Yoshiji Suzuki of Hamamatsu Photonics; Sir William Hawthorne and Edward Hawthorne for reviewing an early draft; Valentin Heuss for many years of collaboration in the field; Praveen Chaudhari of IBM for explaining how scientific research gets done; Paul Henstridge of ICI, Ltd.; Masaharu Yoshida of Kubota Corp.; Dan Dooley of Lasa, Inc.; Ernst Uhlmann of Lasarray SA; Juhani Kuusi and Petri Haavisto of Nokia; Ken Payne for patient tutoring on intellectual property rights for longer than he probably cares to remember; Cees Weijsenfeld of Philips Research; Anthony Pilkington of Pilkington plc for discussion on the float glass technology several years back; Ken Frederick, Joseph G. Wirth, Gary Wiseman, Paul Becker, and several others at Raychem Corp. for sharing their time and experience generously; Franco Sbarro of Sbarro SA; Tatsuya Adachi and Hiroshi Fukino of Seiko Instruments; Toshiyuki Yamada, Takamasa Ito, Stephen Baker, and many others at Sony for helping my research in such a hospitable manner; Lowell Steele for his keen insights and valuable advice; Christian Sturzinger, Matt Simmons, and Hannu Siikala of Sulzer AG; John Seely Brown for several stimulating discussions at Xerox PARC; and Ambros Speiser (formerly of Brown Bovery, Ltd.), for providing the much-needed perspective that experience brings.

Although several individuals at the International Institute for Management Development (IMD) and IMI-Geneva helped to further my work, I would particularly like to acknowledge the individual who got it started, Bohdan Hawrylyshyn. Noritake Kobayashi (Dean, Keio Business School) and Richard Kaehler (Pepperdine University) hosted me during a sabbatical in 1989 in Tokyo and Los Angeles, respectively. I remember their hospitality gratefully, because that was when I decided to start putting my thoughts together. Particular thanks are also due to Andrea von Carlowitz of IMI for typing early drafts and to Myriam Romero of IMD for graciously taking the task over and not reminding the author when the final draft should be final.

Nicholas Philipson and Barbara Roth shepherded the manuscript through publishing with such admirable facility as to make this last stage a pleasure.

My final debt is to my wife, Irma. Without her understanding and support this book would not have been possible.

—Vijay K. Jolly
Blonay, Switzerland

Introduction

Among the exhibits at Geneva's Automobile Show in 1989 was a proverbial "reinvention of the wheel." A clever inventor, Franco Sbarro, demonstrated a hubless wheel that did away with the usual central hub connected to an axle. The interior of the wheel was empty; instead, a lever arm with ball bearings was attached to the interior rim of the wheel at the point where the wheel touched the ground—a kind of skateboard riding on the rim's inner circumference.

As a simplification of the wheel, Sbarro's invention promised lighter constructions. By putting the weight of the vehicle closer to the road, it also offered improved handling and braking as well as the freedom to design wheels of any dimension. Heavy vehicles with multiple wheels on the same axle could run the wheels independently of one another, hence obtaining better suspension and turning.

Equally remarkable was the inventor's runaway enthusiasm for the wheel's potential applications. The wheel had already been adapted to prototype cars and motorcycles, and Sbarro had already designed a bicycle with his wheel. Trains, buses, trucks were only the most obvious among the other applications he had in mind.

How many of these applications will eventually get developed and marketed only time will tell. By the summer of 1996, nothing was on the market, and the initial excitement with which the Sbarro wheel was greeted had begun to fade. Judging from the countless examples of stalled innovation, getting even a few of its applications into marketed products will not be easy.

Many technologies, even those as promising as Sbarro's wheel, actually do not make it to market—let alone become commercial successes. Some end written up as articles in journals, while others are simply forgotten, or find use in products far removed from what the inventor had in mind. And then there are some that find a place in science museums to be remembered for what might have been.

But none of this keeps people from inventing new technologies and investing in their development. Thus, throughout the ups and downs of the venture capital industry in the United States during the 1980s, the number of patents issued to individual inventors continued to grow from 13,000 in 1985 to 18,300 in 1990. Similarly, despite periodic recessions, and reminders that technology is not what makes products sell, companies have generally maintained their levels of R&D investments throughout the world. Also, while U.S. companies have reduced the proportion of their R&D devoted to long-term research somewhat, companies in Europe and Japan have been steadily increasing theirs. R&D investments, in fact, are now close to what many companies spend by way of investment in plant and equipment. In Japan, the amount spent on R&D by the top fifty industrial companies had even exceeded capital spending by 1989.[1]

Justifying these investments is, of course, the hope that some value will be realized in the end. This concern for realizing value from investments in R&D touches not just companies and individuals today but governments as well. The rate at which their technologies have been commercialized, thus far, is not impressive. Hertzfeld's analysis of NASA patents form 1959 to 1979, for example, found that only 1.5 percent of the patents the agency earned were actually used outside the agency. This compared to a less than 5 percent commercialization rate of the 30,000 patents held by the U.S. federal government as a whole.[2] The situation in other parts of the world has been no better.

To find greater uses for the technologies they invest in, governments all around the world have enacted measures to encourage commercialization, especially by private bodies. In the United States, this trend got added impetus with the passage of the Stevenson-Wydler Technology Innovation Act (PL 96-480) and the Baigh-Dole Act (PL 96-517) in 1980. The former aimed to foster technology transfer from the National Laboratories by encouraging cooperative research, visits, and licensing; the latter allowed universities, nonprofit research institutes, and small businesses doing government-funded research to maintain ownership of the technologies they developed and apply for patents in their name. Both laws were expanded and strengthened by the Federal Technology Transfer Act of 1986 (PL 99-502), making technology transfer and the commercialization of new technologies an integral part of the mission of government laboratories. The more recent trend toward converting defense-oriented R&D capacity to civilian use and promoting dual-use technologies is motivated by the same desire to obtain better and wider returns from investments in R&D.

Much the same trend is in evidence in other parts of the world. Whether it is the European Union insisting on industry participation in the funding of various new technology programs, the Japanese government mobilizing private companies in sponsored research, or the Chinese and Indian governments cajoling universities and research institutes to become more commercially oriented, the intention is the same—to move from mere knowledge creation and strategically targeted research to realizing commercial value.

WHY A BOOK ON TECHNOLOGY COMMERCIALIZATION?

The desire and need for realizing greater value from investments made in R&D may be universal, but the subject continues to be approached with trepidation, not least because of the difficulty and unpredictability of the process involved. While our understanding of innovation has shifted in recent years from its being a probabilistic event that we hope will happen but we're not quite sure how, to a process that can be managed, this understanding is still partial. We know now that successful innovation requires:

Understanding the marketplace and the customer well;

Coming up with a superior product that delivers significant, unique benefits to the end-user;

Launching the product in an attractive market, as measured by its rate of growth, size, and competitiveness;

Having a well-planned and coordinated development and marketing process;

Getting customers themselves involved early in the development process and, if necessary, as codevelopers;

Undertaking early and frequent prototyping; and

Undertaking as much of the development process (market assessment, R&D, and manufacturing process development) concurrently as possible, typically through the use of multifunctional teams with top management and supplier and customer involvement.

These actions, and the tools they imply, not only improve the probability of a successful product launch but also aid in compressing the time to market.[3]

All these recommendations, however, apply to a part of the innovation process only—dealing with product development and launch. Technology plays an incidental role in them. In their study of "new" products, authors have seldom discriminated among products based on a new technology, products based on a new marketing concept, and products that were simply new to the firm being studied. Everything from a new formulation of shampoo, a new way to package potato chips, Sony's Walkman, microwave ovens, and nuclear magnetic resonance (NMR) imaging devices were usually treated within the same sample.

As for the "commercialization" part of product innovation, it has typically been seen as merely the final stage of product launch, meriting little or no attention on its own. Building the plant, tooling the production line, and market launch were straightforward extensions that depended on performing all the preceding steps effectively. Those authors who did consider commercialization issues treated them under the rubric of new product marketing, with occasional qualifications to take into account the fact that these were "high-tech" products, and hence different from others.[4]

There are two sets of reasons for studying technology commercialization per se.

First is the role new technologies play in differentiating end products and offering new functions to be performed. With more and more companies mastering the keys to successful product development, one is already beginning to see a plethora of products, all well but indistinguishably conceived, manufactured, and delivered on time—to saturated markets. As Jiro Aoki, general manager of Matsushita's domestic sales planning office, put it recently in reference to VCRs, one of the most successful technology-based products of the 1980s, "At one point there were 220 types of TVs and 62 types of VCRs across the industry but only 10 percent of these sold."[5]

The best antidote to a saturated market is a new functionality, something that technology often provides. Just as we have moved from thinking of quality as avoiding aggravation to conforming to customer-defined expectations, and then on to quality that surprises and delights, the same graduation is now being asked of products—to go from improving the way existing functions are delivered to stoking new latent demands and creating altogether new markets.

The applications need not be particularly earth-shaking either, as the example of "memory shirts" launched in Japan at the end of 1993 shows. Based on shape-memory polymers discovered during the early 1980s, these shirts retain their pristine shape and finish after washing, doing away with the need to iron them. Despite the fact that they cost 20 percent more than conventional shirts, the two companies introducing them, Tomiya Apparel and Choya Corp., can barely keep up with demand—that too in an otherwise recessionary environment.[6]

The only way for companies to grow profitably is to offer high value products, cheaply, to attractive markets and, as far as possible, to do so in a unique way. Technology helps along all four of these dimensions. This explains the finding that leading companies not only commercialize two or three times the number of new products and processes as do their competitors of comparable size, but incorporate two to three times as many technologies in their products as well.[7]

The second set of reasons has to do with the difference between a technology and a new product. A technology is essentially a "capability," often a versatile one, that can be used in more than one product. Products are occasional embodiments of this capability and mediate the process of bringing it to market and realizing value from it. The technology and these products, however, often live separate existences, following their own competitive logic, converging sporadically.

The archetypal example is that of lasers. Ever since the first laser was demonstrated in 1958, a whole galaxy of products has been introduced, all based on the same basic principles. Today lasers range in size from one micron or less to the Nova, which occupies a complete hangar at the Lawrence Livermore National Laboratory in California. The wavelengths they provide go from middle of the infrared band all the way to ultraviolet, with X-ray band lasers being experimented with too. Their power range and applications are equally broad. Some are sensitive enough to move individual molecules and DNA fragments around, while others can cut through inches of steel in seconds.[8] Just about every industry in the world today uses lasers in one form or another, or soon will. Each of these different types of lasers constitutes one event in the commercialization of "laser technology."

This difference between products and technologies influences the way we think about commercialization. In both cases, commercialization is "to cause something having only a potential income-producing value to be sold, manufactured, displayed or utilized so as to yield income or raise capital"[9]—a definition the French capture well in using the term *valorisation*. For products, this means taking a design through development and then manufacturing and marketing it. For technologies, on the other hand, value realization encompasses a broad range of things, including "all stages of commercial development, application and transfer, including the focusing of ideas or inventions toward specific objectives, evaluating these objectives, downstream transfer of research and/or development results, and the eventual broad-based utilization, dissemination and diffusion of the technology-based outcomes."[10] As such, it begins before products are even conceived and stretches out to after they have been developed and launched—the latter to accommodate the influence a proprietary new function has on market acceptance and profit realization. See Table I-1, which summarizes the differences between product and technology commercialization.

Following from this difference in commercialization is the outcome expected and how this outcome is judged. For products, the desired outcome is value to customers, *and it is the latter alone who decide.* In

TABLE I-1

THE MAIN DIFFERENCES BETWEEN PRODUCT INNOVATION AND
TECHNOLOGY COMMERCIALIZATION

Characteristic	Product	Technology
1. **Object to be commercialized**	Singular design	Multifaceted capability
2. **Start of commercialization (and time scale)**	Product conception (1–5 years)	As soon as a potentially valuable technological concept is proposed (10–20 years)
3. **Stakeholders to whom to demonstrate value**	Customers as end-users	Several, whose mix and interests evolve with the technology
4. **Nature of demand**	Final for the segment targeted	Derived from the product(s) made possible
5. **Competition**	Other products for same function	At different levels against other technologies for same product or function
6. **Marketing challenge**	Exploiting unique selling proposition (USP) of finished product	Exploiting whatever the technology can achieve at the point in time
7. **Timing**	End-user market opportunity	The time line of competing inventors, adopters, and resource providers
8. **Opportunity for value creation and appropriation**	Revenue from making and selling products competitively	Product sales and/or collateral benefits over life of technology

contrast, the evolving capability a technology represents means that the stakeholders to be satisfied are of a greater number, whose composition changes over time. Thus, in the beginning, the principal stakeholders to deal with may simply be professional peers whose opinion regarding the quality of the science done and the veracity of the findings can make or break further progression of the technology. Later, as the technology evolves, others become involved: colleagues, outside collaborators, and—especially important for private inventors—resource providers. Each of these stakeholders assigns a value to the technology as it progresses, and they have their own reasons for doing so.

This evolutionary character of technology has meaning for the way one thinks of demand and competition. Rather than the demand emanating from a particular class of customers to whom a product is targeted, the demand for a technology is a derived demand; it comes from the end products made possible. Similarly, while we tend to see market competition as between products and services offered by various companies, technology competition manifests itself at different levels. In the early stages, the competition is between alternative technologies and approaches and is basically a competition among inventors. In addition to fighting the oblivion that comes from being bested by a more cost-effective approach, they struggle for the resources and attention needed to take things further. At late stages, competition involves getting the technology incorporated in products or processes and in gaining market acceptance for the novel function offered.

This multilevel competition, and the changing customers or stakeholders a technology confronts as it progresses, have a bearing on how one judges the need for speed and timing. For products, the window of opportunity depends on what end-users demand at a point in time given what else is available. For technologies, on the other hand, end-product opportunities constitute the upper bound, so to speak, of a time window. But there are several intermediate windows to go through as well, having to do with the time line of resource providers and the host of organizations involved in demonstrating the technology and promoting its adoption in the marketplace.

Finally, the fact of being a general capability gives a number of possibilities for realizing value from technologies not available to most products. In product innovation, value comes at the end of the process when consumers buy the product. Value creation in a new technology is a cumulative, ongoing process, as resources get attracted to it. The latter can take the form of venture capital, attracting public funds for continuing the effort and, within an organizational context, the obtaining of interest and resources from business groups. All "pay" for the technology is in a certain sense based on its evolving potential. Also, if properly managed, ownership rights in a new technology permit premium pricing, delaying the onset of competition, obtaining various nonprice benefits in the context of license agreements, and access to markets that would otherwise be difficult.

WHAT THIS BOOK IS ABOUT

Technology commercialization of the type described above relates to a particular class of innovations that Souder calls "means-generated"—those that are made possible by some new technological capability.[11] Ralph Gomory refers to them as "ladder" innovations (those that stem from scientific breakthroughs) as distinct from "cyclic" ones (the continuous incorporation of product and process inventions in line with market evolution).[12]

The point of departure of this book is the somewhat unsettling finding that successful product development projects tend to be those for which the technology is "available," or based on well-developed science that can be used to create it within the framework of a product development project.[13] This finding is naturally hard to deal with for those whose primary interest has been in creating the technology and developing the science in the hope that it would find applications. What are they to do? Do they stop work, knowing that failure awaits them? Or can they indeed better their chances for making the technology "available" in a form that value can be realized from it?

These questions relate to a broader set of concerns that those engaged in science-based research confront today:

Why do particular technologies succeed and go far while others, apparently equally meritorious, get aborted along the way? What exactly happens along the way, and how much of it can be influenced and managed by an inventor?

How can technology commercialization be made more effective so that those working on early-stage technologies can profit from their investments? Obtaining a better ROR (return on research) is a major concern today. But what actions are needed to achieve it? How, in particular, to marry curiosity-driven fundamental research with the legitimate demand on the part of senior management for a slew of rapidly introduced breakthrough products?

How immutable is the ten- to twenty-year time scale of commercialization, and what, if anything, can be done to speed it? Speed and time-to-market thinking now pervade just about everything companies do. Their role in gaining competitive advantage from the introduction of new products is also generally accepted. But does the same apply to new technologies, or is the dictum "haste makes waste" equally applicable?

How much of the commercialization burden should the proponent of a new technology take on alone versus engaging partners?

Finally, what does effective technology commercialization mean for the way companies manage their innovation process generally?

These are the questions this book addresses. Answering them is to take out some of the guesswork that accompanies technology-based innovation. By seeing the latter as a black box at the front end of product development, managers within companies renege on their responsibility to get the most out of the investments made in R&D.

There has never been a greater need to come up with a better framework for thinking about technology commercialization. While incremental innovations based on process improvements, minor modifications at the product level, and high-quality execution have served many companies well in the 1970s and 1980s, there is mounting evidence that this will be less viable in the future. Devices and equipment based on entirely new principles are being launched with increasing frequency, offering in many cases a step-change in functionality over the incumbent technology. This is particularly true of industrial equipment and analytical instruments, as well as a variety of pharmaceutical products. Also, as Hiroyoshi Rangu, general manager of NEC's Tsukuba-based Fundamental Research Laboratories, put it, "In the past, industry could do without basic research because we were innovative enough to improve products by trial and error. But now, for instance, we're pushing toward the atomic scale [in electronic devices], and to understand how electrons really behave at that level we must have a fundamental understanding of the science."[14]

THE FRAMEWORK ADOPTED AND CHAPTER OUTLINE

To see how new technologies themselves can be commercialized effectively, the book looks at the entire process from the moment a new technological insight is gleaned to the marketing of products or processes incorporating it—hence the subtitle "Getting from Mind to Market." The technological insight could be a concept like Sbarro's wheel, the discovery of a mechanism to suppress tumors, a laboratory process for realigning the microstructure in a ceramic compound, a new type of polymer, or an idea for a special electronic switch that seems to work experimentally. New mathematical algorithms that eventually end up in computer software would belong to this category as well.

Anyone who has observed technological innovation longitudinally, especially over a decade or more, knows that this process cannot be broken down into discrete, linearly arranged activities. There is far too much "backing and forthing" between stages, and stops and starts that seem to occur randomly, to permit such a view. The best one can do is to "parse" the process, breaking it down into component parts to explain relationships, as is done in grammar. If the components end up having a time dimension, it has more to do with the starting or ending points of certain activities than their relay characteristics.

Parsing the overall process from mind to market led to the identification of five key subprocesses, each of which needs to be performed well to get to a successful outcome in the end. Corresponding roughly to the stages of innovation others have described in the past, they constitute the framework on which the book is built.

Admittedly, state-by-stage characterizations of the innovation process are not in fashion today. Repeated failures of the traditional "linear model" (in which research results were transferred to development and then to production and marketing) have caused many to prefer viewing innovation as a single, integrated process coupled to a market opportunity from the beginning. While appropriate for product development and certain types of incremental innovations, especially those for which the enabling technology is available to draw upon when needed, this modern view has several drawbacks when applied to major innovations in which technology plays an important role. Not surprisingly, even those who espouse it today worry about its implications for generating breakthroughs.

Conceiving of technology commercialization as a sequence of distinct subprocesses, it is argued, better captures the reality of technology-based innovations. It permits the use of a sequential investment decision framework based on options theory, which is best suited for accommodating the long time horizons and the nature of the risks involved. It incorporates the development of new technologies explicitly in the innovation process. And, from a managerial standpoint, it recognizes the different mind-sets needed along the way. All inventors know that the process of conceiving an idea is different from that of building products based on it; both, moreover, are different from the mind-set and actions required for introducing new products to the marketplace.

That said, this book is *not* an exhortation for returning to the old linear model. Rather, it presents a different way of thinking about the stages in innovation and the links between them. As such, it offers a new template for guiding inventors in their task. While much has been written about the importance of an "entrepreneurial personality" in successful innovation, the fact is that many entrepreneurs succeed with one idea, only to fail with the next. The cause of the failure was not a personality change. Instead, it was the lack of a model of their process general enough to apply to the new project. This book attempts to address the need for such a model.

The methodological approach derives from this framework. Instead of correlating measures of success or failure at the end of the entire process with particular actions taken at various stages, each segment of the process is analyzed for its own logic, seeing what worked and what didn't. The fact that a technology failed in the end is not important, so long as it was possible to identify where the failure occurred and what caused it. Thus, some early stages may have been performed quite well in a particular case, moving the technology forward despite various odds, only to have the technology stumble at a later stage for unanticipated reasons. Making the early actions hostage to the latter, it is claimed, is to expect more foresight from innovators than is reasonable. By piecing together each stage's successes and failures, it is possible to get a more complete picture of what needs to be done when in the commercialization process, either for a profitable outcome or, equally important, for cutting losses before they mount further.

This book is in the tradition of clinical research, informing the reader about actual choices at each stage. The wide variety of technologies it covers is intended to enrich these choices, not to address the problems unique to a particular industry. Those readers who like to draw ideas and inspirations from a different context than their own will find this useful. It is hoped that others will not be overly frustrated because of the care taken to present the arguments in as conceptual a manner as possible.

The book begins with a complete description of the process of taking technology-based insights to market and realizing value from them. Chapters 2 through 10 then treat each of the activities that are critical to successful commercialization. Chapter 11 puts the entire process together and looks at what needs to be done to close the circle, so to speak, in a timely and effective way. The final chapter (12) concludes with lessons that can be drawn for managing the R&D function for a greater commercial orientation within large companies today.

1

FROM MIND TO MARKET

The Process of Technology Commercialization

MOST TECHNOLOGY-BASED INVENTIONS NEVER GO BEYOND THE CONCEPTION stage. The light bulb in the mind gets lit often, but only occasionally does it leave a trace. Similarly, patents get applied for and granted, but many remain as trophies of the inventor or records of technical achievement. Even more wasteful are the numerous inventions that do get incorporated into products that then fail.

Little wonder that new technology-based businesses have long had a reputation as unsound investments. As Gleason Archer wrote as early as 1938 in the *History of Radio to 1926:* "Fifteen years is about the average period of probation, and during that time the inventor, the promoter and the investor, who see a great future for the invention, generally lose their shirts. Public demand even for a great invention is always slow in developing. That is why the wise capitalist keeps out of exploiting new inventions."[1] Even today, the shares of companies bringing a new technology to market get uncharitably referred to as "binary events": they can either be worth nothing, or a lot, nothing in between.

What causes these failures and why such uncertainty? Why, for instance, did food irradiation with gamma rays using radioactive Cobalt-60 or Cesium-137 not meet with success? Astronauts on the Columbia Space Shuttle flights had already successfully dined on beef, pork, smoked turkey, and corned beef that had been sterilized with such nuclear radiation. Third world countries, where refrigeration is scanty or nonexistent and where stored-food spoilage sometimes claims up to 50 percent of the food crop, could obviously benefit from this technology. So could developed countries where this technology offered a viable alternative to the use of maligned chemical additives and where foods treated by this method were demonstrated to retain more of their original appearance, taste, and texture than canned, heat-treated food.[2] Even now, after the World Health Organization gave strong backing to this technique in October 1994, people remain skeptical.

What is it that causes some technologies to succeed while others, sometimes initially more meritorious, don't even get a chance? There are no simple answers, and each technology's history is unique in some way. Yet, seeking answers is key not only to understanding technological innovation but also to reassuring companies that are looking for new growth opportunities today.

THE FIVE KEY SUBPROCESSES IN TECHNOLOGY COMMERCIALIZATION AND THEIR BRIDGES

Some technologies fail because they get incorporated in products for which the anticipated demand never materializes. Others continue to search for suitable products, sometimes over decades, without being incorporated into any product at all. Then there are those that fail because they cannot live up to their promised capability when being demonstrated, or attract insufficient interest and resources to have such demonstrations made. Finally, the entry to market itself has constituted an intractable obstacle in some cases. Like one-day wonders, some technologies have made a fleeting appearance, never to be heard from again. Their problem was one of positioning and delivery. They could neither gain adequate market penetration, nor could they sustain their commercialization for a variety of competitive reasons.

In understanding what went wrong, one needs to know where in the commercialization chain problems occurred and why. In the dozen or so technologies the author studied over time, the following were the typical activities where things could go wrong:

The linking of a technological discovery to a worthwhile and exciting market opportunity;

Having the technology endorsed early by those whose opinion matters;

Incubating the technology sufficiently to understand its true potential, including whether it will ever be cost-effective enough to merit taking further;

Mobilizing adequate resources for its demonstration;

Successfully demonstrating the technology for the context in which it is to be used;

Mobilizing the market constituents needed for gaining market acceptance and delivering the benefits of the technology;

Promoting the final products and processes to an often skeptical customer group;

Choosing an appropriate business formula for gaining access to the required business system; and

Sustaining commercialization so as to realize value from the technology after it has been launched.

Technology commercialization, in other words, is about performing successfully a range of things, each adding value to the technology as it progresses. Being proficient at one or two of them and clumsy in the remaining brings down the average result; worse, it can abort a technology's progression midstream.

As pictured in Figure 1-1, five of these activities constitute the key subprocesses involved in bringing new technologies to market: *imagining* a techno-market insight; *incubating* the technology to define its commercializability; *demonstrating* it contextually in products and/or processes; *promoting* the latter's adoption; and *sustaining* commercialization. As important as these subprocesses are the four bridges between them. While the former involve problem solving of a technical or marketing nature—doing things to the technology, so to speak—these bridges are associated with mobilizing resources around it. They have to do with satisfying the various stakeholders of the technology at each stage, without whom the technology's value does not get recognized, nor is there an impulse to take it further. Thus the bridges are value-creating activities in their own right.

These bridges evoke an important reality about the innovation process—that it is fundamentally an exercise in stakeholder management. Many technologies fail not because of the technical skills of their proponents, nor because of the market to which they are targeted. They fail simply because no one got sufficiently interested in them at the right time.

What follows is a description of the main issues that arise in managing the five subprocesses and in bridging them successfully. The concluding section then discusses how the overall model presented compares with conventional stage-by-stage descriptions of the innovation process and why it is especially relevant in today's environment.

Imagining

The notion of commercialization as a process of value recognition means that it starts at the idea stage itself. For technology-based innovations, this is when the prospects for a technical breakthrough get combined with a potentially attractive market opportunity.

FIGURE 1-1
THE PROCESS OF TECHNOLOGY COMMERCIALIZATION

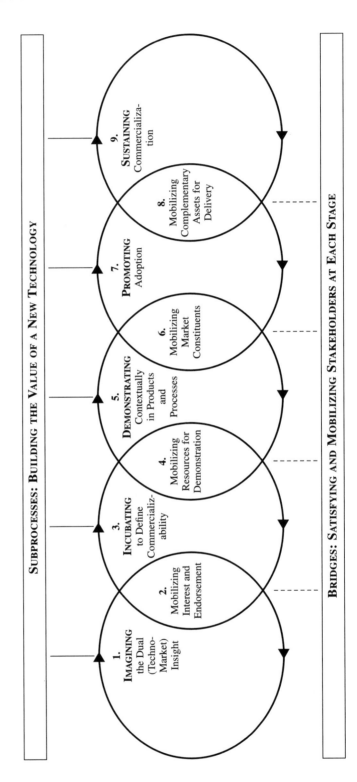

Competition in the commercialization process also actually starts right here. The competition for ideas, if anything, is as keen as the competition one sees between products and services in the marketplace—perhaps more so. It is here that most new technological discoveries get weaned out, despite the enormous work that may have gone into their elaboration.

An illustration of the high attrition rate of ideas is provided by the experience of the Danish Product Idea (PI) support scheme set up in 1972 and administered by the Danish Technological Institute (DTI). With a mission to advise inventors and find partners for them, DTI started a "scout" scheme in 1977 to search out relevant research at institutions of higher education, thereby adding to the ideas directly brought to it by inventors. Between 1985 and 1990, out of the approximately 5,000 ideas collected from inventors and public sector researchers, only 350 (7 percent) were retained as original and worth pursuing; 94 passed the next level of assessment in terms of patentability and got licensed to companies; 30 products actually got produced by the licensee; and 15 products were still in production in 1991.[3] While the PI experience is somewhat more discouraging than comparable ones in Italy and the United Kingdom, it is illustrative nonetheless.

The fact that most inventions do not get commercialized should also be viewed as normal, not attributable to special problems associated with technology commercialization alone. Because ideas come cheap, there are so many of them generated all the time, all clamoring for the attention of resource providers—and their interests at the time determine each idea's fate.

The best and most quoted example is that of Chester Carlson, trying in vain to interest others in his electrophotography (xerography) idea. After filing his patent application in 1937, Carlson approached as many as twenty-one companies, including the likes of IBM, RCA, and Eastman Kodak. While the invention worked, it resulted in copies that were barely legible. No one was willing to commit the funds and research support needed to perfect what to Carlson was an eminently useful invention. After seven years of frustrating search, Battele Development Corporation finally agreed to devote the needed resources in 1944 because one of its physicists became intrigued by the idea.

Contrast this with the more recent experience of Ariad Pharmaceuticals Inc., a biotechnology start-up based in Cambridge, Massachusetts. Set up in 1991 by Harvey J. Berger, the former head of R&D at Centocor, the company's mission was to research new types of drugs based on the phenomenon of signal transduction—the signal sent by a cell's receptor to the DNA within it. While many had speculated about the role these signals play in causing disease, and the potential payoff from interrupting or controlling them, the phenomenon itself was ill understood. Yet, because of the promising nature of the research and the cast of scientists backing it, the company was able to raise $46 million in one round of financing—long before even a proof of principle had been demonstrated.

Given the enormous success Carlson's idea subsequently enjoyed, it is hard to pinpoint the reasons for its being ignored compared to Ariad's idea. Carlson, after all, had already demonstrated a prototype, while Ariad's idea was still unproven. Moreover, while the xerography idea was unique, there were many others thinking about and researching signal transduction at the time Ariad raised its funds.

The judgment of whether ideas are worth pursuing is highly subjective. Some stakeholders place greater importance on ideas' technical merit, while others are more attracted to their market potential. The famous "not invented here" (NIH) syndrome is not simply a manifestation of narrow-mindedness on the part of those judging; it often reflects an alternative view of the future, based on different information perhaps. Compounding this is the "herd instinct" observable in stock markets, which makes the discrepancies between technology valuations even more pronounced. People favor one technology over another in a disproportionate manner at a point in time, as evidenced by recent initial public offerings related to the Internet.

Incubating

Getting a new idea recognized and endorsed to be worth pursuing is, of course, only the start. The commitment of resources and risk capital to develop it requires taking the idea a few steps further. The idea needs to be proved in some unequivocal manner, both technologically and in terms of the need(s) it is supposed to fulfill. This incubation to *define its commercializability* expresses what is required substantively as well as figuratively as the "defining moment"—when considerably greater resources start to be devoted to the technology. Just as the preceding stage represented a competition for *ideas,* this stage has to do with the competition among *technologies* for the application(s) intended and the products to be built.

The need to define commercializability well applies especially to lone inventors, university researchers, and small companies. They need to convince others about the potential a new technology offers in order to secure grants, obtain venture capital, or mobilize research support. Yet they often fail to present their technologies in an attractive enough form to be appreciated by potential partners. They fail to consider what else will be needed to commercialize their invention. They fail to place their intellectual property rights in a commercial context and don't take the trouble to advance the technology to the point when it really becomes attractive.

As those who support early technologies know, judging which technology is commercializable is not easy either. Consequently, many venture capitalists tend to back the proponent of the technology rather than the technology itself. What they expect to do thereby is simply to improve the sheer probability that things will get done right. Brought up and then subsequently annealed by a litany of Murphy's-type laws, they look for a good

Handwritten margin notes:
- IPO
- too early
- ① idea may
- applied
- ② techies
- are not leaders
- Microvision
- ③ Too many
- applications
- ~ focus
- ③ Too in
- w/ idea love

agent to carry things forward—one whose instincts are to correct things when they go wrong, not to discover other grounds to conquer.

One source of difficulty in judging commercializability is an imperfect understanding of the principles underlying the technology itself, which has stymied many discoveries for decades.

A case in point is that of electrorheological fluids. These so-called smart fluids were discovered and patented by Willis Winslow in the late 1940s, and some claim they were first concocted 100 years ago. Consisting of a suspension of fine particles in a nonconducting oil, they have the property of converting themselves into a gel-like solid when subject to an electric voltage. When the current is removed, they revert to the liquid state almost instantaneously (in between 0.0001 to 0.001 seconds). Moreover, this gelling or stiffening is proportional to the voltage applied.[4]

Numerous applications for these smart fluids had been conceived of from the beginning. Voltage-sensitive actuators, clutches, valves, fishing rods that are flexible during casting but stiffen when a fish bites, and even the proofing of buildings against earthquakes were just a few obvious ones. None of these applications, however, was perfected, let alone commercialized. But this has not meant abandoning the principle. As recently as 1989, yet another report claimed that these fluids "will result in the redesign of up to 50 percent of all hydraulic systems and devices."[5] Overall, a $20 billion annual market seems to lie in prospect.

The reasons why no applications have yet been commercialized can all be traced to an inadequate understanding of the principle itself. A number of models have been proposed to explain the phenomenon, but there is no consensus yet. This has made it difficult to tackle a number of practical problems associated with the technology: the settling down of particles, temperature sensitivity, inadequate sheer strength, and the requirement for exceptionally high voltage.

Another concern is uncertainty about the future trajectory of a new technology and the rapidity with which its performance will advance. This causes several technologies to be backed for the same application, hoping one will serve the purpose but diluting the resources available to each.

A good illustration of the competition one sees at the level of technological approaches is that of flat-panel displays. The search for thin displays started almost with the introduction of the first cathode ray tube (CRT), and people imagined "wall television" decades back. With such a large and assured market, the only challenge was a technical one.

Ever since their introduction in the early 1970s in watches and calculators, liquid crystal displays have been the chief contender for flat display. With a power consumption of only 0.002 percent of comparable light-emitting displays, they quickly found applications in a range of portable devices. As progress was made in improving their contrast, broadening their viewing angle, and increasing their response rate to electrical signals, the range of their applications grew, and so did the experience of companies pursuing them. A further impetus was given to this technology in the 1980s with the development of color displays and active matrices using thin film transistors (TFTs). Starting in the mid-1980s, however, a number of other competing technologies emerged to satisfy the need for larger and brighter displays in portable computers and television sets. These included ferroelectric displays (a form of liquid crystal display [LCD] technology that does not require transistors to switch the liquid crystal cells), electroluminescent displays, and plasma displays. More recently, conjugated polymer-based light-emitting diodes have joined the fray because of their structural flexibility and potentially easier and less costly manufacturing process. Judging the commercalizability of any one of these technologies requires assessing the future trajectory of performance of all the others.

A final challenge in defining commercializability has to do with estimating market opportunities and the time frame in which they will materialize. With more and more inventors chasing the same technological discovery and application, periodic shakeouts in R&D programs are inevitable.

This is, for example, what happened to composite materials over the past decade or so. Anticipating a huge market for lightweight, superstrong, heat-resistant materials, virtually all the major chemical companies (as well as some nonchemical ones) launched major research programs in this area starting in the late 1970s. Because of cost and safety concerns in the applications to which they were targeted—mainly aerospace—there was an immediate glut in research capacity. By the early 1990s, many of the early entrants had started either to divest their activities (notably BASF of Germany and Courtaulds PLC of the United Kingdom) or to scale them back (as ICI did with its Advanced Materials division).

Demonstrating

Taking a new technology up to the point where it gets recognized to be commercializable is often easy compared to what comes next—demonstrating it in marketable products or processes. This is the stage associated with product development. Unlike other products, those that derive from a new technological capability require walking a tightrope between conceiving of something customers will buy and being able to implement it with the technology at hand.

An illustration of this tightrope is what happened with picturephones. First offered by AT&T in the mid-1960s, this product was plagued by a combination of technological and design problems for almost three decades. The 1964 picturephone was capable of sending only still, black-and-white pictures, largely on account of the limited carrying capacity of phone lines. With the introduction of color, this limit on transmission capacity became worse. In fact, despite the use of advanced image compression technologies, the videophones being introduced until recently could still send and receive only ten color picture frames a second—too few to give true real-time images. Compact light-sensitive cameras and clear displays are just now beginning to be introduced. But, until such time that all the pieces come together in a form consumers want, the technology will remain on the fringes. And technology is not the only reason for this. Users will need to get used to the product concept itself. Some continue to believe it adds little to phone conversations and sometimes even gets in the way. The acoustical intimacy of a phone call is shattered by visual imagery; while many would like to see their caller, they don't wish to be seen themselves.

Conceiving of products just because technology makes them possible can be treacherous, but this is often less of a problem than actually getting the technology to work. A good example is IBM's beam addressable storage technology. Invented by Praveen Chaudhari, the former vice president of science, and some of his colleagues at IBM's Yorktown Heights laboratory in the early 1970s, this consisted of recording and reading information using a high-speed solid-state laser.

This magneto-optic technology, based on a phenomenon known as ferrimagnetism, today constitutes the heart of all writable compact discs. It is used for everything from data storage to music and multimedia discs. At the time of the invention, however, two things were missing—the necessary complementary technologies and a product concept that fit what the market was demanding.

As for the technology, solid-state lasers were at that time neither reliable nor cheap enough to make this invention a viable competitor to inductive recording. While scaling up the process and improving the basic invention to get adequate signal-to-noise ratios was also considered necessary, this had to wait until the laser problem was solved.

From a product-market standpoint, the new technology's principal advantage lay in creating high-density, decentralized storage media—not central or off-line mass storage devices, which were popular at that time. It was actually the personal computer industry in the late 1980s and erasable compact discs more recently that became significant users of the technology—both totally unanticipated at the time of the invention. In the meantime, IBM had licensed its patents to others, and the first products using the technology started to come from Japan. It is only recently that IBM itself began incorporating the technology in its own disk drives—nearly fifteen years after inventing it.

The challenge of marrying a new technology's function with market-worthy end products lies behind many of the delays and cost overruns in commercialization. In some cases, one needs to expand the scope of the research beyond what was initially foreseen. In others, one ends up making compromises at the product level because that is all the technology can deliver at that time. Often both are involved.

Promoting

Very few inventions, no matter how well conceived and demonstrated, get an automatic reception by the market. As Myers and Sweezy found in studying 200 failed innovations, three-quarters of them were stopped only after they had made it to the pilot test stage; as many as one-fifth were actually stopped at the final, most expensive stage of production installation. In other words, 85 percent of all innovations that ultimately failed continued to be funded beyond the relatively economical phase of assessment and initiation. By far the greatest cause of their subsequent failure lay in the marketplace. As many as 27.5 percent of new product and process technologies were scuttled because of "uncontrollable" market factors. Another 26 percent failed because of limited sales potential and an inability to find buyers for something that was apparently developed "in the public interest."[6]

Regardless of how extensively one performs market research prior to developing a product, acceptance by the market is never assured. Technology-based innovations encounter the same set of problems any new product concept does—the need to create a market where usually none exists. Therefore, market acceptance often involves a complex socioeconomic process over which one seldom has complete control. Steven Lubar, in reviewing a recent book on technological winners, captures the essence of what usually happens:

> Things don't evolve; they are pushed in different directions by the decisions of inventors, manufacturers, marketers, and users, people who have economic, social, and cultural as well as practical reasons to remake technological artifacts in ways that serve them best. For example, people managed just fine without the zipper. It took zipper manufacturers some 20 years of marketing to convince the public it needed zippers. Even then, the zipper was adopted not because of "need" or because button flies failed but because of cultural ideas about modernity and fashion.[7]

For many new technologies the promotional challenge has two dimensions.

One has to do with persuading people to adopt. Whether they do so for the reasons an inventor has in mind, or they invent their own reasons for adoption, they are sometimes discouraged by the effort they need to put in. This is especially true of technologies that require a new set of skills, work procedures, and standards before they become widely commercialized. These are what some refer to as "transilient innovations,"[8] which set in motion a sequence of events that can disrupt, destroy, and make obsolete established competence, or create totally new organizations and industries. One example is the cochlear implant, a biomedical device enabling profoundly deaf people to discriminate sound. Approved by the U.S. Food and Drug Administration (FDA) in November 1984, the cochlear implant is a substitute for conventional hearing aids, which served only individuals with impaired hearing, not the profoundly deaf. Its commercialization has required the development of new diagnostic and surgical procedures, service facilities, and trained technicians, as well as new competencies in R&D, manufacturing, and marketing. It also required the creation of new industry practices and FDA regulations and standards of efficacy and safety for such devices.[9]

The other dimension relates to the infrastructure that has to be created in order to deliver the technology's full benefit. This is the kind of problem Edison had to deal with in getting customers to adopt electric lighting. They were already well served with piped gas, so he had to create an entirely new distribution infrastructure for them, constantly balancing his generation and transmission capacity in line with it.

Delivering a technology's benefits does not necessarily imply the creation of an altogether new infrastructure. Sometimes the challenge is getting parts of the infrastructure already in place to adopt it. The experience the Bakelite Company had in introducing vinyl floor products illustrates the problem well. The product was ready in 1931, and Bakelite even made some vinyl tiles itself, which it installed in its Vinylite Plastics House at the Chicago World Fair in 1933. Yet, despite the demonstrated advantage of the product over existing floor coverings, such as linoleum and rubber, it took until 1947 for the company to convince a floor products manufacturer to start making and selling it.

At first it was a matter of price. During the 1930s, vinyl resin prices were at a level that made it uncompetitive compared to linoleum (based on linseed oil) and asphalt tiles (based on coumarone indene, a coal tar derivative). Later the problem became the process. Vinyl flooring was made by a totally different process from that used for manufacturing linoleum, the floor covering material against which continuous vinyl competed most directly. This made it difficult to convince linoleum producers who saw vinyl not only compete against their existing product but involve additional investments as well.[10]

Existing infrastructures are all vestiges of a predecessor technology. While initially created by companies to commercialize what were then innovative technologies, they gradually become barriers protecting these earlier investments. To change the infrastructure already in place, or worse, to create an altogether new one, requires first the manifestation of sufficient demand for the new technology. But, as many innovators have found, the demand itself presupposes the existence of infrastructure. Breaking out of this chicken-and-egg conundrum takes enormous perseverance and, often, investments greater than those required to develop the technology itself.

Sustaining

The key to realizing value from any new technology, of course, is to make sure the products and processes incorporating it enjoy a long presence on the market and that a fair share of the long-term value they generate are appropriated by the technology's initiator. With rapid product (and technology) obsolescence and the constant entry of new competitors, this is often the hardest part. In fact, it is precisely here that many start-up companies fail.

An important caveat is that sustaining a technology's commercialization does not mean persevering against all odds. That is self-defeating. A technology that is found to be intrinsically deficient should be abandoned quickly unless other good applications are found for it.

This, for example, applies to the Stirling engine. Although it was patented first in 1816 by Robert Stirling and produced more or less continuously between 1818 and 1922, it never quite achieved the same level of acceptance as steam, electric, and spark-ignition technology.

Based on a closed system, where heat is applied from outside the cylinder, Stirling engines are known to have the following major advantages over internal combustion (IC) ones: They are inherently more efficient from an energy standpoint; they can use just about any fuel ranging from liquid hydrocarbons and biomass to radioisotopes without engine modification; they are considerably less polluting; they run more quietly and are free of vibration; and they can be used in a variety of applications where IC engines are impractical.

Since development work on these engines was resuscitated by Philips of Holland in 1938 and by General Motors in 1958, most of their technical drawbacks were also overcome. Yet very few applications for the technology emerged. At times, it was a matter of cost. Mass-produced Stirling engines required expensive heat exchangers (heater, cooler, and regenerator) and needed to be made of strong, heat-resistant materials that are expensive and hard to machine. They also needed to be intricately constructed to give the somewhat larger heat transfer surface area these engines need compared to IC engines. Compared to the other alternatives being pursued for automobiles, they were found to be technically complex, slow-starting, and not sufficiently powerful. The experience and infrastructure established around the Otto cycle IC engine (see Chapter 10) became a progressively greater barrier too. The result of all this is that Stirling engines have rightly attracted only sporadic and low-level interest, relegating them to small niche applications.

For technologies that do offer potential, sustaining commercialization should be seen as a planned activity. It requires taking purposeful measures to bring costs down, constantly improving it, and paying attention to the various forces that influence its use vis-à-vis competing technologies.

One also needs to consider carefully how much to sustain the use of the technology itself versus the business it has helped create. Dropping it too soon can mean truncating the returns from the investments made in it earlier. Staying with it too long, on the other hand, can mean being blindsided by better, more competitive technologies as they emerge.

Closing the Circle of Commercialization—Bridging the Subprocesses in an Effective and Timely Manner

The value of any new technology ultimately lies in the products incorporating it and their success in the marketplace. Yet many technologies are taken to an intermediate stage and either fail there or get inordinately delayed. This is sometimes due to the merits of the technology itself, but it can be due to a failure to bridge the subprocesses effectively.

Bridging the subprocesses is about managing two things: creating enough value in a predecessor stage to make a technology worth taking further, and mobilizing the stakeholders concerned with the next stage and convincing them of its future potential. The former involves insights and problem-solving abilities; the latter is fundamentally a selling exercise.

Refer back to Figure 1-1, which illustrates this dual imperative graphically. As shown on top, each subprocess needs to be seen as building on the value created by the one that preceded it, thereby making it attractive to pursue further. The bridge phases at the bottom relate to satisfying the stakeholders, who often change as the technology moves from one stage to another.

In most technology-based innovations, four bridges need to be built to close the circle of commercialization. The first is between imagining an idea and assembling resources for the research and development phase associated with proving its worth. It involves mobilizing interest on the part of those whose support is needed at that point to take it further. Next is the link between the technology in its generic form and the development of marketable products incorporating it. This involves mobilizing a considerably greater amount of resources and seeking the cooperation of a larger number of actors both within and outside an organization. It involves the transition from interest and encouragement to a commitment on the part of backers.

These two bridges are generally associated with the so-called technology transfer problem. But they are not the only ones to contend with, and may not even be the most important ones required for successful commercialization. Two other, this time market-related, bridges need to be built too.

One relates to the acceptance of the product incorporating a new technology by the first set of customers as well as a host of market constituents. The latter include suppliers of complementary products and the infrastructure needed for users to benefit fully from the technology, competitors helping to get the technology established as a standard solution for a particular problem, as well as "lead users" and third parties that play an important role in any new technology's acceptance. The final bridge relates to a broader diffusion of the technology, without which it will have only an ephemeral impact.

The early bridges correspond roughly to the way companies move their technologies internally and the way transactions for new technologies take place among nonaffiliated organizations. Within large companies, the most common handovers occur between central research laboratories and special development laboratories serving multiple divisions (from imagining to incubating) and between development and divisional laboratories (from incubating to demonstrating). For lone inventors the transition points are similar, though different organizations may be involved at each of them.

A good illustration of the different turns the commercialization process can take just on account of providers of capital at these stages is that of Ebonex, a new ceramic material with applications in the electrochemical field. Invented in 1982 by Peter Hayfield of IMI Ltd., a metals company based in the United Kingdom, Ebonex got bounced around over a range of applications and stakeholders during a ten-year period. The first application was to heat large quantities of custard in institutional kitchens, by passing an electric current through the custard between electrodes made of Ebonex. Very soon, however, the IMI board decided that it did not wish to be in the ceramics field, so sold the patent rights to a group of 75 investors in California. The latter set up a new company, Ebonex Technologies Inc. (ETI), to commercialize the technology.

Unable to raise sufficient capital, ETI brought in ICI of the United Kingdom as a partner at the end of 1986. Probably owing to ICI's longstanding involvement in the chlorine industry, the first application ETI worked on was chlorine generation for swimming pools. This was not a commercial success. When ICI backed out of the company, ETI went looking for other investors and, in 1991, ended up back in the United Kingdom. The latter move was due as much to Britain's low manufacturing costs and strong technical skills as to the availability of fresh capital from Korda & Co, a British venture capital company.[11]

Such unintended technology transfers are symptomatic mostly of the inventors' inability to direct their technology to the appropriate stakeholders and to convince them of its merits. The world is teeming with people who conceive new ideas, but whose actions seldom go beyond the philosophically resigned "if only someone would listen" stage. Yet people with lesser thoughts and more trivial inventions sometimes move ahead because they are better at interesting others, reaching out, and influencing stakeholders and resource providers. One needs to remember that all stakeholders are not obstinate, nor intrinsically recalcitrant. They may simply have a different opinion about a technology. Appreciating these opinions, learning about the assumptions on which they are based, is usually a better attitude to adopt than deriding them as "uninnovative."

CHARACTERISTICS OF THE OVERALL PROCESS

The five subprocesses described above are not in themselves exceptional. In fact, most stage-by-stage descriptions of the innovation process can be mapped onto them, as shown in Table 1-1. Where they differ conceptually and substantively is in the following regard:

They all represent *segments of the innovation process*, each requiring input from a *variety of functions* and external sources as well as different types of research;

Each segment represents an *independent subprocess of value creation;*

Each subprocess needs to contend with its own set of *stakeholders;*

The subprocesses conform approximately to the nature of *competition* and *specialization* in technological innovation today; and

The subprocesses offer a way to think about *entry, exit,* and *alliances* when it comes to bringing new technologies to market.

Multifunctional, Multiresearch Segments

Today's debate regarding how to perceive and, therefore, manage technological innovation posits two extremes: viewing it as a linear process starting with scientific research, going on to development, and then on to production and marketing versus viewing it as a single, market-driven, integrated process. Neither view describes well what successful innovators actually do; when presented as opposites they force companies to choose between either conducting long-term, speculative research or short-term, customer-oriented development projects presenting little risk. This is an unnecessarily constraining choice.

A better approach is one that reconciles and incorporates the advantages of both: seeing innovation as a segmented process, where each segment requires an integrated approach to come up with a valuable outcome.

The point is made graphically by seeing the process not so much as

$$R \rightarrow D \rightarrow E \rightarrow MF \rightarrow MA$$

(where R = Research, D = Development, E = Engineering,
MF = Manufacturing, and MA = Marketing)

but rather as a multifunctional set of several processes:

Not only do all the subprocesses require multifunctional inputs, but they often require *different types of research* as well. Basic research, applied

TABLE 1-1

HOW THE SEGMENTED VIEW OF COMMERCIALIZATION CORRESPONDS WITH
CONVENTIONAL STAGES IN TECHNOLOGICAL INNOVATION

The Segmented, Value Build-up View of Commercialization	Schumpeterian and Traditional 3-Way Classifications	Bright (1970) Stages[a]
1. Imagining		1. Scientific suggestion, discovery, recognition of need or opportunity
		2. Proposal of theory or design concept
2. Incubating	1. Concept development (basic and applied research leading to invention)	3. Laboratory verification of theory or design concept
3. Demonstrating	2. Product development	4. Laboratory demonstration of application
		5. Full-scale or field trial
4. Promoting	3. Market development	6. Commercial introduction or first operational use
5. Sustaining		7. Widespread adoption as indicated by substantial profits, common usage, significant impact
		8. Proliferation

[a]James R. Bright, *Practical Technology Forecasting* (Austin, Tex.: Technology Futures, Inc., 1970).

research, and product development can be associated with all the sub-processes, with the possible exception of promoting. The actual mix depends on the technological challenge that needs to be overcome to arrive at a successful outcome.

Each segment, moreover, represents commercial outcomes rather than research milestones. Table 1-2 summarizes what these expected outcomes are and what one expects at the completion of each segment of the process. Thus, imagining is different from basic research in that it ends with linking findings to some market need—not just some research results that add to an understanding of the technology. It is, moreover, completed only when those whose opinion counts endorse the technology and when sufficient excitement is created to take it further.

TABLE 1-1

continued

Cooper (1986) Seven-Stage New Product Game Plan[b]	National Society of Professional Engineers (1990) Engineering Stages[c]	DuPont (1995)[d]
1. Idea generation	1. Concept	1. Idea
2. Preliminary assessment 3. Concept generation (technological)	2. Technical feasibility	2. Scouting
4. Development (engineering, design, and prototypes) 5. Testing 6. Trial production and test market	3. Development 4. Commercial validation and production preparation 5. Full-scale production	3. Project 4. Prototype
7. Full production and market launch		5. Introduction and commercial
	6. Product support	6. Product support

[b]Robert G. Cooper, *Winning at New Products* (Reading, Mass.: Addison-Wesley Publishing Co., 1986).

[c]William G. Howard, Jr., and Bruce R. Guile, eds., *Profiting from Innovation* (New York: The Free Press, 1992), p.62.

[d]Personal communication from DuPont Lycra® Division, 1995.

Similarly, incubating is about exploring both the technology *and* its application further to characterize its potential more fully. As such, it is a lot more than applied research. It is about seeking market information, seeking legal advice, developing some prototypes, consulting engineers on feasibility, and establishing contact with a wide range of stakeholders.

The same outcome and multifunctional orientation applies to demonstrating, promoting, and sustaining the technology.

TABLE 1-2
THE LINEAR VIEW CONTRASTED WITH THE SEGMENTED VIEW OF THE COMMERCIALIZATION PROCESS

1. THE LINEAR VIEW OF INNOVATION	BASIC RESEARCH	APPLIED RESEARCH AND DEVELOPMENT	PRODUCT DEVELOPMENT AND ENGINEERING	PRODUCTION AND MARKETING	INCREMENTAL R&D
2. THE SEGMENTED VIEW OF SUBPROCESSES	IMAGINING	INCUBATING	DEMONSTRATING	PROMOTING	SUSTAINING
A. Expected outcome	Exciting, preferably unique technology-based idea linked to a market need	Definition of idea's technical feasibility, commercial potential, and plan for taking it further	Incorporating the technology in attractive, market-ready products and/or processes	Getting product or process rapidly accepted by various market constituents	Generating long-term value by entrenching and expanding use of the technology and retaining a lead in it
B. Completion points	Technical proof of principle, filing key patent(s), preliminary vision for the technology	Preparing a business case and plan for commercialization, crafting the technology or product platforms, testing with lead customers	Launch of commercial version of product or process	Capturing a profitable share of market quickly	Adequate return on investments made in technology and infrastructure for commercializing it
C. Main stakeholders	Peers, colleagues, research partners, media	Providers of venture capital, development partners, potential users of technology	Potential customers, suppliers of complementary technologies, internal colleagues in other functions (e.g., manufacturing) and business partners	Customers, end-users, opinion leaders, and market constituents mobilized for delivery	Company management, changing customer segments, business partners

Semi-Independent Processes of Value Creation

The fact that technology commercialization cannot be a fully planned, integrated activity—like constructing a building, for example—does not mean it should be approached haphazardly. Unfortunately, many people see it as an ongoing experiment. They do things every day, meet people, explore, think, and constantly redirect their efforts. Contracts get hastily signed and then regretted. They try one thing, then another, hoping to improve the outcome.

By seeing the five subprocesses as having goals and outcomes to be achieved along the way, it is possible to preserve the advantages of this experimentation while being more consequential. It is true what people say: If the cost of discovery is $1, developing it to a prototype costs $10, and getting a marketable product ready is $100. But this is how *cost* is distributed, not *value*. What we need to do is to see each subprocess as contributing the greatest value relevant to its mission.

The basic message is that the investments made in a technology need to match the value it creates at a point in time—either in the form of what someone is willing to pay to buy an option on it or, if a public company, the market capitalization investors assign. One can overinvest in a technology just as one can underinvest in it. Thus, if the time it is likely to take to bring the technology to market is long and uncertain, the best approach consists in maintaining a low level of effort and doing only those things that do add value in the early stages, such as obtaining good patents, promoting to mobilize research partners, and so on. Conversely, crash programs are warranted when the technology's marketability is imminent and there is the potential of competing technologies getting in first.

The value at intermediate stages of the commercialization is naturally expectation-driven. This explains why company valuations change when they are granted patents. David Austin's study of the 565 patents granted to the twenty largest biotechnology firms until November 1991, for example, found significant excess returns being created when these grants were made. Product-linked patents created a mean excess return of 1.9 percent; those patents that got press coverage in the *Wall Street Journal* created mean excess returns of as much as 6.8 percent.[12] Kelm et al. found a positive correlation between excess stock market returns and each of the stages of R&D project initiation, continuation, and new-product launch—with biotechnology firms being particularly well rewarded when announcing the initiation and continuation of projects.[13] The most dramatic recent illustration of the latter is the £2 billion market capitalization assigned to British Biotechnology in the spring of 1996, largely for its anti-cancer drug Marimastat—even though the latter was still in phase II trials.

The value perceived in a new technology does not, of course, evolve linearly. Sitting one day in Raychem Corp.'s Menlo Park office, the author noticed a picture entitled the "Business Enthusiasm Curve" (Figure 1-2). It

FIGURE 1-2
THE NEW BUSINESS ENTHUSIASM CURVE

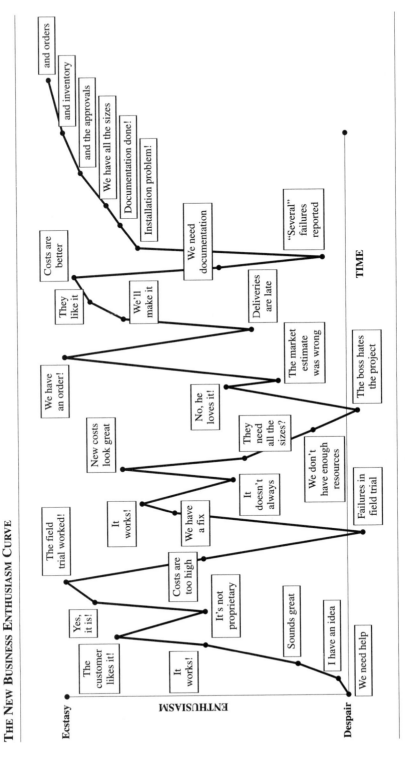

SOURCE: R.J. Saldich, October 11, 1984. Reprinted with permission.

was drawn in 1984 by Robert J. Saldich, who later became president and CEO of the company. At first, it was dismissed as an interesting expression of the type of humor common to Silicon Valley. But, as the research on the book advanced, its message stuck. Relating to a part of the technology commercialization process, it describes well how the overall process often turns out—frequent bouts of enthusiasm followed by disappointments, delays, and then enthusiasm again.

Figure 1-3 illustrates the three *general* paths that perceived value in a new technology can take as it progresses through the five stages of commercialization. The first (path I) corresponds to ideas like the Sony Walkman—one person's vision for a product that receives only moderate enthusiasm followed by exemplary development and commercial delivery.

The opposite (path II) is what happened in the case of food irradiation mentioned earlier. The idea itself was initially perceived to be promising. A number of companies in different parts of the world got attracted to it and invested large sums in exploring it further during the 1970s. By trying out different intensities of radiation and times of exposure, most also were able to demonstrate that the technology worked as intended. The problems turned up in the delivery stage, partly in the form of consumer resistance—which was not adequately sensed in the market studies done during demonstration—and partly in mobilizing the needed infrastructure to treat perishable foods on a commercial scale.

Path III, finally, is a stylized version of Robert Saldich's Business Enthusiasm Curve. It portrays all technological innovations that occur in fits and starts. It reflects, moreover, the complex set of forces that influence the perception of value in practice. According to one research manager:

> The building up of a technology's potential does not proceed linearly. A number of things come into play beyond the technical progress being made. First, there is the inevitable second-guessing by people who are influential but who really don't understand the technology fully. Then there is the annual funding system to contend with. With several competing priorities, decisions need to be made not just on how much to fund a particular project but whether to do it at all! Finally, every now and then, there is the issue of the credibility of the research group and whether they are really working in the best interest of the company.[14]

The opportunities for speculative gains implied by path II notwithstanding, the kind of value buildup one would like to see, of course, is that illustrated by path I. Starting off high, by imagining something unique and useful, needs to be followed by actions to build on this potential steadily. It is like companies who want their share price to grow continuously, not in fits and starts. Performing the various activities involved at each stage in a proficient manner enables an inventor to, as Gregory Smith, Vice President,

FIGURE 1-3

THE DIFFERENT PATHS THAT PERCEIVED VALUE IN A TECHNOLOGY CAN TAKE

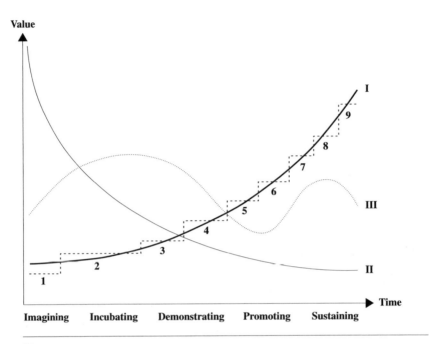

KEY

I   The most natural path based on closing the circle of commercialization progressively

II   Good definition followed by disappointing demonstration and no delivery on time

III The most commonly observed path

Research and Technology of AlliedSignal, put it, "buy the right to keep going by having successes along the way."

Progressive value buildup often requires performing each subprocess for its own logic too. The fact that a scientific insight gets demonstrated in the laboratory, for example, has no bearing on whether it is robust enough to work in the real world. Pharmaceutical companies know this well. A promising new chemical entity may bind to the receptors it is targeted to but may prove fatal to the mice into which they are injected, let alone cure whatever disease they have been made to have. Also, what works in mice may not work in humans, especially for breakthrough therapies for which animal models have not been well established yet. This is only at the research level. As the technology moves from the laboratory to a production environment and then to the market, the vastly different nature of the context means that conditional probabilities quickly drop to zero. A technological breakthrough geared to a useful function does not mean that it will yield a good application; further downstream, successful product demonstration is no guarantee that the product will be a winner in the marketplace. The more these activities are spaced in time, the more independent their probabilities of success from one another.

The independent nature of the subprocesses means that uncertainty is equally high throughout. What changes is the source of the uncertainty, directing attention to a different body of information each time. The accomplishment of one stage successfully reduces the *total* uncertainty remaining, but does not necessarily increase the probability of accomplishing a subsequent stage. The latter requires addressing the unique logic of that particular stage, aided perhaps by new information that becomes available when it begins. This segmented character of technological innovation has led many to think about it in terms of sequential investment decisions based on options theory.[15] Spending money on one stage, according to this view, represents the price paid for an option to work on the next stage, whose investment represents the exercise or strike price of the option. As with financial options, one has the right, but not the obligation, to start work on this next stage, depending on how things evolve.

Referring to Figure 1-3, the value the technology represents at a point in time determines whether or not to proceed. This value consists of two things: the discounted future earnings from whatever has already been sold, such as a license on a particular facet of the technology that was spun off, plus the option value of the stages further downstream. If the latter is greater than the investments needed to continue, then it makes sense to move on to the next stage. If not, the appropriate course is to wait until circumstances become more favorable or to terminate the project at that stage. As the commercialization process advances, the more "real" this option value grows, becoming equivalent to the discounted free cash flow that products incorporating the new technology generate after they are launched on the market. Before then, they are option values representing potential only.

This thinking explains the kind of research-funding agreements that pharmaceutical companies enter into with small biotechnology companies and universities in order to gain access to research projects in their early stages. Business agreements are often structured as a combination of an upfront payment (the option price) followed by a series of progress payments that can be terminated at will. The latter represent ongoing option payments, guaranteeing the pharmaceutical company the right to invest to take a discovery further, provided it sees continuing promise in it.

Options thinking is particularly relevant to technology-based projects involving separable stages, long time periods during which circumstances change unexpectedly and in which there is persisting uncertainty regarding the ultimate value that can be realized. However, these are also the conditions that make the computation of option values and an optimal investment strategy difficult. The best one can obtain are ballpark estimates, which then need to be modified with good judgment or form the basis of negotiating transactions.

This said, it is the intuitive insights that the framework provides that matter. There are, moreover, two things to bear in mind when applying the framework to technology commercialization. One is the treatment of value. While the ultimate value that the technology represents may be uncertain, it is controllable to some extent by the actions taken. Just as competitors might suddenly preempt the technology midway, one has the possibility of increasing the value of the technology at each stage consciously by, for example, redirecting it to better uses. The other concerns the market for the options generated. The appreciation of value is highly subjective and subject to biases, especially for early-stage technologies. Potential buyers generally undervalue technology options because they lack all the information and knowledge of a seller. Conversely, if they have better opportunities for taking the technology further, they can be made to pay more than what the inventor thinks it is worth. How and to whom the technology is targeted, in other words, determines its value as much as its intrinsic merits.

The Changing Cast of Stakeholders to Be Mobilized

The value of a technology at each stage is ultimately not measured by the investments made, nor by the standards of technical achievement, nor even by the knowledge accumulated over time. It is measured by what stakeholders relevant to that stage perceive in the technology.

In the early stages, when the technology is being defined, the relevant stakeholders might be scientific peers or venture capitalists; later, during the demonstration phase, the primary stakeholders might be various resource providers and potential customers; finally, when the finished product or process is ready for market launch, a host of market constituents, including suppliers, intermediate adopters, competitors, and end-users can be involved. Performing the various technical and marketing activities proficiently at each stage, therefore, needs to be combined with actively interesting the relevant stakeholders and managing their expectations. Refer back to Table 1-2, which summarizes who these stakeholders tend to be at each stage.

Whether it is peers endorsing the technology and dispelling skepticism, management and colleagues providing resources to continue work on it, or outside parties contributing capital, no technology has ever been developed without the assistance, or at least the indulgence, of others. Short-circuiting some early stakeholders and precipitating the technology's incorporation in end products can lead either to the latter being resisted or to critical support being withheld at times when it is most needed. Moving a technology from one stage to the next, in other words, is not just a "technical handover" but an overlapping process of interest and resource mobilization.

This stakeholder management challenge is particularly great for technologies that change the basis of competition and that require a new pattern of delivery. Here, not only are the usual early-stage stakeholders to be satisfied but a number of downstream market constituents mobilized as well. The same applies to some "social technologies" where the technology is easy to develop but a number of institutions need to be involved in commercializing it. Antipollution technologies, nonconventional energy, cheap housing, and many agricultural innovations belong to this category. For them, politics is often the overriding influence on commercialization success.

Match with Competition and Specialization in the Innovation Process Today

Competition, as pointed out, occurs throughout the process, starting at the idea stage. One sees competition among alternative technologies offering a similar function, competition among different product concepts that users find appealing, and sometimes competition among alternative approaches to the market.

An illustration today would be that of photovoltaic technologies. As we enter the late-1990s, there are at least seven contenders: crystalline silicon, amorphous silicon, copper indium diselenide (CIS), cadmium telluride (CdTe), thin film silicon, gallium arsenide, and nanocrystalline semiconducting films coupled with organic dyes that mimic natural photosynthesis. Within each, furthermore, are a multitude of different approaches, all aiming to increase the efficiency of solar energy conversion in a stable manner.

There is then the competition at the application and product level. Some technologies are being aimed consciously at the requirements of electricity grids, which means large and robust arrays that can be manufactured cheaply and that can withstand open-air environments for a long period of time. For them what counts is low cost, ease of panel construction, and minimal maintenance. Other technologies are geared to maximum conversion efficiency and a minimization of space, features that are vital in applications such as satellites and hand-held devices. Nanocrystalline semiconducting films with organic dyes, on the other hand, are seen as potentially low-cost, transparent photovoltaic systems for use in a variety of large consumer electronics products and glass windows for home and office generation of electricity. Each technology naturally wishes to be a contender for the product applications others are coveting. It wants to be *the* photovoltaic technology of tomorrow.

This multilevel competition translates into a competition for stakeholder attention and funds too. The five value-adding subprocesses correspond roughly to the manner in which funding is structured today as shown in Table 1-3. Competition for funds occurs at each stage, and each stage has

TABLE 1-3

ROUGH CORRESPONDENCE BETWEEN COMMERCIALIZATION STAGES AND EXTERNAL FUNDING

Commercialization Stage	Type of Financing	Source of Funds
1. Imagining	Seed or zero-stage financing	Government R&D support, family and friends, special early-stage venture capitalists
2. Incubating	First-stage or start-up financing	Government R&D support and venture capitalists
3. Demonstrating	Second-stage financing	Venture capitalists and government technology development programs
4. Promoting	Third-stage and other expansion-related financing (called development capital in the United Kingdom)	Banks and other commercial lending organizations
5. Sustaining	Traditional corporate finance	Banks and retained earnings

its own criteria for attracting resources. Thus, those who imagine and define a technology well in the beginning get to amass a large war chest of funds. Others have to accumulate resources more progressively in line with achievements made from one stage to another.

A more recent trend is that different people are tending to specialize in different stages of innovation. Separate actors are inventing technologies, defining and incubating them, and demonstrating them in products and processes. And there are even some whose sole mission is to help with marketing the latter on a global basis. This also leaves room for today's inconveniently but evocatively named "virtual organization" —whose main business is to connect and integrate the outputs of such a kaleidoscope of organizations, each providing a different function or service independently.

One is already beginning to see more and more individuals setting themselves up as independent inventors, partly as a result of downsizing in R&D organizations. Universities and research institutes worldwide are beginning to actively market their technological ideas at an ever earlier stage. Some former central research laboratories of companies have joined in too, such as RCA's David Sarnoff laboratory (now part of SRI International) in the United States and Thorn EMI's Central Research Laboratories (CRL) in the United Kingdom. Whereas the latter worked exclusively for

EMI businesses previously, including inventing the CT scanner, external customers now account for 95 percent of its business.

Specialization along the commercialization chain is particularly advanced in the pharmaceutical industry today, where small research companies have built the needed critical mass to do pioneering research in a number of cutting-edge fields. They see their role as providers of new drug candidates and innovative therapies, while letting others commercialize them. In that, they are aided by the emergence of specialist product development companies. A number of companies such as Pharmaceutical Product Development, Inc. now offer their services for conducting clinical trials efficiently and dealing with regulatory authorities. They not only understand the full context of drug demonstration but are equipped to undertake the demonstration on behalf of the owners of new chemical entities. Further downstream in the chain, specialists have also already emerged in encapsulation methods and drug delivery.

The reason specialized R&D companies are growing in importance is that there are more "buyers" for their output. In the United States, some companies are even abandoning their commitment to research on generic technologies, relegating this to universities or to consortia such as MCC, SEMATECH, and others. Judging from the rapid increase in the payments for technology, more and more companies are realizing the benefits of paying the 5 to 10 percent royalty rates needed to access good modern technologies than to spend on (often duplicative) research themselves and build up a critical mass of research talents. With an infrastructure to support product manufacturing and marketing already in place, many have now a declared policy of rapidly introducing new products in response to the needs of their customers and are willing to buy in the technologies required if necessary. This is, for example, what ICI is now emphasizing after having been a "science based" company for a long time. Its main focus is on the downstream end of the commercialization chain.

Finally, when time comes to gaining widespread and early market introduction, there is also a growing preference toward mobilizing others who are specialized in various downstream elements of the business system. The latter can include major distributors buying on an original equipment manufacturer (OEM) basis, suppliers of joint-products, licensees with better access to particular market segments, or the many trading companies seeking a role in high-technology industries today.

Match with Entry, Exit, and Alliance Possibilities

The consequence of this specialization along the commercialization chain is that it is possible to enter or exit a new technology at different stages. Thus, it is possible to focus one's effort on the very early stages and exit, or partner with others for the downstream stages (with companies who have product ideas and the means to commercialize them), or vice versa. The inventor of a new technology, in other words, does not have to be the one to close the circle of commercialization. Conversely, competitors and imitators can enter the cycle at any stage, thereby eroding the share of the technology's potential the inventors themselves can appropriate.

While much has been written about inventors who lose out *after* they have launched their products, the fact is that many lose out long *before* that stage is even reached. They may start the process but may not be the ones who see it to the end. Conversely, many fast-followers pick up a technology only late in the demonstration phase and then market and deliver products successfully—as Sun Microsystem, Inc., did with its RISC workstations and GE with NMR imagers.

Such a strategy of waiting to enter a technology when it gets more ripe for commercialization seems to have worked for companies in certain long-gestation technologies in the past. In the new materials industry, for example, where twenty years from invention to widespread use has been the norm, very few companies inventing the substance made money. Rather, it was companies that entered midway through the process, as Kyocera did with ceramic technology for semiconductors, who came to dominate the industry and gain the bulk of the profits created—while many of the early entrants with strong patent positions, notably several U.S. companies, abandoned their efforts at that point.[16]

Similarly, exiting a technology midway in its commercialization may be the most sensible decision in particular circumstances. Doing so is not always easy. Apart from the ego and personal commitment of the technologist himself, those championing and funding his efforts have a stake in continuing things "just in case something valuable might be found." It is not a profitable attitude in most cases[17] but an altogether human response to obstacles. What the value build-up model offers is to relate entry and exit to achievements along the way and what needs to be done to demonstrate commercial value at each stage. To exit a technology successfully and profit from it means establishing the best value up to that stage.

Virtually all the research managers the author spoke to identified stopping projects and exiting from a technology as one of their most difficult yet important tasks. The need to perform it well is, if anything, greater today than at any time in the past. Companies don't want to take on too many projects in R&D because of limits on management time and, as Lowell Steele, the former head of technology planning at GE, puts it, "Companies are running out of risk tolerance in today's environment; moving a technology project forward inevitably means moving on to a higher risk tolerance level. The fact is that one must kill some projects in order to focus greater resources on those that are presumably more attractive."[18]

The traditional, functionally based conception of the innovation process is not well suited to the making of entry and exit choices. It sees the process as a linear sequence of activities whose value can be judged only at the end. The segmented, outcome-based approach adopted here not only gives a better feel for what value has already been achieved but points out what needs to be done before a go/no-go decision gets made. Rather than relating this decision to project objectives and milestones that may have been set a long time back, it has the virtue of using current information for judging the project's merit.

A final aspect concerns alliance possibilities that have made research specialization even more attractive than was hitherto the case.

A bit more than a decade ago, most thoughtful students and practitioners in the field of technology commercialization saw alliances as a way to bring a new technology to market *after* it had been fully developed. One could either license the technology (patents and know-how), spin it off, establish a joint venture (to retain some equity interest and thereby a continuing share of its future profits), or develop and market products and processes on one's own. Licensing and spin-offs were instruments for exiting from the technology itself, or from markets the technology owner considered unattractive or unfeasible to enter alone; undertaking the entire process of commercialization to the end on one's own was typically seen as a "first-best" choice for those who could afford to do so; joint ventures, finally, were seen as an in-between choice and a compromise; one entered into them because licensing did not provide adequate long-term rewards but a partner was nevertheless needed to supply one or the other complementary assets required for effective commercialization.

The situation in the 1990s is dramatically different. The spectrum of choice in itself has not changed. Technology can still be commercialized either passively (licensing patents and know-how or spinning off the technology), in collaboration with others (such as joint ventures), or on one's own. What has changed is the way these instruments can be combined and used at different stages of the commercialization process. Thus, one possibility is to collaborate during the incubation and demonstration stages but do the actual delivery on one's own. Another is to conduct the entire incubation and demonstration phases on one's own and then collaborate with others at the final stage of market launch. Other variations have become increasingly common too—doing *parts* of each of the stages on one's own while either licensing or collaborating with others on other activities involved.

Thinking about alliance possibilities by subprocess offers two main advantages: it indicates what needs to be done in a preceding stage to make the technology attractive to potential partners and it provides a goal to the alliance. A major reason why alliances fail today is that the objectives of the partners begin to diverge over time, usually on account of changes in the market environment itself. The narrower the scope of an agreement and the better defined it is, the fewer the chances of this occurring. Multiple, "spot" alliances by stage are superior to long-term business commitments where the reasons for this commitment can often change.

SUMMARY

Commercializing a new technology involves performing nine different activities well. Five of these correspond roughly to traditional stages of the innovation process but are best seen as independent subprocesses of value creation in their own right. The remaining four activities constitute the bridges connecting these subprocesses. They capture the role stakeholders play in determining which technologies get taken further and which get stalled in their commercialization.

Although such a stage-by-stage view of the innovation process lost some of its credibility and utility in recent years, the way in which it is modeled for the purposes of this book is a more real-life rendition of what happens to new ideas as they go from mind to market.

There are several advantages to looking at the process of technology commercialization in these terms:

It conforms to the growing specialization within the commercialization chain today;

It offers a way to manage the process in time, based on external, value-based criteria, rather than internally set project objectives that can be flawed;

It suggests corrective actions to take at logical intervals, including whether and when to drop a particular idea;

It accommodates technologies with different time frames within a single framework; the five subprocesses can be accomplished in one year or in twenty, yet all technologies need to go through them in the same manner; and

It allows investment decisions to be made in discrete intervals, going from one stage to the next as more information about the market and the technology becomes known.

Taken together, all these advantages translate into reducing the guesswork traditionally associated with technological innovation.

2

IMAGINING THE DUAL (TECHNO-MARKET) INSIGHT TO START COMMERCIALIZATION

SUPPOSE YOU WERE GIVEN THE TASK OF CONVERTING METALLIC GOLD INTO a soft, claylike substance—one that could be easily molded by hand or put through a tea strainer. Would you (1) accept the R&D challenge, and (2) know what to do with the result, provided, of course, you were successful?

Knowing how the problem might be approached technically depends on one's background and competence. Finding out what, if anything, to do with the outcome is marketing flair. The two together make for the techno-market insight, whose imagination lies at the heart of all successful technology-based innovations.

As it turns out, Mitsubishi Materials Corp. of Japan did imagine such a link. Using its know-how in powder metal technology, it formulated a mixture of gold powder, less than 20 microns in diameter, added some water and a unique organic binder, and came up with gold clay. It is as malleable as potter's clay, but after being left to dry for two days and then fired at 1,000°C in a kiln—to burn off the binder and evaporate the water—it emerges as solid gold, harder, in fact, than gold fabricated by conventional methods. It can thus be used in applications where it would otherwise be too soft.

The company spent two years developing the clay and has patented the process throughout the world. It was launched in the summer of 1995. Jewelers are among the most enthusiastic potential users of the product. It allows them greater scope in designing and fabricating jewelry and gives the latter an entirely new look. To broaden its market, Mitsubishi is also offering silver and platinum in clay form now.[1] What gave researchers at

Mitsubishi the opportunity to get to this point was the quality of their initial insight. It combined a market need, even if in imprecise terms, with some proof that the technology considered had a fair chance of fulfilling the requirements of this need.

Because needs tend to be imagined in broad terms in the early stages of most technology programs, the onus of making the insight convincing often falls on the technology dimension. Typically, this means at least an initial demonstration of the principle underlying the technology to distinguish it from pure speculation. Figure 2-1 illustrates where such a "proof of principle" fits into the research process generally and of what it consists. While a great deal of research may have been done up to this point, most of it was associated with building an understanding of technologies in the field and catching up with the state of the art. More likely than not, this precommercial research was motivated by past knowledge and the curiosity of a researcher, particular competencies an organization wishes to develop for the future, or the mere fact that a generous research grant was available for pursuing it. The value it represents is similar to that of investments made in education and training—a sunk-cost that *may* prove useful should an appropriate opportunity present itself. It has social, but little commercial, value.

Commercial value in the technology starts to be recognized when something new gets elucidated with some confidence. It is when probing new principles and mechanisms, scoping out the properties of whatever is being studied, and formulating new hypotheses culminates in a good model and some proof that one is on the right track. The greater the market opportunity to which such proof is directed, the greater the *potential value,* meaning that it merits a closer look.

Hesselink's Holographic Storage Principle

One example of such a proof of principle linked to an unequivocal market opportunity is the recent demonstration of holographic storage.

The fact that a holographic system can store considerably greater information than two-dimensional disks has been speculated about ever since the first lasers hit the market in the 1960s. Dennis Gabor's hologram principle enunciated in 1947 is based on a coherent light beam scattering off an object and intersecting with another coherent beam; the interference pattern created where the beams cross harbors a three-dimensional image of the object that can be recorded in some medium such as a doped photorefractive crystal; when this hologram is probed with a third beam of coherent light, the original image reappears three-dimensionally.

Lasers constituted a ready source of coherent light and, therefore, a key enabling technology to make Gabor's principle practicable. But the availability of lasers was in itself not enough. To make holographic storage of digital data work, one needed a way to imprint the data on a laser beam; a

FIGURE 2-1

ARRIVING AT THE DUAL INSIGHT TO START COMMERCIALIZATION

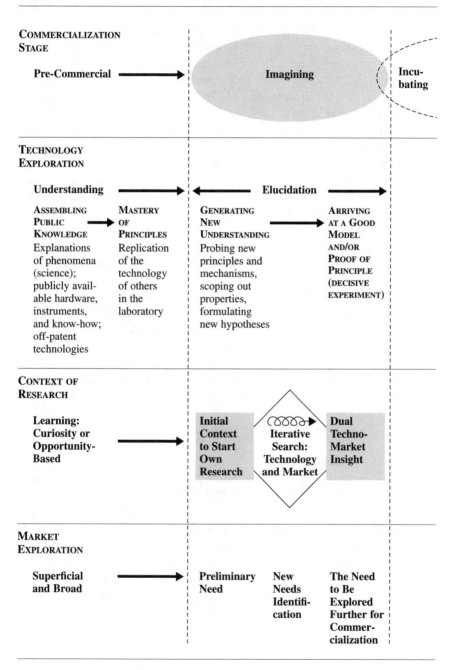

sensitive recording medium also needed to be found as well as a method to link the data to electron-based computers.

Almost thirty years after the invention of lasers, these other enabling technologies started to become available. In August 1994, a team at Stanford University led by physicist Lambertus Hesselink reported the first demonstration of a holographic storage system that read and wrote digital information while connected to a computer's hard drive.[2] In this demonstration, they were able to store 163 kilobytes of data with an error rate of about one bit in a million.

Both the storage amount and the error rate were orders of magnitude inferior to existing magnetic and optical storage systems—let alone the theoretical potential of a holographic system. But it was a proof of principle nevertheless. The Stanford team showed a Mona Lisa portrait copied from the holographic data storage system that was remarkably close to the original. The team was confident that the error rate could come down by several orders of magnitude and that, with the help of better light modulators and laser systems, the information density could be boosted to as much as 10 to 100 gigabytes—the equivalent of several hundred hard disk drives—per cubic centimeter of crystal.[3]

What Hesselink and his team have come up with is a potentially commercializable technology. Some knowledgeable observers feel that a working device is still five to ten years away and depends on future progress in the key enabling technologies. If incumbent technologies such as magneto-optics continue to progress at their current rates, they may even surpass the capabilities offered by holograms. But the first breakthrough has been made, and holographic systems for the storage of digital information now seek their place in the sun. Their potential is realistic enough for Hesselink to have started his own spin-off company, called Optitek, Inc., to bring the technology to market.

The intrinsic worth of Hesselink's technology comes from two facts simultaneously—the laboratory proof of principle achieved and the vast market opportunities that await it. The ability to store not just discrete bits but an entire page of data (or picture frames) at a time makes holographic storage ideal for applications such as video servers. Mathematical operations too can be performed not on numbers but on arrays of numbers, thereby turning a computer's memory into a processing unit of sorts.[4] With a worldwide market for information storage and retrieval products on the order of $50 billion in 1996, an attractive market awaits the technology if it is successful.

ARRIVING AT THE DUAL INSIGHT

Getting to the point illustrated by the Hesselink example is, of course, not easy. Yet to ascribe this to genius and serendipity only is to shroud technology in more mystery than it deserves. After all, most companies do fine with just above-average research talent. They simply have a better understanding of how to get to the point where commercialization starts and what to do next. They know how to convert research programs into commercially valuable technologies, regardless of what got the research started.

In practice, research gets initiated on the basis of a variety of impulses: an idea for a future new product; solving a customer's problem; a reaction to competitor moves or other threats to a business; and exploiting new principles to build a capability. All these impulses derive from a recognized need of one kind or another. What is different about them is how determinate (or precisely characterized) the end product is. In some cases, a specific product whose design attributes are known in advance is involved; in others, one knows the problem to be solved but not the precise product that will be needed. Depending on how the research gets pursued subsequently, all these starting points offer the promise of a technological breakthrough.

An Idea for a Future New Product

Perhaps the most common context in which research is undertaken today is where someone has an idea for a future new product—inventing a three-dimensional television, for example. The idea could be suggested by customers or by a researcher's own convictions. Either way, the specifications of the product determine the technological path to be taken.

A company that personifies this form of innovation today is Sony. As Kozo Ohsone, Senior General Manager of the Audio Group, put it in a speech given to the first-year students of the Harvard Business School in January 1988:

> We always have an image of how an ideal product would look and perform in our minds. This is not wishful thinking on our part, but a concrete plan for which exact product specifications have been drawn up. Unfortunately, it is usually impossible for us to begin producing this ideal version of our product immediately. Instead, a step-by-step plan must be formulated to guide us in reaching our goal. There are a number of factors which determine how quickly this can be accomplished, but the three most important ones have always been *size, weight* and *performance.* In order to reduce the size and weight of our Walkman without sacrificing quality, we have had to develop new integrated circuits, batteries, motors, recording heads and transport systems, and to fit everything into a case the size of a cassette tape.[5]

Sony TR-55 Camcorder

One case in which significant developments were needed in key enabling technologies was the lightweight Hi-8 video camcorder known internally as

TR-55. The TR-55 was conceived in 1985 as a successor to the company's first CCD camcorder (Video-8), which had just been launched that year. Planned to weigh a mere 1.7 pounds, the TR-55 was designed to incorporate a six-time power zoom lens, a variable-speed digital shutter, and a digital superimpose function.

During the four years it took to develop it, progress had to be made on several fronts: development of a new four-layer printed circuit board, a new low-melting-point solder and soldering process, a new set of miniaturized components, a new recording head, and a variety of new production equipment. Although all these technologies built on Sony's long-term thrust in increasing recording and component mounting density and in reducing size and weight generally, they were intended for a very specific design concept.

Solving a Customer's Problem

Another reason for starting a research program is to solve a customer's problem. Unlike the previous case, there is usually no product idea behind such research in the beginning; the hope, however, is that the problem will be generic enough to lead to products later.

An example is how Raychem recently developed its gel technology. As a seller of heat-shrink plastics used in splicing cables, the company was long familiar with the telecommunications industry. During the early 1980s, its field technicians began reporting problems of circuit shorting in terminal boxes, especially after floods and heavy rainfall. Although not a supplier of these boxes (which connected main lines to individual houses), the company decided to look into what the cause was. Intriguingly enough, most complaints turned out to be nuisance calls in that when repairmen showed up the problem had disappeared. Apparently, spiders were getting into the boxes and making webs on which water and dew collected, causing circuit shorting; this water would then evaporate, eliminating the problem later in the day.

What was needed was a better method for encapsulating the terminal posts. Being a materials-driven company, Raychem had already been experimenting with gels for many years. Within two years of recognizing the problem, its R&D department designed a cap filled with gel that simply screwed onto the posts. Developing a cap that was watertight but could be unscrewed when required did not involve a great deal of research and used an existing material, polyurethane.

Another source of ideas is problems being encountered by one's research colleagues. The invention of the scanning tunnelling microscope (STM) in IBM's research laboratory in Zurich is a case in point. The problem Heinrich Rohrer, one of the inventors of the device, was attempting to solve had nothing to do with microscopy as such. Rather, he had chosen to help some colleagues with tolerance problems they were encountering in the fabrication of Josephson junctions. Oxidation at the surface of these junctions was creating a thin film of insulating material, and the idea was to study these films through local spectroscopic and probing techniques. Lacking an appropriate tool to do the latter, Rohrer and his colleague Gerd Binning tried to develop their own local spectroscopic probe and, in the process, realized they could obtain topographic images down to the atomic level.

Reaction to Competitor Moves or Other Threats to a Business

Defensive motives for undertaking research are actually more common than the literature on innovation implies. The threat to an existing product line, either for environmental reasons or on account of products recently launched by competitors, acts as a spur to come up with new solutions and products. If a proprietary position is simultaneously sought, this can translate into a fairly significant research commitment.

ICI's FM-21 Membrane Cell

An example is the FM-21 membrane cell project undertaken by ICI in the 1970s to come up with a better way to produce chlorine and caustic soda.

The traditional way to produce chlorine and caustic soda on an industrial scale was through the electrolysis of brine using either a mercury cell or an asbestos diaphragm cell. Given the environmental and energy problems associated with these cells, many companies had started experimenting with a third technology—the membrane cell—beginning in the 1950s. Using a polymer-based ion-selective membrane, such cells would not only eliminate the need for mercury and asbestos, but were expected to yield purer products and use less power.

ICI's early work in membrane technology had resulted in its being granted a patent in 1961 on a zero gap membrane cell design. However, the nonavailability of viable membrane materials had prevented this work from advancing further. During the early 1970s a number of things happened to revive the company's interest in the field. Both mercury and asbestos had become environmentally suspect, the former partly on account of the Minamata tragedy in Japan. Companies such as DuPont and Asahi Chemical had also by then come up with new ion-selective membranes suitable for electrolizer cells. With several companies launching membrane cells on the market, ICI accelerated its efforts and, after an expenditure of some $20 million, developed its own design, named the FM-21. As Paul Henstridge, the project manager, recalls, "We were really responding to an environmental threat but could have bought in the technology from others. However, being a big company, we didn't want to be at the mercy of others."[6]

Exploiting New Principles to Build a Capability

Muscling into an existing market based on a new discovery that one, or even someone else, has made, is yet another common motive to start research. Whether it is a drug company wanting to develop a more efficacious delivery mechanism, or a semiconductor company aiming to come up with high-performance integrated circuits, newly discovered principles offer a unique opportunity to try different routes to solving known problems and coming up with superior products. In the case of software, mathematical algorithms serve the role of these new principles, offering more efficient ways to solve numerical problems.

In all such cases, what companies and individuals look for is a relatively underexploited principle that could distinguish their research from others'. While some potential applications may have been considered as part of the research (or search), these usually address a broad class of problems, rather than specific products.

Raychem's Surge Arrester

A good case in point is the way Raychem, Inc., got into ceramics technology. It all started in the early 1980s with Richard Sovish, then head of corporate R&D in Raychem's Swindon Lab in the United Kingdom, becoming convinced that Raychem ought to be in ceramics. While the company had established a leading position in conductive polymers, it needed to broaden its materials know-how to remain competitive in the future. Ceramics was this future.

The path to entering the ceramics field occurred to Sovish while attending a conference in France, where a presentation on the chemical processing of ceramics caught his attention. This was a new, although much talked-about, principle in 1983, and it offered a way to improve the performance of a variety of ceramics products. When he got transferred to the company's Menlo Park site the following year to head R&D in the Electronics Division, this is the principle he wanted to exploit. Hiring about a dozen people with different disciplinary backgrounds, he started a program to research these ceramics. Since the work was done within the electronics division, the applications Sovish had in mind were mainly in that field. But there was nothing concrete about these applications. The new ceramics capability based on chemical processing that Raychem acquired during the 1980s eventually resulted in a successful new venture selling surge arresters. But that was not among the applications thought of in the beginning.

This is the kind of technological innovation that is sometimes uncharitably referred to as "happy engineering"—where both the technology's outcome and the market need are unknown in advance. However, while there may be no product ideas driving such research, it tends to be based on a belief that whatever new functionality is developed *will* have some valuable use. Typically, it is about developing a new capability relevant to a class of problems.

Which of these paths get followed depends on the nature of a company and the strategy it adopts for directing its R&D. In a 1992 study of 200 Swedish companies of all sizes done by the Swedish IVA, only in 10 percent of the cases was academic R&D a significant source for a commercializable idea. By far the greatest source was customers' wishes and the behavior of competitors.[7] Large, science-based companies have a more even distribution of approaches; within them, furthermore, central R&D laboratories naturally tend to favor the last approach, while development laboratories concentrate on customer problems and product development needs. Table 2-1, for example, summarizes an approximate distribution for the central research laboratory of Brown Boveri Ltd (BBC, now part of ABB) during the period it was led by Ambros Speiser (from 1966 to 1987).

BREAKTHROUGHS CAN BE PATH-INDEPENDENT

Any of these reasons for starting to research a particular field can lead to a breakthrough idea linking a new technology to a market need. It all depends on how this research gets pursued. The current exhortation that research should be customer-driven, in other words, needs to be considered in a nuanced manner. Yes, customers must be at the center of one's development focus, but they are neither the sole source of initial ideas nor the best

TABLE 2-1

APPROXIMATE DISTRIBUTION OF IDEAS FOR STARTING RESEARCH AT BROWN BOVERI IN THE 1970S AND 1980S

		Approximate Percentage
1.	Idea for a future product	15
2.	Solving a customer's problem	15
3.	Reaction to competitor moves	20
4.	Exploiting new principles to build a capability	
	Own principles[a]	35
	Principles discovered by others	15
	TOTAL	100

SOURCE: Professor Ambros Speiser, interview, December 1995.
[a]Where the core patent belonged to Brown Boveri.

arbitrators for how these ideas should be pursued in research. Their role is critical only when actual products start to get developed.

What the history of a large number of recent breakthroughs tells us is that commercially valuable ideas come from: pursuing a particular problem deeply; being prepared to interpret and exploit serendipitous events by taking a broad view of the goal of research; and alternating between the technology and its uses in a purposeful manner.

Pursuing a Problem Deeply

Most breakthroughs come from exploring a problem deeply and thoroughly, regardless of how the problem originated. As Chester Carlson summed it in a 1964 lecture: "First of all you find a need that isn't supplied and then you immerse yourself completely in it for ten years or so; and just keep working and apply everything you see and read to the problem at hand and perhaps you will succeed."[8]

If breakthroughs are indeed associated with a deep understanding of the underlying phenomena, they can occur in any of the research modes described. Thus, although product-initiated research is the most determinate in terms of starting context, it too does not preclude major technological advances—provided the scope is broad enough. As Akio Morita of Sony stated:

> This approach does not prevent our people from doing basic research. We authorize a lot of it. For example, we use a new exotic kind of material for our Video 8 recording head, and that new material was developed by our metallurgists in our research center. There was no project for Video 8 when the new material search was authorized, but we knew that high-density recording would be an important field, and so we authorized the project. At the same time, even though we didn't have eight millimetre in mind, we knew that we needed to research new kinds of recording head systems. It developed that, for the new heads, new materials would be welcome, perhaps needed, and so the research projects came together at about the right time.[9]

Ambition, and not the source of the idea is, in other words, what results in a breakthrough. The design of the FM-21, for instance, could have been a simple, me-too one, just to give ICI its own membrane cell capability. But a conscious decision was made to differentiate it from competitive offerings and to exploit the advantages offered by the technology itself. As explained by Paul Henstridge, the business manager later put in charge to commercialize the FM-21,

> At an early stage in the development of ICI's ion-exchange membrane cell it was realised that here, for the first time in nearly eighty years, there was an opportunity to develop a radically new technology for the production of

chlorine. There was a determination to take full benefit of this opportunity and to immediately set challenging targets that had been found to be unattainable with mercury and diaphragm cell technologies. There was also a deliberate attempt to disregard much of what had gone before in the design of membrane cells for chlorine production; this had led to relatively large and complex fabrications relying on hydraulic rams for closure. From the very outset it appeared that there had to be scope for a significant step forward.[10]

Often, pursuing a technology deeply serves the purpose of expanding its context, so that researchers hope to come up with a better techno-market idea than the original one. The notion of depth, in other words, is partly one of going to the source of a technology and partly one of having different problems to solve.

In the case of Raychem's gel technology, for example, the research effort continued long after the initial problem had been solved. As the company's understanding of gels advanced, it naturally began looking for a wider range of sealing problems to solve. Following the terminal posts, it first leveraged its gel sealant technology to redesign the entire terminal block itself—something that had not been done for almost fifty years. Then, it delved deeper in understanding the chemistry and thermodynamics of gels, their structural properties, and ways of controlling the "tack" or stickiness of the material. This research, in turn, led to exploring other properties and applications, allowing the company's project team to imagine wholly new product platforms for things like sensors, actuators, and even artificial muscle.

Being Prepared for Serendipitous Events

Depth is often the handmaiden of serendipity too, which explains why major breakthroughs have occurred while researchers were pursuing R&D that is not mission-oriented. A good example is that of 3M's Scotchgard brand fabric protector.

Having acquired the rights to a unique electrochemical process from a chemistry professor in 1945, 3M launched an extensive program exploring the chemistry of reactive fluorochemicals in particular. The product that eventually became Scotchgard was based on a new route to fluorine containing acrylate monomers. However, while its initial nonwetting (by oil or water) properties had been discovered as early as 1952, it took another five or six years for a marketable version to emerge. As Donald LaZerte, a recently retired technical director involved with the Scotchgard brand since 1949 recalled, accidental events played a role too. "One day, one of those lucky accidents occurred that finally got us all going in the right direction. One of our lab technicians spilled a diluted polymer sample on her tennis shoes. When she tried to wash it off a few minutes later, she astutely observed the polymer's repellency and durability to the washing. At last, we were on our way."[11]

Serendipitous events, of course, occur all the time, and most go unrecognized. To marshal them in one's favor requires looking out for them constantly and keeping a broad enough view of the mission to be achieved. It requires a willingness to explore around the corners of a given problem and an open mind regarding what one might stumble upon.

This has occurred often in the pharmaceutical industry. In fact, many useful drugs have *not* come from searching for them in the laboratory. An example is antiarrhythmic drugs. Dilantin, one such drug, was shown by Merritt and Putnam in 1938 to be useful for epilepsy, and almost by chance it was brought into the treatment of cardiac arrhythmias. Lidocaine, another popular version, was first conceived of as a local anesthetic.

The changing context of research leading to a breakthrough is also illustrated by the invention of Xylocaine in 1942. Launched by Astra AB of Sweden in 1948 as a dental anesthetic, it became the most successful local anesthetic of all time. The research on which it was based began in 1932 and had nothing to do with anesthetics. Hans von Euler and his colleagues in Stockholm were interested in finding out the chemical link between genes and enzymes in order to map out the process of inheritance in purely chemical terms. One of the things they looked into was why individual strains of barley were so resistant to certain pests. During the course of these investigations, one of the researchers, Harry Hellström, isolated a poisonous alkaloid, which they called gramine, found only in plants deficient in chlorophyll. The hope then was that this toxin might lead to the development of an agricultural pesticide. When attempting to synthesize gramine in the laboratory, however, the researcher produced the wrong isomer (isogramine); when he tasted this, it produced a numbing effect on the tongue and lips. Although highly toxic by itself, it was felt that the anesthetic effect was due to an intermediate compound in the synthesis. That was the hypothesis picked up by Nils Löfgren, one of von Euler's students, in 1936. Over the next six years he and an associate, Bengt Lundqvist, synthesized dozens of compounds. The thirtieth compound, which they named LL30 (standing for their names and the synthesis sample), turned out to be Xylocaine.[12]

Such examples in the pharmaceutical field are legion. A Sandoz drug currently in early testing as a treatment for Alzheimer's disease, for instance, was initially discovered by researchers looking for new antihistamine medicines. And the pharmaceutical industry is by no means unique.

Alternating Between the Technology and Its Applications Purposefully

Deep research, without any context or problem to solve, is inevitably hostage to serendipity alone. Not everyone is as lucky and perspicacious as 3M's lab technician.

A more productive approach usually is to actively manage both the technology and its context simultaneously as research progresses. Such real-time coupling, rather than jumping to assessing the feasibility of the first idea one had, reduces the risk of poor judgments made at the beginning. It also opens up avenues that may not have been thought of and that become attractive with changes that might have occurred in the meantime. The spiral in Figure 2-1 illustrates what the process looks like in going from the initial context of the research to the final techno-market vision.

Belland AG

One illustration of this process is how Roland Belz got to invent his "intelligent plastics."

As a frequent traveler between Munich and Stuttgart, Roland Belz, the founder of Belland AG in Solothurn, Switzerland, was struck by the condition of public toilets, particularly the dirty and unhygienic state of toilet seats. While paper and "one-way" roller hand towels had already been introduced, why, he thought, was there no equally hygienic system for toilet seats? It seemed to him that the hygienic requirement for sitting down was much greater than for a towel to dry hands that were already clean.

Noting that there must be a business in addressing such a public nuisance, he dreamed up a number of ways to cope with it. A patent search was also done and, "I was surprised by how many clever techniques had already been proposed, ranging from a continuously pullable cover all the way to a disposable paper system," he said. "None of these ideas had been commercialized, probably because they were unworkable in practice or economically unfeasible."

Belz's idea in 1973 was to solve the problem with a plastic film that would be placed on the toilet seat and then flushed down after using. The problem was, however, that the water-resistant plastic would be nondegradable. It would not only clog pipes but would present environmental problems of disposal common to many plastics. The solution, he thought, would be a plastic that was water-resistant while in use but dissolvable in water later. All the work he did over the next few years, partly on his own and partly with the help of Battele in Germany, was geared to coming up with such a plastic for toilet seat covers. The development of these plastics involved a twelve-year effort (1973 to 1985) and cost $25 million.

Unlike other plastics, which are either always soluble in water (such as polyvinyl alcohol, polyacrylic acid, or polyacrylamide) or not water-soluble (most conventional plastics such as polyethylene, polyamide, polyvinyl chloride, or polystyrene), Belland's plastics have the property of remaining water-resistant while in use but can be dissolved in water after the addition of a reagent. The rate at which the plastics dissolve is, moreover, programmable.

This programmable water solubility feature caused some to refer to the Belland materials as "intelligent plastics." They had all the characteristics of conventional plastics, including water resistance and processability, but could be dissolved after their useful life was over. Unlike biodegradable and photodegradable plastics, their degradation was controllable. Also, compared to these environmentally friendly plastics, the Belland materials were easy to separate from other substances through dissolution and could be easily recovered from their solution for recycling purposes. Even without recovery, the resulting solution was environmentally harmless, promising to complete the hitherto broken cycle of biomass-oil-plastic-biomass.

Although making toilet seat covers motivated the development of these plastics, this application was only the beginning. Soon after the plastic was demonstrated in the laboratory, toilet seat covers were abandoned in pursuit of other, more useful and profitable applications. Through internal brainstorming sessions and the help of A.D. Little, Inc., Belland AG came up with over 200 possible uses for intelligent plastics. Some were direct replacements for existing plastic and paper products, while others represented whole new areas the material made possible. These applications included everything from agricultural films to protect seeds all the way to humidity sensors, hospital bedding, diapers, and camouflage coatings for the military. Just nine of these promised a market of nearly $1 billion in the United States alone. It was among the latter that Belland AG subsequently redirected its efforts.

Some would naturally criticize such lack of focus and dragging out of research. But toilet seat covers were not a great idea to begin with—there was indeed a need for them, but their economics and the technical challenge they posed turned out to be unattractive. Rather, it was the expanded scope of the technology that attracted investors to continue supporting it. The technology of intelligent plastics was also in itself quite unexceptional and, until very recently, there were some who doubted the claims Belz and his colleagues made about it. What made Belland AG one of the most talked about and richly funded start-up companies in Switzerland was the sheer attractiveness of the applications the technology could access. Not only was their variety immense, but they all addressed problems of an environmental nature at a time when Europe's "green movement" was gathering widespread support.

Trying to understand what Belz, and many inventors like him, did in terms of "technology push" versus "market pull" is to oversimplify. It can be misleading too.

The distinction between "market pull" and "technology push" has actually always been more rhetorical than real. While practically all the studies aimed at understanding the sources of innovation—and why some innovations succeed more than others—came out in favor of "market pull," they address the distinction tangentially at best. Other studies done later, moreover, either rejected the proposition based on empirical findings or found sufficient weaknesses in the way the proposition was framed and tested to declare a draw. Furthermore, as Mowery and Rosenberg point out, the methodological weaknesses of these studies, and the definition of what constitutes "market pull" used by them, makes their conclusions suspect, especially for major innovations.[13]

A better way to think about the process at the research stage is in terms of *alternating* between solving problems in Klondike Spaces and Homing Spaces. Klondike Spaces get their name from the exploration for gold in the Alaskan Klondike region at the end of the last century. With no clues to narrow their search, gold explorers looked everywhere they could, abandoning one area after another as they encountered dead ends. Inventors who put their faith in a combination of hard work (meaning exhaustive research) and serendipity are like these Alaskan explorers. Others pick up on a clue and "home in" to a target. They invest time and effort in understanding what clues to look for and then follow through to where it leads systematically. Good inventors have the capacity to engage in both types of problem solving, alternately widening the search and zeroing in on a potential clue that they recognize before others.[14]

Such alternative paths to discovery can be seen in the pharmaceutical industry today. Some companies first identify a disease, then identify models to predict drug behavior pertaining to that disease in animals and humans, and only then identify drugs that work in these models. Others, however, adopt a "mechanism-based" philosophy. They first find a receptor, a drug target, or an enzyme and then try to find compounds that interact with that target in some way. Using the new discipline of combinatorial chemistry, they are able to do this automatically, screening thousands of molecules a day. It is only once the compound has been identified that they look for the disease in which it might work. As Anthony Pottage, Director of Clinical Affairs at Astra AB, puts it, "Both approaches have their own merits and there is no way of telling which is the more effective way to a new chemical entity or drug candidate." For this reason, Astra encourages both approaches in its laboratories.

The same considerations apply at the market level. Market determinateness (the precision of a need) is indeed associated with successful innovations, but this is not to say that it must precede technological research. After all, one can be as wrong about a market as about the prospects of completing a new technology. Who among us, bemoaning the intrusion of the telephone in offices and homes, would have said cellular phones are exactly what we need, or that a very attractive niche existed between the telephone and mailed letters in the form of fax machines? The "market first" approach is a relative notion anyway. Is a single market study enough? What should the contents of this study be? How many potential customers to talk to and, more importantly, how thoroughly?

More important than which dimension leads innovation is maintaining a commercial focus throughout. As Mark F. Bregman, technical adviser to IBM's chairman and CEO, put it,

> Any good research, any high-quality research is ultimately driven by curiosity of the researchers and the real issue is: Are the researchers curious within the right context in which to be curious? And that context has to be one that is very much in contact with the needs that the marketplace has. And I think that is the biggest change in our view of R&D over the last several years.[15]

Establishing this context in advance is, of course, the hard part. Overspecifying it, moreover, can result in compromising the creativity of research.

[handwritten margin note: Cross-functional teams]

Seiko's FIB

An illustration of searching for context while the technology itself is being explored is that of the development of a new and highly successful focused ion beam system by Seiko Instruments, Inc. (SII) recently. Long known as a watch manufacturer, SII began to diversify in the early 1970s with a goal to add a major core competency, or technology, every decade. Starting with its precision mechanical engineering and design miniaturization base, the company first entered the field of electronics. Work done in the 1970s in this field led to the invention of the electronic quartz watch and later to products such as liquid crystal displays, integrated circuits, and quartz crystals.

The development of the focused ion beam (FIB) had its origins in the second wave of diversification—that into scientific instruments. Begun in the early 1970s, this business had grown to a significant size by the end of the decade. With a mandate by Seiko's president to grow this further, the company started a search for technologies that would result in new instruments to commercialize.

The three-man team that was put together in 1981 for the purpose were all former employees of JEOL, a manufacturer of electron microscopes and other beam instruments. In examining what general area of technology to concentrate on, they settled on two key words: semiconductors and vacuum. As Tatsuya Adachi, one of the team members, recalls,

> Although we had no capabilities in either field, the interface between semiconductors and vacuum looked like a promising area at that time. Our first thought was to make semiconductor production line equipment. But there were strong competitors already in the field and we were not geared up as a company to sell and maintain such equipment. In searching for what to concentrate on, we came across a paper on ion beam sources written in 1979

by a researcher at AT&T. Although there were twenty other companies and universities working in this area too we decided to explore it further.[16]

Exploring ion beam technology and building capabilities in semiconductors and vacuum proved fortuitous in the end, but only in hindsight. Gallium ion source emission had been known since the 1930s, but progress in the field had been held up for lack of good, high-quality vacuum and a stable ion source. Seiko's approach consisted in exploring the technology broadly, trying to find areas where it could make a contribution. Between 1981 and 1983, Seiko hired some thirty engineers knowledgeable in the field and spent $10 million in learning about and developing different components of an ion beam system—notably a stable ion source, beam control mechanisms, and a stable and accurately positioned stage (x-y-z table).

In developing different components of the technology, it was not clear exactly what product Seiko wished to or could commercialize. Early applications pursued included repairing photomasks and lithography, but neither was successful. An unexpected application then emerged. Drawing on his earlier experience with electron microscopes at JEOL, Adachi started experimenting with ion beams as an imaging tool. It turned out that ion beams actually offered better image quality than scanning electron microscopes (SEM). Imaging, therefore, became the key feature of the first prototype of the FIB built in 1984.

This prototype was a small piece of equipment, suitable just for scanning ion microscopy (SIM). If this was where things stopped, it is unlikely that the technology would have had much success. As Adachi put it,

> Although the microscope worked we knew the technology could do more. Being an electric design engineer, I was used to repairing printed circuit boards with cuts and solder. Why not, I thought, focus the beam more and make active chip modifications too? We began with making sharp, deep craters on a circuit and then gradually expanded our research to include the deposition of metals and insulators.[17]

This work led to another fortuitous discovery—that the FIB could become an imaging-cum-microfabrication tool. Although lasers were quite adequate for making small chip repairs and modifications, especially given the relatively undemanding requirements of the semiconductor industry in the mid-1980s, they needed a separate optical microscope for positioning. The FIB, on the other hand, not only offered better image quality but could both image and process on the same equipment. It was this dual function that finally drove the company's development effort, which resulted in the first commercial product Seiko launched in 1985. Successfully positioned among all the competing technologies, the FIB was an immediate hit.

As the Seiko FIB example suggests, the quality of a techno-market insight is actually an additive one. It comes from a clever imagination of *both* the technology and the context. One needs to give enough latitude and room for creativity on both dimensions for effective new techno-market insights to emerge. Companies highly proficient in technology creation often fail to introduce radical innovations because they define their own context (read strategy) too narrowly and rigidly. This is why it was the likes of Netscape and Sun Microsystem that launched the key enabling technologies for the Internet and not companies like DEC or IBM, which were better equipped to do so from both a technical and business standpoint.

GETTING TO A TECHNO-MARKET VISION QUICKLY

With depth and flexible contexts at the heart of the invention process, it is easy to condone delays and apparently aimless research. Many researchers, in fact, continue their work hoping to come up with a truly great idea. Not deciding on what to commercialize is a way for them to push at the frontiers more. Continuing exploration helps them refine the market opportunities identified or try out some other approaches that might benefit the technology itself. Research follows search, which then yields directions for further research, both with regard to the technology and the market. As Praveen Chaudhari of IBM put it in reference to the technology dimension,

> Researchers always want to do more because they still haven't figured everything out; they want to fully understand the basis of the technology before they put it into an application. After all, if you have done something creative you want to make sure you've done the best you can, that you haven't left something out. For a scientist, producing a product is trivial. He would like to move on to something more challenging once he has demonstrated his idea.[18]

Yet the process of exploration has to stop sometime if value is to be generated. Constant iteration between progress in a technology and its application possibilities does not mean going in ever widening circles. The start of commercialization is a willful act, not a natural transition that occurs automatically. One needs to settle on a techno-market combination, imprecise as it may be. An envelope needs to be drawn both around the technology's basic parameters and characteristics and around the attributes of the application(s) in which it will be used. This, incidentally, scopes out the territory to be patented and over which a proprietary position will eventually be sought. It is also the package that needs to be presented to the first set of stakeholders in the commercialization process—a lab director, some divisional colleagues, peers, and venture capitalists. Failing to decide on the package for too long a period of time is not only "happy engineering" at its best, but a recipe for being cut off from those whose support can be essential to go further.

Getting to an idea worthy of commercialization as quickly as possible is also an undeniable priority today. After all, research is a competitive arena too, with an increasingly narrow window of opportunity to prove a point. IBM is one company that has stated its intention to "make bets earlier" on which technologies to develop, eliminating costly duplication and the great debates within IBM over alternative solutions, which have slowed product introductions in the past. While shortcuts can be dangerous and counterproductive, there are certain things inventors and R&D managers can do to accelerate the start of the commercialization process. These include accelerating the rate of experimentation, grounding the research in known problems from the start, and intensifying contacts between researchers and the market.

Accelerating the Rate of Experimentation

Some companies today believe that the best way to come to a breakthrough insight is to leave researchers alone. Such a policy of benign neglect is seen as encouraging creativity. Constant reviews and screenings pose the danger of prematurely killing what might turn into a valuable new opportunity. Since insights cannot be programmed, management's greatest opportunity to add value is to let researchers plow away at their own rhythm.

While such a view did sometimes serve companies well in the past, it is becoming less and less tenable. Conjuring "big bang" innovations as the natural reward for supporting scientific inquiry, especially if the latter is curiosity-driven, is to chase an expensive illusion. Recent, rapid-fire innovations from some companies belie this view of the world. By using brainstorming and formal creativity techniques, involving the inventor as well as other colleagues, they have not only accelerated the search for solutions but defined inventions early. In today's corporation, they argue, there is no room to hide, nor the necessity of doing so. The Japanese, with their belief in "Three heads having the wisdom of Manjushiri," have been particularly zealous in transforming inventions into a collective endeavor from the beginning.

Active management of research basically means encouraging rapid experimentation. Progress in a technology does tend to be largely determined by the number of successful experiments made per unit of time[19] or, as Thomas Watson, the founder of IBM, used to say, "If you want to succeed double your failure rate."

For those who cannot afford these real experiments, "thought experiments" are a poor but nevertheless viable alternative. This is where structured problem-solving and creativity techniques involving the participation of a heterogeneous group of individuals have proved useful. An example was a recent session at Synectics, Inc., a creativity training company based in Cambridge, Massachusetts. Using analogies, even irrelevant ones, the purpose of this session was to generate alternative uses for a client company's music synthesis technology. Literally dozens of possibilities were generated and examined over a two-day period involving twenty participants. Among the more promising uses found for the technology was in hearing aids. By programming hearing aids for a dozen different frequencies, wearers could tune their own aids for their particular hearing defect. This was the birth of the ENSONIQ hearing aid.

While generating alternatives in this manner is useful, it should be remembered that it is no substitute for the kind of spiral search one sees inventors going through in their own minds. The "aha" they arrive at is often a refinement and confirmation of a mental picture of a technology they had already imagined. The adage that luck strikes the prepared mind is as evocative of the role an inventor's vision plays in coming to a breakthrough idea as it is a reflection on the tortuous search needed to get to it.

Grounding the Research in Known Problems from the Start

The main reason why some companies shy away from basic research is that they don't know, or cannot imagine, what it might be useful for. DuPont, which is among the disillusioned, actually has the answer in the history of its own Pioneering Research Lab. William Hale Charch, who ran this laboratory in the 1930s and 1940s, was unusual in two respects—in the way he defined pioneering research and in the precise manner in which he established context.

Pioneering research, for him, was not only methodological research; it was "any kind of experimental or research work which is directed toward the development of a comparatively radical new type of Cellophane [the product category to which his lab was dedicated] or Cellophane by a radically new process." Any means of getting there was equally legitimate in Charch's eyes. All the work this laboratory did, first in rayon and then in acrylics and polyester, was geared to finding "a wool substitute, a fur substitute, or bristle substitute, or special fibers for a multitude of industrial uses." Wool was one of the main targets throughout the late 1930s and the 1940s. Rather than just working on polymer chemistry, the laboratory embarked on a long quest to understand what gave wool its characteristics. Finding resilience the major property, Charch made "synthesizing for resilience" the goal. Out of this focus on wool came the invention of Orlon acrylic and Dacron polyester fibers.[20]

Curiosity-driven research, in other words, does not have to be context-free research. In fact, the more research is allowed to proceed deeply in a recognized problem area, the quicker and often better the outcome.

A good illustration is the self-aligning silicon gate invention made by Robert Kerwin of AT&T Bell Labs. In his words,

The invention itself was conceived in one afternoon's discussion with co-workers in February 1966. There was a recognized need at that time for a

[handwritten margin notes: although natural benefits from switching strategies periodically between non contextual experimentation and focused. Change is more key]

high yield process to make integrated circuits and the bottleneck appeared to be one of aligning gates accurately in a small area. The insight we had was not to think of the electrodes as metal only but to conceive of silicon as an electrode material as well. After figuring out how best to deposit the silicon gate and in what sequence we were able to reduce the invention to practice in three months' time. Subsequent development such as self-limiting etching, use of dual dielectrics, etc. took a bit more work, but we had enough put together to file a patent already in December 1966.[21]

Since the problem addressed was a pending one, commercialization was immediate. Robert Noyce and Gordon Moore at Fairchild Semiconductor, Inc., had already conceived of memories based on unipolar transistors and "clicked" immediately. They ran some experiments on the new gate and got the funding to establish Intel.

Xerox PARC's PaperWorks Project

A recent proponent of such research is John Seely Brown of Xerox PARC. "At PARC we want our researchers to be firmly grounded in the real world and in real problems. We want them to go to the root of the problem and come up with breakthroughs that address the problem as well as the problem space they are symptomatic of. If necessary, we want the problem space to drive the reframing of the problem itself."[22] The expression Brown uses to describe such research is "marinating in a space of reality."

Making connections with real problems does not render such research unsuited to breakthroughs, nor does it limit its applicability. Compared to mission-oriented research, which often implies going around barriers encountered in achieving a pre-set objective, grounded research attacks the root of the problem itself. As Brown puts it, "In solving root problems you sometimes do come up with a fundamental breakthrough that not only solves the problem at hand, but opens up new possibilities."

An example is that of Xerox's new PaperWorks family of products. As a "documents" company, Xerox had launched several programs in optical character recognition technology, all related to reading a document and converting it into digitally editable form. The problem, however, was what to do when the original document itself was dirty or degraded. One of the research projects, therefore, focused its attention on image interpretation in the presence of "noise." In the process of attacking this problem, one of the researchers started to reframe the problem itself. Rather than come up with a way to interpret soiled documents, he started to work on a way to digitally encode separately everything that was on the document. Thus, in addition to a normal printed text, each document would contain a small space in which the entire document was reproduced in digitally readable characters. The latter, consisting of rows of tiny forward and back slashes, could be hidden in the background of text or disguised as a decorative page border.

Such a *glyph* encoding not only meant a duplicate record but also an additional means by which the document could interface with a machine—reconceiving the document itself as a user interface. Thus, for example, users can access their personal computers from fax machines directly, and instruct the computer to store, retrieve, and distribute a file in one's absence. A soiled original poses less of a problem since all the information is encoded digitally with error-correcting codes; the latter, moreover, facilitate "reading" of the document more expeditiously than with conventional scanners.

What one sees good research directors doing today is to keep a problem context in mind from the beginning and then shape it on a real-time basis. The initial context tends to be followed by an exploratory phase covering both the technology and the market. But they try to limit and control this exploration to come as quickly as possible to a refined context—the idea truly worth pursuing.

Grounded research, in other words, is not short-term, problem-solving research. It is akin to basic research in the sense that it tackles problems in depth, going to their root and understanding the principles driving them. The only difference lies in the nature of the problem being solved. Rather than researching just the principles for their own sake, it is about researching principles fundamentally but in a given context.

The role of governments in articulating needs can sometimes aid the process as well. Whether it was the Apollo program in the United States, the fast breeder reactor program in France, or a host of national projects undertaken by MITI in Japan, they all served to stretch the imagination of researchers. Not all the technologies developed for these programs found use as intended, but they were at least grounded in concrete product ideas from the start.

Big, eye-catching programs are not the only way for governments to encourage context. Even modest efforts to get researchers to address societal concerns can be mutually beneficial—both to society and to the researcher concerned. The Dutch have created a network of thirty-eight public "science shops," which are university-based centers where community groups, public interest organizations, local governments, and labor unions can commission faculty and students to investigate societal concerns. A similar initiative is being planned in the United States and Canada.[23] While some of the problems these science shops bring to the attention of researchers may seem trivial, they should be seen for what they are—providers of an *initial* context for profound research.

Intensifying Contacts Between Researchers and the Market

While structured problem-solving and creativity techniques are indeed helpful, they are not the only way of getting to new ideas quickly. What aids the process is bringing different perspectives to bear on a problem on a continuing basis. This can be done by creating a climate of dialogue and sharing within a company or by instituting formal venues where technological issues get discussed on a regular basis.

An example of the latter are the science policy committees many companies have established. While their main role is to approve and review projects, they can often be a vehicle for new ideas because of their broad perspective. A by no means atypical case is that of American Cyanamid's launch of its Combat insecticide.

The story of Combat goes back to 1979, when American Cyanamid set up an interdivisional research policy committee. One of the topics at a meeting of this committee in 1979 was how research in other business groups could better benefit the company's Consumer Group. After a series of meetings between the Consumer Group and the Agricultural Research Division, aimed at generating and ranking ideas for commercialization, an idea for commercializing a roach control product emerged. Using insecticide technology from the Agricultural Division as well as the help of outside consultants with knowledge of cockroaches, the Combat roach control system was developed—which *Fortune* magazine named as one of the ten best product developments of 1985.[24]

Many companies have now realized that innovative ideas come more from active interaction among researchers than from people working away on their own in a cloistered environment. Whether it is by forming cross-disciplinary teams (called *benkyoukai* in Japan), creating open space offices, or instituting structured brainstorming sessions on a regular basis, the purpose is to speed up and multiply ideas generated. The more people talk to one another and exchange ideas, whether it is through electronic media or white boards installed in cafeteria and meeting rooms, the greater the chances that creative technical insights will emerge *and* be linked to market opportunities that the original proposer may not have thought of.

The logic of cross-pollination explains the many alliances one sees at the research stage these days. Companies with complementary skills get together to generate new product ideas and technologies without necessarily engaging in a long-term contractual relationship or even exchanging money. Their hope is that, if and when something new is developed by fusing their expertise, all parties will get to commercialize a piece of the end product or system. Thus, in HP's alliance with Nokia Oy at its Bristol laboratory, HP is contributing its computer skills, and Nokia its expertise in wireless communication. The product being developed jointly, called OmniGo 700, is a computer with a docking port into which a cellular phone can be plugged, creating a wireless device about the size of a hardcover novel that can send and receive data. The hope is that the OmniGo 700 will eventually become a mainstay for mobile computer users.[25]

A great deal of what laboratory researchers work on often goes unnoticed, not because of incompetence or malice, but because no one was around to place the discovery in a useful context. To some extent, large companies have an advantage over lone inventors here. Not only do they offer greater opportunities for interacting with colleagues and "internal" customers, but their research directors tend to have a wider reference base to draw upon. Thus, as Robert Kerwin of AT&T Bell Labs recalls,

> I would not have been able to make my gate process discovery in a university. The reason corporate laboratories are making most of the "basic" discoveries today is that their scientists are stimulated by the demands from other scientists working on a problem. Corporate scientists team more than university scientists do.[26]

The role research directors can play in making connections is illustrated by how IBM came up with its magneto-optic technology. As Praveen Chaudhari, one of the inventors, put it,

> The initial work we did was for our magnetic bubble program. However, it soon occurred to me that the same material was excellent for magneto-optic applications. The reason that occurred to me—and that is important—is that I was also responsible for the magneto-optic program at that time. So I was aware of the need for a material there and I could then make that connection.[27]

The important role context plays lies behind why so many inventions get made by the user community. As Eric von Hippel found in studying the locus of innovation in several industries, it is only in some industries that a "manufacturer" of a piece of equipment or device accounted for a bulk of the inventions. These industries were typically those where manufacturers possessed most of the technical know-how and experience and where they were best positioned to exploit the economic benefits accruing from the invention. In scientific instruments and certain equipment technologies, on the other hand, users accounted for most of the innovations. They not only perceived a need for the invention but invented the instrument itself, built a prototype, and proved the prototype's value by applying it. They were the ones most qualified to do so and needed the innovation to advance their own research.[28]

The way context gets established sometimes is actually counterproductive: not enough of it in the early stages and then too much of it later. While the former results in aimless research in the hope of a "scientific" breakthrough, the latter either leads to application-specific technological blind alleys or to inadequate (even inappropriate) exploitation of research results. What is needed is an evenly rich context throughout.

A Japanese company, Hamamatsu Photonics K.K., has found several ways to offer its researchers a rich context from the beginning. Founded in

1948, this $300 million company is best known as a leading supplier of photomultiplier tubes that are used in a variety of imaging devices. In parallel with the basic research it does on the nature of light, Hamamatsu is in constant touch with researchers in a variety of areas, such as medicine, biotechnology, physics, and astrophysics, to find out how photonics technology can help them in their work. Whereas, previously, it asked these "customers" how its products were being used and could be improved, it now engages in research alongside them to define future applications. Thus, in 1985, it set up a lab in Tsukuba to carry out research in the life sciences. As Teruo Hiruma, president of the company, explains,

> After we set up our instruments we found a lot of biology people from other institutions coming in to use them. To better understand their needs, we hired some biochemists of our own to work with them and to suggest what kind of instruments we should build. One of the ideas we found was a way to measure DNA sequences very fast. Another was in the study of electroporation [making cell membranes permeable by exposing them to a short electric pulse]. These ideas led to the development of our ultra-fast streak camera.[29]

A more ambitious program in a similar vein is "The International Conference on Peace Through Mind/Brain Science" that Hamamatsu has been sponsoring since 1987. Held regularly every one and a half years, this conference brings together experts in photonics technology and mind science from around the world. The purpose is to understand how one might carry out real-time observations of the functioning of the human brain as it exercises control over mental activities. Researchers who attend the conference come to understand not only new scientific challenges but also concrete uses to which their discoveries can be put as soon as they succeed.

SUMMARY

The caricature of inventors waking up in the middle of the night with a full-blown clever idea to be marketed is just that, a caricature. Most ideas evolve through constant iteration between a new technological capability and a market need. There are, moreover, several paths leading to the combination (techno-market insight) that starts the process of commercialization.

Getting to a valuable insight quickly is partly a serendipitous event. But it can be "engineered" somewhat. The start of the process of technology commercialization, in other words, should be seen as a willful act, not something one stumbles into after some research results have been obtained. The engineered insight may not be the one that gets pursued in the end. It simply should be seen as creating enough excitement to take things further.

In practice, there are three ways to come to a techno-market insight speedily: accelerating the rate of experimentation, using formal creativity techniques if necessary; grounding the research in known problems from the start and pursuing the latter deeply; and intensifying contacts between researchers and the market, allowing them to anticipate uses they may not normally think of.

The first task in technology commercialization involves managing this process of idea creation effectively. Both for research managers within companies and for government agencies, this translates into:

Providing as wide and rich a commercial context as possible, including scenarios of the future;

Creating the conditions wherein chosen problems are pursued deeply and in a nonobvious fashion for a while; and

Encouraging contacts, brainstorms, and idea exchanges, rather than encouraging solitary, withdrawn research and skunkwork over a long period of time.

Market Study / FDA regs / Category anal.
    before   Clinical Trials end

    FACTORS : - 2 yrs coding
              - FDA regs
              - journal publications

                                        Clin
                                        Trials

                                        Focused
                                        experimtn

3

MOBILIZING INTEREST
AND ENDORSEMENT

EVERYTHING—EVEN TECHNOLOGY—IS POLITICS. BRINGING A NEW TECH-
nology to market is above all an exercise in resource assembly and a collective enterprise. Failure to recognize this explains why many otherwise
meritorious discoveries lie idle or get delayed in their commercialization,
sometimes by decades. A perverse corollary is that economically efficient
technologies can be superseded by less meritorious ones.

Imagining a breakthrough idea, as all inventors come to realize, is often
the easy part of innovation. Taking it the next few steps—proving the concepts underlying it, finding robust uses for it, and interesting others—is
where many run into a wall. What is needed is not large sums of money, nor
the approval of a large number of people, but enough support to convert an
insight into a project worth pursuing. Without such support progress is
invariably slow; worse, its absence can translate into widespread skepticism
when the technology actually hits the market.

In a less hurried and competitive world there was little need to sell a
new technology's potential in advance. Inventors usually plowed ahead on
their own, convinced of the value of what they were doing and taking the
time necessary to convert an idea into a marketable product. If resources
were a constraint, they were usually coped with through relatives and
friends and by implementing the process gradually.

With so many new technologies vying for the attention of resource
providers, choices about which technologies to fund must be made early
and more confidently than in the past. In fact, the greatest leverage in
time to market for technology-based products lies in recognizing which

technology to back. Those who take the plunge early with conviction are the ones who establish leadership in a technology, gain a proprietary position, and then dominate the products emanating from it.

As for inventors, reaching out to external stakeholders early may not be easy, but it plays an important role in the commercialization process. The fact that their ideas are still tentative naturally makes them reluctant to seek feedback. Likewise, reaching out to resource providers to speed their work, they fear, will limit their freedom to explore and hence compromise the breakthrough they have in mind. But, if approached in a considered manner, such feedback and support not only facilitate getting started but improve the chances of subsequent success.

As Brown and colleagues found in comparing the performance of inventors who obtained grants under the U.S. Department of Energy's (DOE) Energy-Related Inventions Program (ERIP) instituted in 1974, with those who may have qualified (had their proposals offered sufficient energy benefits) but didn't, the former outperformed the latter on several measures—the proportion that entered the market finally, cumulative sales per technology, patent protection obtained, cumulative funds raised, percentage of funds raised from nonpersonal sources, employment creation, and long-term survival. Apart from the initial funding, ERIP provided these inventors greater credibility in raising funds subsequently from other sources, and technical and market feedback as part of the approval process.[1]

Garnering support for an idea early to speed up the innovation process and facilitate its subsequent marketing requires paying attention to the following: dispelling skepticism and having the idea endorsed by colleagues and peers; understanding the criteria and process people use to support early-stage research; reaching out to others in the research community in order to obtain their cooperation in problem solving and application definition; and communicating the idea effectively to those whose interest really matters.

DISPELLING SKEPTICISM

Just as there are well-established protocols for conducting research, the scientific community has evolved certain criteria for supporting new ideas. Not following these commercialization protocols and pushing ahead single-mindedly may result in a breakthrough product. But chances are it won't be accepted, and the inventor will have to retrace his steps.

One important aspect of this protocol is the need for early endorsement by those whose opinion matters. Skepticism, not optimism, tends to accompany most new discoveries and technology-based ideas, which explains the often heard maxim, "In science, the credit goes to the man who convinces the world, not to the man to whom the idea first occurred."

[handwritten margin notes: wrong in thinking; IPO $; validates business]

Inventors who have not taken the trouble to disclose the technology, with appropriate safeguards, and plowed ahead on their own to incorporate it later in a functioning device face two barriers: one relating to what the device can and cannot do and the other relating to the underlying technology itself. If the latter comes as a surprise, unverified and unendorsed by opinion leaders, the normal reaction is to dismiss it as voodoo technology. Controversy and reexperimentation are sometimes politically motivated. But they can lead to considerable delays and doubts about the device itself.

Haber's EMP

Consider, for example, the case of electromolecular propulsion that Haber Inc. recently brought to market. After years of often frustrating research, Norman Haber of Towaco, New Jersey, had come up with what he considered a breakthrough technology in the late 1960s. This had to do with a hitherto unknown electrokinetic effect with potential applications in a wide range of industries.

Prior to Haber's discovery there were four known electrokinetic effects—electrophoresis, electroendoosmosis, streaming potential, and electrosedimentation. They described how charged molecules migrated through fluids and gels when subject to an electric potential and were used for identifying large molecules contained in a sample and for separation purposes. Electrophoresis, for example, is commonly used today for separating DNA molecules according to their molecular weight and plays an important role in the identification of genetic codes.[2]

All these principles had been discovered in the early years of the twentieth century and had been fully described mathematically by the 1950s. What Haber had discovered was a fifth principle that, unlike the known ones, involved nonlinear and nonelectrolytic processes. It too utilized a DC electric field to cause molecules to migrate as in electrophoresis, but could be used with a variety of media, both aqueous and nonaqueous. By using very little current, it made high driving voltages possible without the need for cooling, thereby allowing quicker analysis. Unlike the previously known principles, its advantage was also that it permitted the separation of nonpolar, uncharged molecules, something that could not be done by the other electrokinetic effects. The name given to the new principle was electromolecular propulsion (EMP).

Like many basic discoveries, a virtually unlimited number of applications could be envisioned for EMP. Figure 3-1 summarizes the three main areas of practical applications Norman Haber and his colleagues had thought of.

Haber's claims were not just hyperbole. No less an authority than Rollin Hotchkiss of the Rockefeller Institute and Member of the National Academy of Sciences put the discovery in the ranks of a new paradigm:

FIGURE 3-1
EMP—ELECTROMOLECULAR PROPULSION

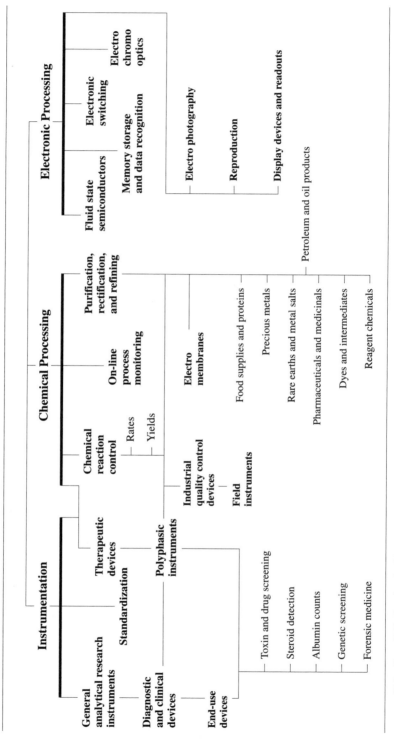

SOURCE: Haber Inc., 1991. Reprinted with permission.

It is a very powerful theory and a very rare one, indeed, that predicts well beyond experiments that have already been done. . . . The applications are so enormous I can't imagine how many of them there are or what future ones there will be . . . A lot of theoretical and, eventually, practical biological applications [will] be forthcoming. . . .[3]

Professor L. Pierce Williams of the New York Academy of Sciences was equally rapturous:

Norman Haber's discovery of Electromolecular Propulsion will lead to a radical new theory of the liquid state and to our understanding of inter-molecular actions. . . . It seems to me to be quite analogous to the discovery of X rays by Roentgen, which ultimately led to a revolution in our understanding of matter.[4]

Unfortunately, apart from the two professors and Norman Haber himself, few others thought the discovery merited any attention. Some, such as Andreas Chrambach, a specialist on electrophoresis at the National Institute of Health, were downright dismissive: "There is no such thing as EMP," he said, criticizing the fact that Haber had not sufficiently subjected himself to peer review. The patent office was not convinced about the validity of the invention either, despite the fact that Haber brought along a prototype device to demonstrate his principle when applying for a patent in 1969. With input from nineteen different examiners it turned down all of Haber's claims in the beginning. When the U.S. patent was finally issued in 1976 it failed to convince patent offices in other countries. It took until 1990 for the EMP patent to be granted in Japan and Sweden, and the German patent was not issued until May 1991.

During the twenty-five years following the discovery of EMP, and the more than twenty years after it had been demonstrated in the laboratory, the interest in the technology has been minimal. Only nominal amounts of venture capital could be raised. Several companies in the instrumentation field were approached to help commercialize the technology but, as Haber said, "only one was interested but offered what amounted to a secretary's salary for one year."[5]

Because of the general skepticism Norman Haber encountered, he had little choice but to demonstrate the EMP principle in working applications himself. The application he chose in 1992 was an analytical instrument (called the 15K-1 EMP) that could be used in laboratories for separating a narrow range of molecules. Priced at $12,500, the 15K-1 even had to be offered as a complete system including trial supplies of different substrates, gels, and solvents for media formulation. An instructor's manual accompanied the package, explaining not just how to operate the instrument but which solvents to use on particular substrates and how they were to be handled to obtain the promised results. This was done at enormous expense for a company that was facing constant financial pressures. What Haber really needed was a strong industrial partner to exploit the many uses his invention could be put to.

The EMP story is a good illustration of a potentially valuable technology, developed within a valid and attractive market context, that then went nowhere. It stalled because Norman Haber was unable to mobilize the interest of all of the key stakeholders one sees in early-stage technologies. And, absent interest, there was little support.

Allowing Others to Verify the Idea

Other scientists are often the first "customer" for a new technology. They are by nature a skeptical and iconoclastic lot. They have seen too many instances of pathological science, or what Irving Langmuir, the 1932 Nobel Prize winner in chemistry, called "the science of things that aren't so." Citing "discoveries" of new phenomena such as mitogenetic rays, N-rays, the Allison effect, and the Davis-Barnes effect earlier this century, he referred to these as cases "where there is no dishonesty involved but where people are tricked into false results by a lack of understanding about what human beings can do to themselves in the way of being led astray by subjective effects, wishful thinking or threshold interactions."[6]

A recent example of pathological science was the discovery of polywater by Nikolai Fedyakin, a Russian chemist, in the early 1960s. As Gary Taubes put it in his history of the controversy surrounding cold fusion, "Polywater was purported to be a variant of water which neither froze nor boiled. In fact, it had few of the same properties as water except that it seemed to be made of water and nothing else. Indeed, the parallels between the two episodes (polywater and cold fusion) are striking, and one wonders if pathological science is a kind of infection, like the measles, that attacks the scientific community periodically and has to run its predestined course."[7]

The polywater research community had become polarized into believers and skeptics—the latter suggesting that polywater was no more than contaminated water while the former blamed lack of confirmation on careless experimentation. With polywater researchers refusing to exchange samples with other laboratories, especially those run by skeptics, there was no way to reconcile the points of view. Until the polywater episode finally died, as much from disinterest as an inability to come up with a demonstrable proof, the scientific community fought the issue outside the traditional peer-reviewed literature,[8] much the same as in cold fusion.

It is naturally difficult to state in advance whether a particular discovery belongs to the category of scientific pathologies or breakthroughs—especially if its proponent is an eminent scientist. Much depends on events immediately following it, particularly whether other scientists succeed in verifying the discovery.

This need to be able to reproduce an experimental phenomenon has long been part of the tradition of scientific inquiry. Ideally, scientists want to know both that something really works and why. However, given the confidentiality that may surround the details of the why, they are content, at a minimum, to be able to reproduce a finding in their own laboratory based on the technique suggested by the pioneer. The latter is no more than a safeguard against exaggerated or, worse, wrong claims.

Intra-lab results (handwritten margin note)

Having a Good Model Helps

While both Haber's EMP process and Roland Belz's intelligent plastics were received with the same amount of skepticism initially, the latter was able to mobilize considerably greater resources over the ten years following the first laboratory demonstration. The difference, in retrospect, did not lie in the relative market opportunity each represented. If the EMP process promised a somewhat smaller market, there were immediate applications available and considerably fewer infrastructural barriers. The cost benefits of Haber's process were also more evident right from the beginning than was the case with Belz's water-soluble-on-demand plastics, which required an expensive manufacturing process and far greater investments in downstream infrastructure to be viable. The difference primarily lay in the credibility of the underlying principle that was advanced. The EMP was totally mysterious, even to experts. While there was skepticism also around what Belz had achieved, at least people understood the approach he was taking. Having Battele as an early research partner gave confidence too.

With so much hype in the technology business, the best antidote to skepticism is a good theory—one that can be understood, analyzed, and reproduced if necessary. The scope of the theory, moreover, needs to extend beyond one particular phenomenon; it needs to include an understanding of how the phenomenon is manifest under a range of conditions, how it can be manipulated, and what its practical limitations are. Using scientifically acceptable methodologies not only gives confidence in a technology, it makes it easier for resource providers to imagine scaled-up and commercial versions of it. With today's concern over things like safety and environmental impact, one not only wants to know how something works but why, and what its consequences might be.

The O-Ring

An old but still illustrative example of the need for understanding why something works is that of the famous O-ring, invented by Niels Christensen in 1933. Although it did not make its inventor as rich as it could have, this simple component ranks along with the safety pin and the paper clip as one of the world's most useful inventions applied in numerous fields. Placing a simple rubber ring in a straight-sided groove, Christensen had addressed a problem that had long challenged the mechanical industry—how to seal pistons so that they could slide easily while blocking the flow of fluids such as lubricants or gases. The cleverness was not so much in the rubber ring, which had been used before but tended to wear out too quickly. Rather, it was in the dimension of the groove in which it was placed—a width of roughly one and a half times the ring's diameter. If too big or too small, the seal was not effective; either the piston would not slide smoothly or the ring would wear out fast.

Today O-rings are to be found in a variety of products ranging from fountain pens and liquid soap dispensers to hydraulic presses and reciprocating engines. Yet, despite its obvious utility, despite the fact that it worked the first time it was tried, and despite the fact that it required little effort to be incorporated in end products, the O-ring was not accepted immediately. In fact, it was not until 1940—seven years after the patent was issued—that the first application for it was found. This application was, moreover, in the military, a particularly aggressive user of new technologies. The opportunity came accidentally too in that this was the period when Franklin D. Roosevelt's defense buildup started in the United States. Tens of thousands of airplanes were to be built, and each would have hydraulic systems controlling doors, landing gear, and surface actuators. Millions of hydraulic shafts would need to be sealed. Fortunately for Christensen, two U.S. Army Air Corps engineers, Nicholas Bashark and Elworth M. Polk, agreed to give O-rings a try. They installed some on the worn, rusty landing gear of a Northrop A-17A, and the seal held up through eighty-eight bumpy landings. They then ran controlled, quantitative laboratory tests—all at military expense over a two-year period. Because the O-ring passed all these tests it became specified as the seal of choice in virtually every application on aircraft where it could be used.

Outside this military application, however, the O-ring experienced further delays in commercialization. One source of inertia was the use of alternative components, notably V-rings and U-rings, each employing a different geometry of groove and seal and considered adequate for the purpose assigned. Even the minimal amount of rework called for by the O-ring acted as a barrier. More important a barrier was the perceived risk. The O-ring obviously worked, but no one could figure out why it did—in fact, even Christensen had misinterpreted the mechanism underlying the component in his 1933 patent. This naturally created skepticism on the part of eventual users who wanted to understand the ring's technical possibilities and limitations before switching to it. It was only in 1941, using transparent cylinders and slow-motion photography, that the ring's functioning was completely understood.[9]

Arriving at a good theory marks an important watershed in the commercialization process, assuaging the skepticism of resource providers as well as providing a jumping-off point to those who want to use it later and follow its progress. It allows the accumulation of extensive experimental data while permitting others, often less qualified than the inventor, to practice the technology.

UNDERSTANDING THE CRITERIA AND PROCESS FOR SUPPORTING EARLY-STAGE RESEARCH

Supporting early-stage research is nearly always the taking of a bet. There are no simple rules, whether for zero-stage funding intrepid venture capitalists provide; grants given by public agencies; or the backing research directors provide to equip laboratories, assemble researchers around an idea, and release time to pursue it. The best the proponent can do is to understand the criteria generally used by these stakeholders and the process by which judgments get made.

Regardless of whose support is sought, two criteria invariably surface: the credibility and reputation of the individual(s) proposing the idea, and the quality of science being used.

Given the uncertain nature of the outcome of such research, it is only natural that the greatest weight is often placed on the individuals themselves. As stated by Ambros Speiser, the former head of BBC's research, "Resource allocation in the beginning is a matter of intuition regarding the idea and judgment about the individual(s) proposing it. I mainly looked for a researcher's judgment in the past, his originality and his discipline to carry things forward. Although hard to admit, the fact is that some people are more consistently right than others."[10] Empirical studies on research productivity confirm Speiser's observation. As Narin and Breitzman report, a small number of researchers in most research organizations account for a disproportionate share of inventions. The most productive inventors may be five to ten times as productive as the average inventor.[11]

As for the quality of science, this pertains to the originality of the approach, the potential the approach offers to get around constraints and limitations in the incumbent technology, and the promise it holds for providing a clear pathway to improving the characteristics of the function to which it is targeted. The reason early-stage stakeholders attach importance to all this is not so much to choose among competing approaches but to know whether researchers have thought through all the pitfalls in advance and know where they are going.

Beyond these two criteria, the factors that get taken into account depend on the stakeholder addressed. Venture capitalists are particularly attracted by two things: the individuals involved and the commercial potential offered within a reasonable period of time. Private companies, on the other hand, look for strategic fit in addition to this, but each company has its own time and risk profile. Government agencies, finally, are motivated by sociopolitical and macroeconomic considerations in addition to the intrinsic merits of a project.

Public and Government-Supported Technologies

The criteria become particularly jumbled when noncommercial considerations enter the calculus—something inevitable in government funding of basic research. Why is it, for example, that many of the problems addressable by technologies already available lie unattended, while major resources flow to seemingly less useful and uncertain projects such as atom smashers of various kinds or the Gravity Probe? The latter is one among many of the expensive experiments that have been conducted over the years to confirm (or contradict) various theories advanced by Einstein. One recent case is that of Gravity Probe B. This experiment, to be conducted by Stanford University and Lockheed, involves measuring a single parameter characterizing the spin of a gravitational field predicted by general relativity. It involves launching a satellite gyroscope experiment scheduled for 1999 at a reputed cost of $500 million. As Joseph Silk of the Department of Astronomy and Physics at the University of California put it in a letter to *Science,*

> Some scientists consider that the result is already known; others doubt that the degree of accuracy required for the gyroscope to remain stable—a thousandfold better than has been achieved on the ground—can be attained in space; and still others note that even if Gravity Probe B were to find a discrepant result, the only sensible reaction would be to lobby for funds to refly an independent experiment. So complex is Gravity Probe B that only if the anomaly were confirmed would it be believed. These tests of Einstein's theory are beautiful in concept. The reality is that in times of budget compromise and cuts, more tangible science is being sacrificed to test fundamental ideas that no one really disputes.[12]

Judging the relevance of such experiments to human and even economic concerns stretches most people's logic. But logic there is, and it lies in domains not amenable to economic analysis. One could say that these projects will act as a spur to the supplying industries, create jobs and other new technologies, be vital for national security, and so on, but so will many other uses of scarce resources.

An important reason why the Gravity Probe B project continues to be funded is also the selling skills of its main proponent, Professor Francis Everitt of Stanford University. Since 1980, "This English-born mustachioed scientist [has] assembled an impressive political coalition that has fended off six attempts by the White House, the National Aeronautics and Space Administration (NASA), and Congress to cancel the project."[13]

When they do appeal to economic logic, governments tend to support new technologies where:

> Generic enabling technologies are involved, which are in the nature of nonrival, public goods, meaning that they have to be produced only once for many people to benefit and that one person's benefit does not reduce its value to others;

> Private inventors and companies either find the technology too onerous and risky for them individually or are incapable of appropriating its resulting benefits to make their investments worthwhile;

> Needed technical standards are best established through the aegis of a "neutral" body with the power to police them later;

> Government intervention can signal endorsement of the technology and hence motivate private companies to join in the effort more confidently; and

> Private companies would benefit from information exchanges and the establishment of communication networks among them but are hesitant or incapable of doing this on their own.

The last two criteria have become increasingly important today based on the experience of Japan and the European Union. Thus, the Japanese Economic Planning Agency makes periodic forecasts of future technology utilization taking into account what is already available and what the government perceives to be important for the nation. Whether right or wrong in a predictive sense, these forecasts capture the imagination of a broad cross-section of individuals and mobilize companies to start working in particular areas. Even more important than signalling is the promotion of communication channels between researchers. Recognizing the need for such contacts and cross-disciplinary research, Japan's Science and Technology Agency (STA), for example, initiated its System for Incubating Novel Ideas in 1992. Although the level of funding is small (about $1 million in 1993), it encourages meetings among talented researchers from various disciplines and organizations representing industry, universities, and government.

More controversially, some government agencies are also starting to bring "commercial use" as an explicit criterion in judging even early-stage research projects to support. The country with the most explicit policy in this regard is the United Kingdom. Following its white paper (policy document) on the subject released in 1993, it has directed its various research councils to include relevance to industry or to an identified user group as an important consideration in the allocation of funds to researchers, whether in universities or in companies. To signal its seriousness, the government has also appointed a leading industrialist as part-time chairperson in each of the six research councils—whose full-time chief executive will continue to be drawn from the ranks of academia. While many think the United Kingdom has gone too far in this regard, preferring that government research be based on the economic criteria listed above for early-stage research, they generally endorse greater commercial orientation later in the R&D process (see Chapter 5).

Private Company Projects

Private companies are naturally more focused in their criteria and are primarily concerned with obtaining a successful commercial outcome for the research they support. However, recognizing the uncertainties inherent in early-stage projects, and not wanting to suppress the exploration of ideas too early, they tend to take a flexible approach. Thus, when it comes to estimating commercial potential, they rely more on broad estimates of need instead of precise demand—which presupposes a knowledge of ultimate product features, price, and the segments targeted. In the pharmaceutical industry, for example, the attractiveness of a particular therapeutic area tends to be approximated by reference to the existence of an unmet medical need and the potential patient population that could theoretically be concerned. The overall portfolio of projects is usually more important for companies in that industry than are individual project characteristics.

Astra AB

An illustrative example of the way early-stage technologies get looked at in science-based industries is offered by Astra AB.

In order to evaluate and support early-stage projects more purposefully than it used to, the company set up a project evaluation group (PEG) in 1992. It consists of six people—one pharmacologist, one physiologist/pharmacologist, one chemist, two clinical pharmacologists, and one toxicologist—all of whom had previously held senior positions in R&D management (research director level) but who no longer have line management responsibility in the organization.

Once a year in August, the PEG meets to review all Astra projects in the synthesis/screening, IND documentation, and phase 1 stage—the earliest stages in drug development. Meeting in isolation for four to five days, the group rates these projects along two main dimensions: project potential and medical value (see Table 3-1). Medical value refers to the result that can be expected in the form of a new drug and is relatively easy to judge. More difficult and judgmental is assessing potential, which encompasses things like the uniqueness of the approach, technical merit or feasibility, and the scientific merit of the approach. As Anthony Pottage, the Director of Clinical Affairs of Astra and member of PEG, put it,

TABLE 3-1

CRITERIA USED BY ASTRA'S PROJECT EVALUATION GROUP (PEG) FOR
JUDGING EARLY-STAGE (PRE-IND AND PHASE-I) PROJECTS

		Score
A.	**Project Potential**	
	1. Uniqueness (approach, mechanism of action, competition)	1–3
	2. Technical Merit (animal models, clinical models, synthesis, formulation, manufacture)	1–3
	3. Scientific Merit (target definition, lead compounds, candidate drugs, problems, expertise available)	1–3
	SUBTOTAL	3–9
B.	**Medical Value** (me-too, significant advance, breakthrough)	1–3

SOURCE: Astra AB. Reprinted with permission.

> In exploratory research you are really judging the idea itself because you don't have much data. Potential is whether we, as a group, like the idea; do we like the science, do we think it has a chance of success, has the researcher thought through what problems might arise later and are we comfortable with the approach taken. We are essentially interested in the quality of the science, the way the project is being managed and whether the researchers have a good model to work with.[14]

Apart from assessing each project individually, the PEG also looks at how these projects fit within the overall research portfolio of the company. As illustrated in Figure 3-2, individual projects and the resources devoted to them (the size of each circle indicating the manpower behind it) are laid out in a matrix for *each* product company, with the vertical axis indicating potential on a 0–9 scale as defined previously, and the horizontal axis the status of the projects. Projects in category A are advanced enough to have reached the stage of an IND for tests in humans, B projects have crossed the screening stage for efficacy, and C projects are those still in the exploratory phase. The idea is to have a reasonably balanced research portfolio within each product company and to ensure that projects are resourced in accordance with their potential and stage.

FIGURE 3-2

EARLY-STAGE RESEARCH PORTFOLIO IN ONE OF ASTRA AB'S
PRODUCT COMPANIES

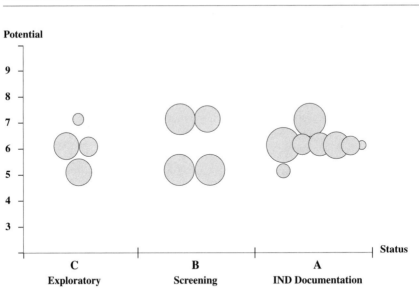

NOTE: Size of circle denotes manpower allocated to the project. Reprinted with permission.

Adapting the Criteria to an Industry's Competitive Profile—
Sandoz Agro AG

The broad criteria used by the pharmaceutical industry are justified because
of the uncertainties that exist both in the preclinical phase and further
downstream when clinical trials begin. Where the latter are more predictable, or at least more easily managed, finer criteria tend to be used incorporating both product-specific and competitive features. Sandoz Agro AG,
for example, evaluates its early-stage projects for herbicides and fungicides
using the criteria summarized in Table 3-2. Because of the focus on a well-
defined effect, the company is also able to identify the most critical issues
in each project. These indicate to R&D managers the areas where bottle-
necks might occur and where to spend money for a successful outcome.

Process Overrides Criteria

Both Astra and Sandoz Agro admit to the imprecise nature of the criteria
they use and the need for exercising judgment on the part of those who
assess projects.

   The size and composition of Astra's project evaluation group helps ensure against biases. Each individual member completes a score card for

TABLE 3-2

SANDOZ AGRO AG'S EVALUATION CRITERIA FOR
EARLY-STAGE RESEARCH PROJECTS

Project Profile	Valuation					Most Critical Issues
	1	2	3	4	5	
Rate at which herbicide/fungicide will be applied (g/ha)—lower the better						
Projected cost to produce—lower the better						
Spectrum of effect (example, number of weeds eliminated)—broader the better						
Selectivity (not affecting crops or crop plants to be protected)						
Chemical potential (how chemistry compares with what competitors are using)						
Patentability						
Duration of activity (should be long enough to protect for entire season but short enough not to harm following culture)						
Ecology						
Safety (for crop and those applying herbicide/fungicide)						

SOURCE: Sandoz Agro AG. Reprinted with permission.

each project, but the final score card is not just an average. It comes out of a debate lasting four to five days, representing a consensus on the group's views. During this, the PEG visits each product company in turn, spending two days in each location, listening to presentations, and questioning the project teams directly. The interesting aspect of the PEG evaluation is that neither its recommendations on individual projects nor the consequences to be drawn from the portfolio matrix are binding on the product companies. The PEG's role is strictly advisory. Its impact is through dialogue and influence rather than executive authority.

Some public funding organizations have also started to emphasize the *process* of arriving at judgments as much as the criteria themselves. The Dutch Technology Foundation (STW), for example, attributes its relatively high success rate to the process it employs. This three-step process consists first in obtaining comments from a relatively small number of peers. The person or team making the proposal is then given the opportunity to respond to these comments. The final step involves the actual judgment. Rather than assigning the judgment of technical quality and utilization potential to a separate group of individuals, both dimensions are judged by a specially constituted jury of twelve "laypeople." The latter represent different positions in society, such as research directors from small, medium, or large firms; senior researchers; university professors; and representatives of government organizations and institutions. To avoid influence by others, each member judges independently—and no one serves more than once on such juries.[15] A recent study of its first round of grants awarded in 1981 and 1982 found not only a higher success rate (in terms of the use of the technology ten years later), but a high correlation between the ranking of projects by the jury and their subsequent rate of success as measured by actual utilization in commercial applications.[16]

REACHING OUT TO OTHERS IN THE RESEARCH COMMUNITY

Intrinsic to mobilizing interest is also an attitude of sharing. There are some technologists who keep their insights under wraps until the end, secretly imagining product ideas and trying them out. While the advantage of doing this is obvious, they are sometimes wrong about the product and find out too late when prototypes have already been built. The opposite approach is to reach out to others early for confirming the technology, application suggestions, and product ideas, thereby also creating a pull for the technology.

Sharing to Gain Peer Support

From the moment Pons and Fleischman announced cold fusion in Utah on March 27, 1989, an entire cross-section of the scientific community worldwide mobilized itself around the discovery. This initial burst of enthusiasm, however, quickly turned to disappointment and controversy. No one could replicate the results precisely. Many who did get excess heat in their experiments disagreed with the hypothesis, claiming the phenomenon to be an electrochemical rather than nuclear one. Many got no excess heat at all, or got it so sporadically as to fear errors in their experimentation. Then there were others who dismissed the whole thing outright as being contrary to any known (or knowable) principle of nature. Except for some diehard optimists, the level of interest in the field and the importance of cold fusion as a potentially commercializable technology dropped as quickly as it had arisen.

Part of the blame for why interest was not sustained rested with Pons and Fleischman themselves. Their attitude of "I don't know fully why it works, but if you had my secret recipe it will," alternately challenged and frustrated others. Reluctant to provide details of their experimental techniques to competitors, they inevitably aroused skepticism.

Sharing discoveries with scientific peers helps establish authorship and peer respect. From a commercialization viewpoint, the purpose served is that of mobilizing the so-called invisible college of influential leaders in the field[17] to endorse the findings. One researcher's laboratory proof of principle has never been a match for the collective endorsement of a scientific community, or the second proof that experts and other (sometimes better regarded) labs bring. The latter not only lends credence when the findings are published, or when patents are applied for, but gives confidence to eventual providers of capital and other resources to advance the technology further.

Mobilizing Other Researchers for Problem Solving

Regardless of how many financial resources one is able to garner from in-house or external sources to pursue an idea, they are never enough. In today's world, those who pull ahead reach out to other researchers within the same as well as other organizations for help in advancing the research too. They share their discoveries, with appropriate safeguards, so that others will not only endorse what they are doing but also assist in problem solving to get things done quickly. Rather than dismissing peer skepticism, they try to dispel it; instead of monopolizing the discovery, they try to be open to coauthorship and coownership.

There is ample evidence to suggest that research benefits from feedback and advice from others, yet many scientists and engineers prefer not to reach out to other experts. This is for a variety of reasons: the culture of the organization in which they work, their own fear of being ridiculed or disappointed at the lack of enthusiastic endorsement of what they have achieved, or simply the fact that others may be busy and preoccupied.[18]

Successful innovators do tend to exchange more information and establish more efficient external communication links than their less successful counterparts. At the research stage, communication with others helps generate new ideas, stimulates creativity, and becomes a valuable source of information to aid problem solving. As Yar Ebadi and James Utterback found in their study of 117 Sea Grant research projects, funded by the U.S. Department of Commerce for the purpose of developing use of marine resources, the greater the frequency of communication and the greater its diversity, the more successful was the outcome. The position of a project within the communication network was important too. Projects to which most communications were directed, thereby being central to the communication network, tended to have a higher probability of success than those that were at the periphery and exposed to only a part of the information exchange.[19]

neg process

The peer network among researchers is intensifying each day, aided by new communication and information technologies. Entire research corpuses are today linked together through E-mail regardless of their geographic location or organizational affiliation. More and more research findings are being distributed through the Internet, which promises faster peer reviews and interaction with others than traditional refereed journals allow. These electronic networks, in fact, almost amount to joint research and problem solving, bringing together the thoughts and even experimental data of a dispersed community of researchers.

An associated phenomenon is the dramatic increase in collaborative research in recent years. In the United States, only 13 percent of all research papers written by industry scientists in 1973 referred to the participation of university researchers; in 1982, the figure was 24 percent and climbing. The change, as one might expect, was most marked in biology, up from 19 to 46 percent; in engineering the comparable figures were 9 and 17 percent, while clinical medicine saw an increase from 21 percent to 34 percent.[20] Today, about 35 percent of all U.S. patents issued to industry have arisen from collaborations between basic scientists working in universities and industrial scientists working in their laboratories.[21]

Such participation in scientific communities creates a real risk of multiple, "independent" discoveries, as the history of several technologies indicates. But it is unlikely that the risk can be altogether avoided by a firm or individual volunteering to forsake such exchanges. Also, since researchers in other organizations latch onto breaking technologies anyhow, the better attitude is to mobilize their contributions to one's own cause than to always compete with them.

As demonstrated by Michael Rappa for the case of compound semiconductor technology (such as gallium arsenide), a scientific community committed to a newly emerging technology not only grows faster than the scientific community in general, but this growth is also associated with an increase in the number of university graduates familiar with the technology and the movement of researchers between organizations. This growth in the overall scientific community—consisting of researchers in firms, universities, and industrial laboratories—provides a critical mass needed for advancing the new technology in terms of concrete inventions. Equally important are the knowledge and publicity engendered in preparing the market for when these inventions are launched.[22]

Coproducing Ideas to Gain Buy-in and Assistance

Interest in ideas is keenest when they are coproduced between the parties involved. John Seely Brown of Xerox PARC is one advocate of this. Some years ago, PARC created a video called the "unfinished document" in which it tried to portray how digital copying would transform people's work. As Brown put it,

> We thought of the unfinished document as a "conceptual envisioning experiment"—an attempt to imagine how a technology might be used before we started building it. We showed the video to some top corporate officers to get their intuitional juices flowing. The document was "unfinished" in the sense that the whole point of the exercise was to get the viewers to complete the video by suggesting their own ideas for how they might use the new technology and what these new uses might mean for the business. In the process, they weren't just learning about a new technology; they were creating a new mental model of the business.[23]

This kind of coproduction is now being adopted by several companies. Rather than being restricted to top management, it includes lower-level employees, suppliers, and—most importantly—customers.

EMI's CT Scanner

An important way such coproduction helps is in defining the context of a breakthrough. Such was, for example, the role the U.K. Department of Health and Social Security (DHSS) played in the development of the first computed axial tomography (CT) scanner.

The technology itself grew out of two discoveries made several years back. One was the principle of mapping complex structures in two—and three—dimensions from an infinite set of projections. This principle had been first described by Johann Radon, an Austrian mathematician, in 1917 and had immediately found potential application in fields ranging from radio astronomy to crystallography, microscopy, and radiology. However, since it involved a large number of computations, its use had to wait until the development of modern computers in the 1950s and 1960s.

In radiology, another technique had meanwhile been developed to localize pathologies in the human body three-dimensionally. This technique, called tomography, entailed moving the X rays relative to the body in one direction while at the same time moving the film in a parallel plane in the other direction. Discovered in the 1920s and early 1930s, tomography had become the main method by which radiologists obtained three-dimensional information. However, the approach had several defects, and radiologists throughout the world were hoping for something better.

The first application of Radon's principle in medical imaging was made in 1961 by W. H. Oldendorf, a University of California neurologist. Unfortunately, although Oldendorf went on to construct a working model, and in 1963 to take out a patent, he was unable to interest either radiologists or industry in his idea. The same fate befell A. M. Cormack, a Tufts

University physicist, who too tried to measure transmission profiles in order to reconstruct three-dimensional images in 1963. Like Oldendorf, Cormack was unable to process the many computations needed to make pattern recognition possible on a real-time basis.

The person who succeeding in mitigating the drawbacks of the new technology and generating interest in it was Godfrey Hounsfield, a British electronics engineer working at Electrical & Musical Industries Ltd (EMI), in Middlesex, United Kingdom. Hounsfield's solution was to first store the tomographic information in a computer's memory, remove redundant information from it, and then "approximate" the projections instead of working on an infinite number of mathematically precise projections as Radon suggested. Being an expert in computer technology, he was able to work out a method for reconstructing an image from its projections using an iterative procedure based on what is known as the algebraic reconstruction technique, or ART algorithm. As such he is credited with the invention of the first working CT scanner in 1969, for which he earned a Nobel Prize, together with Cormack, ten years later.

Unlike Oldendorf and Cormack, Hounsfield was fortunate in having the support both of his employer, EMI, as well as the external community. Despite its lack of experience in the medical market, EMI's management was quick to realize the enormous potential of CT scanners. The funds available for such research, however, proved inadequate for completing a prototype. Rather than abandon the project, the company next turned to the DHSS for help.

Apart from providing financial assistance, the DHSS was instrumental in facilitating a much-needed collaboration between EMI and the radiological community. This focused the development toward more precise applications; rather than completing the device for mass screening—which would have been uneconomical—the DHSS encouraged EMI to concentrate on a brain scanner. In addition to being functionally superior and cost-effective compared to existing alternatives, this application was technically easier. Brain imaging did not pose problems of involuntary movements (heartbeat, for example, or twitching of muscles). Since scanning took several minutes, these would be problematic in imaging many other areas of the body.

The DHSS provided both credibility and resources for Hounsfield's project. When time came to test the first scanner on living patients, it set up an advisory team to oversee these tests at a hospital near London. There, a leading neuroradiologist, James Ambrose, collaborated with Hounsfield in further development of the scanner from an expert user's standpoint. By purchasing one prototype and underwriting the construction costs for four more, the DHSS gave a much-needed boost for completing the project.[24]

Apart from anything else, such contacts with the user community constitute "preselling" of a new technology. The sooner and more effectively this selling begins—even in the absence of commercial products—the earlier and more widely a new technology gets adopted when it is ready.

The role of this early promotion among peers also explains in part how RCA came to dominate the electron microscope business in the United States during the 1940s and 1950s in competition with GE. The technology the two companies adopted did indeed differ: While RCA chose electromagnetic lenses for magnification, GE chose electrostatic ones in the hope of developing a more robust, smaller, and cheaper instrument. The fact that electromagnetic lenses took a bulk of the market was due, however, more to the approach RCA took than to the presumed technical superiority of such lenses.

RCA's approach was to maintain active involvement with the scientific community from the beginning. Its leading scientist in the field, James Hillier, became a regular attendee at professional gatherings such as those of the Electron Microscopy Society of America (EMSA). The company invited a leading expert in electron microscopy, Thomas Anderson, to set up his lab within RCA and encouraged his contacts with the research community, notably in the biosciences. Other researchers, both inside and outside of RCA, were encouraged to use the company's instrument in their work and soon began publishing research referring to it. All this, combined with an attitude that users could contact the research laboratory directly if they had questions, contributed to making electron microscopes a credible research tool and to the visibility of RCA's instrument in particular.

GE, though its technology and product concept were arguably superior, assumed a low profile by comparison. Its scientists were rarely seen at professional meetings; internally, organizational support for the electron microscope business was ambivalent at best; and customers were urged to contact "the nearest GE sales office" rather than the laboratory staff directly.[25]

COMMUNICATING TO MOBILIZE INTEREST

The mobilization of interest in any idea ultimately depends on the effectiveness with which it is communicated to others. When it comes to early-stage technologies, the communication strategy needs to strike a balance among several things: the need for promotion versus secrecy, evoking interest versus excessive hype that can backfire, and targeting a message versus allowing interest to come from a variety of sources that one does not know about initially.

Balancing Promotion and Secrecy

Many inventors manifest a schizophrenic attitude when it comes to promoting their early-stage ideas, never quite sure how much to disclose and how much to keep secret. The psychological need to protect an unfinished product, however, often creates its own barrier to acceptance.

When and how much to communicate about an early-stage idea naturally involves trade-offs, especially for basic technologies. Too early a disclosure can compromise one's ability to obtain intellectual property rights and incite others to start working on the same discovery before it is even ready for commercialization. Holding back for too long, on the other hand, risks losing the benefits of early feedback from peers and potential users and having to devote greater resources to the promotion effort later. It also means struggling alone in a new direction, with all that implies for resources and probable errors of judgment.

Rather than be content to simply publish the results of experiments concerning a new phenomenon or hypothesis, more and more scientists today are taking the additional step of demonstrating their discoveries in concrete and "useful" applications in the hope of obtaining patents. Instead of following their natural inclination to publish results early and widely, they now systematically file disclosures (records of invention to establish priority), delay publications by as much as six to twelve months, and refrain from making announcements that might compromise their chances. Publication in a journal is more and more a reward or a consecration of the discovery. In many basic technologies, the findings were probably already shown to peers for review and feedback and presented in seminars and the like.

The problem with pursuing intellectual property rights early is the constraints it places on scientific dialogue. Thus, Pons and Fleischman had already applied for nine patents before they had convincing proof that cold fusion worked. Partly because of this, the two professors preferred not to intervene in the frenetic worldwide effort that got launched to replicate their findings.

The issue of comprehension and reproducibility by peers plagued the commercialization of AT&T Bell Labs' Karmarkar algorithm too. Announced in 1984, this linear programming algorithm represented a considerable improvement over the Simplex method devised by George Dantzig in 1947. Depending on the application, it was 4 to 250 times faster and was particularly suited to optimization programs involving thousands of variables and constraints.

Although a generous trader of technical information in the past, AT&T saw the commercial potential this new algorithm offered and decided to keep it proprietary. The result was that it created much less enthusiasm and fewer commercial opportunities than it otherwise would have. Although the principle of projective transformations it used was published and well understood by peers, the latter were unable to reproduce the results AT&T was claiming without more details from the company. Roy Marsten, professor of management information systems at the University of Arizona, captured the general sentiment well: "The mathematics of his [Karmarkar] algorithm are wonderful. My personal feeling is that he got some good results on certain types of problems. I don't think he's going to be able to do it on general classes of problems." Professor David Shanno of the University of California at Davis was equally skeptical: "I don't disbelieve him, but no one can duplicate his results. Right now, it's a mystery."[26] The most convincing (though perhaps not optimal) way of commercializing the new algorithm turned out to be in the form of a complete computer system—the AT&T KORBX System, costing $8 million to $9 million—both for external and internal use within AT&T.

The question of disclosure is actually best approached in stages. For those working in the very early phases of a new technology, when different approaches are still being tried, the benefits of trading information outweigh its drawbacks in terms of appropriability. Not only are other researchers likely to be working on the problem simultaneously anyhow, but the knowledge traded itself is probably partial and hypothetical. A reasonable stance, therefore, is one of actively participating in such information exchanges and interorganizational collaboration to benefit from all its advantages but then timing one's withdrawal to pursue more specialized and potentially proprietary facets of the technology later.

Creating Pull Without Hype

Attracting attention to a new technology is in the end a competitive endeavor, more so today than at any time in the past. Apart from targeting scarce resources, mobilizing interest in a technology is a bit like what companies do by way of competitive signalling—announcing half-baked products or partnerships and staking out a market arena. The purpose is partly to preempt the moves of others. But it is equally a verbal battle for stakeholders' attention, in hopes of mobilizing their support early on. The excitement created, moreover, has to be great enough to overcome the many hurdles that lie ahead and to assemble as many resources up front as possible.

The ability to link a technology to an important unmet need and to sell its potential has actually always been the stock in trade of most successful start-up companies. The best illustrations of salesmanship and interest mobilization in technology commercialization are to be seen in the multimedia industry today, where partners have been pursued with almost as much zeal as the technology itself. Speaking of Marc Porat, the founder of General Magic, Inc., the *Wall Street Journal* captured the phenomenon well:

> Marc Porat is a silver-tongued devil. The president of General Magic, Inc., is credited with creating a spellbinding vision of the electronics future. . . . His dream-yet-to-come-true of a vast array of electronic networks able to fulfil a user's every wish resulted in an announcement here yesterday that American Telephone & Telegraph Co., Sony Corp., Motorola Inc., Philips Electronics NV and Matsushita Electric Industrial Co. are investing in

General Magic, a secretive, three-year-old venture started by Apple Computer Inc. They are hoping that their membership will give them an opportunity to reap big profits from the advent of small devices called personal intelligent communicators, or PICs.[27]

Although some dismissed PICs as "vaporware"—innovations that are promised but never delivered—the above partners were sufficiently impressed by Porat's vision to make the commitment they did.

The battle for stakeholder attention does not, however, mean unethically distorting facts pertaining to the technology. Not only is this uncondonable, but it often results in Pyrrhic victories. One has to communicate in a measured way—providing enough exciting information to create a stir but eschewing excessive hype.

An aspect of measure is the need to abide by established protocols. Thus, a highly controversial trend established over the past decade or so concerns scientists announcing new discoveries in the public media simultaneously with peer reviews, in some cases even prior to the latter. As the discussion in this chapter highlights, there is little to be gained in sidestepping early stakeholders in a technology—even if their intentions are noncommercial.

The Two Levels of Communication

To be effective in mobilizing interest in a new technological idea, communication needs to be at two levels—at a mass level in order to create excitement and "pull" for the discovery, and at an individual level to explain what the technology is about and persuade interested stakeholders to support it.

Broad-based media campaigns are especially useful when:

The technology covers a wide spectrum of uses that many companies can identify with;

Companies that might be interested have different appreciations of the technology and different time lines of need; and

The technology can be couched in broad market terms addressing a commonly felt need.

These reasons lay behind the approach that Belland took when starting the commercialization of its intelligent plastics in 1984. Because of its small size and relatively limited financial resources, it would have had difficulty approaching the various makers and users of plastics individually. Instead, playing mainly on the environmental merits of its technology (not the equally or more important technical ones), it launched a campaign aimed at the public media. This included television reports, articles in trade journals (such as *Modern Plastics International*) as well as in the popular press (*Fortune* and even newspapers such as *The Observer*). Literally hundreds of companies wrote in to inquire further about what Belland had developed, and most wanted to know what its commercialization strategy was and how they might contribute to it, including by developing applications they had conceived.

Belland's approach was to publicize the technology widely and let others think about uses for it. In fact, starting with the first fund-raising campaign, in which many investors wanted exclusive rights to certain applications in return for investing in Belland, over 200 companies wrote in to inquire whether the applications they had in mind were feasible.

By reaching out to a disparate group of stakeholders, mass media campaigns provide a surer means of interesting those who might find the technology attractive. They cause a process of self-selection, in which only those who are seriously interested approach the inventor. They also have the virtue of sidestepping what is often the biggest hurdle to evincing interest— dealing with technical people within companies instead of senior general managers. Catching the latter's attention early through the popular and trade press is a good way to gain support; discussions with technical people can occur later.

A highly targeted and personalized approach, usually encompassing technical people, is often also required in parallel. It is particularly important when:

> The technology can be described only in functional (rather then in market) terms;
>
> The breakthrough is accompanied by a discovery of a hard-to-explain principle or major heuristic know-how; and
>
> A unique application is involved, but one that involves considerable investment on the part of the actors involved.

Not paying adequate attention to this level of communication explains the generally disappointing result universities and national research organizations have obtained in promoting their inventions. While many listed their technologies on electronic bulletin boards and on-line data bases such as *Dialog, Knowledge Express, Quorum,* and *Corp Tech* (which lists over 35,000 high-technology companies along with their products and research interests), they failed to get the kind of response they hoped for. As stated by Hans Wiesendanger, senior associate at Stanford University's Office of Technology Licensing, where roughly 50 percent of patents granted now get licensed:

> There is no substitute for personalized communication. One needs to target buyers and to offer them the information in the form they really want— what the technology is all about, its commercial uses, how it compares with competing technologies and, perhaps the most important, the steps needed to take it further.[28]

Sustaining Stakeholder Interest

While stakeholders relevant to the early stages of a new technology do tend to be more indulgent and long-term-oriented than others, they still want to see progress at regular intervals. They want to be reassured that the project they are supporting continues to exhibit the potential they saw initially.

The closer one can bring aspects of the technology to practical problems as it advances, the more comfortable they feel. This is illustrated by the work recently done at AT&T Bell Labs on submicron technology. When it began working on 0.1 micron CMOS circuits in 1992, most people assumed it was an impossible task. The laboratory demonstration made in 1994 was found interesting, but product applications were still considered years away. Partly as a means to sustain what looked like a long-term research program, the group working on the technology turned immediately to addressing some short-term needs with the capability they had acquired. They applied the knowledge they had gained in advanced circuit design, transistor thresholds, and power supply to lower voltages in the company's existing half-micron products.

Sustaining interest in the technology by finding more proximate uses for it is one challenge. Another is sustaining interest in the research group itself. The more willing researchers are to demonstrate concern for the preoccupations of those providing support, the greater the chances of their being funded over long periods of time.

The current trend among some companies to ask their research staff to divide their time between pursuing long-term exploratory research and solving engineering or customer-related problems is actually a step in the right direction. At Bellcore, for example, research staff are sent on "internships," working directly with regional phone companies. One researcher, who had previously been working on high-speed networks, for example, spent three months helping a department write technical requirements for nascent portable communication services. As George H. Heilmeier, CEO of Bellcore, put it, "You've got to be willing to do near term work because it helps build credibility. Then, when you have something longer range, they're willing to listen."[29]

Summary

Arriving at a seemingly attractive techno-market vision quickly is of little use if no one expresses an interest in it. The first challenge any inventor confronts, therefore, is that of identifying the stakeholders whose support is needed in the beginning and getting them to back the idea.

While a single, highly placed "idea champion" may be the principal stakeholder in some corporate settings, this is more the exception than the rule. In most cases, one needs to satisfy a variety of different stakeholders simultaneously—peers, colleagues, funding agencies, and outside partners. From some, it is mainly endorsement that one is looking for. From others, it is resources to examine the idea further or technical help in developing it.

With so many ideas competing for the attention of these early stakeholders, missteps can be costly. The selling skills of the proponent are important, but it is usually also necessary to follow certain long-established protocols. A protocol-based strategy of interest mobilization consists in the following in practice:

Making sure that the scientific basis of the idea has been well thought through;

Getting the endorsement of peers early;

Sharing the idea to gain peer support and assistance in problem solving;

Aligning proposals to the priorities and criteria used by early-stage resource providers; and

Formulating a communication strategy that balances interest creation with secrecy, evoking interest without excessive hype, and the need for face-to-face explanations with casting a wide net in the hope of evoking pull from unexpected sources.

4

INCUBATING TO DEFINE COMMERCIALIZABILITY

WHILE A CONSIDERABLE AMOUNT OF TIME AND RESOURCES MAY HAVE GONE into arriving at a techno-market insight, the stages that follow require the commitment of far greater resources. They may confront fewer uncertainties, but they involve the assumption of far greater risks.

Deciding whether and how to take a technology further is what the incubating stage is about. Companies with several projects in their R&D pipeline use this stage as an opportunity to screen those they think offer the best potential. For lone inventors, on the other hand, this intermediate stage between imagining an idea and building products around it involves making the idea more attractive to resource providers and other stakeholders who can help in taking it further. In either case, incubating involves exploring the technology further and getting a better feel for its true worth.

Many companies and, increasingly, universities and research institutes recognize the value of this stage in technology commercialization and have instituted organizational mechanisms for managing it. Raychem, for example, has formal "business incubators" attached to its central R&D organization. Consisting of small, focused teams with multifunctional skills (mainly technical and marketing), their mission is to take laboratory discoveries and to determine more accurately whether or not to proceed with them. The work of these groups typically involves researching the technology further, incorporating it in a precommercial product or process, building prototypes, and testing them with lead customers. It also involves a more thorough analysis of the market and the steps needed to reach it effectively. While the outcome management expects is a good business plan, or a recommendation to terminate, these incubators may even ring up sales of $1 million to $2 million during this phase.

The value that such special incubators contribute is demonstrated by the experience of Eastman Chemical Co. of Kingsport, Tennessee. In the 1980s, the company's R&D department did most of the customer-need identification and verification. Of the several hundred projects the company tracked during this period, 40 percent were not successful due to either a change in the marketplace or an invalid original need. Since 1991, need analysis and validation have been the responsibility of dedicated technology-and-innovation-management teams within each business. The improved quality of the information assembled by these teams has resulted in two useful outcomes: incorrectly identified needs have been cut to 21 percent in 1996, and the value of new and improved products has more than doubled from 1993 to 1995.[1]

The point is that no technology-based idea is intrinsically more commercializable than another at the start. It has to be made so. Just screening ideas for "golden birds," as some companies do, is seldom enough. The process of enhancing the value of ideas, or coming to an unequivocal decision to abandon them or hold them on ice for a while, is a value-creating activity in its own right. What steps need to be taken, and how this value should be judged, is a central theme of this chapter.

WHAT DEFINING COMMERCIALIZABILITY IS ABOUT

However it is done, defining commercializability is about building *expected value* in the eyes of those whose support is sought. Like all expected value judgments, it is a combination of two things: the size of the potential payoff and the probability of realizing it within a reasonable time frame.

Because so many variables are involved, a range of outcomes is possible. Robert Kerwin, however, captures the essence well: "Commercializability for me means two things: Whether others endorse the technical achievement made, which avoids the danger that the technologist may have misread the findings or missed out on something important, and whether there is an immediate need that the technology fulfills." Subjective preferences play a role too. For some, like John Seely Brown of Xerox PARC, it is when there is "the creation of the seeds for an order of magnitude change in the way things are done." Others, like Hiroshi Fukino of Seiko Instruments, mark the event more modestly: "It is when we have the ability and confidence to communicate with customers on their problems."

In general, however, the process is about building confidence. This means eliminating 50 to 80 percent of the risk (depending on the risk threshold of concerned stakeholders) that it can be scaled up, can be manufactured at competitive prices, and will work under normal operating conditions. Furthermore, to compensate for the risk that remains, it means explaining (not proving) that a significant market potential exists and how the technology will remain proprietary and profits realized from it.

It is this confidence-building aspect of incubation that DuPont's Lycra division stresses too. As indicated in Table 1-1, incubation corresponds roughly to what it terms the "Scouting" phase. Norman D'Allura, technical manager of the division's European operation, summarizes the mission of this phase as follows:

> The Idea stage is about concepts, taking them to the point where someone in the organization might be interested in them. From a technical standpoint this usually means obtaining a proof of principle. The Scouting stage involves defining avenues towards commercialization, understanding the practical aspects of the technology as well as its economics. This stage also requires an in-depth understanding of market needs and how the technology fits into a Du Pont division's product vision; it is about undertaking all the activities required for coming up with a business plan so that it can be taken to the more expensive and resource consuming Project phase.[2]

Three things usually need to be accomplished to establish the commercializability of many generic inventions:

Achieving certain technical milestones and showing that the technology will progress rapidly from that point on;

Conceiving of an attractive set of applications and a plan for pursuing them that optimizes returns on the investments to make; and

Assembling intellectual property rights (IPRs) linked to the strategy of commercialization planned.

Which of the three factors to stress in practice depends on the nature of the technology. Sometimes the market opportunity is so compelling that only a credible approach outlined for the technology suffices. In other cases, if a demonstrated breakthrough in a "potentially valuable" technology is achieved, one need only devote a small effort to analyzing its market opportunities. The more one can cover all three aspects, however, the greater the perceived value of the technology. Thus, for example, among the two most valuable technologies in the semiconductor field were Robert Kerwin's invention of silicon gate technology at AT&T and Robert Dennard's invention of three-dimensional circuits at IBM. Both technologies had been well demonstrated in the laboratory, made rapid progress in functionality once they started to be used, were targeted to an immediate problem confronting a large and growing industry, and were protected by unassailable patents that could be licensed if necessary. Moreover, referring to the discussion in Chapter 3, the fact that both technologies had been immediately endorsed by peers working in reputable organizations helped in addition.

Giant Magnetoresistance

A good example of this combination of factors is that of a technology that recently created a flurry of interest—giant magnetoresistance (GMR). The effect involved in this case is the change in the electrical resistance of a material when it is placed in a magnetic field. Ordinary magnetoresistance (MR), which has been known for some time now, was too feeble to be of much practical use—with MR materials showing resistance changes of around 4 percent. GMR, first discovered in 1988 at the Université de Paris-Sud, showed resistance changes of up to 50 percent at a temperature of 4.2°K. With this level of response, GMR was immediately seen as a potential substitute technology for the induction "read" heads in computer disk drives, allowing for a considerably greater storage density.

To be seriously considered for this application, however, materials had to exhibit GMR at room temperatures and with relatively low magnetic fields. After the first discovery at the Université de Paris-Sud, researchers were able to make quick progress on the first criterion, developing GMR materials whose resistance changed by as much as 65 percent at room temperature. The second criterion, however, proved more intractable. Achieving such resistance changes required very high magnetic fields—typically 250 oersteds, or 500 times the earth's magnetic field.

Despite the rudimentary nature of the breakthrough and the amount of effort needed to take it further, the technology was immediately heralded as one of today's "big impact technologies," on par with high-temperature superconductivity.

One reason was the quick progress made in improving on its performance and the optimism of the scientific community regarding the potential it offered. In August 1993, five years after the phenomenon was first reported, researchers at IBM ADSTAR in San Jose, California, were able to demonstrate GMR at much smaller magnetic fields—between 5 and 10 oersteds. To achieve this they created alternating layers of nickel-iron and silver only a few nanometers thick, then annealed the material by quickly heating and cooling it. Although they were able to report resistance changes of only 4 percent to 6 percent, their work was seen as proof that GMR was a practical and (perhaps) feasible technology for disk drives.

The second reason had to do with the sheer volume of its applications. If proven, the technology could be used in a wide variety of fields ranging from automobile sensors in engines, suspensions, and brakes; in computer disk drives, where it offered a seventeenfold increase in storage capacity; and in memory chips that retained their information even when the power was turned off. Collectively, all these applications represented billions of dollars' worth of sales.

TECHNICAL MILESTONES AND FUTURE PROGRESS

How far to take the technology's own development before reaching out for major resource commitments depends on several things. Thus, Ariad Pharmaceuticals Inc. was able to raise $46 million in a single round of financing with no more than a conceptual model of the technology it was attempting to use. Hesselink, on the other hand, had to achieve a proof of principle before he could mobilize serious interest and resources in his holographic storage technology.

Technologies with an obvious and immediate commercial use can attract significant resources soon after a convincing model has been advanced or a proof of principle demonstrated—progress associated with the imagining stage discussed earlier. In most cases, however, a bit more needs to be done, achieving a functional threshold and providing a credible plan for the future evolution of the technology (see Figure 4-1).

Crossing a Functional Threshold

The functional threshold in any technology is the point at which it can be *demonstrated* successfully in a particular use. This usually involves assembling a broad range of process concepts, data, and heuristics to be able to do something *concrete* with the idea one has. As such, it requires considerably more work than is associated with laboratory proofs of principle. While prototype devices tend to be associated with this stage, they are not mandatory. But there must be a demonstration of application-specific utility that those judging the technology find convincing. This is, for example, the stage reached by GMR in 1994. Compared with Hesselink's holographic storage technology, which still has major application-related hurdles to overcome, GMR's incorporation in end products is both more imminent and more predictable.

The system of patenting has long recognized what the crossing of a functional threshold means. Within the hierarchy of science and technology that went from pure research (the pursuit of knowledge for its own sake) to applied and development research (the invention of something tangible), there was some point at which "science" became "technology." Although it was seldom clear where this point lay, patent offices around the world were expected to separate mere ideas from industrially applicable discoveries. Only if a new insight could be directly incorporated in some statutorily acceptable form—a process, a machine, a manufactured good, or a

FIGURE 4-1

THE TECHNOLOGY AND MARKET EXPLORATION INVOLVED IN INCUBATION

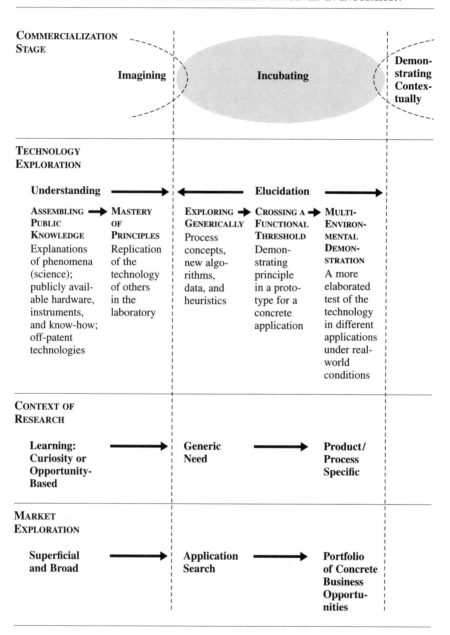

new composition of matter—would it qualify for patent protection, provided, of course, that it also met the other patenting criteria of novelty and inventiveness.

Recombinant DNA Technology

An example of crossing a functional threshold is the Cohen-Boyer break-through in recombinant DNA. The technology we now call gene manipulation actually traces its foundations to the early 1940s, when Oswald Avery and his colleagues at the Rockefeller Institute in New York first determined that genes were made of DNA. Aided by new techniques and instruments that had been developed around this time, such as chromatographic separation, electron microscopes, and X-ray diffraction, the next challenge was to determine what DNA molecules themselves looked like and what their constituent molecules were. This effort led to the identification of the four base pairs: adenine (A), thymine (T), guanine (G), and cytosine (C). It also led in 1953 to the well-known postulate by James Watson and Francis Crick that DNA had a double-helical structure within which the base molecules were paired in a complementary fashion (A with T and G with C).

The hypothesis that the genetic messages of DNA were carried in the sequence of these base pairs was empirically proven in 1956. However, it took another ten years for the genetic code to be fully deciphered by H. Gobind Khorana in June 1966. In the meantime, several important discoveries were made that later contributed to our understanding of gene manipulation itself. These included, among others, the proof in 1958 that DNA replication involved the complementary strands of the double helix; the isolation of the enzyme, DNA Polymerase I, which makes DNA; and the role of RNA in carrying information that orders amino acids in proteins. It also included in 1965 a discovery, which considerably facilitated subsequent experimental work, that genetic information is carried not just in the main chromosome (with millions of base pairs) but also in so-called plasmids—tiny circular DNA molecules containing only several thousand base pairs.

While all these discoveries elucidated how heredity worked, they were still inadequate for actually effecting a genetic change. Nothing tangible could be done with them. The same could be said of the two other important discoveries that followed them—the discovery in 1967 of the enzyme DNA ligase, which can join DNA chains together, and the isolation of the first restriction enzyme in 1970, which could cut DNA molecules at specific sites.

Translating all these important discoveries into a functional technology occurred in 1972 at Stanford University. That was the first time that a DNA molecule was actually broken into identifiable fragments using a restriction enzyme and then rejoined using the enzyme DNA ligase. The following year, in 1973, Cohen and Boyer were able to extend this physical transformation by inserting a foreign DNA fragment into a plasmid DNA to create the world's first chimeric plasmid. They were, furthermore, able to reinsert this chimera or hybrid DNA into a bacterium *E. coli*. That was the start of what we now term recombinant DNA technology.

Rapidity of Progress

Crossing a functional threshold is, of course, only a mark of achievement to date. What resource providers are really interested in is what happens next: how robust the technology is in terms of standing up to real-world product requirements and how quickly it will progress to yield its promised function. The more amenable a new technology is to rapid improvements in its functional characteristics, the greater the likelihood of it being pushed through to commercialization.

The most dramatic illustration of this, in fact, is to be found in recombinant DNA technology. If expressing hybrid DNA in *E. coli* was as far as we could get, and that too in time-consuming and error-prone laboratory experiments, it is unlikely that anyone would have shown much interest in the Cohen-Boyer patents. Fortunately for Cohen and Boyer, as well as the nascent biotechnology industry, a number of advances followed in rapid succession to permit the actual use of their principle.

When gene splicing and sequencing techniques were first discovered in the early 1970s, it took months and often years to successfully clone a single gene, making each new gene cloned a media event of sorts. As a result of subsequent advances, particularly the discovery of hundreds of restriction enzymes, better ways of mapping plasmids, and automated sequencing techniques, the efficiency of cloning has increased a thousandfold. An important contributor was the polymerase chain reaction (PCR) process invented at CETUS by Karry Mullis in 1983. This simple technique for replicating fragments of DNA quickly and in large amounts has found use in a variety of applications. Prior to its development, DNA replication was done by the lengthy and tedious process of isolating the targeted DNA fragment, purifying it, cloning it within bacteria or other cells, and growing the latter in culture. The PCR method worked directly with the DNA itself, separating its two strands, growing complementary copies on each to build duplicates, and repeating the cycle every minute or so. It not only yielded exponentially growing quantities of the DNA fragment but avoided many of the tricky steps associated with cloning. Today, isolating and cloning genes is a common process, often done in a matter of days.

Similarly, one of the reasons why Hesselink's holographic storage of digital data has caused so much excitement is the sheer potential for improvements in functionality the basic technology offers. While the Mona Lisa demonstration involved storing just 50 kilobytes of data—representing but a small patch on a modern laser disk—the technology could go up to storing 1.2 billion bytes per cubic centimeter with certain improvements over the demonstration version, making it competitive with the best magnetic hard drives.

The point about future trajectories is that one needs to anticipate and work toward them. The approach one takes in mobilizing other researchers and in sharing the initial discovery with them plays an important role in influencing how quickly a technology progresses. Thus, the fact that Stanford University licensed the Cohen-Boyer patents on recombinant DNA early and widely (see Chapter 5) contributed greatly to the rapidity with which the technology advanced. Working out a strategy for engaging other researchers is as much a part of building value in an idea as latching onto a promising technology from a scientific point of view.

Thus, in order to tackle the many technical problems that need to be solved before holographic storage becomes a viable technology, and to generate momentum around it, Hesselink became a principal researcher in a $32 million Advanced Research Project Agency (ARPA) project in November 1995. This five-year project is being funded 50 percent by ARPA and 50 percent by twelve industry and university participants. Different organizations will focus on different facets of the technology; for example, Hesselink, along with GTE, Inc., will work on telecommunications services and systems, and IBM on applications that would benefit from high-speed random access to large data bases. Without the mobilization of such an array of research talent, it is unlikely that holographic storage technology will advance quickly enough to interest major resource providers.

CONCEIVING OF ATTRACTIVE APPLICATIONS

Except for technologies that are developed expressly for a single product or process, many early-stage discoveries have the potential to be used in a variety of applications and products. The scope and attractiveness of the latter contribute as much to a technology's commercializability as the progress achieved in its functional parameters. This is the reason why the discovery of high-temperature superconductivity got such an enthusiastic reception. Despite major technological hurdles the discovery posed, mostly associated with an incomplete understanding of the phenomenon and the nature of the material giving rise to it, there was little doubt about its enormous economic potential.

Exploring the different uses of a discovery and how they should be pursued is a key aspect of defining its commercializability. Unfortunately, as Robert Kerwin put it, "The way scientists and engineers are trained is that they achieve great satisfaction through solving a particular technical problem; they don't feel the drive to think 'What else can I do with this, or what is needed to commercialize it.' "[3]

Ken Frederick, director of business development at Raychem, elaborates as follows:

> If you don't have access to potential applications the functional breakthrough achieved in the technology will die. If you choose the wrong applications you will suboptimize. You may also be talking to customers who have incredible applications, but you don't have the technology proven.

When Raychem started to commercialize its Nickel-Titanium shape memory alloys it transferred the technology from the Central Laboratories to the Electronics Division. Unspoken, unsaid were the words *military* and *aerospace*. We told them that the only reason you are in the Electronics Division is that we need a home for you. But, naturally, the bonding was made with that Division's sales force. We did find the best applications for the technology in the Division's marketplace, but we didn't find the best applications for the technology. We made no money out of it. Now, these alloys are finding applications in the medical field as we expand the search.[4]

To get the most out of a new discovery, its various uses need to be explored thoroughly and systematically *before* going on to product development. In most process-based technologies, this involves looking at different fields of use; in device-related technologies, on the other hand, this phase consists in conceiving the right product platforms, which will then be leveraged across a family of different products.

Doing all this in advance provides some security against errors in market assessment and preempts others from staking a claim on the technology later. Thus, when Amgen looked at one of its first gene-spliced drugs, erythropoietin (EPO)—a protein that stimulates the body to produce red blood cells—it thought that it was only good for end-stage renal failure, that is, in the most severe of dialysis cases. Later it discovered that almost 80 to 90 percent of the market lay in areas it had not even identified—cancer, rheumatoid arthritis, anemia, and, of course, normal dialysis.[5]

Searching for applications before moving on to product development also offers an opportunity to gain from scale economies in utilizing the technology. This explains why Martin Marietta, when it came up with its XD alloys, a proprietary family of high-temperature metal matrix materials, looked into both defense and commercial applications concurrently. In addition to their application in hypersonic vehicles (for example, tactical missiles) it looked for automotive applications as turbochargers, connecting rods, or valve materials to create sufficient volume and sales to develop acceptable pricing structures.[6]

How extensive the search for applications should be and how to choose among the applications generated depends on the technology and the company commercializing it. In general, however, the following considerations need to be taken into account in designing one's approach:

Consciously looking beyond the initial context for which the technology was developed;

Avoiding predictive biases by defining applications from a use standpoint; and

Constructing a portfolio of applications that optimizes returns on the investments to be made over time.

Looking Beyond the Initial Context

Just as the difference between good research and bad research lies in finding good problems to solve, the ultimate value of a new technology lies in the applications in which it gets incorporated. A fertilizing molecule to make geraniums grow faster and last until winter may not have the success its inventor thinks it deserves—especially if it costs as much as a small greenhouse—but it will be a sure winner if it grows hair on people's heads instead. Not knowing what the technology's best applications are at the start runs the danger of protecting the wrong facet, or protecting too much.

Many inventors do not take the trouble to step back from their discoveries and reexamine what its best application will be. The consequence is that they fall victim to their own, or their organization's, context, which may not be what the market needs most. To see the kind of trap an inappropriate characterization of a technology can result in, consider the example of an inventor who, after years of effort, has come up with a new design for an automobile engine. "It will change forever the economics of internal combustion engines," he might say. His hyperbole may even have some merit. What he has actually found is a new design for a piston crown that improves combustion efficiency by 15 percent and reduces hydrocarbon emissions by twice as much. But this too was only because he first began by discovering a three-dimensional fluid flow algorithm. The automobile application may have followed because of his familiarity with the industry, or because he happened to work for a car company. In terms of the marketability of his algorithm, stationary gas turbines may have been a more appropriate application. To blame him for indulging in "happy engineering" and seeing too big is to miss the point. His technology was badly defined, that is all.

Sometimes the application is uniquely defined by the technology itself and is so obvious that little thought is given to exploring further. When Percy Spencer, a Raytheon engineer, placed a bag of popcorn in front of the waveguide driven by the magnetron from a military radar set in 1945, the popping of kernels inside the bag immediately pointed to cooking applications. Two years later the company introduced its first microwave oven for restaurants and then licensed the technology to others for similar applications.

Mostly, however, it is the inventor's background and interests that determines how a technology gets targeted. A typical example is the invention of the maser and the first optical ruby laser. The principles underlying both had been described in Einstein's 1916 work on stimulated emission and involved an understanding of the energy levels of molecules and solids. The technology needed to apply the principle, however, was not developed until World War II—magnetron and klystron sources, semiconductor detectors, and waveguiding networks. The fact that the first device to use these principles and accompanying technologies turned out to be a microwave (maser), and not optical one (laser), was because of Townes's interest and background in the noise problems of microwave amplifiers. It was Townes's interest in microwave spectroscopy and communication that also explained why the initial applications for the maser were in amplifiers and oscillators. The Soviet maser pioneers N. G. Basov and A. M. Prokhorov too were radio and microwave spectroscopists.[7]

When the laser came along in the early 1960s, it too was perceived as a tool for extending radio and microwave circuit functions into the optical region. Furthermore, Maiman, who demonstrated the first optical laser, used ruby because he had worked with ruby as a material for masers, knew its energy levels well, and had calculated the optical pumping power necessary for the laser action. Although ruby is scarcely the easiest material to lase, its use was determined by familiarity, just as Townes's discovery of the maser was.[8]

A company's mission and rules of exclusion can play a role too. Thus, one of the reasons why ATM (asynchronous transfer mode) telecommunication switches have been delayed in their commercialization is the context in which they were developed. Compared to traditional digital switches, which contain fixed links between subscribers, ATM switches offer much greater capacity by flexibly combining low bandwidth (voice, for example) traffic with high bandwidth (video, for example). Thus, customers can buy the bandwidth they need, when they need it, rather than having to invest in a dedicated high-capacity network. Although technically ready around 1990, ATM switches have yet to find a niche in the marketplace. Promoted mainly by telecommunication suppliers, they were offered as a way to integrate voice, data, and video traffic—the business of telecommunication companies. Its immediate benefits, on the other hand, were found to lie in high-speed data services instead—in implementing intranets, for example—which interested companies in another segment of the industry.[9]

Overcoming such contextual myopia requires a conscious effort in expanding the search for a technology's uses between the time when the initial techno-market insight was arrived at and the start of product development. Conducting such searches in moderation helps identify uses one may not have thought of initially, and it updates the context in which the technology was first developed.

Avoiding Predictive Biases

As those who have been involved in exercises aimed at generating new applications find out, many of the ideas that come up relate to *future* uses of a technology. While this is good from the standpoint of developing unique products, one needs to bear in mind an admonition often given to economists: Forecast a number, or a date, never both together! The fact is that while many thoughtful predictions about future uses of a new technology do come true, they seldom occur in the time frame one first imagines. Conversely, while one may be right about the time horizon, one may be completely off the mark insofar as the use is concerned.

The biases one encounters in predicting use of a new technology have their origin in two things: an incomplete understanding of its potential and applications, and an excessive preoccupation with what is fashionable at the time forecasts are made.

On the first point, the U.S. National Academy of Sciences (NAS) has on several occasions asked leading scientists of various disciplines to outline the futures of their professions. The Westheimer report of 1965, *Chemistry: Opportunities and Needs,* and the Pimentel report of 1970, *Opportunities in Chemistry,* predicted the progress in chemistry. Leading physicists speculated about advances in their discipline in the Pake report, *Physics: Survey and Outlook,* in 1966, and later in the Brinkman report of 1986, *Physics Through the 1990s.* In 1970, Philip Handler, Chairman of the NAS Survey Committee on the Life Sciences, edited opinions of prominent biologists on future directions of research in *Biology and the Future of Man.* As Daniel E. Koshland Jr., editor-in-chief of *Science* magazine, put it recently,

> The predictions made in these excellent volumes have, for the most part, been fulfilled—except that the most revolutionary and unexpected findings were not predicted. Physicists did not suggest the transistor and the laser, chemists missed buckyballs, biologists did not foresee recombinant DNA. Thus, history would suggest that scientists tend to understate the future.[10]

The difficulty of linking scientific breakthroughs to concrete applications is illustrated by what Carl Gosline, vice president, University Patents Inc. (UPI), said during a workshop sponsored by the Licensing Executive Society in 1970. Describing some of the technologies that his company was involved with, he singled out two: the work Sol Spiegelman had been doing since the late 1950s on nucleic acid hybridization methods, and the UPI pico voltmeter. Speaking of Spiegelman's work, he rightly claimed, "The most profound scientific development in which UPI is involved is the invention of Dr. Spiegelman of a way to cause the RNA molecule to replicate in a test tube." However, as he continued, "That has great scientific import. Whether it will ever have economic or social value remains to be seen." The same misjudgment applied to the pico voltmeter. "The pico voltmeter is an intriguing device for measuring extremely small voltages, but then there aren't huge numbers who want to do that and so its economic significance is relatively low."[11]

As for the preoccupation with current fashion, this is related to a phenomenon psychologists term "projection"—we assume that others will want what we want and behave in ways we ourselves wish to. This bias can be collective also. Steven Schnaars in a book called *Megamistakes*[12] tells of a number of technology forecasts made by eminent people this century, very few of which materialized. While some were victims of misjudging technological capabilities, many were simply on account of projecting the "Zeitgeist," or spirit of the times.

An example of judgment colored by a mood in a particular epoch is that of ultrasonics technology. By the 1960s, it had become one of the "in" technologies; naturally, therefore, many technology forecasts made at that time saw a widespread need for it. *Newsweek* predicted that we would be taking ultrasonic showers by 1970. Water would be obsolete, and dirt would be beaten off your body by sound waves. In 1967, *Fortune* foresaw ultrasonic cleaning for dishes—and perhaps even for clothes. A few years later, *Fortune* described an ultrasonic sewing machine that would use high-frequency vibrations to weld, rather than stitch, synthetic fibers—hence speeding up the attachment of buttons, for example.[13]

The same bias applies to forecasts being made today. Consider the technologies the *New York Times* chose in January 1991 as having the greatest potential for the remainder of this decade. After "Consultation with experts at universities and in government and industry," these included micromachines, parallel processing computers, superconductors, new tough materials, solar power, genetically modified plants and animals, and, of course, software engineering.[14] If the list looks obvious, it should. After all, each of these technologies has progressed sufficiently to graduate from science fiction. Moreover, the symptoms they address are all part of our collective Zeitgeist at the moment—health consciousness, environmental concerns, the price performance of devices, and intelligence augmentation. How many of these concerns will still be around even a decade from now is anyone's guess. The fact is that these technologies are being developed to address today's issues, in the expectation that they will have relevance to those for whom they will become available.

One way to avoid such predictive biases is to forecast both the technology's trajectory and the problems likely to be encountered in the future together. Rather than see the future as no more than a resolution of the unsolved problems of today, one needs to see it as a source of *new* problems to which the technology could be targeted. For shorter-term uses, on the other hand, applications need to be imagined from a user standpoint. The latter's perception of discontinuities, after all, is more relevant than what the proponent of the technology imagines.

Creativity techniques that seek out the unusual are valuable for establishing the *initial* context of the research, finding hitherto unimagined problems to solve in coming up with an exciting techno-market vision. But subsequent shaping of the invention and targeting it to a commercial orientation requires real-world insights, discouraging as they might be. In the half-dozen or so application brainstorm sessions the author sat in himself, virtually none of the *imagined* uses of a technology got marketed in the end. However, the applications suggested by industry experts did prove consequential. These experts not only defined the applications in more concrete terms but were able to point quite accurately to the pitfalls, the time scales, and the investment requirements.

A case in point is ultrasonic cleaning technology, referred to by Steven Schnaars. Its functional merit lies in cleaning hard-to-access nooks and cavities in objects. Defining applications so broadly will generate a long list of applications, many of which either can be treated by alternative technologies or find ultrasonics too expensive for the amount of cleaning desired. What is required is also an in-depth understanding of each of these applications. And it is precisely here that many companies shortcut the process and arrive at misleading or plainly wrong conclusions.

Leveraging a new technology's distinctive advantages, in other words, requires understanding its uses thoroughly, application by application. One way to achieve this is to get those concerned with these applications directly involved in the definition process. This is, for example, what Finnsonic Oy, based in Lahti, Finland, does with its ultrasonic cleaning technology today. Rather than producing standard cleaning plants, it recognizes the individuality of cleaning problems and develops custom-designed ultrasonic cleaning plants based on a customer's own needs and requirements. It engages customers for determining their cleaning objectives, the level of cleanliness they desire, and the speed with which they want to perform this. The design engineering work it then undertakes seeks to optimize a solution based on the customer's needs, not what the technology itself can deliver by way of ultimate performance. This includes the degree of automation required, the resources available, and the premises the client already possesses.

The more completely an application is thought through from a use standpoint, the better. This requires not just conceiving products but the complete business concept too. A case in point is the ceramics injection molding technology being pursued at AlliedSignal, Inc. The idea Clifford Ballard, the manager of this project, had was not just to develop particular ceramic parts but to imagine a whole new way of doing so. While plastic parts could be simply and cheaply produced by a number of injection molders using standard compounds, ceramic parts were made by job-shops, each employing different methods and using its own batch formulations. Drawing a parallel from the plastics industry, he thought of a future where ceramics too could be made in a high-volume, automated environment using injection molding.

Injection molding was only part of Ballard's vision. He imagined an entire business for AlliedSignal where the latter would act as a supplier of ceramic molding compounds to a large number of independent molders; the technology could be further leveraged by supplying these molders with a service consisting of automated parts prototyping and mold design and fabrication. Thus, when a customer came to one of these molders with a parts request, the latter would digitize the drawing and send it to AlliedSignal electronically. Using automated prototyping methods, AlliedSignal would quickly send over a part prototype for confirmation as well as a mold designed specifically to match the company's compound, allowing the molder to start series production within a couple of weeks.

As discussed in Chapter 5, the completeness of this vision and its business orientation was an important factor in mobilizing the resources needed for demonstrating it.

Constructing a Portfolio to Optimize Returns

Generating a list of potential applications is often the easy part. More difficult in practice is deciding on which among these applications to pursue and when.

A way to approach this issue of selection is to do so in stages. As shown in Table 4-1, a first level of screening consists in weeding out applications that have little business interest. This is then followed by evaluating those that remain for their intrinsic commercializability. The actual weights to assign to individual criteria and how many applications to pursue, and in which sequence, depends on a company's circumstances. What is required in many cases, however, is a portfolio of applications that optimizes long-term returns on the investments planned.

Preliminary Screen (Business Interest)

Generally speaking, applications of interest are those targeted to attractive markets and, for existing companies, those that leverage the skills and infrastructure already in place. The latter is naturally more relevant to existing companies than to start-ups with nothing to relate applications to. Attractive markets are large markets that exhibit high and stable (noncyclic) growth rates and ones in which potential customers themselves are very profitable. As for specific customers and segments within the market, attractive ones are those for which the product represents an essential need and where customers tend to be relatively price-insensitive innovative adopters, amenable to trying new products. These attributes, taken together, tend to favor the successful introduction of new products as measured by profitability and time-to-market.[15]

As for relating applications to a company's existing business, the reasons for this are obvious: familiarity with the technology reduces the perceived level of risk, hence ensuring resource commitment from senior management; the availability of competences means that progress can be made more quickly and securely; the presence of a business infrastructure

TABLE 4-1

Screening for Attractive Applications

Preliminary Screen (Business Interest)

Market Attractiveness

Size

Growth

Customer profitability

Customer receptivity to innovation

Leveraging Existing Skills and Infrastructure

Technical synergy

Commercial synergy

Conformity with future strategy

Secondary Screen (Commercializability)

Ease of Commercialization

Addressing a pending problem

Resources available in niche

Downstream barriers to commercialization

Readiness of technology for application

Uniqueness of Application

Most cost-effective solution

Unique technical solution

Scope of Problems Addressed

Helps expand product scope

Helps expand the core technology and widens patent coverage

already in place ensures that the product(s) will be brought to market with minimal new downstream investments; and, perhaps most importantly, the fit ensures that user requirements and the total context of the product are well understood in advance.

As Peter Larsson, who became manager of Raychem's surge arrester venture mentioned in Chapter 2, put it:

> We were fortunate in having a good fit with a technology we had long dominated (cross-linked polymers) and were able to offer the arrester housing along with the new ceramic discs. We also sold it to the same customers, even the same pole, to which we supplied cable accessories. And we kept the entire set of capabilities close to the company. Instead of spinning out the venture entirely, we only half spun it off. The project stayed an integral

part of the Electrical Division and could draw upon the work in related fields being done within corporate R&D.[16]

This dual criterion has been empirically validated too.[17] As the work of the Boston Consulting Group, McKinsey & Co., and, more recently, the Strategic Planning Institute's PIMS program, have shown, profit potential in a business tends to be a function of strong competitive positions in attractive markets. The same applies to the introduction of new products. Hewing to the factors constituting competitive position and market attractiveness has been shown to improve the chances of launching new products successfully.

Existing competencies are, of course, not the only criteria that companies use. As illustrated by the example of Seiko's pursuit of the FIB project, the need to build new competencies in a particular area may be an equally valid reason for deciding whether or not to pursue a particular technology and its applications. Sumitomo Electric is another company that takes this explicitly into account when judging whether or not to fund particular projects. For it, conformity to a business area *targeted for the future,* and the potential for creating an independent business area with growth prospects, are criteria as legitimate as the feasibility of the technology and its fit with *existing* businesses.[18]

Secondary Screen (Commercializability)

As a recent study on the factors leading to the cancellation of research projects at Alcoa found, four main categories of factors were involved: lack of market potential, lack of company support, technical barriers, and economic barriers.[19] While the first two relate to what has just been discussed, the latter two relate to the commercialization of the technology itself. It is no good just targeting applications that are attractive from a market standpoint and that fit a company's existing strategy and business. Equally important are the factors bearing on the technology itself. Applications that pass the preliminary screen must then be judged by the intrinsic commercializability of the technology.

As shown in Table 4-1, there are three main things to consider when relating applications to their commercializability. The first concerns the ease of commercialization. Far too many technologies languish for a long time and get overtaken by competing ones simply because they are targeted to the most attractive applications. Going after less attractive but also less demanding applications is often a good way to start.

The importance of considering ease of implementation as one of the desirable paths was also confirmed by John Ettlie's study of forty federally sponsored innovation projects in 1982. The probability of commercial success for these projects was, in fact, mainly influenced by three factors—the use of incremental rather than radical technologies, ease of introduction and implementation, and what he termed pricing potential, meaning that no subsidy was needed to make the technology cost-efficient. Market potential, interestingly enough (though curious to Ettlie), had a *negative* impact on the probability of commercial success.[20]

Recognition of the importance of an early start to the commercialization process also formed the basis on which A. D. Little, Inc., evaluated the most promising commercialization options for Belland's intelligent plastics. From the 200-odd applications generated initially, some were first discarded as being technically impossible to implement. The remaining fifty-four were then evaluated for potential market size and profitability, as well as for commercial and technical feasibility to determine which of the technically feasible projects could be developed in less than two years.

Easy applications both permit learning to occur in the marketplace and prevent technology-based ventures from turning into black holes, straining the patience of early backers. Even if these applications seem trivial given the science on which they are based, searching for them in the beginning and gearing up to launch them can be a precondition for other applications to be pursued. Any step taken to reduce the perception of interminable funding requirements helps sustain interest in the technology and ensure a base level of cash flow.

A number of factors determine what makes an application easy. Some have to do with the technology, while others relate to resource mobilization or to the marketing of the end product or process. In general, four main things are involved:

Whether it addresses a pending problem;

The resources available in the niches to which the application is targeted;

The downstream barriers to commercialization it is likely to encounter; and

The readiness of the technology for particular applications.

Pending problems are those for which an industry has been searching for a solution for a long time and is, therefore, receptive to its adoption. This is, for example, what explains the rapidity with which ion-selective membranes got applied soon after they were discovered in the early 1970s. Their use in the electrolysis of brine to yield chlorine and caustic soda was immediate, not only because the industry had been searching for an alternative to mercury and diaphragm cells for nearly two decades, but because some companies had anticipated and conceptualized their use in a membrane cell ten years before they came along. The same occurred in their other major application—electrodialysis. By permitting the exchange of cations and anions while holding large protein molecules in one chamber, these membranes allowed the purification of feed solutions, which was either impossible or uneconomical using electrochemical methods in the past.

Urgency does not, of course, always translate into a willingness to pay. If technology commercialization is really about resource mobilization—a central argument throughout this book—then an easy application is really one to which people are willing to devote money immediately. This is particularly important for technologies being brought to market by small, resource-poor companies and to lone inventors.

Capital is more forthcoming in some fields and sectors of the economy than others. Thus, even after the development of niobium-titanium superconducting alloys in the 1960s, their main use soon became restricted to large, government-funded research efforts. These included applications such as bubble chambers, super colliders, and magnetically levitated trains, all of which required huge, nationally funded research programs. The main commercial application pursued was in the medical field—in the form of magnetic resonance imaging (MRI)—which has also been traditionally characterized by high up-front risk investments. The mature and conservative electric utility industry, in which the application of superconductivity promised the greatest rewards, largely ignored the principle for nearly three decades.

Resource availability also explains the way biotechnology first got targeted to the pharmaceutical industry. While the technology could be used from the beginning in a wide range of fields, including pharmaceuticals, animal and plant agriculture, speciality chemicals and food additives, environmental areas, and bioelectronics, its first major applications were in the pharmaceutical field. Given the long lead times and expensive developments associated with the latter, one would not have normally expected that to happen. Biotechnology products, because of their relative newness and the unfamiliar manufacturing process associated with them, were from the beginning perceived to be more risky than drugs developed the traditional way. The clinical and market disappointments that have accompanied products introduced in recent years by companies such as Genentech, Centocor Inc., and Xoma Corp. have vindicated this risk perception too. In hindsight, several reasons can be advanced for why pharmaceuticals became the key application area:

> Compared to other fields, a much larger proportion of public funding was being channelled into biomedical research generally, especially in the United States, where the technology got started. The first biotechnology products, such as DNA-produced human insulin, interferon, and MAb diagnostic kits, were a direct result of the biomedical nature of the basic research that led to these new technologies.

> Pharmaceutical companies had already accumulated several years of experience with biological production methods, and the experience enabled them to take advantage of the new technologies.

Pharmaceutical products were high in value-added and could be priced to recover costs incurred during R&D, making that sector a good place to begin the costly process of developing a new technology.[21]

The role of downstream commercialization barriers in determining ease of bringing new technologies to market is well recognized. This also explains the approach taken by most biotechnology companies within the pharmaceutical field. Most of their initial products were conscious replacements or improvements of products already on the market: insulin, human growth hormone, interferon, and tissue plasminogen activator. Not only were the clinical properties of these products known, hence accelerating the obtaining of approvals, but potential buyers were already familiar with them. Early products also included monoclonal antibody (MAb) in vitro diagnostic kits and DNA probes. The time and the number of tests required for these in vitro products was much less than that required for in vivo products generally. The same argument explains why many companies have targeted gene probe diagnostics as the first major application in genomics (of which the Human Genome Project is a part). Compared to actual gene therapy, which confronts both developmental and regulatory hurdles, this area is closer to market.

Because of the role downstream barriers play, easy applications tend to be those in which the technology's particular function has some precedence. This not only saves a great deal of applied research but also reduces commercial uncertainties.

A good example of this is the application of lasers in the medical field. Ever since the first ruby laser was invented in 1960 by Theodor Maiman, a number of medical uses were immediately thought of. People knew that lasers could do things other instruments could not. However, the first applications tended to be in areas where light and heat were already a part of therapeutic remedies. For example, ophthalmologists had been using xenon lamp photocoagulators for decades to treat a wide variety of eye disorders. Lasers merely provided a more controllable, monochromatic, intense beam of light; the principles involved in healing detached retinas, for instance, were the same.

Finally, in many situations, technology readiness determines which applications ought to be taken first. The way photovoltaics were introduced to the market illustrates this. When serious attention was devoted to photovoltaics during the 1970s, for example, the route that practically all research organizations took was to enhance conversion efficiency in order to compete with existing sources of electric energy. This fixation on a single variable, conversion efficiency, often led to seeking more expensive solutions. It was the Japanese who first broke this spiral of technical perfection by applying photovoltaics to alternative devices such as hand calculators and watches, where conversion efficiency was less important a barrier.

The Japanese have, in fact, been particularly good at targeting "trivial" or nondemanding applications early in a new technology's development; often these also happen to be high-volume applications that help in reducing cost while demonstrating the technology's utility, justifying its use elsewhere. While the Americans used shape-memory alloys first in step ladders for the Apollo moon landing program, the Japanese used them in women's brassieres as reinforcing wire. Similarly, while the Americans were targeting carbon fiber for jumbo jets, the Japanese put it in golf clubs instead.

Taking easy applications first in order to commercialize a new technology quickly means finding the path of least resistance among all of these four variables. What the path is depends on the technology in question and the nature of its market opportunities.

Sometimes, technology readiness for particular uses is most important, as demonstrated by the approach taken recently by companies trying to commercialize high-temperature superconductors (HTSC). In high-temperature superconductivity, the largest markets are indeed in the power and transportation fields. The problems associated with these applications, however, relate to the high current densities involved and the ductility of the material needed for drawing wires. The most feasible applications, therefore, tend to be mostly in the electronics area, where low current densities and thin films can be used. In order to pursue these applications and move the technology forward, one company, Conductus Inc., founded in 1987 in Sunnyvale, California, decided to take a systematic evolutionary approach —what Linda Capuano, vice president of operations and business development, terms a "food-chain" approach.

Since yttrium barium copper oxide (YBCO) was the only high-temperature superconducting material then available in bulk form, that is what the company started with. It first established capability in making very high-quality YBCO films. After successfully depositing a single layer of the film, it looked around to see what applications such single-layer films might have. Among the devices it came up with were passive microwave components (resonators and antennas) and infrared sensors (bolometers). These became the first commercializable items.

As the company gained expertise in depositing multiple layers, the complexity of devices it worked on expanded. In 1989 it was able to deposit three layers, which made simple active devices like SQUID magnetometers possible. By the end of 1990, the company was working on seven layers and had mastered the use of grain boundaries to build more complex circuits. This allowed the company to demonstrate the world's first integrated high-temperature magnetometer, with the YBCO SQUID and flux transformer integrated on one chip. As Linda Capuano put it:

> Creativity lies in staging the products derived from a new technology. The tendency is to jump to more complex systems because there are more profits there and larger volumes. Everyone wants to move up the food chain, but

how do you support yourself while you are moving up to that? Computers and satellites are where these YBCO technologies will eventually end up but that is some years ahead.[22]

What Conductus Inc. basically did was to marry the known and proven technologies of SQUIDs and Josephson junctions to develop early products that could be used in known applications—such as diagnosing heart disease.

Conductus has been one of the few companies in the HTSC field to sustain itself, mainly because of its flexible and progressive approach to applications. While many companies targeted difficult applications such as HTSC wire and high-power systems, it went from making magnetometers to a simple demonstration kit for explaining superconductivity in schools and universities. More recently, instead of making HTSC chips themselves—which was part of its founding mission—it began to work on just the chip packaging unit.

Hesselink's Optitek, Inc., mentioned in Chapter 2 is stressing technical feasibility too. In order to bring a product to market within the next two or three years, Hesselink has chosen video-on-demand as the first niche to target. It is an application that requires downloading the high volumes of data best suited to holographic systems while, at the same time, tolerating the fairly high error rates the system will need to contend with while some of its enabling technologies evolve. Unlike computer applications it would, furthermore, require only a read-only memory (ROM) for which Hesselink thinks present photorefractive materials could suffice.[23]

In other situations, like the pharmaceutical and medical examples cited above, it is resource availability that is the overriding factor in determining which applications get chosen first. A recent example of a technology being first targeted to a resource-rich niche where it addresses a pending problem is what happened with Xerox's DataGlyph invention referred to in Chapter 2. While initially developed for use in the office environment in line with the company's business mission, its first big use will actually be "smart" ID cards. Sandia Imaging Systems, of Carrolton, Texas, recently bought the rights to the DataGlyph technology for use in a $275 million project of the U.S. Immigration and Naturalization Service to create a new generation of employment authorization cards, border-crossing cards, and green cards that can, for example, store the bearer's palm print in a glyph-encoded format on one side. Compared to cards with magnetic strips or silicon chips, these cards are expected to be cheaper and more fraud-resistant.[24]

The second factor is the technology's differentiable advantages vis-à-vis competing solutions. This can be in the form of offering either the most cost-effective solution or a *unique* technical function. Naturally, the more both are provided together the greater the chances of successful commercialization. It is this factor that causes new technologies to seek out specialized niche applications in the beginning.

Such applications eventually result in end products uniquely based on the new technology. They are the ones that help sustain a technology's commercialization profitably and over a period of time.

One caution about easy applications: They often tend to be substitutes in a known product. Like all substitutes, they themselves are vulnerable to encroachment from other technologies. The best guarantee for a long-term presence of the technology is to seek new applications that uniquely derive from the technology's own characteristics. As Kataoka Shoei, executive director of Sharp Corporation, put it with regard to liquid crystal displays:

> There are limits to the demand for liquid crystal displays if they are treated merely as a replacement for other display technologies currently in use. We must take the lead to develop new uses that will expand the market for liquid display panels. The idea is to create next-generation products centered on LCDs as a key device that create their own demand. The unique characteristics of liquid crystal displays must be put to use to create products that did not exist up until now, products that will make the consumer say, "Ah, I've always wanted something like this."[25]

The final commercializability-related factor concerns the scope of problems an application addresses. Following the notion that a technology is really a capability that can be leveraged across a wide number of applications, the more a particular application permits expanding the future scope of products and the technology itself, the better. Apart from the economies in R&D one can enjoy later, this permits obtaining a broad patent coverage before competitors start to enter the technology. Such scoping applications get chosen more for long-term technical reasons than for any concrete immediate application. Starting work on them during the incubation process helps demonstrate what a technology can do and what its limitations are.

The Application Portfolio

The important point about these commercializability factors is that they can serve as a guide for either selecting the best application to start with or constructing a portfolio of applications to pursue. An ideal portfolio, in fact, is one where all three factors get considered—an easy application to gain experience and generate early cash flow, a unique application to establish the technology, and a scoping application that permits demonstrating the technology across a wide variety of potential uses for the future. If a single application meets all three requirements, it is the best one to pursue. More typically, however, one needs different applications in each category.

While one observes several start-up companies proposing more than one product or application when going out to raise funds, they do not always look at these in the light of the above portfolio. Formulating such a portfolio, furthermore, should not be seen as a one-time decision. Rather, it is an evolving, experimental process based on progress in the underlying technology and searching for opportunities actively.

AlliedSignal's Optically Responsive Polymer Research Program

An example of such an experimental approach comprising different kinds of applications is offered by a recent technology program undertaken at AlliedSignal.

In line with its effort to find new technologies and businesses around its traditional polymer know-how, AlliedSignal had started a program on optically responsive polymers in 1986. Such polymers offered the capability to fabricate simple and inexpensive electro-optic devices on a variety of substrates. Their low dielectric constants (or refractive indexes) would allow devices to operate at higher efficiencies. Optical wave guides, one of the major application areas foreseen, could be readily processed and chemically modified to optimize performance too.

While these theoretical advantages of the technology had been recognized since the early 1980s, practical applications required considerable progress to be made in the materials themselves, in device architectures and fabrication techniques appropriate for them. Specific applications to be worked on depended on how much progress was made in these areas.

"Early in the effort I thought of a 'holy grail' that would revolutionize how electro-optics was done," says Jim Yardley, head of the program. "With the 30–100 pico-meter/volt electro-optic coefficient we have today you get some applications, but you don't revolutionize electro-optic devices. At an electro-optic response of 3,000 pico-meter/volt you can, for example, build auto-focus cameras that focus electronically rather than with a motor; you can control one light beam with another at this level of performance, opening up really attractive market opportunities in optical processing."[26]

Realizing that such optical processing applications lay far out in the future, Yardley and his team constantly redefined the focus of the program in line with the progress they made in the generic technology. Figure 4-2 summarizes this changing composition of investment in the principal application areas. The first near-term application area chosen was optical interconnections used in electro-optic devices. In order to access a large-volume application simultaneously, a parallel effort began in photopolymer waveguides. In 1989, these were the two areas of focus. Neither, however, was expected to result in a near-term commercial opportunity. This led to adding a third area in 1990—that of clarity enhancement coatings—which the team saw as easy to implement given the progress that had been made in the generic technology by then. After trying various uses for these coatings, including spectacles, windows, and even greeting cards, the team found a near-term opportunity in enhancing the quality of LCDs. While

FIGURE 4-2

INVESTMENT IN OPTICALLY RESPONSIVE POLYMERS

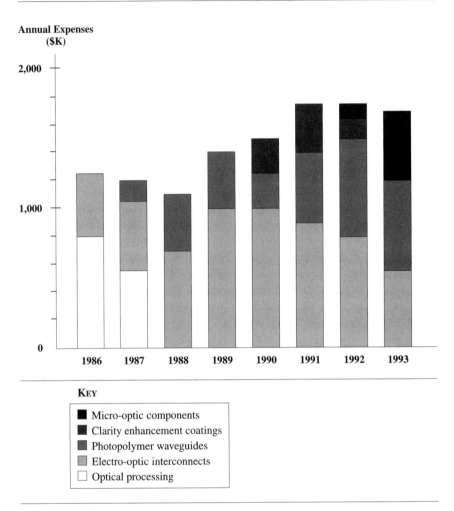

KEY

■ Micro-optic components
■ Clarity enhancement coatings
■ Photopolymer waveguides
▨ Electro-optic interconnects
□ Optical processing

SOURCE: AlliedSignal, 1994. Reprinted with permission.

research in waveguides and optical processing continues, it was the LCD application that started to drive commercialization by 1996.

ASSEMBLING INTELLECTUAL PROPERTY RIGHTS LINKED TO COMMERCIALIZATION STRATEGY

Among the most valuable technologies invented in recent years has been that of dimensionally stable anodes (DSA) for chlorine and caustic soda production through the electrolysis of brine, invented by Henri Beer. According to Vittorio de Nora, who helped commercialize DSA, three things explained its phenomenal success: luck in having a good product, luck in there being a need for the product, and luck in being alone. "Luck in being alone" was as much a result of Henri Beer's ingenuity as the farsighted manner in which the DSA technology was protected. The basic invention was patented in 1957. This was then followed by another patent in 1967 relating to the commercial product and several improvement patents later. The approach not only gradually expanded the coverage of the patents to include 95 percent of the market but extended the life of the protection afforded to the technology. Each patent built on a better knowledge of the prior art and a better knowledge of the commercial opportunities.[27]

The importance of protecting technology and the role such protection plays in technology commercialization has been the subject of considerable debate in recent years. Questions such as whether the cost of obtaining (and maintaining) rights is commensurate with their strength and the benefits they provide, which rights to choose, when to protect, and the scope of intellectual property rights to obtain, are far from settled.

Intellectual property rights are worth nothing if the cost benefits of the invention are such that customers end up buying something else. As the findings of several studies show, things like a company's reputation, possessing lead time advantages, exploiting learning curve effects aggressively, and superior marketing contribute as much, if not more, to success than these rights.[28]

Even so, no one denies that, if properly thought through and managed, the various instruments for the protection of intellectual property rights available today (Table 4-2) play an important role in technology commercialization. Not only do they help appropriate the benefits of an invention, but they provide a wider range of possibilities for bringing it to market.

Because of this book's focus on new-to-the-world technologies, the intellectual property rights of real interest are patents for invention. Trademark and copyright protection is relatively inexpensive to obtain and applies to end products introduced in commerce. The same applies to semiconductor chip protection where no disclosure of substance is involved.

For patents, one issue in the past used to be the trade-off between their cost (and disclosure) versus their validity when challenged. To patent an invention costs $10,000–$15,000 in most industrialized countries. If patents are sought in all major countries where the invention might be practiced, say a dozen countries, the cost is of the order of $100,000 per patent. Since most inventions tend to be covered by more than a single patent, the cost can easily exceed that. To this one-time expense needs to be added periodic renewal fees and, of course, the vastly greater costs associated with litigations, should they arise.

The prospect of litigation has, in fact, been a major deterrent for some

TABLE 4-2
SUMMARY OF THE MAIN INSTRUMENTS AVAILABLE
FOR PROTECTING TECHNOLOGY

Instrument	Requirements to Be Fulfilled	Term of Grant	Protection Against
1. Patent for invention	Novel, useful, and inventive industrial method	20 years from date of application	Manufacture, use, or sale of claimed features of product or process
2. Patent for utility model (petty patent)	Industrially applicable devices with novel shape or construction	3–10 years depending on country	Object similarity
3. Patent for industrial design	Original, ornamental design (nonfunctional) reproducible industrially	Between 1 and 25 years depending on country and applicant's desire	Design similarity
4. Patent for plant varieties	New plant variety produced asexually or through seeds	Similar to patent for invention	Reproduction of plant
5. Copyright	Original literary, artistic, or software work; registration and notice required if publicly distributed	Life of author plus 50 years, except for designs	Copying the form of expression
6. Protection of mask works	Original circuit design embedded in photographic mask or equivalent	10 years from registration	Reproduction and/or importation of protected circuit layout
7. Trademark	Commercial use and registration	Indefinite, provided it is used	Confusing resemblance
8. Trade secret	Substantial know-how that is novel and kept confidential	Indefinite, as long as kept secret	Derived work

SOURCE: David A. Burge, *Patent and Trademark Tactics and Practice* (New York: John Wiley & Sons, 1980); Kenneth E. Payne, personal communication to the author, June 1996; personal updates.

inventors considering whether to file for patents. The situation is, however, changing. In the United States, a new court of appeals for the federal circuit was established in 1982 and was charged with handling all patent infringement appeals. While formed partly in an attempt to foster uniformity and predictability in rulings on patents, this court has tended to be more propatent than was the case before. While prior to the establishment of this court as many as 70 percent of all patent challenges were successful, the proportion had been reversed by 1991, with just one-third being declared invalid. Not only are preliminary and permanent injunctions being issued against infringers more often, but the penalties for infringements have also grown—treble damages based on lost profits (and legal costs) rather than simply foregone royalties as in the past.

This strengthening of patent rights is occurring on a worldwide basis, too. Recent negotiations within the World Intellectual Property Organization (WIPO) and in the context of the Trade Related Aspects of Intellectual Property Rights (TRIPs) agreement within the General Agreement on Tariffs and Trade (GATT) have led more countries not only to become signatories to patent conventions but also to tighten their approach to infringements.

The strengthening of patent rights still begs many of the questions inventors have traditionally faced: whether to apply for patents or keep the technology secret, when to apply for patents, and what scope of coverage to seek. As with other aspects of technology commercialization, these questions are best addressed in stages.

Patents on Basic Inventions

At the imagining stage, applying for patents represents as much of a gamble as the techno-market insight itself. This is when fundamental inventions get made without full knowledge of the course they will eventually take. As Ambros Speiser recollects from experience:

> During my thirty-year association with Brown Boveri we obtained nearly 1,000 patents at the Research Center—about one patent application for every three disclosures that got made. Perhaps only ten or twenty of these patents turned out to be truly valuable. But we didn't know which in advance. Also, one of these valuable patents—relating to the supertwist nematic principle for LCDs—was filed just four weeks before a Japanese company. Had we delayed the patent application we would have lost out on a major income opportunity.[29]

Knowing whether to file patents on basic inventions continues to pose a challenge today. If anything, competitive pressures force companies to file for more applications than they would like. In countries where patent examinations are voluntary, this is less of a problem. One can apply for a number of patents but then not go through all the other steps needed to obtain a grant. The propensity of several Japanese companies to file patent applications on superconductors is a case in point. Thus, by the end of 1987, Sumitomo Electric Industries had filed for more than 700 superconductivity patents in Japan, more than most big U.S. companies apply for in a year in all fields. In addition to preempting others from filing similar applications and thus circumscribing its own freedom to pursue the technology, Sumitomo could then later decide to pursue the especially promising ones to obtain a grant. In countries where all patent applications get examined automatically, such broad-based filings can be wasteful.

Recognizing this, many companies have started to bring a business perspective to bear on their patenting decisions as early as possible. The trend is to aim for fewer, high-quality patents, which will provide long-term marketplace dominance in an attractive technology. AlliedSignal is one such case. As Roger H. Criss, the chief patent counsel for the company's Engineered Materials Sector, explains:

> Whereas, in the past, patent applications were mainly driven by technical people, we now have a patent committee which includes sales and marketing for deciding what patents to seek. Like other companies, we have too many inventions that we can file patents on and maintain. We now examine whether there is real value in a concept either from selling product, licensing or simply keeping people away from it. This has led to reducing the number of patents we file each year and a narrowing of the fields we cover in some cases.[30]

At Philips, too, patenting is increasingly being seen as a joint responsibility of R&D, the Central Patents and Trademark Department, and the involved product division or business group. R&D people are expected to know the patent portfolio of competitors and to actively seek routes to optimize the company's position. The generation of patents, in fact, is one of the ten processes Philips has identified for measuring the effectiveness of its R&D (see Chapter 12).

Patenting for a Commercial Mission

Filing patents on basic inventions mainly serves a defensive purpose, staking out a proprietary domain an inventor *might* want to pursue further on an exclusive basis. The decision-making process leading to it also helps identify those areas that should remain secret and those that should be published to prevent others from compromising the inventor's research freedom. It is later in the commercialization process that a more proactive approach to patenting is needed, filing follow-on patents to strengthen coverage and to support the commercialization strategy envisaged. This is when patent costs really start to mount. The reason for treating the subject in this chapter is that the formulation of the approach to take is best done as part of the incubation process itself. The approach needs to be grounded in the actual commercial opportunities one plans to pursue as well as the strategy for pursuing them.

Patents versus Trade Secrets

For inventions one does wish to take further, the first issue concerns whether to keep a technology secret or to seek patents on it. Table 4-3 summarizes the main arguments favoring each.

Like all issues that get posed in the form of pros and cons, the choice depends on the purpose to be served. In general, patenting is preferred when competitors are likely to invent a similar technology soon, when partnerships and cross-licensing arrangements are foreseen as part of the commercialization strategy, when patent infringements are easy to track down, and when capital needs to be attracted from external sources. The latter is especially relevant to start-up companies. While founders and other "human assets" of a start-up company may leave, intellectual property rights are tangible-enough assets to merit investment on their own. Many

TABLE 4-3

ARGUMENTS FOR AND AGAINST PATENTING

For Patenting	For Keeping Technology Secret
• Patents provide a defined period of exclusivity during which others can be prohibited from commercializing the invention even if independently developed.	• Patents are expensive to obtain and offer weak protection.
• Patents establish ownership distinct from teams and individuals.	• Secrets can be kept indefinitely if well protected, while patents force early disclosure.
• Market protection is assured longer if technology is easy to reverse-engineer.	• One can control the timing of disclosure to suit market opportunities.
• Patents prevent others from preempting the technology in a world where first to file patenting has become the norm.	• Sometimes it is impossible to prove that an end product infringes a patent.
• Patents give something to exchange if in-licensing is desired.	
• Patents facilitate and clarify research collaboration and technology marketing agreements.	
• Patents allow greater freedom in choice of business formula.	
• Patents can impose more restrictions on a licensee than is possible in know-how licenses, including, in some countries, longer contract durations.	
• Patents motivate inventors and are a sign of achievement.	

venture capitalists prefer to back technologies that are covered by patents for this reason.

This said, it is important to see patents and trade secrets as complements, not as substitutes for each other. For the reasons listed in Table 4-3, some facets of a technology are best patented and others kept secret. Thus, many computer companies keep their technology for wiring printed circuit boards confidential because it changes every few years but patent their computer architecture, which can last much longer.

When to Patent

All technologies do not gain market acceptance immediately. One needs, therefore, to balance early patenting for preemptive reasons with the assurance that patents remain valid after products are launched. Because of the time it takes for a radical innovation to gain widespread market acceptance, many otherwise important patents expire before they can exercise any competitive leverage. Most of the basic patents on holography, for example, are now expiring because applications have developed slowly. The Holotron Corporation, a joint venture between Battelle and DuPont, which owned all of the key patents issued in the United States during the 1960s, did try to force holographers in various industries to take licenses, but had little success. The major licensee of what remains of the holography patents today is the American Bank Note Corporation, a maker of embossed holograms for checks and credit cards—a far cry from the initial idea Dennis Gabor, the principle's inventor, had in 1947, which was to use holography to improve the resolution of electron microscopes.

Most companies today file their patents as late as possible, unless there are compelling reasons to do otherwise. Typically, this means filing after a prototype is ready and when the first customer is about to be approached— especially one who refuses to sign a confidentiality agreement. Such late applications maximize the effective life of a patent and also tend to result in a stronger patent after the development work has been completed.

Early patenting is the norm today mostly in highly competitive industries. This explains why most pharmaceutical companies continue to file patent applications on their new chemical entities almost immediately after discovering them, knowing fully well that it will be several years before these entities will result in marketable products. It is only in less competitive therapeutic areas that one sees pharmaceutical companies waiting awhile and filing their patents just before clinical trials begin.

How Much to Patent

Incubating a new technology is as much about expanding its technical possibilities as it is about establishing an optimal proprietary domain around it.

The scope of this domain, moreover, must cover the inventor's plans for the technology as well as what competitors might do.

Broad-based patenting is usually justified when a great deal of technology sharing is intended and when different facets of the technology are commercialized independently.

These reasons explain the approach taken by Belland AG. As Roland Belz and his colleagues continued experimenting with their intelligent plastics, practically every aspect of the company's technology was protected one way or another. The chemistry, consisting of formulae and process parameters, was held in secret; the process control technology was covered by some important patents, notably on the thin-film extruder reactor, as well as secret know-how on how to conduct polymerization optimally. Some applications had also already been patented by Belland, and the intention was to maintain at least a part ownership in future applications.

These intellectual property rights corresponded to each of the separate markets in which the Belland technology could be used: market for intelligent plastics (Belland Chemistry); market for Belland's process linked to the productions of intelligent plastics (Belland Hardware); and the market for Belland's process in applications other than intelligent plastics (Customer Chemistry and Belland Hardware).

While some companies commercializing applications based on the intelligent plastics were expected to eventually own in-house production facilities, there were others whose volume would never justify investments in an extruder-reactor line. By owning rights to the polymer, its applications, as well as the production technology, Belland was able to avoid diluting the worth of particular facets of its technology while sharing it broadly. Thus, for example, a buyer of the extruder-reactor was free to produce any conventional plastic but needed to license when making water-soluble-on-demand plastics based on Belland's chemistry. Since a separate license was needed to commercialize a particular application, people with a production license could sell only to authorized application licensees.

Belland's approach applies to most materials technologies. Thus Allied-Signal, too, patents its new materials technologies broadly to give itself greater freedom in commercialization. Its patenting approach is illustrated in Figure 4-3, covering composition of matter, the core process, and major applications as well as a host of derivative materials and applications. Only narrow, customer-specific applications are left to customers to write.

Where broad-based patenting is required, one needs to research beyond the base patent on one's own. Unfortunately, in many large research organizations, there is no incentive to do this. Inventors think of a problem, solve it, demonstrate it preliminarily in the lab to get the base patent, and then go back to do other things. That is what their job description tells them to do. A virtue of having an express incubation program is that it forces

FIGURE 4-3

PATENT STRATEGY AS APPLIED TO NEW MATERIALS DEVELOPMENT

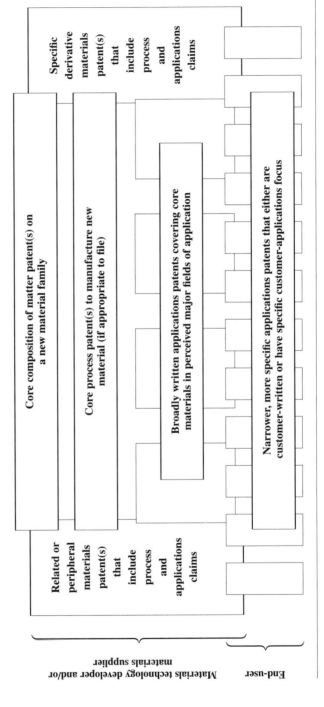

SOURCE: Personal communication from Gregory Smith, AlliedSignal Corp., 1996. Reprinted with permission.

them to look downstream in the commercialization process and stake out the appropriate proprietary domain.

Doing this additional development work in neighboring fields is necessary not only to gain better control over a new technology but to prevent others from hijacking it through a tactic known as "patent flooding." In the latter, rivals file a number of narrow patents closely related to the core patent without directly infringing on it. The consequence is that the company owning the core patent cannot improve its own technology or market its products without the permission of the "flooder" and is thus forced to enter into a cross-licensing agreement.

Bringing Commercializability Forward

The challenge in incubating a new technology is to obtain a favorable judgment of commercializability *and* to have this judgment made as early as possible. The alternative is to have resources committed slowly in small amounts, hence delaying commercialization or compromising the demonstration of the technology.

There is little one can do in practice to accelerate the development of the technology itself, except perhaps to engage in more collaborative research. The role of the latter should not be underestimated either. The fact is that the trajectory of a new technology is never preordained. While one can estimate its theoretical limits in advance, it is far from obvious how quickly these limits will be approached in practice—if ever. What the history of several technologies does show, however, is that progress is a function of how many researchers are mobilized to experiment with the technology.

Apart from the strategy proposed to get others involved in moving the technology forward quickly, the greatest leverage in bringing the judgment of commercializability forward comes from two main things: assembling as much information concerning the technology's market potential up front as possible, and proposing a credible to-do plan that takes into account the uncertainties likely to be encountered.

The need to assemble as much information up front as possible was confirmed by a 1971 survey on the abandonment of R&D projects in the United Kingdom. While only nontechnical reasons were surveyed, they all pointed to a failure to consider some obvious things at the start of projects. Projects were abandoned because it was found that only a small, unattractive market existed, there was one (monopsonistic) buyer who changed his mind, and the level of competition in the product made it unattractive to commercialize. In addition to these environmental factors, projects also got abandoned because the company lacked marketing or production capacity and expertise. The majority of these things should have been anticipated in advance but were not. In fact, rather than culling projects in their early stages, most companies took the projects further, often to the prototype and even market launch stage, before shelving them.[31]

Naturally, technical factors need to be assessed too in looking ahead, particularly those that may act as a hindrance. Resource providers want to know about the latter and the steps one intends to take to circumvent them. Most people judging commercializability want to know the specific hurdles that need to be crossed before a technology's potential can start to be realized and what needs to be done commercially to start the process. They particularly want to know about the critical immediate steps and the approximate time needed to complete the technology for the product class to which it is initially targeted.

As the example of Trilogy Inc. illustrates, the more carefully thought through and credible the to-do plan, the greater the support.

Trilogy Inc.

Founded in 1980 by Gene Amdahl to develop computers based on wafer scale integration semiconductor technology, the company began by raising $51 million through an R&D partnership. It raised another $150 million through a public stock offering and investments by DEC and Sperry by 1985—the year it proposed shipping the first product.

What enabled Trilogy to become the richest-funded start-up until then was a combination of its founder's reputation and the promise of its technology. A well-known former IBM computer designer, Gene Amdahl had further distinguished himself as founder of Amdahl Corp. But reputation alone is never enough. Equally attractive to resource providers was the potential of the new technology, the way it would be positioned, and how value would be realized. With wafer scale integration, 40 wafers would replace as many as 4,000 separate silicon chips and be able to perform over 32 million instructions per second (MIPS). Compared to IBM's top-of-the-line 3084 computer of the early 1980s, a computer based on the new technology would occupy 10 percent of the floor space, perform 30 percent better than two IBM computers together, and sell for about 50 percent of the IBM selling price. The strategy proposed for capturing value was appealing too. Rather than selling these chips alone, the intention was to develop an IBM look-alike computer around them, something Gene Amdahl had already done successfully at Amdahl Corp. With the new computer priced at around $4 million, it was not unreasonable to foresee a $1 billion turnover for the company just two years after the proposed launch date of 1985. The total market for computers of this size was expected to be around $25 billion by that time.

As for meeting the deadline, some precautions had been incorporated in the plan too. Wafer scale integration was obviously a difficult technology with a high risk that malfunctions would occur. Bearing this in mind, Amdahl proposed making chips that would compensate for a malfunctioning part. He put two to three times as many circuits on each wafer as are actually needed to perform a single task, so that special diagnostic circuits would detect failure and divert signals to another set of circuits.[32]

As it turned out, Trilogy failed to live up to its plan (see Chapter 6). But it did make a convincing enough case to raise an unprecedented amount of capital. Those who supported it were, to some extent, supporting Gene Amdahl himself. But they presumably knew of the technical challenges that remained to be solved. They were simply convinced by the plan and its apparent reasonableness.

The Trilogy case is indeed somewhat unusual. Many generic technologies do not have such a precise product in view in the early stages, which is partly why they have difficulty in attracting substantial resources early. The main thing their plan needs to address is the evolution of the technology's perceived value in relation to the costs that are likely to be incurred. Cost overruns are not in themselves fatal. What kills support for a technology is the perception that its potential value no longer matches the investments required to complete it. Since a great deal of work still needs to be done to reach the stage when market-related issues can be confidently addressed, the plan needs to focus the future trajectory of the technology, its speed of progress, and the actions needed to demonstrate it adequately.

SUMMARY

No technology-based idea is intrinsically commercializable. It has to be made so. Many inventors (and company research groups) ignore this fact and precipitate the incorporation of the technology in the first application that occurred to them. This not only suboptimizes the potential of the technology but allows competitors to enter and stake their own claims on it.

Many companies today recognize the value of incubating ideas to judge whether to take them forward, and to build a better case for those they retain. For lone inventors, with a single idea to commercialize, it is the latter aspect of incubation that is important. In practice, it consists in:

Taking the technology a few steps further and exploring the best applications for it;

Drawing up an attractive strategy of pursuing these applications, so as to mobilize resources easily while demonstrating the technology;

Protecting different facets of the technology based on the commercialization strategy to be adopted; and

Having a clear idea about what the next steps will be.

The emphasis should be on making the technology "commercializable" (attractive to commercialize) as quickly as possible. Usually, the better this is done, the greater the prospects for mobilizing large sums of money and other needed resources up front.

5

MOBILIZING RESOURCES FOR DEMONSTRATION

THE REASON WHY THE MOST "ATTRACTIVE" APPLICATIONS DO NOT GET pursued is sometimes that no one other than the inventor is really interested in them. It is here that many lone inventors drop out and researchers in large corporations become frustrated. They become victims of the "development gap"—the inability to translate applications conceived into concrete products.

With technology demonstration costing more than the research leading up to it, money is often the key constraint. Philosopher Nicholas Rescher summarized the issue well in writing: "As best we can tell, the limits of science are economic; we reach them not because we have exhausted the novelties of nature but because we have come to the end of our economic tether."[1] Or as Henri Beer, the inventor of dimensionally stable anodes, put it in a speech at the Centennial Celebration of Case Institute of Technology in October 1990:

> The greatest problem for me and probably for most of the independent inventors has always been to find the financial means for the necessary research work. . . . [I]n the future this will become an even greater difficulty for the free-lance inventor . . . because inventions tend to become more and more technical and sophisticated, which implies that longer and costlier research work will have to be done. For many inventors this will be a serious additional obstacle. Most of the cheap inventions have already been made.[2]

Whether one agrees with Beer's remark about cheap inventions, the fact is that money advances technology. This is true whether it is federally funded research in the United States on defense, health, or the space program; European Union projects in several high-technology fields; or MITI's initiatives in Japan. Also, as Roberts and Hauptman found, underfunded companies underperform the better funded ones in the biomedical field.[3] The latter simply have greater opportunities to experiment and a bigger cushion against error.

Yet large "war chests" of the type Trilogy Inc. and Ariad Pharmaceuticals Inc. assembled are hard to find, especially outside the United States. Thus, 56 percent of U.K. biotechnology firms established in recent years relied on personal savings rather then venture capital, and 26 percent of them relied on self-generated profits as their main source of investment capital later; in the electronics field the reliance on personal savings and profits was even greater, with 73 percent of U.K. instrument and electronics firms having reinvested profits as their main source of capital. In the United States, the situation is not much different with, for example, three-quarters of the twenty-three spin-off firms of the University of Texas at Austin that were examined in 1989 relying mainly on personal capital from the founders and borrowings from banks and savings institutions.[4]

In today's fast-moving and competitive environment, capital is only one of the resources that anyone demonstrating a new technology needs to mobilize. Equally important are two other things—context and capabilities. Context relates to concrete product opportunities and knowledge of what to demonstrate and how. For first-time inventors and those unfamiliar with an industry, this knowledge can be critical to success. Capabilities refer to the research infrastructure and skills required for bringing together enabling technologies and performing product development efficiently. They include not just R&D but, increasingly, project management skills, ways to integrate marketing and manufacturing considerations, and dealing with a host of suppliers and research partners.

The simultaneous need for capital, context, and capability explains why many inventors have traditionally preferred to partner with large, experienced companies at this stage. But this is not always possible or desirable: Large companies, already inundated with requests for collaboration, are hard to sell ideas to; mindful of the contribution they can make, they also demand a higher share of the resulting benefits than a small partner might.

Aligning with large companies does not have to be the sole option. As this chapter illustrates, there are several venues available today for gaining access to the needed resources. The more carefully all the things described in the previous chapter to make an idea commercializable are done, the greater the chances for attracting these resources. Even so, the demonstration stage often involves a new campaign of interest and resource mobilization, not least because of the new cast of stakeholders to be engaged compared to those who may have supported the technology in its early stages.

THE NEED FOR A PURPOSEFUL APPROACH TO RESOURCE MOBILIZATION

Figure 5-1 summarizes the many options available today for mobilizing the three types of resources needed for demonstration. Following the logic of most new technologies, they are arranged in order of the extent to which the core technology has been developed and the extent to which applications have been defined.

Implicit in such a representation is the association between sharing a technology and mobilizing the resources needed to demonstrate it. Thus, in the very early stages, when others are called upon to contribute capital and technical expertise to develop the generic technology, the amount of sharing is greatest. Those who help with the demonstration inevitably also end up controlling part of the technology. Conversely, the more the proponent of a technology can take it further alone, both in terms of its generic features and its use in particular applications, the less he or she needs to share later.

There are a few things that should be noted about these options from the standpoint of the mid-1990s. One is that they do *not* track capital availability exclusively. In other words, sharing the technology early should not be seen only as an alternative to the inability to raise sufficient capital. This

FIGURE 5-1

TRADITIONAL OPTIONS FOR MOBILIZING RESOURCES FOR DEMONSTRATION

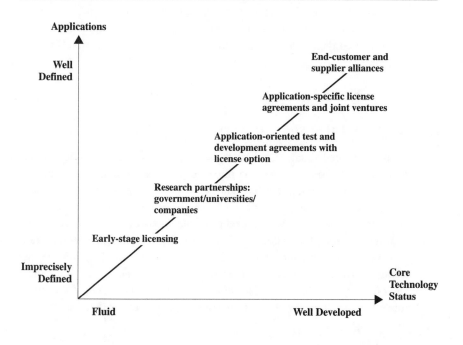

may have been the case in the past but is no longer. Sharing a technology early can be the most reasonable approach to take, even for well-endowed companies, to gain access to critical research capabilities or to application-specific knowledge. This could be for time-to-market reasons or because the needed knowledge is unlikely to find permanent use in the company to justify creating it in-house.

Second, whereas previously, government funding, university work, research partnerships, private venture capital, and application-specific corporate alliances complemented one another *sequentially* along the chain of demonstration, they are increasingly *converging* with common interests throughout. They all span the entire chain with a common interest in bringing a new technology to market as quickly as possible. While the nature of this convergence varies from country to country, its consequence everywhere has been to expand the choice inventors have at each stage. Benefiting from this expanded choice, therefore, requires reaching out to a broad stakeholder community *simultaneously* from the start. It involves targeting each group for its own interests in the technology. Contracting multiple, "spot" alliances with each not only offers access to a broader range of resources, it enhances the prospects of retaining greater ownership in the technology itself.

Finally, as with the other activities associated with technology commercialization, one needs to *anticipate* the commercialization stages further downstream and design a resource mobilization strategy in a purposeful manner. One needs to decide in advance why the technology is being shared in the first place, what precise contribution is expected from potential partners, and what role the inventor foresees later. Far too many inventors have failed to run such downstream scenarios through their minds and, as a result, denied themselves a fair share of the value their inventions created for others.

EARLY-STAGE LICENSING TO EXIT

There are indeed situations where the best course of action is to license the invention itself to one or more companies, who then assume full responsibility for demonstrating the technology and creating products or commercial processes around it. For the inventor it amounts to exiting the technology and cashing in on the value created up to that stage. This is what Rex Whinfield and his colleagues at Calico Printers Association did after they invented polyester fiber in the United Kingdom. Not having the resources to take the invention further, they approached ICI and then DuPont. After the latter bought the U.S. version of the patent (for a lump sum), ICI took a royalty-bearing license. Both DuPont and ICI then went on to develop the technology, with Rex Whinfield working on it at ICI as a consultant.

What Calico Printers Association had given to ICI and DuPont is often referred to as a master license or general license. One level down from an assignment—where the right to patent itself is given to the assignee of the technology—such licenses transfer all substantive rights to the technology, usually on an exclusive or semiexclusive basis, to the licensee. These rights permit a licensee to practice the technology unhindered, usually in any field of use, either on a global basis or, as in the case of polyester, in a broadly defined region.

Similar in effect to master licenses are broad, nonexclusive licenses given to a large number of licensees. They permit the latter to practice the invention in any way they want and usually imply no downstream rights for the inventor. A licensee who comes up with some concrete products based on the technology has full rights over it, subject to the payment of royalties to the licensor based on the sales generated.

Such early-stage licensing, allowing little subsequent control over its commercialization, is usually appropriate when:

The inventing organization lacks the infrastructure and ambition to participate in taking the technology further, as was the case with Rex Whinfield;

The technology's applications are numerous and ill-defined, each of which requires significant R&D commitment before products can be developed;

The mission of the organization requires it to share the technology with several licensees, usually on a nonexclusive basis; or

The patents are so all-encompassing that others are bound to challenge their validity or work around them.

All these reasons applied in one way or another to Stanford University's licensing of the Cohen-Boyer patents. These basic patents covered a wide range of processes and end products, each of which required a great deal of additional R&D to use or bring to market. Although exclusive licenses in limited fields of use were initially considered, the approach ultimately chosen was to license on a nonexclusive basis and on reasonable terms so as to allow as many companies as possible to practice the technology. The earlier the licenses were signed, the better too since it would take several years before royalty-bearing end products could be envisaged. In fact, an incentive was even provided to encourage companies to take the license early. The result of this approach was that, by June 1991, over 120 companies around the world had signed agreements with Stanford. Each paid $10,000 per year in a nonexclusive arrangement with royalty positions varying between 0.5 percent and 2 percent depending on the end product.

The fact that a university was the owner of the technology certainly played a role in the decision to license the technology widely. But it is arguable that a private company would have done likewise. There was no way a single company, even the largest, could have realized its full potential alone or successfully defended against those contesting the validity of the patent. With regard to the latter, not only were the fourteen claims in the patent judged excessive by many in the industry, but the technology itself was hard to distinguish from all the scientific contributions that others had made prior to it.

DEMONSTRATING GENERIC TECHNOLOGIES WITH RESEARCH PARTNERS AND GOVERNMENT SUPPORT

For inventors who do wish to retain a long-term position in their technology and participate in its demonstration, there are today a number of possibilities for mobilizing external resources. Apart from an increased availability of private venture capital, two things are new: the growth in collaborative research among private companies, and the commercial orientation of government research support.

Intercompany Partnerships

Cooperation between private companies and venture capitalists in early-stage research got boosted in the United States during the 1960s and 1970s in the form of R&D partnerships. Investors in such limited partnerships were allowed to deduct their investments for income tax purposes and were offered a share of the royalties when the products were marketed. While popular in the early 1980s, a number of factors contributed to a decline in their use more recently.

The decline in R&D partnerships has, however, coincided with the emergence of multicompany consortia for precompetitive research, which seemed to have worked so well in Japan under MITI's sponsorship. Although all parties may share ownership in the outcome, there is usually a mutual agreement as to who will commercialize what or where.

Such joint R&D ventures, especially among large companies, tended to be viewed unfavorably by antitrust authorities until recently. With rising research costs and risks in several areas, and the fact that many foreign countries not only permitted but actively supported such joint efforts, the U.S. Justice Department issued a new set of guidelines in 1980 making it easier for companies to undertake such ventures. According to this *Antitrust Guide Concerning Research Joint Ventures* (November 1980), the closer the activity is to "basic" research, the greater the number of actual and potential competitors, and the narrower the field of the joint activity, the greater the chances that the project will be acceptable to the Justice Department. In 1984 a new law was passed in the United States, the Cooperative Research and Development Act of 1984, formally allowing competitors to join in consortia for precompetitive research. Between 1985 and 1994, more than 450 such research consortia had been registered under this act.

Today, joint research agreements take a variety of forms depending on the stage a technology is in, the variety of its applications, and how complementary the involved companies are. Instead of being designed mainly to share cost, they bring together a variety of companies and institutions, each possessing different skills and playing a complementary role when the technology is ready. Illustrative of the general trend is the kind of research-based cooperative network recently set up by Rhône-Poulenc Rorer's (RPR) Gencell division.

RPR Gencell Network

In order to be among the first in cell and gene therapy—a field in which it has already invested over $300 million—RPR created what it called a "decentralized interactive research network with complementary technology, common goals and focus." The idea behind this network of fourteen participating companies and research institutes around the world is to give RPR Gencell access to most of the enabling technologies needed for gene therapy, which it can then contract for on an as-needed basis. The network allows RPR to combine its own dedicated team of 150 in-house researchers with the expertise of a large number of external researchers engaged in different facets of the technology, thereby accelerating the development of new therapies in a number of disease areas.

Being at the center of the network, RPR's role is to provide funding and research support to member organizations in return for certain commercialization rights. Although relationships are one-on-one with RPR, interaction among partners is encouraged, fostered by a network meeting in which many participate. While specific arrangements with partner companies differs in each case, the Gencell network involves a collective sharing of information among members.

By making its own capabilities in certain therapeutic areas (notably oncology, cardiovascular disease, and nervous system disorder) available to members and engaging in joint research, RPR gets an early insight into what member organizations are doing. With worldwide clinical research facilities and the planned creation of cell processing centers in different regions, RPR provides those interested with a ready-made outlet for their technology.

This wide and loosely connected research network offers several advantages:

It helps assemble the needed "toolbox" of technologies for cell and gene therapy (cell selection, gene sequencing, vector technology, and control of gene expression) earlier than would otherwise happen;

It leverages RPR's own investments by drawing on other funds available to member organizations, including public monies in some cases; and

It provides RPR with a broader pipeline of therapeutics as well as multiple approaches to a few selected targets, thereby improving the probability of a successful outcome—including allowing for combined approaches when this is better than a single therapy.

The loose network allows all members to pursue their own work independently and at their own pace while providing a forum for linking up with someone—in this case preferably RPR—when there is something of interest. As Josef Bossart, vice president, business and marketing development, explained,

It's like suppliers of components for an automobile. They can suggest new types of components to the automobile assembler [RPR] at any time and, knowing others in the network, get their ideas accepted for quick commercialization instead of launching on a major sales campaign each time. Furthermore, just because they have come up with a new design for head-lamps does not mean they have to think in terms of getting into automobile manufacturing on their own.[5]

Government Support

For reasons given in Chapter 3, governments have traditionally supported mainly basic research, and that too in universities and in specialized (often government-owned or -sponsored) research institutes. To the extent that private companies got involved, it was as subcontractors in government programs in fields such as defense and aerospace. The notable exception was that of Japan, where the Science and Technology Agency (STA) and MITI supported applied research during that country's "catch-up phase" and involved themselves in the actual commercialization of technologies.

The situation has changed dramatically since the late 1970s in most countries. Governments now also play a role in the demonstration of new technologies as a partner to private industry. This takes two main forms: funding private research which is commercially oriented and closer to the market and making government laboratories and institutions available to private industry. While the actual amount of funding that governments provide may have gone down as a percentage of the R&D done in many countries, the scope of government involvement has expanded.

Research Funding with a Commercial Orientation

Although the case for governments to support research is well established in the economic literature, pursuing this case has not been free of controversy. Governments, in the name of market failure, have often turned into the greatest instigators of technology push, resulting in perhaps more technologies being supported than warranted.

The first set of policies aimed at addressing this mainly concerned fiscal incentives. These typically covered tax write-offs and credits aimed at motivating private companies to invest more in R&D. Companies themselves decided what they wanted to work on, and the government merely "topped off" their resources. As for contract research, governments realized that transferring ownership on some technologies would give an incentive to take the results of such research further. Whereas, previously, patents emanating from government-funded research belonged automatically to the government, the Baigh-Dole Act of 1980 in the United States allowed universities, nonprofit research institutes, and small businesses to maintain ownership of the technologies they developed and to apply for patents in their name.

More significant than these measures has been the change in government funding priorities and in the mechanisms for bringing about a greater commercial orientation. Influenced, to some extent, by the successful promotion of commercial technologies by Japan, many countries now explicitly fund purely commercial (or dual-use) technologies. A case in point is the U.S. Advanced Technology Program (ATP) administered by the National Institute of Standards and Technology (NIST). ATP's 1995 budget was around $450 million, and ATP assistance takes the form of direct funding to universities and private organizations, as well as work performed within government laboratories, usually on a shared-cost basis. Although this program is likely to be cut back or eliminated in the near future,[6] it marked an important policy watershed in the United States.

Characteristic of such programs is governments' preference to share only part of the R&D costs and to have multiple institutions involved. Thus, roughly 50 percent of SEMATECH's $200 million annual budget is funded by the government and the rest by consortium partners themselves. European Union (EU) funding is restricted to 50 percent of a project's cost too. Starting in 1984, all EU R&D programs have been grouped in a series of multiannual framework programs that today, in their fourth phase (1994 to 1998), cover seventeen specific areas with a five-year budget of around $14 billion ECUs.[7] Targeted to basic and applied research, the aim of these framework programs is to reduce technical but not commercial risks in the development and market introduction of new technologies. These programs are complemented by the EUREKA program launched in 1985, which aims to strengthen European competitiveness through research collaborations among companies, research institutes, and governments for technologies that are closer to the market. The governments of the project partners decide on the support and public funding to be allocated directly. This program had generated over 880 projects by 1993, with significant involvement of small and medium-sized enterprises.

The results of these European programs have been impressive, too. Thus, the EU ESPRIT program (one of the framework programs targeted to information technologies) claimed credit for more than 700 information-technology prototypes, tools, or standards by mid-1992. These included a microprocessor chip for Apple's Newton and a prototype system for storing and retrieving images on which Philips based its CD-I technology. In fact, big European electronics firms reckoned by then that about one-fifth of their recent products contained technology arising from ESPRIT projects.[8]

While the aim of cost sharing is to ensure the commitment of private companies, the encouragement of collaborative effort serves many purposes. It makes governments not seem discriminatory, maximizes the return on scarce resources, exploits synergies among participants, accelerates research, and substitutes scientific peer reviews for industrial peer pressure. It also builds networks among partners, in hopes that the market/user context will be brought in sooner and that there will be a pull-through to commercialization when the technology gets demonstrated. All this explains why government agencies today prefer to fund projects put forward by teams comprising researchers from several companies and institutes. As Clifford Ballard explains how he obtained an ATP grant for AlliedSignal's ceramic injection molding project (referred to in the previous chapter):

> Our success with the ATP grant was partly due to our scientific approach and the thoroughness with which we had thought through all the hurdles to be overcome. It was equally due to the team we had assembled, not just for problem solving and to demonstrate the technology, but to prepare the ground for its subsequent commercialization. In addition to AlliedSignal's Research and Technology unit [the potential developer and supplier of ceramic compounds] we mobilized the Pennsylvania State University [for expertise in rheology and intelligent process control], Cincinnati Milacron [for developing injection molding equipment suitable for ceramics] and various product fabricators. The latter included two of AlliedSignal's own divisions as well as Golden Technologies, a division of Coors Ceramics, Inc. We had, furthermore, also proposed recruiting a manufacturer of injection molded plastics within the first year of the four-year program to bring in a potential customer's viewpoint.[9]

Japan has a longer history of such multifirm research collaboration agreements. Its system dates back to 1956, which was consecrated by the Act on the Mining and Manufacturing Industry Technology Research Association of 1961. Fashioned after a British World War I program aimed at forming cooperative research ventures among small and medium-sized companies that could not afford their own R&D activities, this act legitimized (and encouraged) the formation of so-called engineering research associations (ERAs). In addition to bringing together a variety of firms, including competitors, to tackle particular technological challenges, these ERAs have benefited from fairly generous government funding. The latter took the form either of a research contract, in which the government owned the research results but typically licensed patents back to the association on favorable terms, or a forgivable loan, where the ERA owned the technology but was obliged to repay the loan if the project was successful.[10]

Several things distinguish Japanese ERAs from U.S. cooperative research agreements. Rather than instituting measures to limit anticompetitive behavior, the Japanese encourage interfirm cooperation fairly downstream in the commercialization process. The latter is also reflected in the applied nature of ERAs, often including prototype and pilot plant development; with the exception of some ATP projects, U.S. agreements tend to be mainly for early-stage research and "idea generation." Whereas U.S. agreements are the result of private initiatives (SEMATECH being an exception), Japanese ERAs have invariably had a government sponsoring agency— MITI in nearly 90 percent of the cases. Finally, while U.S. cooperative research agreements are often implemented in a joint facility, most Japanese companies prefer to do their work in their own facilities and simply coordinate with others.

A final scheme involving direct support of commercial technologies is intervening as a venture capitalist. One form this takes is the funding of early-stage technologies by regional development agencies, who hitherto mainly attracted production facilities to create jobs. A second is the trend among many European governments to become active cofinanceers in private venture capital deals, providing matching funds but letting venture capital organizations do the due diligence. Thus, in Germany, a new agency called TBG (Technologie-Beteiligungs-Gesellschaft, or Technology Investment Co.) has taken over a program previously administered by the Research and Technology Ministry. It gave $37 million in ten-year loans in 1995, mostly to projects private venture capitalists had scrutinized and backed. Its policy is to match private-sector investments of up to $2 million per company. The European Investment Bank based in Luxembourg is starting a similar coinvestment scheme Europewide, and many other European countries are evolving such schemes of their own.[11]

Access to Government Laboratories

When private companies provide the context and the government provides the capital, some researchers find this combination inadequate, especially lone inventors and small companies. What they often need is help with problem solving and access to R&D facilities. To assist with this, many countries are now providing access to government laboratories and creating mechanisms for researchers to interact with experts from a variety of disciplines within them.

The use of government laboratories by private individuals and companies has been a common phenomenon in many European countries. More recently, the United States embarked on the same path. By allowing, and even encouraging, them to enter into cooperative research and development agreements (CRADAs) with these laboratories, the government is trying to help private companies perform certain types of research for which they lack competence and laboratory facilities. Made possible by the Federal Technology Transfer Act of 1986 (modified and improved under the National Competitiveness Technology Transfer Act of 1989), CRADAs involve agreements between federal laboratories and companies in which each side typically contributes personnel, services, facilities, and equipment on a 50/50 basis toward specific research efforts. In cases where small companies or a significant amount of basic research is involved, federal laboratories may even bear more than a 50 percent share. Sandia, belonging to the U.S. Department of Energy (DOE), is one such laboratory active in CRADAs. By 1994, it had operated around 200 of them, involving a total investment of over $620 million, of which 60 percent came from the government.

In addition to collaborative research, these laboratories are also participating in early product testing of privately developed technologies, acting as a Beta site of sorts. For small and medium-sized companies, the laboratories field technical inquiries too, including offering a toll-free number that industries can call when they need quick solutions to technical problems. Sandia alone had assisted in solving 300 such problems by 1994, with most of the resources for small inquiries provided by the government.[12]

In Germany, the best parallel to U.S. CRADAs is the way the Fraunhofer Institute functions. With forty-six specialized institutes, a staff of nearly 8,000, and a budget of DM 1 billion, it is one of the world's leading applied research bodies. With funding from the federal government, regional states, and business, its activities today mainly cover lasers, robots, environmental protection, electronics, materials, and optics. The institute works most closely with companies that have little research capability of their own. Around 60 percent of its industrial contracts are with small and medium-sized companies (Mittelstand). Recently it even established a center in Michigan in the United States and plans to do the same in Singapore.[13]

The use of government labs for helping private individuals and companies solve problems and demonstrate their ideas is not altogether free of controversy, with the recently commissioned Galvin Report in the United States recommending that these labs revert to their original mission of contributing to science and major national priorities. Even so, there is an active discussion in many parts of the world to "privatize" such laboratories—the United Kingdom being the most advanced in this direction.

Multi-Stakeholder Convergence in Technology Demonstration

The basic message in all this is that the demonstration of generic technologies is no more either a solitary challenge or hostage to just one stakeholder group. Provided the technology is promising and the technology's proponent is willing to reach out to others during this phase, there are more resources available than at any time in the past. With all resource providers avowing to a commercial orientation, there is even some synergy in the support they provide.

Many of the recent initiatives governments have taken are actually aimed at bringing about such synergy among actors. Building on their preference for collaborative research and the participation of government laboratories in commercial projects, they are combining the two to encourage faster technology generation and commercialization, with government labs acting as a catalyst for some large-scale projects. One example of a partnership between industry and the U.S. federal government is the Partnership for a New Generation of Vehicles, whose goal is to find a vehicle that will be three times as fuel-efficient as comparable vehicles today and yet sell at the same price.

The Japanese Key Technology Center (Japan Key-TEC) initiative is a similar hybrid. Set up in 1985 with an initial investment of $210 million from the government, the Japan Development Bank, and private industry, its mission is to assist companies to develop leading-edge technologies. In addition to its founding capital, it receives around $300 million a year from the Ministry of Posts and Telecommunications (MPT)—from dividends received out of government-held shares in NTT—and MITI. About 75 percent of its funds go to a variety of research institutes established as partnerships between the government and private industry. These research institutes are set up with a fixed life span, ten years in many cases subject to renewal, so as to allow flexibility in terms of what gets supported. The rest is provided to companies as interest-free loans in order to develop their own technologies. These loans are repaid with interest if a successful product is developed. No interest is payable if the research is not commercially successful.[14]

The way some countries are pulling ahead in gene therapy today illustrates the role multiple stakeholders play in technology demonstration, especially avant-garde or controversial technologies. Thus, while DNA manipulation has become subject to regulatory constraints in some European countries, French companies are turning out to be the pioneers because they had an early start and because public opinion is staunchly behind gene research. The latter is largely the result of aggressive lobbying by France's influential Muscular Dystrophy Association, which also provides funding for gene therapy research. The French government plays a promotional role too. In addition to its $200 million research funding, it is setting up a network of gene-therapy centers around the country. As Athos Gianella-Borradori, head of Sandoz's gene-therapy program, put it enviously, "Gene-therapy in France is a mixture of science, finance and politics."[15]

France, in fact, probably has the most concerted program and policies to promote technology demonstration. In addition to a burgeoning venture capital industry and active participation in extramural research on the part of big companies, a number of government agencies are involved in promoting and sharing the cost of research. Its "Programme Mobilisateur" in the biotechnology field evokes this. In addition to the role of ANVAR (L'Agence Nationale de Valorisation de la Recherche), which spent $300 million on the transfer of public sector research to industry in 1992 alone, the statutes of national research organizations such as CNRS (Centre National de la Recherche Scientifique), INSERM (Institut National de la Santé et de la Recherche Médicale), and INRA (Institut National de la Recherche Agronomique) were changed in 1982 in order to encourage them to exploit their findings commercially. Joint CNRS/industry development teams have been established, and public sector researchers may now be seconded to industry on full salary, some of them for the purpose of setting up their own firms. ANVAR, likewise, subsidizes 50 percent of the cost of the first year's employment of a researcher by a small or medium-sized firm as part of its policy of encouraging links between public research and industry. In fact, as many as 72 percent of French biotechnology firms have received public funds of one kind or another (whether from national or local and regional bodies) in recent years.[16]

APPLICATION-SPECIFIC DEVELOPMENT

Although government institutions do sometimes help with concrete applications, this is primarily left to agreements between private companies. They are, after all, the ones who understand the commercial context best and are responsible for bringing specific products to market and profiting directly from the technology.

The nature of inter-company agreements one sees for application development fall into two broad categories: test and development agreements with a license option, and application-specific licenses and joint ventures.

Test and Development Agreements with a License Option

Such agreements, as their name implies, are used when applications are in their early stages of development, often involving considerable research beyond what the technology owner has done. As such, they usually result in a sharing of downstream commercial rights and, depending on how the agreement is framed, coownership of intellectual property rights. The general practice is to proceed in a stepwise manner: first a secrecy agreement, then the option agreement, followed by the negotiation of the license agreement itself.

Secrecy agreements are commonplace whenever some disclosure of a technology is needed for someone to evaluate it. In the case of pharmaceuticals, this often consists of disclosing a fairly considerable amount of scientific data regarding the compound as well as providing samples of the compound itself. While some companies provide this free of charge, others regularly demand a small payment as part of the secrecy agreement. In both cases, the party to whom the information is disclosed is obliged to conduct an evaluation within a reasonable amount of time. The result of this evaluation, moreover, needs to be passed on to the party making the disclosure without disclosing it to third parties.

Either concurrently with the secrecy agreement, or immediately following the evaluation of the sample and data, a development cum option agreement is signed, spelling out the way the data can be used and the broad terms of the license on which an option is given. This agreement also provides a potential licensee with the right to conduct further scientific studies and assemble test data of its own for eventual submission to its country's drug registration body.

The scope of such development cum option agreements can vary a great deal depending on the technology, how advanced it already is, and the capabilities of the potential licensee. It can range from minimal involvement on the part of the technology owner, as in the case of many test licenses, to a full-fledged research cooperation and joint development agreement where both parties are actively involved.

In most contracts of this type, each stage is costed separately, and the party interested in the technology is given the option to terminate the cooperation at the end of any stage. The party is usually also given an option to subsequently take an exclusive license (usually worldwide and only for the field covered by the research agreement) at the end of the entire project.

Carlson and Xerography

The approach used in the pharmaceutical industry applies to many technologies that go through progressive demonstrations before they can be incorporated in end products. Chester Carlson employed a variant of such a development license to have his xerography invention demonstrated by the Battelle Development Corporation (BDC). Although maintaining ownership rights to his patents, he transferred substantially all his rights to the latter to exploit the technology. The main terms of this agreement consisted in the following:

BDC was to fund the further research needed to demonstrate the invention more convincingly;

BDC would assist in licensing the technology and keep 60 percent of the royalty income, with Carlson keeping the remaining 40 percent; and

Carlson would receive a minimum royalty of $500 in 1948 and $1,000 a year thereafter. Carlson's royalty would, however, be reduced to 25 percent of gross on the basis of a 1 percent reduction for each $1,000 in excess of $10,000 spent by BDC for research unless he matched BDC expenses in excess of $10,000.

During 1944 and 1945, the research conducted at Battelle made three very important contributions to the advancement of xerography. These were: (1) the use of selenium as the photoconductive coating and a high-vacuum technique for coating plates with selenium; (2) a corona discharge wire to apply a charge to the plate and subsequently to the paper to effect transfer of the image; and (3) the resin that would form the print on the copy. With these Battelle contributions adding to the original Carlson concept, the feasibility of xerography as a dry copying method got firmly established. When the technology reached this stage, Battelle then entered into a license agreement with the Haloid Company (now Xerox) in 1947 to commercialize it further.

Application-Specific License and Joint-Venture Agreements

In cases where the potential applications of a technology are known in advance (perhaps even listed among the claims of the inventor's patent), and the development work needed is less risky, a more focused approach is often preferred. By partitioning rights according to field of use—breaking down the field of use for, say, a new type of photovoltaic cell either by some physical level of performance (applications above a certain peak-watt threshold) or by product (cellular phones, for example)—one can achieve several advantages simultaneously. The commercialization process is started across a broad front; the company best equipped to exploit a particular application will work on it; and each company is provided with an incentive through global exclusive rights in its chosen field. Such application-specific partitioning of rights can be implemented by licensing the basic technology, forming joint ventures, or using a combination of the two.

The Example of Lanxide Corp.

One company that has successfully accelerated the commercialization of specific applications of its technology through a wide range of focused partnerships is Lanxide Corp., based in Newark, Delaware. The company was founded in 1983 to develop and commercialize ceramic/metal composites using a patented vapor-phase oxidation process called PRIMEX (pressureless metal infiltration) that allows near-net shape fabrication. These composites combine many of the features of ceramics and metals, providing a new class of structural materials.

Between 1983 and 1993, Lanxide Corp. collected some 1,000 patents (123 U.S. patents and 900 foreign patents) covering its reinforced ceramic and metallic product technologies—quite an achievement for a 400-employee company that received its first patent in 1987. This extensive patent portfolio gives the company considerable leverage in mobilizing partners for the commercialization of particular end products, both within the United States and abroad.

Among the first instruments used for mobilizing funds was an R&D limited partnership that owned the Lanxide technology. Alcan Aluminium, Ltd., of Canada bought a 40 percent interest in this partnership (Alanx Products L.P.) along with a 12.6 percent equity interest in the company itself. Following this, Lanxide Corp. entered into a number of application-specific joint ventures and license agreements. The most notable among these were the license agreement with Alcan (to make pumps and ceramic "chokes" linking pipes carrying slurry from mines) and joint ventures with DuPont, with whom the company now has three separate joint ventures: Lanxide Armor Products, Inc. (formed in 1987 for advanced armor components for ground vehicles, aircraft, marine, personnel, and space applications); DuPont Lanxide Composites, Inc. (also formed in 1987 for aerospace, gas turbine engine, and process heat exchanger applications); and Lanxide Electronic Components, L.P. (formed in 1990 for hybrid circuit electronic packages, carrier plates, substrates, chassis, and support structures).

Lanxide Corp. also formed a joint venture in 1992 with a Japanese trading company, Kanematsu Corp., to market the entire range of its technologies in that country. Lanxide Corp. held 65 percent of the equity in Lanxide KK and Kanematsu held 35 percent. Among the first arrangements made for "retailing" different facets of the technology was another 50/50 joint venture set up in 1993 between Lanxide KK and Nihon Cement Co. to manufacture and market ceramic matrix composites (CMCs) and metal matrix composites (MMCs). Lanxide was to contribute its commercial production technology for CMCs and MMCs to the joint venture, while Nihon Cement would contribute its technology in fine ceramics.

All of these arrangements allowed the company to focus its own efforts on the core technology itself. It also allowed the company to introduce its first commercial product—wear-resistant parts for the mining industry—in 1989, six years after being founded.

END-CUSTOMER AND SUPPLIER ALLIANCES FOR PRODUCT COMPLETION

The final stage of technology demonstration involves the development of end products themselves. While capital and technical resources are needed here too, three other things are necessary: complete knowledge about product characteristics, an opportunity for testing products, and access to certain key components and materials for implementing the product. Inventors who have taken their technology to this stage on their own have access to help here, too.

Product Knowledge

Outside potential users can be an important source of help in defining what form the technology should take quickly and effectively. A typical case is that of the alliance between Applied Materials, Inc., a producer of etching, ion implantation, and deposition equipment for the semiconductor industry, and CNET (Centre National d'Etudes des Telecommunications), a research and development group within France Telecom. When introducing its new tungsten deposition system (Applied Precision 5000), a critical technology in the fabrication of submicron metal-oxide-semiconductors (MOS) devices, it shipped over the equipment to CNET's facilities in Grenoble, France, and trained engineers there in process development. As James Bagley, president and chief operating officer of Applied explained, "We can put down tungsten layers all day long in our laboratory facilities. But without building devices in an actual customer environment, we don't know whether there's any real benefit to the device [semiconductor] maker. This kind of alliance ultimately brings us closer to our marketplace."[17]

The best way to design in user requirements is by developing the product jointly with users. This is essentially what Alcoa did with its Spaceframe program for developing aluminum car bodies. Started in 1985, the Spaceframe was developed right from the beginning as a joint project between Alcoa and Audi. While Alcoa provided assistance relating to the capabilities and behavior of aluminum structures, the concept itself was engineered by Audi's predevelopment staff working in close cooperation with Alcoa engineers and scientists. At Alcoa Laboratories near Pittsburgh, new aluminum alloys, advanced vacuum die casting, extrusion processes, and improved robot-welding techniques were developed and refined. After the development work was done, Alcoa set up a $70 million factory in Soest, Germany, in 1992—with Audi as its first customer. This plant was built adjacent to the existing Soest facility of Hönsel-Werke AG, a German manufacturer of aluminum castings, extrusions, and sheet products. By cooperating with Hönsel-Werke, Alcoa was able to develop its production capabilities and to obtain a supply of extrusions for the subassemblies it shipped to Audi.[18]

Product Testing

For many technology-based products, in-house laboratory tests (sometimes known as Alpha tests) are often not sufficient. Further testing in a real-world environment, preferably with the active involvement of potential users, is needed to surface problems that either may have been overlooked or would not become apparent in the artificial conditions of a laboratory. These Beta tests serve a number of purposes beyond just the verification of performance. They provide information on refinements to be made to the core product design, including the addition of features desired by customers; completing the product offering in terms of documentation and training, for instance; and the marketing mix to support product introduction. When they are successful and well managed, Beta tests also serve a promotional purpose. They help develop account relationships, identify the path to purchase decisions, and provide confidence to the general market.

Although potential customers are sometimes keen to offer themselves as Beta test sites to show how avant-garde they are, mobilizing them is not always easy. The greater a technology's potential—as described in the preceding chapter—and the more a Beta site customer expects to profit from the demonstration personally, the more likely the customer is to cooperate voluntarily. This was, for example, the experience of an Israeli company, Electric Fuel Corporation, when it tried to demonstrate its new zinc-air battery in Europe recently. Targeted to automotive applications, this battery offered several advantages over competing battery technologies, including what is probably the leading contender in this field—nickel metal hydride batteries. The main advantage of a zinc-air battery is that, instead of having to be recharged electrically, its electrolyte can be physically drained and fresh electrolyte pumped in as fuel, in the same amount of time it takes to refuel a gasoline car. This feature solves the two key problems that might hinder the commercialization of other batteries: the time of recharge (which can be anything from fifteen minutes for a 60 percent recharge for nickel metal hydride batteries to several hours in other batteries), and the need to create a special infrastructure of recharging stations and electrical connections throughout the transport network.[19]

Although Electric Fuel Corporation was not alone in the field, the technology's intrinsic merits, and the prospects for others to participate in and benefit from its commercialization, enabled Electric Fuel to mobilize a vast array of demonstration partners within a few months. Thus, Italy's largest private energy supplier, Edison SpA, paid $7 million in 1995 for equipment and exclusive rights to market the technology in Italy, France, Spain, and Portugal. A consortium of German companies, including the national post office, Siemens AG, Mercedes-Benz AG, and Adam Opel AG, agreed to run a $15 million, two-year field test program starting in late 1995. If successful, the pilot program could open the door for Electric Fuel to equip some 40,000 delivery vehicles for the fleets of Germany's postal service and its phone company, Deutsche Telecom, as early as 1998. The Swedish post and Vattenfall AB, a utility company, are also expected to become associate partners in the German field test project. Vattenfall AB will later act as the strategic partner in Scandinavia, setting up a regeneration facility for the batteries, seeking new additional users for the technology, and providing refuelling and regeneration services to those new customers.[20]

Supply of Key Components and Materials

In several industries, suppliers can act as crucial development partners too. This is typically so when they see the prospects of supplying a major component to an invention, preferably on an exclusive basis.

An illustrative case is the role ICI of the United Kingdom is playing in developing film for Clive Bilbie's Re-Mark-It label. Clive Bilbie, a New Zealand entrepreneur, invented a new type of erasable label for products such as videotapes, computer disks, and the like. Similar in principle to "magic slates" and erasable pads already on the market, erasing is done by pushing air through the label instead of physically separating the layers.

The key component for implementing this invention is a five-layer polyester film strong enough to be written on and erased more than 1,000 times without being stretched or damaged. After failing to interest manufacturers in the Asia Pacific region over the five years it took to finalize the concept, Bilbie turned to ICI. The latter quickly agreed to undertake the challenge and spent $375,000 in developing the needed film.[21]

The motivation of suppliers in participating in someone else's technology is similar to that of customers who volunteer for Beta site tests—they want a window on new developments that will stimulate their own R&D and an opportunity to participate in a new business on a privileged basis.

COMBINING MULTIPLE SOURCES OF FUNDING AND SUPPORT

With such a variety of sources to turn to for demonstrating a new technology today, inventors face two dangers: loss of control over their core technology and loss of business focus.

The experience of Alcoa with structural laminates (available commercially as Arall and Glare) illustrates the first danger. These laminates consist of thin sheets of high-strength aluminum sandwiching either aramid fibers (Arall) or glass fibers (Glare) bonded together by an epoxy. Alcoa entered the field by first taking a license from Delft University in Holland, where much of the early work had been done in the 1970s. It then co-opted the 3M company in a joint-development program to develop the adhesive system and to optimize the aramid fiber/epoxy resin prepreg system. For expertise on aramid fibers, Alcoa then formed a joint venture with Akzo, the

Dutch chemical company that, along with DuPont, is a world leader in aramid fibers. However, as one Alcoa staff member recalls,

> The development may have been facilitated [by these alliances] but then there were delays because no one knew who "owned" the technology—Akzo, 3M, Delft or Alcoa? A great deal of energy went into figuring out who was going to commercialize the products, energy that could have been spent better in working with customers. We had competition before we had a product. These commercialization rights were sorted out only in 1991.[22]

The only way to cope with the issue of control is to stake out one's own proprietary domain as precisely as possible *before* engaging partners. Possessing some key patents, or some special know-how, at the start of the process helps in this regard. This is what Radiant Technologies, Inc., did. Established in 1990, the company first built up a strong patent position in ferroelectric ceramic thin films for use in integrated circuits. Using this patent position as a lever, it entered into development contracts with some semiconductor and computer firms that wanted to commercialize the technology. In parallel, it entered into CRADAs with certain national laboratories to gain access to additional technical expertise and hard-to-come-by equipment and modeling capabilities. It guarded for itself, however, the responsibility for designing and manufacturing prototypes and equipment.[23]

As important as ownership and control over the technology is the need to preserve a commercialization focus, not being distracted or pulled in unwanted directions. Thus, you need to see government support and funding as a resource for demonstrating something *you* want to commercialize—not as an opportunity to do contract research on its behalf, interesting as this might be. This is the lesson the Celanese Research Company learned in developing polybenzimidazole fiber (PBI) for the U.S. Air Force. Celanese won the contract to develop this high thermal stability fiber in 1963 and succeeded in developing it a few years later. But neither the Air Force nor Celanese was willing to take things further through to scale-up and marketing—the Air Force because of a lack of immediate need and Celanese because of not wanting to depend on a single customer. It was only in 1974 that Celanese took on the commercialization on its own as a diversification venture.[24]

The Example of Amgen

Some companies have been particularly good at reaching out for external support from a number of partners, yet maintaining control and focus in their commercialization strategy. One company that has used all the modes described is Amgen Inc. of Thousand Oaks, California. Founded in 1980 in order to develop products based on DNA technology primarily for the human health care market, its initial funding came from the venture capital community and Abbot Laboratories. After one of its scientists, Fu-Kuen Lin, successfully cloned erythropoietin (or EPO, a natural hormone that stimulates red blood cell production) in 1983, the company entered into a joint venture with Kirin Brewery Company of Japan in order to fund further work. The entire worldwide rights to EPO as well as two other products (G-CSF, a protein that stimulates the production of white blood cells known as granulocytes, and GM-CSF, a granulocyte-macrophage colony stimulating factor) were vested by Amgen in this joint venture along with $4 million for a 50 percent share. Kirin paid $12 million for its 50 percent share. As shown in Figure 5-2, the joint venture was to fund Amgen's R&D in these products on a contract basis as well as pay license fees once they became commercialized. As for the commercialization rights to EPO itself, Amgen obtained an exclusive license to manufacture and sell in the United States, while Kirin obtained a similar right for Japan. The joint venture retained the rights of commercialization elsewhere in the world.

Somewhat prior to this joint venture, Amgen had also signed an R&D agreement with Abbot Laboratories in 1983. This five-year agreement concerned the development of certain diagnostic and therapeutic technologies unrelated to the EPO/CSF products. In addition to paying some $15 million to Amgen over the period of the contract, Abbot Laboratories also undertook to pay royalties on net sales to the year 2000 on products eventually developed.

By 1985, however, the funds obtained from these two agreements proved inadequate. As a result, Amgen signed another cooperation agreement with Ortho Pharmaceutical Corp., a subsidiary of Johnson & Johnson, in September 1985. This covered the development and commercialization of Interleukin-2 (for cancer and immune regulation) and hepatitis-B vaccine as well as EPO. Johnson & Johnson undertook to fund Amgen's research (about $17 million from 1986 to 1989) and undertook to conduct clinical trials and seek regulatory approval for all three products. In return Amgen ceded part of its own rights to EPO. While it retained the rights to EPO for kidney dialysis patients in the United States, it gave Johnson & Johnson exclusive marketing rights in the rest of the world, except Japan where Kirin had rights. At the same time, Kirin-Amgen also ceded its non-U.S. rights (notably European) to Johnson & Johnson in return for a royalty based on sales.

Among the other agreements Amgen entered into was also a limited partnership formed in 1987. In this private placement worth approximately $75 million, Amgen served as the general partner with a 1 percent share. According to the agreement between Amgen and Amgen Clinical Partners, L.P., the company undertook to develop G-CSF and certain recombinant growth factors on the partnership's behalf. Amgen was to be paid for this at an amount equal to its actual costs plus a management fee equal to a stated percentage of such costs. If the research and development efforts are

FIGURE 5-2

MAJOR COOPERATION AGREEMENTS ENTERED INTO BY AMGEN

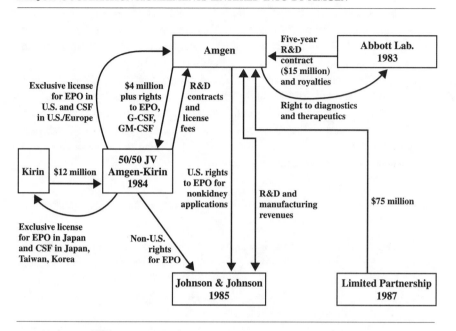

SOURCE: Amgen, 1990.

successful and the necessary FDA approvals are obtained, Amgen will also be responsible for manufacturing and marketing the resulting products in the United States on behalf of the partnership.

What enabled Amgen to mobilize such a broad range of resources and yet keep some control over downstream commercialization was its ownership of the basic technology and its ability to separate out different facets of its technology—similar, in many ways, to Lanxide Corp. Amgen also had a clear vision of where it wanted to go on its own—to some day become a fully integrated biopharmaceutical company. The rights that it did give away on certain products and geographic areas were seen as a necessary cost to pay for achieving that goal in the markets it reserved for itself.

CREATING THE PULL FOR RESOURCE MOBILIZATION

The extent to which an active promotion strategy is needed for mobilizing resources depends on how much interest was created around a technology earlier and the steps taken to make it commercializable. If the two are done well, the task is easy. The world may not beat a path to the inventor's door, but it will at least be receptive to any overtures the inventor makes.

As the experience of many inventors, research institutes, and universities shows, however, active promotion is nevertheless required in practice. This is partly because of the number of competing technologies making claims on the same set of resources. But it is equally due to the asymmetry of information and understanding when technology is concerned; the inventor simply knows more about it than any potential customer.

To be successful in mobilizing resources for demonstration, one needs to understand and follow the time line of intermediate adopters of the technology; cast the net widely; reduce the perceived risk in the technology by taking it a step further if necessary; lower the barrier and cost of entry to potential partners; and sustain interest through regular achievements, such as taking at least one application to the end.

Following the Interests and Time Line of Intermediate Adopters

The key to accessing partners for specific demonstration needs is to align one's effort to the interest of those targeted. This can mean pursuing applications they want most, sensing *their* needs and aspirations, and empathizing with their criteria for providing support. They need to be seen as "customers" of the technology just as peers and other scientists were for endorsing the technology earlier.

Knowing about the time line of intermediate adopters of a technology—those who will help take it further—is, of course, the difficult part. External events, such as a pressing national need or a major environmental accident, can be used to time one's approach, but they can seldom be anticipated. Similarly, while researching a broad range of industries and companies helps, the cost of doing so is often incommensurate with the benefits obtained in practice. A better stance is to keep an open mind vis-à-vis the partners (internal or external) one deals with and respond to their changing needs promptly and in a flexible manner.

The latter is what enables many technologies within Raychem to find a home. Project leaders are encouraged by senior management to reach out to anyone in the company who might have an interest in what they are doing and to shape their development programs accordingly. For example, the company's surge arrester program failed to get the needed support from its initial sponsor, the electronics division, because the latter chose to proceed with another overvoltage-protection technology that had been developed in another part of the company. So the surge arrester team went over to see the energy division. As it turned out, the latter had just completed a study on surge arresters and had identified an opportunity in providing better housings for them using the company's polymers as a replacement for porcelain. The head of the ceramics group within the energy division, Peter Larsson, immediately made the connection with what was being offered—developing a nonfragmenting housing along with the new zinc-oxide varistor disc the group within the electronics division was working on to come up with a totally new surge arrester.

The same openness to new impulses better timed to the requirements of a "customer" characterizes how the company seeks out applications to work on externally. This is how it got its PolySwitch technology established in various uses. By their nature, polymer PTC (positive temperature coefficient) devices were easiest to implement for low-voltage applications, and these were the ones Raychem had concentrated on in the late 1970s and early 1980s. Since production scale-up still posed problems, the idea was to go after small-volume applications and try out the device with customers. A first lucky break came with Kodak in 1982. The latter was developing its lithium battery operated disc camera and wanted a small, resettable fuse to protect the battery, which could explode if short-circuited. Though the PolySwitch group managed to sell some fuses for this application, Kodak's disc camera itself failed in the market, causing Raychem to write off its investments in this particular project.

"The next major break came with AT&T, which was about to introduce its first digital switch [the ESS] in 1983," recalls Hundi Kamath, a member of the PolySwitch group at that time. "It, however, required a fuse that could stand 600 volts, not the 20 to 40 volt capability Raychem possessed at that time. A fresh program of research was launched immediately to meet AT&T's specifications. Since a conventional fuse would have meant removing a whole card and shutting the line down, AT&T was willing to pay a premium."

Simultaneously, Raychem set up a small group of two to three people in Japan to look at electronics-oriented applications, about which it had gathered some experience from Kodak. "There we ran into Matsushita," Kamath recalls. "They were the ones actually making the lithium batteries for Kodak and wanted to supply them to 35 mm cameras as well. After we designed a new part to fit their pack we got a similar order from Sanyo. It was these battery applications and the AT&T switch which launched PolySwitch commercially in 1983."[25]

Casting a Wide Net

Targeting the needs and time lines of one or two resource providers is seldom enough. As many inventors come to realize, needs and time lines do change and often unexpectedly. What looked like a sure-fire application and a solid partner when planning a demonstration program can quickly lead to disappointment.

The only way to reduce such vulnerability is to reach out to a wide range of potential partners from the beginning and adapt the resource mobilization program to their requirements. This is particularly important in countries where large sums of venture capital are hard to come by.

Belland AG

One company that has successfully followed this route is Belland AG, raising far more resources than is the norm in Germany and Switzerland. The research leading up to the proof of principle and functional breakthrough had taken five years (1974 to 1979) and cost about $700,000. Yet a great deal of further work and investment was needed before any marketable products could be made. At this time, Roland Belz had also decided to leave the single application he had been pursuing—toilet seat covers—to go deeper into the technology and make it useful for the many other applications he had begun to foresee by then. "I could already make toilet seats, even with cotton flakes to make them more agreeable to sit on, but they were either too water-soluble or too water-resistant."

Depending on the strategy to be pursued, anything between $7 million and $20 million was needed. The first thing the company did was to approach venture capital firms and banks in Switzerland and Germany in 1982. This proved fruitless. Advertisements were then placed in newspapers to attract individual investors. About 180 individuals responded. However, after meeting with all of them, only $800,000 got raised from 9 investors.

With no more private money forthcoming, the company then made the rounds of all the German state governments and visited Ireland, Austria, the United States, and Switzerland in search of subsidies. It was in the Canton of Solothurn, Switzerland, that it found the warmest reception. With a decline in the Canton's traditional watch-making industry, the authorities there were actively seeking out new opportunities for balanced regional development. After a brief preliminary feasibility study, they offered to guarantee and subsidize $8 million in loans to Belland, covering about half the contemplated investment for 1983 and 1984. To qualify for this aid the company moved to Solothurn, where it set up both its administrative headquarters and its first plant.

Finding the remaining half of the funds needed was not easy. Belland reached out to over 100 companies that were close to its technology and familiar with its potential. One such company was Hermann Berstorff Maschinenbau GmbH, a Hannover-based maker of extruder-reactors, the key piece of equipment the company needed. Instead of cash, Berstorff offered its equipment on concessional terms, which Belland readily accepted. Some of the other companies Belland approached wanted end products to test but were not prepared to fund a major development program. A couple of others were prepared to pay a large sum but wanted to own the technology outright. Being unable to get suitable development partners, the company didn't hesitate when an Australian company came to it with a request it had not even thought of in 1985—an exclusive license for the *entire* technology for Australia and some neighboring countries. In return, the company was willing to pay $5 million up front and to advance a loan of $2.5 million, at a time when Belland needed cash. This Australian company, in fact, turned out to be the biggest private resource provider until new partners came in the late 1980s. Rather than see its offer as a distraction, Belland saw it for what it really was: part and parcel of its resource mobilization effort on the road to making and selling its plastics in Europe and North America.

Without such perseverance, and an open mind as to who to partner with, it is unlikely that Belland would have gotten as far as it did with its technology. Many inventors, unfortunately, either underestimate the scope of the effort needed to mobilize adequate resources or give up too soon after the first refusal of support. Casting a wide net, while keeping a clear goal in mind, often makes the difference between technologies that succeed and those, probably equally meritorious, that don't.

Reducing Perceived Risks by Taking the Technology a Few Steps Further

To interest potential resource providers one sometimes needs to go a few steps further in the commercialization process on one's own. This can mean producing some sample end products or demonstrating that a process yields sufficient testable quantities of the end product. As Peter Ridley, director of corporate relations at the University of California College of Medicine, Irvine, put it, "Most people want a prototype: at least some good solid concepts that can be reduced to practice. Without this, interest in a new technology tends to wane no matter how attractive the potential might be."

An example of a company that did this successfully is Applied Microbiology, Inc., of Brooklyn, New York. Formed in 1983 to commercialize research emanating from the Public Health Research Institute (PHRI) of New York, it quickly settled on a couple of "niche" applications of just one of the institute's technologies—antibacterial agents. Founded in 1942 by Mayor Fiorello La Guardia "to conduct research in areas critical to the health and well-being of the people in New York City," the PHRI was engaged in researching a wide spectrum of diseases and had made important contributions toward the understanding of poliomyelitis, cancer, influenza, diphtheria, and toxic shock syndrome. With over 100 research scientists on its staff, it was undertaking basic research on AIDS, malaria, anticancer drugs, and antibiotic-resistant infections.

After Applied Microbiology purchased the commercialization rights for all of PHRI's technologies, it reviewed the various research programs and settled on a couple of compounds that were most immediately commercializable in markets that were sufficiently focused and defined. One of these was bacteriocins, which are protein alternatives to antibiotics. Bacteriocins had been known and researched since the 1950s. Not only were they potentially effective against antibiotic-resistant strains of bacteria but killed bacteria much more rapidly than conventional antibiotics, even within a few seconds after contact. As such, they offered immediate applications as "biological disinfectants" and as "biological preservatives." Because they are generally targeted toward a narrow range of related bacteria only, they were of little interest to the large pharmaceutical companies engaged in antibacteriological research. Applied Microbiology was, therefore, quickly able to line up companies as partners for applications in fields such as oral care (mouthwash, toothpaste, denture cleaners, and chewing gum), dermatologicals (topical disinfectants such as soaps, creams, and lotions; wound control; cosmetics; and deodorants), veterinary medicine (bovine mastitis and fish farming), and food (salmonellosis and listeriosis prevention.)

Characteristic of all these applications is the fact that they require a minimum of regulatory approvals prior to mass commercialization. The bacteriocin compounds had been known for a long time, and research had already shown their effectiveness in preventing and treating gum disease— hence the idea of the mouthwash.

Despite the relative ease with which its chosen products could be commercialized, Applied Microbiology went a step further. It set up its own laboratory (called Applied Genetics Laboratory) on the premises of the New York PHRI as part of its commercialization agreement with the latter. Having settled on the compound Lysostaphin, the new bacteriocin cloned by the PHRI, it conducted some further research in this laboratory to develop a patented one-step purification process yielding large quantities of the protein. Apart from demonstrating commercial feasibility, this made it easier for the company to attract large companies as partners on favorable terms soon thereafter.

Lowering the Barrier to Entry

A rule often ignored by inventors is that one needs to *lower* the barriers of entry into a new technology in its early phases of commercialization and *raise* them later, when the technology is in the market—that is, during the sustaining stage. The less well defined the market, and the more difficult the economic conditions are, the greater the need to do this.

Sbarro's Wheel

Failure to heed this is a main reason why Sbarro's hubless wheel has been stalled in its commercialization since it was announced in 1989. Despite the media attention the wheel drew and despite the prototype motorcycles and race cars built to demonstrate it, there are no commercial uses yet.

Lacking adequate resources himself, Sbarro vested patents rights on the wheel and some of its application in a new company, Société Brevets et

Licenses SA, in which he was given a minority interest. A few local investors put in money to pay for the patents and various prototypes and commercializing the invention. As Sbarro reflects on what happened,

> Two things went wrong. First was the state of the world economy. . . . The hub-less wheel would have been more expensive than conventional ones and the specialized niches to which it would normally have been targeted started to prove unattractive. Second, the approach we took may have created a barrier too. One or two companies would have probably gone ahead if we asked for a small test license fee with an option to a license later. Instead, we were looking for the "big contract" from the beginning. Given the change in the business environment, these companies were unprepared for a large up-front commitment.[26]

While several inventors are concerned by the prospects of technology "leakage" when entering into alliances, one needs to view this in perspective. Some leakage is actually healthy in the early stages of a technology. By reducing the barriers to assessing and experimenting with a technology, it helps mobilize a wider research community around it. What is required is a way to manage this leakage while safeguarding one's downstream options through the agreements one enters. Achieving good secrecy agreements and reasonably priced options, followed by high royalties later, when products reach the market, is better than seeking expensive comprehensive agreements from the beginning.

Taking One, Any, Application to the End Quickly

If curiosity can kill cats, going from one application to another in search of ever more attractive markets can lead to a technology's burial. The important thing is not to keep hesitating between applications or pursue too many of them half-heartedly. The temptation to do so is great. Most generic and multifaceted technologies offer an embarrassingly large number of possibilities that can collectively add up to a significant value. Keeping all these possibilities in sight and pursuing them across a broad front in the hope of eventually interesting someone and not missing out on the most attractive markets is a trap into which many inventors fall. The spreading of attention and effort and the expenditure of resources in multiple and dissimilar fields can often lead to supporters losing interest long before the technology has a chance to prove itself in the market.

A better commercialization stance is to take one application to the end first and as quickly as possible. This is yet another reason to look for an easy application in the beginning, as was pointed out in Chapter 4. It demonstrates that the technology works, thereby attracting potential partners for other applications. It starts to generate revenue early, small as this might be, and it gives confidence to those backing the technology. Most importantly, it establishes a precedence for end-users to refer to and permits cost estimates to be established.

SUMMARY

Demonstrating a new technology requires three things: context, capability, and capital. Large firms have an advantage in that they possess, or have easy access to, all three. For lone inventors, and large firms unwilling to make big bets on a particular technology, the best course is to assemble as much capital in the beginning as possible. The more the effort put into making the technology commercializable, the easier this is.

The absence of sufficient capital up front is, however, less of a constraint today than in the past. With the convergence in the interests of several resource providers—governments, venture capitalists, and other companies—a wide range of options are available at each stage of the demonstration program. Accessing them simultaneously through multiple alliances offers the prospects of assembling a greater range of resources, having the technology demonstrated expeditiously, and also retaining a greater ownership in the core technology.

Mobilizing resources for demonstration is a competitive endeavor, as competitive in fact as the competition one sees between end products in the marketplace. This is the stage in the commercialization process where most inventors either fall behind or lose their stake in their technology. Mobilizing resources successfully requires reaching out to a wide range of potential partners in a purposeful manner. Among the key things to keep in mind are looking for the interests and time lines of each stakeholder; reducing their perceived risk in the technology; and showing quick progress in the demonstration, in order to sustain interest.

6

DEMONSTRATING CONTEXTUALLY IN PRODUCTS AND PROCESSES

ALTHOUGH SUCCESSFUL IN CONCEPTUALIZING A HIGH-PERFORMANCE IBM-compatible computer based on wafer scale integration chips and raising an exceptional amount of interest and resources from the beginning, Trilogy failed in the end. It failed because it could not develop the four key things needed for its computer while the opportunity existed: (1) the interconnecting high-density, high-speed semiconductor circuitry on a single wafer; (2) a scheme to ensure defect-free parts using redundant parts of a wafer; (3) the packaging needed; and (4) the computer-aided design system to manage the redundancy-based logic design and interconnect scheme.[1]

Progress had indeed been made in all these areas, but not enough to launch a competitive product. Perhaps the goals were ambitious from a technological viewpoint. But they were essential for achieving the price-performance target Gene Amdahl had set for himself.

Contrast this case with that of DuPont's Corfam leather substitute. The origins of Corfam went back to the 1930s, when DuPont's first fundamental research on porous polymeric film took place. Nothing was done to exploit this work until the 1950s, when the fabrics and finishes department began to look seriously at the market for shoe uppers. A special poromeric—a two-layered material made up of a web base and a porous coating on top—was developed for this purpose and named Corfam.

Announced in 1963, Corfam was immediately seen as another nylon, a product that would transform an industry and bring fortune to the company launching it. Corfam did have the potential, too. As a leather substitute it offered certain advantages over real leather that would make it an excellent replacement for leather in shoe uppers. It flexed easily without losing its shape and "breathed" to some extent like leather. It weighed only one-third as much as leather and could be advertised as more comfortable. It was highly resistant to abrasion and water-repellent. Unlike leather, it did not have to be polished; merely wiping with a damp cloth renewed the shine.

Its uniformity as a synthetic material also offered definite advantages over natural leather to shoe manufacturers. While it cost somewhat more ($1.05 to $1.35 per square foot at the time, versus 50 cents to $1.00 per square foot for leather), these costs could be partly offset by other savings in terms of waste and machine cutting. A predicted future shortage of leather also seemed to endorse the usefulness of Corfam.

In spite of all these advantages, Corfam sales fell somewhat below expectations while production and other costs far exceeded planned levels, resulting in losses estimated between $80 million and $100 million by 1971. At that time Corfam was withdrawn by DuPont.

The problem with Corfam, in retrospect, was a combination of high cost and incommensurate benefit to those to whom it was targeted. Realizing that it cost somewhat more than natural leather, DuPont had aimed the product at the high-fashion, high-quality, and high-price segment of the shoe market, representing only 10 percent of the total shoe market. Although prelaunch tests had indicated that 8 percent of wearers experienced some discomfort with Corfam shoes, this was taken as reassurance since 24 percent of the users of vinyl-coated fabric shoes also felt discomfort (compared with only 3 percent for leather). As it turned out, the discomfort issue, and the inability of Corfam to adapt to a wearer's feet after some time, was more important than foreseen for the segment to which the shoes were targeted. Thus, while vinyl-coated fashion shoes priced well below leather ones did well, Corfam, whose price exceeded that of leather, failed. Corfam failed because it never gave the extra value that would motivate the segments at which it was aimed.[2]

SEEING PRODUCT DEVELOPMENT AS AN INDEPENDENT SUBPROCESS

The Trilogy and Corfam examples illustrate the two things that need to be simultaneously managed when demonstrating a new technology in end products: the conception of products that the market requires and making sure the technology itself is ready to be incorporated in them at the right time. Often this means walking a tightrope between market-driven product requirements and leveraging as many of the distinctive features of the technology as possible. The starting technology enables new product designs, but it can also act as a constraint to coming up with products in the form customers want.

Walking this tightrope requires seeing product (and process) development as an independent subprocess in commercialization with its own logic. The necessary change in mind-set is underscored by the title of the subprocess—demonstrating the technology "contextually," where the context relates to the end product and no longer to the technology.

Figure 6-1 illustrates how a typical product development sequence fits into the technology's own development. Stages 1 through 4 represent exploring and developing the technology itself, and are best seen as part of the incubating process discussed earlier. Product development involves all the stages from design to the readying of products for market.

FIGURE 6-1

STAGES IN THE DEMONSTRATION OF A TECHNOLOGY IN PRODUCTS

1. Assessment of the enabling technology's current capability and likely trajectory

2. Preliminary ideas to focus development on a class of products

3. Pursuing parallel developments in complementary technologies

4. Recognizing and defining concrete product ideas

5. Product development

    (i)   Idea selection

    (ii)   Preliminary assessment

        • Design requirements and feasibility

        • Market potential and profitability

    (iii) Elaboration of design specifications and development requirements

    (iv) Development

    (v)   Preliminary design of manufacturing system

    (vi) Building of prototypes

    (vii) Testing and product validation

    (viii) Refining product and manufacturing system

    (ix) Test marketing and certifications

    (x)   Production start and market launch

6. Repeat 1–5

In recognition of the special logic of product development, many companies prefer to have separate groups implementing technology and product development, often with different leaders. Apart from the change in mind-set required, this facilitates looking at the technology in a more detached, emotion-free manner. Perhaps the enabling technology wasn't all that it was billed to be or, more likely, was not a sufficient basis for a new product. Perhaps the technology required more exploration and work. Those going directly from technology to product development sometimes resist admitting these things, or do not have the needed motivation to do something about them.

One company that explicitly recognizes the managerial and psychological need to distinguish product development from the earlier phases of technology commercialization is Raychem. While technology development is the responsibility of corporate R&D—albeit with divisional funding and involvement—products are designed and developed within product design labs in the business divisions. The latter are also typically led by a marketing or general management executive, whereas researchers had led the effort earlier.

DuPont also separates its scouting phase from what it calls the project and prototype phases, having to do with product development (See Table 1-1 in Chapter 1). Whereas, in the scouting phase, the project was led by a technical person, project leadership gets transferred to someone from the business center when product development gets authorized. This authorization, moreover, is typically given after a thorough needs analysis has been done—and when the technical department shows that the technology is *ready* for product development.

Looking at products independently from the technology(ies) being commercialized does not, of course, mean ignoring the latter. What is required at this stage is managing the transition from one to the other effectively so as to get the most out of the investments previously (or concurrently) made in the technology itself. In practice, this means:

Seeing good designs as the main outcome of the process, not what the technology can achieve;

Managing technology and product/process development in parallel for their own logic with periodic coupling between them;

Timing the start of product development to leverage progress in the technology while meeting a market window of opportunity;

Optimizing the overlap between technology and product development for purposes of speed;

Handling some compromises the technology forces through market repositioning later; and

Incorporating certain left-over technologies in successor models of the product.

The remainder of this chapter is devoted to discussing each of these concepts in turn.

GOOD DESIGN AS THE MAIN OUTCOME

Regardless of what a technology can do at a given point in time, value lies in coming up with a good end product or process design. That is what customers are ready to pay for. The more this design leverages the new technology, the better in the sense of promising a proprietary position or a distinctive functionality. But that should never be an objective in itself. The end result needs to be a superior product.

Product superiority, in fact, has been found to be one of the most important factors contributing to successful innovation.[3] It can mean many things—offering unique features not available on competing products, meeting customer needs better than competitors, possessing higher relative quality, solving a problem the customer had, reducing the customer's total cost, and simply being innovative.

Attributes of a Good Design

The term "good design" is used here to embrace all these attributes of product superiority. In giving expression to these attributes, it transforms a hypothetical *need* for a new technology-based function into something tangible whose *demand* can be estimated. It includes both the distinguishing features of the product, which set it apart from competition, and the features pertaining to its use. The latter include things like ease of use, aesthetics, the affordance of maximum utility for the price, few negative externalities and side effects, and the like. Thus good design includes the input of industrial designers, design engineers, and, where relevant, application development engineers.

Design is fundamentally about bringing about a synthesis among many different options. This, moreover, applies as much to consumer products as it does to the implementation of a new process technology in a piece of equipment. There is seldom one, unambiguous solution, but rather a range of alternatives from which a "best" design emerges. If good science is about creativity in analysis, good design involves making creative trade-offs and exercising judgment over a large number of variables. As Norman put it:

> If everyday design were ruled by aesthetics, life might be more pleasing to the eye but less comfortable; if ruled by usability, it might be more comfortable but uglier. If cost or ease of manufacture dominated, products might not be attractive, functional, or durable. Clearly, each consideration has its place. Trouble occurs when one dominates all the others.[4]

The term "design," as used here, relates to all the use-related attributes of a product. In general, the key variables to consider in arriving at it are the paradigm of use intended, the core benefits or utilities it is expected to provide, the completeness of the product for its intended use, price, and the time window to be met.

Use Paradigm

The paradigm of use refers to the broad pattern of interaction between a product and the user. It is the gestalt of the design, so to speak, and constitutes the fundamental basis for positioning products in the marketplace. Get this wrong and everything else one does to a product becomes futile.

To illustrate the notion of a use paradigm, consider the case of interactive multimedia today. On the basis of recent consumer tests conducted by AT&T and others, it is still not clear what people will do with the new technology. Uses range all the way from playing games, accessing information, and making certain transactions (teleshopping, for example) to a sophisticated version of E-mail. As AT&T found out from its focus group, most people took a passive stance vis-à-vis what was being offered. As Vincent Grosso, the AT&T executive who led the tests, concluded, "It's a TV paradigm. To succeed in this game, whatever you provide will have to look like a TV, not a computer."[5]

While a TV versus PC paradigm for multimedia may seem like a trivial distinction, it illustrates a point many innovators fail to address when establishing the context of technology demonstration—that things have to work from a use point of view, not just technically or functionally. It is attention to this broad use paradigm that explains why the microwave oven comes out as the product that most "made life a lot better," with the VCR being second.[6] Like all paradigms, it is a reflection of a condition in society. Although introduced in the early 1960s, the microwave's widespread acceptance by consumers began in the 1980s. While price and concerns over safety and taste played a role in this late start, changing lifestyles influenced its adoption too: the realization of the value of time, smaller families, working mothers, an uncritical attitude toward meals, and the like.

The important thing to remember also is that a use paradigm is mainly intended to facilitate the adoption of a new technology, not to position it vis-à-vis competing offerings. That comes later.

Central Utility Factors

One level lower than the paradigm of use are the attributes potential buyers expect in a product or process. Variously known as core benefit propositions (CBPs) or central utility factors (CUFs), these specify the utility buyers derive and form the basis for both the design and competitive positioning of the new product.

CUFs involve considering all the attributes of a product. As mentioned earlier, many of these attributes are constrained by the technology itself. Creativity lies in judiciously emphasizing the positive features afforded by the technology while not letting the constraints come in the way. These features, moreover, need to be made explicit in the beginning and guide the development work.

ICI's FM-21 Membrane Cell. An example of a successful use of CUFs in design is that of ICI's development of the FM-21 membrane cell referred to in Chapter 2. The latter's main attributes were decided from the outset to be low total energy consumption, low installed cost, simple maintenance procedures, optimum performance readily reproducible after each electrolyzer rebuild, simple electrode recoating, and maintenance interval to be determined only by membrane life (which should be maximized). The idea was to make the FM-21 into an "operator's cell"—economical, easy to use, and energy-efficient. These attributes then drove the technology choices made during the development program as well as the detailed features of the design.

The most important choice was to opt for a monopolar construction, where the electrodes would be connected in parallel, rather than the bipolar (series connection) design chosen by others. To achieve low manufacturing costs, the cell was designed with a minimum number of simple components. Mounted on a simple steel frame with tie rods, the entire cell could be moved around by a forklift truck, and the assembly and stripping work carried out on a simple workbench by two workers in only a few hours. Bipolar cells, in comparison, needed days to install or rebuild.

As often happens, the achievement of all the design objectives implied making some compromises. As Paul Henstridge put it, "It was quickly appreciated that an electrolyser designed primarily to achieve minimum energy consumption would always tend to frustrate achievement of the other objectives. The approach used, therefore, was to tackle each of these other objectives and to ensure that the goal of low energy consumption was always kept to the fore."[7]

Henstridge's remark about low energy consumption also highlights an important thing about CUFs: they should be rank ordered to signify where compromises can be made. Apart from guiding the development effort, such a rank ordering helps to isolate the dominant attribute(s) to be used in promoting the technology later.

Completeness in Use

Customers don't buy a product; they buy an effect. And they want that effect in the most cost-effective manner possible. Going from a technology to a product involves bringing together in a single, coherent package, all of the attributes needed for delivering the benefits that the *user* expects. The technology may permit a new kind of use pattern, but it is one among many factors contributing to it.

The distinction Davidow makes between a "device" and a "product" in the computer industry is in line with this notion:

> The complete product called a "computer," consists of system hardware and a wide array of associated options, an operating system, application languages, application programs, documentation, customer training, salesman and presale application support, postsale application support, the maintenance organization and the logistic system that supports it with spare parts, the brand image of the company, the advertising and public relations about the system, and most importantly the feeling of confidence the customer has in the supplier. A company with only a few of those characteristics faces a problem similar to trying to sell an unpainted car. A customer will purchase it, but only at a very cut rate.[8]

The notion of what a product ought to be varies according to the industry. Laying stress on completeness in use, however, signals its main characteristic: it must provide the *total function* a customer expects. If this means broadening the scope of the development, so be it.

Price

The price for which a product is designed has become *the* critical variable for many technologies today. Not only is it key to market acceptance, but it also needs to be established early as a guide to product and process design. As Bacon and colleagues found, "[development] teams that positioned their products vis-à-vis competition on the basis of price experienced slightly less revision in their product definition over time than did the teams that positioned their product on the basis of features. In other words, the discipline exercised by a target price may be greater than that associated with target product features."[9]

What price to design for is ultimately a function of the value offered. There are, however, four things to note about what is otherwise an unexceptional statement. One is that the relationship between price and value is highly complex, except when the function offered itself is reasonably constant. The latter is, for example, true in the computer industry. Although many disagree, the price for a given number of millions of instructions per second (MIPS) is a reasonable measure for the competitiveness of computer systems. Each system starts with a new $/MIPS ratio, which positions it vis-à-vis other systems.

More difficult to judge target prices for are situations where the function is new or significantly different from what was hitherto available. It is also difficult when multiple product attributes are involved, as in the case of some new materials, for example. Material properties can span a wide range depending on the microstructure utilized and the method of manufacture chosen. Properties such as heat resistance, mechanical integrity, elasticity, sheer strength, degradation, and so on are all relevant. Which of these properties is of greatest value to a buyer depends on the application envisaged, making it hard to determine a standard or even benchmark price for the material. The best way to cope with such situations is to relate price systematically to value on a case-by-case basis.

Second, value is as much a function of the segment targeted as it is of comparative worth vis-à-vis another product. This is the lesson Sony learned when it launched its MiniDisc in December 1992. Positioned as a digital and recordable substitute for the company's highly successful cassette-based Walkman, the product was a flop, especially in the United States. The "MTV generation," to whom it was targeted, couldn't afford the extra price the company demanded for the new technology.

Third, following price/performance characteristics is seldom enough. More often than not, one needs a quantum leap in price/performance to dislodge an entrenched technology, as DEC found out with its Alpha Chip. Although somewhat superior to Intel's Pentium Chip introduced around the same time, it faced all the barriers that a new architecture presents— lack of software, habit, and purchasing relationships. As Michael Danner, a test engineer with Reliance Electric, put it, "HP is the favorite at our company. The difference of 10 to 15 percent between the Specmark rating of the PA-RISC Chip [of HP] and the Alpha Chip is not significant. It's only important if it's no contest. Unless there's a doubling of speed, people don't notice."[10]

The final qualification is related to this. Increasingly, the trade-off between costs and benefits is turning around costs per se. In other words, what adopters of a new technology demand is not just a new functionality in a product but at a lower cost than what is being replaced. The best illustration is in the automobile industry, where customers expect constant improvements each year but at affordable prices. They are habituated to a certain category of automobile, and any dramatic change in its relative price causes confusion and disenchantment.

The reason why such budgetary constraints have become important today can be traced to the growing number of substitutes available for any given function. For industrial customers, an additional factor is the need to amortize investments more quickly (because of obsolescence), while maintaining *their* prices vis-à-vis end customers. Naturally, if a technology makes a major contribution to enhancing value but constitutes a small component in an overall system, it can justifiably be priced high. Thus, one of the reason microfibers that have the feel of silk have done so well is that, although 30 percent to 50 percent more expensive than normal-gauge filament, the material cost represents a small fraction of the cost of clothes one buys in a store.

Where they are present, however, budgetary constraints make premium pricing less viable as a marketing strategy. This explains the current trend within many companies today to design explicitly for lower costs. If a trade-off should be made between elaborate and unique CUFs and cost, it is the latter that ought to override. Far too many inventors overload their CUFs, adding costs unnecessarily, whereas they ought to be aiming for cost parity with incumbent or competing technologies at the least.

Time

Although rarely considered in the same way as other product attributes, time is key to a successful design today. Whatever the other attributes built into a product, they are usually relevant to a narrow window of opportunity. The challenge in product demonstration is to strike a balance between the features to incorporate and the competitive time window available.

This is the lesson Texas Instruments Inc. learned with its magnetic bubble memory program. Although potentially superior to conventional dynamic random access memory (DRAM) technology, the company spent seven years perfecting its technology. By the time magnetic bubble memories were ready for the market, progress in DRAMs had made the latter more capable and cheaper than anticipated.

In many cases, meeting a time window for a design requires introducing a simpler and less demanding version from a development standpoint first. Thus, while General Magic Inc. was experiencing delays in getting its Telescript software, which allows users to send "agents" throughout a network to perform certain tasks, others introduced simpler versions for use on the Internet. Among the latter was Oracle Corp., whose software allows users to send automated agents directly to a designated server only. Although more limited in scope, it has an advance over Telescript, which has so far been incorporated only in AT&T's PersonaLink network. General Magic is now planning to offer stripped-down versions of Telescript at lower prices in order to compete.[11]

Processes and Tools for Arriving at Good Designs

In the end, a good design is one that appeals to the stakeholders most concerned by a technology. For certain large-scale technologies, the range of stakeholders who influence a design can include resource providers, suppliers of complementary technologies, and even political actors. For consumer devices, on the other hand, it is primarily the voice of customers that counts. Industrial equipment falls somewhere in between, depending on its size and importance.

Where a wide range of stakeholders are involved, interaction among them can result in designs that may not be optimal, but that satisfy the majority or those whose influence is greatest. As Fries illustrates in her study of NASA's space station design, which changed from a torroidal or wheel-shaped spacecraft to a pair of orbiting stations, and then to a "power tower" with "dual keel" configuration, the design was as much a product of the political environment and the various constituencies that needed to be satisfied as of the engineers designing it.[12]

Chance can play a role too, with the design becoming a hostage to some past event. One example of chance factors at work is offered by nuclear reactor technology. In 1956, when the United States embarked on its nuclear power program, a number of designs were proposed: reactors cooled by gas, light water, heavy water, even liquid sodium. Then a series of trivial circumstances locked virtually the entire U.S. nuclear industry into light water. These happened to be the reactors the U.S. Navy wanted for nuclear submarines because they were compact; the National Security Council at the same time wanted to get a reactor—any reactor—working on land in the wake of the 1957 *Sputnik* launch; some key officials, moreover, also happened to prefer the light water technology.[13] Once light water reactors had been accepted by the U.S. Navy, and design improvements had been made after experience with building them, these reactors became the dominant technology by the mid-1960s—even though high-temperature, gas-cooled reactors would have been technically better.[14]

No tools exist for coping with the events and forces influencing such large-scale technologies. The best one can do is to be sensitive to the forces at work and to the preferences various stakeholders express. For most consumer and industrial devices, however, a number of methods exist today for finding out what design attributes to build into a product in order to be successful.

Product Features

Not long ago, companies such as Hewlett-Packard and Tektronix saw little reason to conduct formal market research when developing sophisticated new products. They simply used their own engineers as surrogates for customers. If their own engineers liked a product, it was assumed that other engineers would too. As the breadth of the customer base expanded, however, this approach to design became increasingly error-prone. Rather than targeting customers that resembled their own engineers, the companies had to target "average" customers, including some nonsophisticated ones, and design a product that met a wider set of use conditions.

A number of formal techniques exist today for finding out the needs of average customers and designing products to fulfill these needs. The most commonly used tend to be those that involve direct interaction with potential buyers, such as focus groups and limited rollouts.[15] Large-sample statistical tools, such as conjoint analysis (based on finding out what individuals prefer in a product and then mathematically inferring the value system underlying their preferences to select among alternative product designs),[16] or structured techniques like quality function deployment (QFD) (which provides an explicit match between customer expectations of a product and its functional characteristics),[17] are gaining in popularity, but mainly in the consumer goods industry.

The reason companies most often resort to direct interaction with a small number of potential customers is the interactive dialogue it permits. This allows the company to adapt products to specific needs as well as to conduct more robust testing prior to launch.

Related to this is the present trend toward early and multiple prototyping. Instead of the traditional approach to product development, in which the end products are visualized in the abstract and prototypes made toward the end of the development program, early prototyping is based on simulating use from the beginning. As such it is an inductive approach, allowing developers to experience the possibilities of use before finalizing what technologies need to be incorporated.

As to how many prototypes to build and test, and how complete prototypes need to be, there are basically two schools of thought. There are some who subscribe to the belief that a prototype should resemble as closely as possible the device that will eventually be sold, thereby permitting accurate feedback to be obtained. There are others who see prototyping as a guide and a learning tool. For them, it is preferable to have a series of representations, starting with early mock-ups and computer simulations, with each prototype reflecting the requirements of all the functions involved in commercializing the end product in the spirit of concurrent engineering.[18]

The point to remember about all these techniques is that creative designs come from surfacing and deeply understanding *problems* customers are facing, not by simply conforming to their wish list. Customers don't design products; designers do.

Simply questioning a large sample of potential customers assumes that they know what they want and are able to articulate these wants in terms of design features. This is not only a wrong assumption[19] but a dangerous one if the customers whose opinion is sought are using an incumbent technology. The latter are usually committed to a package of attributes that makes them blind to new, disruptive technologies.[20]

Sony is one company that places greater trust in its own expert judgment rather than deriving designs from what customers have to say. Thus, as Koichi Tagawa, manager of Sony's corporate R&D strategy department, explains:

> For new business categories, where it is difficult to know customer requirements in detail, we rely more on internal discussions between the designer,

the marketing department, the quality department, and other relevant departments to define the requirements against which the prototype will be designed and evaluated. For more established products, the company already has good knowledge from experience as to how products will be used. We don't need things in writing always. By involving staff from an independent quality management department, we make sure that all the needed product features as well as issues regarding manufacturability get taken into account at the design phase. The overriding consideration that everyone involved in the process has in mind is that the product must enhance Sony's brand image.[21]

Effective Manufacturing

Just as important as the use characteristics of a product are its cost and the time needed to make it available. These two attributes have made manufacturability an intrinsic part of contextual demonstration today.

Traditionally, this demonstration of manufacturability tended to follow an evolutionary path. One first demonstrated the product in a pilot plant, then in a precommercial version, followed by a full-scale commercial version. Going from laboratory to pilot and then on to full-scale production had two major advantages: it permitted technical problems to be solved one by one while the product's own design got fine-tuned, and it allowed the production system to follow the evolution of the market. The kind of production system (manufacturing process) needed could be matched to the product's own life cycle, thereby reducing investment risks and developing the best production system when adequate volume had been achieved. For people in manufacturing, it also allowed a more gradual introduction of new technologies, thereby alleviating their concerns regarding risks.

Such an evolutionary approach is no longer viable today. With the emphasis on time to market, on getting it right the first time, and on gaining rapid worldwide market penetration, the design of a cost-effective manufacturing system needs to be undertaken simultaneously with product development. One also needs to go as quickly as possible to an optimum, full-scale production system right from the beginning, as Steve Jobs, for example, did when introducing the Macintosh line at Apple and then at Next Inc.

There are several techniques in use today to help design products for better manufacturability. These range from organizational improvements (getting design, engineering, manufacturing, purchasing, finance, marketing, and service to work together), design automation (computer-aided design and computer-aided engineering that allow simulating production and assembly), rapid prototyping (solid modeling by various methods), and statistical quality control and design analysis (which help predict defect rates of products while they are still being designed).

Both product features and manufacturing effectiveness need, of course, to be judged simultaneously. What is needed is to relate the value of the function being offered to its cost. This is where cost modeling techniques[22] help. By making the value of each function explicit and working out all the costs needed for delivering it, one can simulate different designs to come up with the one most likely to succeed.

MANAGING TECHNOLOGY AND PRODUCT DEVELOPMENT IN PARALLEL WITH PERIODIC COUPLING

Arriving at a good design does not mean ignoring the technology enabling it. The latter is what makes one product different from another and offers the prospect of a long-term proprietary position in the market. The challenge, rather, is to find ways of aligning the two so that one gets to a good design that also leverages a key enabling technology.

The Variables to Be Managed

As shown in Figure 6-2, one commonly needs to manage four technology-related streams in order to implement product designs successfully. The first two streams relate to the enabling technology itself. In most cases, both a product and a process are involved, each with its own set of enablers. These are what result in a unique and proprietary product and give the functionality imagined for the design.

Complementary technologies, as their name implies, are needed to complete the design. Who develops them in practice is less important than their availability at the right time. They could be a component based on a technology different from the enabling one being commercialized or other devices needed to construct a system of benefits.

Raw materials can be important contributors to successful designs in some cases too. Many process-based technologies have been held up for long periods of time simply because the material inputs they required were unavailable or too expensive.

Product designs, as indicated in the figure, represent the incorporation of all four streams at different points in time. Each design is timed to exploit a convergence between the availability of these components and a market opportunity prevailing at that point. As such, it is about making trade-offs between which attributes to plan for, and when to offer them. One can wait for the design that leverages a particular enabling technology most (Design 3), or one can introduce several intermediate designs that the market will accept, but that don't exploit the technology's potential as fully (Designs 1 and 2).

FIGURE 6-2

THE PARALLEL-TRACK NATURE OF TECHNOLOGY DEMONSTRATION

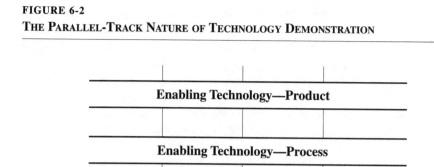

Enabling Technology—Product

Enabling Technology—Process

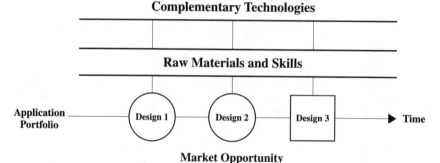

Complementary Technologies

Raw Materials and Skills

Application Portfolio ——— (Design 1) ——— (Design 2) ——— [Design 3] ———▶ Time

Market Opportunity

Deciding What to Emphasize: Product versus Technology

For many technologies, the choice inventors need to make in the beginning concerns the priority to attach to a market-driven design (in the sense discussed earlier) versus the technology's own uniqueness. While the former promises easier acceptance, the latter has the virtue of establishing a proprietary position and a long-term capability that can be leveraged through follow-on products and models. Trying to aim for both advantages simultaneously is the most dangerous, as RCA found out with its VideoDisc.

RCA's VideoDisc

When launching its development program in 1964, RCA wanted an audiovisual player that would sell for under $500 and that would run affordable prerecorded programs—much the same way as had become the norm in the audio industry. Repeated market surveys in the United States and elsewhere since the 1960s had clearly established a need for such a device as an alternative to broadcast television. Anyone who came up with a reasonably priced, reliable, and easy-to-use player was assured of a potentially huge market.

RCA, like many other companies that undertook to develop the device, used audioplayers as a business analogy and saw the technical challenge as one of downsizing professional equipment that had already been on the market since the dawn of television broadcasting, notably the videotape machines introduced in the early 1950s. As vacuum tubes started to be replaced by solid-state transistors, and as high-density recording techniques were already being experimented with, the technical challenge did not seem impossible. After pursuing several different technical solutions, including holographic tapes, magnetic tapes, and capacitance grooved discs, RCA had settled on the latter as the best way to achieve its product objectives. In fact, when it launched its Selectavision VideoDisc in 1981, the price of the player was indeed $499 and prerecorded two-hour discs were made available at $14.98 to $24.98 retail.

What turned out to be a mistake was not so much the choice of technology—since the quality of the picture seen with VideoDisc was actually superior to both broadcast television and magnetically recorded videocassettes—but the assumption regarding the product and what consumers really wanted. Had the VideoDisc been launched five years earlier, as originally planned, it might have been a success. By 1981, however, consumers had a choice between these nonrecordable discs and videocassette recorders that the Japanese had already introduced. Although more expensive and inferior in image quality, the latter were what consumers preferred. The ability to record programs off the air for later viewing was one advantage. Another turned out to be the preference for renting prerecorded cassettes rather than buying discs as RCA's audio analogy dictated.

Once videocassettes got established, it became an uphill battle to introduce discs too. Dealers had become used to VCRs and their service requirements, and they were reluctant to switch to a new technology so soon. Contributing to this reluctance was the fact that dealers did not have to stock videocassettes along with players (which was not the case with RCA's VideoDisc) and the higher margins they were earning with the more expensive VCRs. In the end, RCA lost some $580 million on the VideoDisc. After selling just 550,000 units, it decided to discontinue production in April 1984, three years after the product's launch.

Making continuous trade-offs regarding the scope and depth of technology has both product as well as strategic implications. Thus, focusing at a device level inevitably means delinking one's R&D in basic technologies from the device itself. As RCA realized with its VideoDisc, a breakthrough achieved in a key component technology (e.g., capacitance recording of two-hour programs on a disc) does not mean that the device itself would be successful. To its credit, the company did pursue multiple approaches to the device concept, including holographic tapes, optical recording, and magnetic tapes. However, by going too deep in each of these alternative technologies and having them managed as separate ventures (rather than as one), it went from one missed deadline to another, ending up with the wrong device supplied too late.[23]

The importance of timing the launch of individual products and processes naturally means certain compromises at the level of technology development. In particular, it means scoping out the terrain one wants to cover oneself, and reaching out to others for parts of it. The choice, more-over, covers the underlying technology, the parts of the product developed, and certain collateral features that are needed.

Focusing at the device level is what Hewlett-Packard did with its laser printers. Although it had already built a complete printer on its own, including the laser engine, it started to buy the latter from Canon Inc. This not only allowed it to enter the market faster but to concentrate its own R&D on the software linking the printer and the computer (PCL) as well as the configuration of the text and graphics, which customers appreciate. Although sometimes reported as a victory for Canon, in that the latter benefited from economies of scale and a proprietary strength in a key component, Hewlett-Packard was able to maintain a leading market position because of the investment it made on the end device's software. This PCL software was not licensed to Canon as part of the agreement.

TIMING PRODUCT DEVELOPMENT TO MATCH PROGRESS IN THE TECHNOLOGY AND CHANGES IN MARKET CONDITIONS

When to *start* conceiving of products is largely a function of the confidence one has in making the needed technologies available on time. Thus, when Klaas Compaan of Philips first conceived of the idea of a compact disc in 1969, he knew more or less which enabling technologies would be needed in advance. In fact, barely two years into the effort, his group was able to demonstrate a prototype that could read a black and white video signal off a spinning glass disc. Although this prototype used a helium-neon gas laser that was four feet long and cost more than $20,000—far too expensive and cumbersome for a home entertainment device—the group was confident that a solid-state laser being developed within the company would be available by the end of the 1970s. When the group's focus shifted in July 1972 from pursuing a video disc to an audio one—which required far fewer data to be recorded—the feasibility of the project was seen as even greater.

Being able to time the start of product, and of product development—and then complete the latter on time—requires anticipating progress in the key enabling technologies, making sure that the latter are "robust" when development begins, and using a predevelopment phase with low-level effort if necessary.

Anticipating Progress

Knowing when needed technologies will become available comes from mastering their progress and being able to forecast their future evolution with confidence. This explains why many of the companies that leverage important new technologies into products also tend to be vertically integrated into processes and components or, at least, have a good understanding of them through their network of alliances.

Sony's Enabling Technologies and the TR-55 Camcorder

To see what is involved, consider the interaction between technologies and products at Sony for the period 1960 to 1990 (Table 6-1). The key technologies worked on throughout this period consisted of a mix of functionally defined capabilities (high-precision recording and signal processing, for example), some key components (such as the charge-coupled device (CCD) and recording heads), and a variety of production technologies. All of these had their own trajectory of performance and were seen as contributing in some way to the company's entertainment electronics business.

Occasionally, as with the famous Walkman, these component technologies were simply put together with minor modification. When the Walkman project was announced in 1978, the company had already introduced a portable stereo cassette recorder called the Pressman (TCM-100) the previous year. By developing only a play-back version of the TCM-100, modified for stereo channels, it was possible to obtain the size, weight, and sound reproduction quality that Akio Morita felt were needed to make the product a success. As it turned out, unknown to the group working on the cassette recorder, a prototype, lightweight headphone had also already been developed in another department of Sony.

To the extent that some new technology had to be perfected in order to launch the Walkman, it was the headphone. Until then, even the world's lightest headphones weighed about 100 grams (3.5 ounces) and were of closed-air type. Starting in 1975, under the expressive phrase "zero-fit," Sony's headphones department had started work on a headphone that would be both comfortable and light. When the commitment to the Walkman was made, the headphone research team had most of the technical features mastered to come up with the lightweight (30 grams or 1 ounce) headphone (the MDR-3L2) needed for the TPS-L2, the original Walkman. Riding partly on the success of the Walkman, Sony's open-air "H.AIR" series of headphones and its "Nude" in-the-ear types turned into significant businesses as well.

Compared to the Walkman, Sony's TR-55 camcorder project referred to in Chapter 2 was more challenging technically. It involved setting some design attributes out into the future and *anticipating* the development of the key enabling technologies needed. As with many of Sony's products, the inspiration to design the TR-55 came from marketing. With its strength in

TABLE 6-1
THE INTERACTION BETWEEN TECHNOLOGIES AND PRODUCTS AT SONY

		1960	1970	1980	1990
High-Precision Recording Technology	Technology magnetic tape	γ-Fe₂O₃ (1st gen.)	CrO_2 · CrO_2-Fe_2O_3 (2nd gen.)	Metal powder (3rd gen.)	Metal evaporate
	Recording density (µm²)	1000 · 500	100 · 100 · 50	10 · 10	5
	Tape consumption (m²/hr)	100 · 10	100 · 50	0.5	0.1
	Tape width	2″ · 1″	3/4″ · 3/4″ · 1/2″	8 mm	8 mm
	Components	TR	IC · LSI	VLSI	
Audio Signal Processing	Digital signal processing	Analog — PCM work at NHK (1965)	PCM development at Sony '71 (Start) · '76 (Prototype)	'77 (β-max Audio) (Commercial)	
PRODUCTS	VTRs	INDUSTRIAL VTR CV-2000 U-MATIC (HELICAL SCAN)	Betamax (Azimuth Rec.) (1975)		8 mm Video (1985)
	Audio	COMPACT CASSETTE RECORDER (1965)		WALKMAN (1979) · CD PLAYER (1982)	DAT (1987) · CD COMPACT (1988)
	Video cameras		Betamax Camcorder	"Video-8" CCD Camcorder (1985)	Hi-8 (TR-55) Camcorder (1989)
Charge-Coupled Device (CCD)	Chronology of CCD	BELL LABS RESEARCH	BASIC RESEARCH (1969–72) · DEVELOPMENT (1973–78)	MFG. DEV. (1978–83)	
	CCD camera		CCD CAMERA DEVELOPMENT		
Production Technologies	Percent automatic insertion	Start of automatic insertion	50%≈60%	75%≈80%	90%≈95%
	Soldering	Through-hole and soldering iron	Wave soldering · Surface mount (SMT)	3% SMT · Reflow solder	60% SMT · (1989) air reflow with screen printing
	Mounting accuracy			Pattern rule 300 µm mounting accuracy ± 250 µm	200 µm · 150µm ±50µm · Four-layer mount (1989) · High-density packaging
Complementary Technologies	Recording head	Permalloy head	Ferrite head		Narrow gap MIG (metal in gap)
	Optical recording		Compact disc development	Laser diode	

SOURCE: Compiled using information from various departments of Sony Corporation.

miniaturization and recording technology, the company had become convinced in 1986 that a miniature version of a personal video camera cum recorder would be an instant hit. It would moreover expand the use of its just-introduced 8 mm video recording technology. The ambitious size, weight, and performance specifications set for the product, however, required several new technologies. While some components were brought in, most of the development effort consisted in leveraging technologies that were already being developed within Sony and whose near-term trajectories the company understood well. While the TR-55's design requirements were ambitious and called for a three-year development program, the technological path to achieving them was foreseeable and doable within the time set for product launch.

The Need for "Robust" Technologies at the Start

Companies that launch products successfully and quickly not only define them precisely early but limit the new technologies they put into each, taking what becomes available in subsequent product models.[24] Products that are conceived before one has sufficient confidence in the enabling technologies inevitably result in long-drawn-out and risky development programs.

Once a product gets defined, the fewer the changes introduced the better. The use of a priority criteria list, such as a rank ordering of key product features, as mentioned in relation to the FM-21 development, helps in this regard. Such a list has also been found to be an important aspect of successful product definition.[25] Changes in product definition, when they occur, should be minimal and restricted to the important CUFs, keeping major changes on other attributes for a follow-on product.

The same point is made by Genichi Taguchi when referring to the tasks involved in the product development process and how best to accomplish them. In his words:

> To ensure that Product Planning, Product Design and Process Design are performed smoothly and efficiently, all the technologies needed to design and manufacture new products must be completely developed even before new products are planned. . . . Component suppliers should likewise be utilizing robust technologies to keep apace of new product development. If all the technologies are in place before new products are planned, one only needs to make very simple adjustments in the actual production process in order to begin mass production of new products.[26]

Taguchi uses the term "robust" to describe technologies that are complete and ready. Such technologies have all the information required for a functional design, are flexible in that they can be applied to the development of many new types of products, and reproducible under different operating conditions ranging from the research laboratory to actual mass production. Robustness is, of course, more than just a technical notion. In many cases the author encountered, reluctance to use an otherwise complete and ready technology stemmed from a lack of proper endorsement from those whose opinion matters. Thus, if a new material has not been tested and characterized by appropriate certifying bodies, it will not get used regardless of its functional properties.

This said, a major advantage of scheduling products close to the time when needed technologies are available is the clear product definition it allows. It permits what Conner Peripherals Inc. calls a "sell, design, build" philosophy, consisting in first defining specific customer needs and then designing and building products to meet those requirements. Not only does it provide a strong customer orientation but it also significantly reduces the risk of bringing new products to market.

Timing the start of product development at the last moment of a market opportunity also allows the use of the latest available technology. Ed McCracken, CEO of Silicon Graphics, put it this way in speaking of the company's new desktop computer, the Indy, which took two years to develop:

> I'm convinced that if we had started the Indy three months before we did, we would not have included a digital camera. Our customers were telling us that they wanted video conferencing capabilities, and the technology became available just in time. . . . Long-term product planning is dangerous . . . because it forces companies to make wild guesses about what customers might want. . . . [It] weds companies to approaches and technologies too early, which is deadly in our marketplace and many others.[27]

Using a Predevelopment Phase to Time the Start of Product Development

The important point to note about "robust" technologies is that one does not have to fall back on off-the-shelf technologies that have been ready for some time. Using the latter can result in uninnovative products that can lead to commercial disappointment in markets where innovation is prized. Relying on robust technologies does mean that *start* of product development needs to be timed carefully.

The only way to link product development to market needs is to time its start when sufficient information on the enabling technology, the market, and the requirements for design become available. For many technology-based products, this means allowing for a low-level, predevelopment phase. Major resource commitments and product development proper should begin only when both the design attributes and the positioning message become clear.

Astra Turbuhaler

A good example of this is how Astra's successful inhalation device for asthma treatment (the Turbuhaler) got developed. Until the early 1970s, the main inhalation system used in asthma treatment was the pressurized metered dose inhaler (MDI), which Glaxo had also popularized with Ventolin. MDIs were based on a chlorofluorocarbon (CFC) propellant with drug particles suspended in it. By pushing on the canister, the patient released a precisely measured dose of drug under pressure into the buccal cavity and the lungs. The advantage of the device was its portability and convenience and, when properly coordinated with inhalation, the immediate deposition of the drug within the lungs. The pressure with which the drug was administered also afforded patients a sensation of immediate relief, albeit more psychological than real.

There were, however, several drawbacks too. One was the need for good coordination. The MDI had to be activated at the start of inhalation for best results. Not inhaling properly, or exhaling while activating the device, resulted in depositing the drug in the mouth and the back of the throat. This often caused patients to activate the device several times, making it hard to control the dose taken. The other major problem related to the construction of the device. CFCs were gradually becoming environmentally suspect; the inhalation of the gas mixed with lubricants was also felt to be unnecessary, if not potentially harmful.

The first metered dose powder inhaler (PI) was introduced in 1969 by Fisons. Its pharmaceutical product, Intal, had to be dosed in amounts (about 20 mg) too large to be handled in an MDI at that time. Glaxo's Rotahaler (launched in 1977 with Ventolin) and Boehringer-Ingelheim's Inhalator (launched in 1982) were introduced next in response to the drawbacks of MDIs and explicitly intended for patients who could not use MDIs properly.

These devices required a hard gelatin capsule containing the drug to be loaded and then punctured prior to inhalation. Since the powder was inhaled only when breathing in, the coordination problem associated with MDIs was avoided. However, all the early models were single-dose devices, compared to about 200 doses a typical MDI contained. This meant constantly searching for a capsule, loading it, and puncturing it; patients sometimes had difficulty in loading the device correctly and emptying it reliably. In addition, the active drug was mixed with a carrier substance, usually lactose. This caused a rather large quantity of powder (about 25 mg) to be delivered to the lungs, like a puff of dust; the lactose, moreover, often caused lung irritation. Finally, the proper functioning of the system called for a large inhalation rate, making it unsuitable for small children and those with acute asthma.

As head of organic chemistry at Draco, one of Astra's product companies, Kjell Wetterlin had been involved in asthma research for many years, including as member of the 1960s project group that invented the company's bronchodilator Bricanyl. "Even as a chemist, however, it was natural to be thinking about the product as well as its delivery," recalls Wetterlin. "I was particularly concerned by the drawbacks of the MDI at that time, especially the use of CFCs and lubricants. My daughter had asthma and she would often complain about the bad taste these additives left in the mouth, too. It was obvious that an inhaler that delivered just the pure drug would be a superior solution medically."[28]

The idea Wetterlin started to work on in 1972 was to develop a device that delivered only pure drug to the lungs; contained multiple doses as the MDI did; and dosed less than 1 mg in each activation like MDIs, compared to 25 mg (including carrier substances) delivered by powder inhalers.

Between 1972 and 1980, Wetterlin worked mainly alone. While Astra management knew of his project, and even provided a modest amount of funds, it stopped short of pushing the idea in a major way. The company had not succeeded in getting a strong enough foothold in the inhaled therapy market with its Bricanyl MDI and saw little need to enter the powder inhaler market, unless the product was clearly superior.

What finally got Astra management's attention was when the first clinical trials of a hand-made device in 1980 resulted in a surprising finding—that the new powder inhaler was as good as MDIs, something no other powder inhaler could claim. This promised a product that would not only substitute for existing powder inhalers but provide an alternative to MDIs too—a much larger market.

These were, of course, only preliminary findings and, as one observer put it, "had more extensive tests been done, we probably would have concluded that this initial prototype was actually not as effective." But it was enough to launch the Turbuhaler as a formal development project within Astra with considerably greater resources.

The decision to delay actual product development until the point when the company had a truly superior design concept accounted for part of the success the Turbuhaler enjoyed.

OPTIMIZING THE OVERLAP BETWEEN TECHNOLOGY AND PRODUCT DEVELOPMENT

The main purpose of timing the start of product development to match technology availability is, of course, to minimize technical uncertainty. It does not, however, mean that technology development should be excluded from product development projects altogether. Some products and processes are too intimately linked to a technology for this to be possible. Moreover, to fully leverage a technology in products, one needs to incorporate its latest version—one that may have come after the product was conceived. What one needs to aim for, therefore, is an optimum overlap between the two—not concurrent engineering where everything is done together while the product itself is undergoing redefinition. Several things help in keeping the right balance: choosing easier applications and designs first, defining products precisely in the beginning, maintaining close customer contact, and keeping complementary technologies out of the critical path of product development.

Choosing Easier Applications and Designs First

One of the reasons Philips was able to deliver on its compact disc within a reasonable period of time was the decision made in July 1972 (three years into the development program) to switch from a video to an audio application. This was done despite the fact that the product would cannibalize the company's highly successful casette-tape business launched in the 1960s and despite the fact that customers seemed reluctant to adopt yet another medium in addition to vinyl long-playing records and cassette tapes.

Raychem's surge arrester team heeded this need to start with easier products, too. Although the company's technology could be leveraged best in large, station-class arresters (in the 36 to 760 KV range), a decision was made early to go after the less demanding distribution class arrester market (12 to 36 KV) first. Apart from being technically easier, this allowed the company to build a reputation in order to be credible in the station class segment later.

Staying close to one's existing technological base serves a similar purpose. Sharp's approach to the burgeoning multimedia market illustrates one way of doing this. Its technology road map consists in building new products mainly around technologies in which it is already a leader or, at least, is already known for—liquid crystal displays (LCDs), laser diodes, miniaturization, and flash memory chips. It is, moreover, taking a dual development approach. One approach, which it calls "bottom-up," consists in equipping its existing products with multimedia elements, such as telecommunications or image processing, to turn them into new products. An example is the novel use of three- and four-inch LCD panels as viewfinders on camcorders, replacing conventional eyepieces. The other approach, termed "top-down," will develop totally new products based on novel system elements and technology, such as those explicitly targeted to the Internet. As a conscious decision, it is the "bottom-up" approach that will be taken first.[29]

Defining the Product Precisely in the Beginning

Demonstrating a new technology, like many of the other phases of commercialization, is in the end a process of experimentation. Unfortunately, unlike good experimenters, many inventors agonize over this phase because they are too wedded to the hypotheses they start with. They see technology demonstration as yet another opportunity to prove their theories right instead of what this phase really is—that of a transition from invention to marketable products. This has proved an expensive obsession, as many people funding new technologies will attest. What is required instead is to define products to be developed precisely and to manage the scope of the new technologies to incorporate in them.

The need for devoting adequate time and effort to researching the market and coming up with a good product definition *prior* to starting the development program has been demonstrated in several studies on product innovation. As Robert Cooper concluded in a recent study of projects from the chemical industry,

> Homework undertaken before the project proceeds into Development is critical. Projects that boasted superb up-front homework achieved a 43 percent higher success rate and were rated significantly more profitable; they were more likely to be successful technically, and they had a greater impact on the company. Most important, better homework reduced cycle time; such projects were undertaken in a more time-efficient manner, and stayed on-schedule.[30]

Sharp product definition before starting the development program provides a clear set of objectives for the development team to strive toward; it avoids the need (and temptation) to drag out the process in the name of flexibility; and, depending on the way information relating to it is assembled, results in buy-in across functional areas and potential customers. Also, as Arno Penzias, the head of Bell Labs, put it,

> The more you define the context precisely, the less the technical challenge. Short-cuts and design compromises can be made by focusing on a particular function; as you expand the functional scope of the technology, for example, in a speech recognition system from phonetic to personal recognition, the greater the technical challenge.[31]

Keeping Complementary Technologies Out of the Critical Path of Product Development

The point made earlier about anticipating progress in the key enabling technologies applies to complementary technologies as well. While they might be less important from the standpoint of leveraging proprietary technologies, they need to be kept out of the critical path of development. They should not become the obstacle to commercializing the enabling technologies themselves.

One such complementary technology is manufacturing. Manufacturing engineering programs follow two, sometimes quite independent, objectives.

One consists in adapting a product for the manufacturing environment and designing an efficient production process. The other, which has tended to receive somewhat less attention, is the incorporation and development of *new* manufacturing techniques to accommodate future product requirements. In the case of the electronics industry, for example, the constant push toward circuit miniaturization, higher capacities, and hybrid solutions (optoelectronic for the moment, but with bioelectronic to follow soon) puts as much of the development burden on processing and testing technologies as on product design itself. New processing, bonding, mounting, packaging, and testing technologies drive product innovation as much as product technologies.

Alcatel has realized the importance of driving its product and manufacturing research in parallel, rather than wait for specialist equipment manufacturers to step in on time. It has its own research program in tape automated bonding (TAB), which is seen as a logical successor to surface mounted device (SMD) technology; it works on its own thin film and fiber processing technologies; and it has set up its own testing and calibration facilities since test equipment manufacturers are limited in this area.[32]

For many products, manufacturing is just one complementary technology. In certain electronic devices, for instance, a whole range of things need to be assembled in order to offer what was described earlier as a "complete product." These include the setting of technical standards, the availability of software, and a variety of complementary devices that provide the effect customers want. It is in recognition of this that Philips extrapolates complete road maps comprising all the elements that need to come together at different points in time for designs to be successful.

Alliances naturally play a key role in bringing all these complementary technologies together on time. Philips's approach to developing its audio compact disc is exemplary in this regard. Knowing that software developers and owners would convert to the new technology only if it became a standard that other consumer electronics companies also adopted, it tried to get the latter interested in its project early. In fact, weeks after it had demonstrated a working prototype to internal management in spring 1979, albeit an imperfect one, it flew the same prototype over to Japan to interest companies there. Matsushita, with whom the company had a long-standing cooperation relationship, turned down the offer to work on a standard. But Sony agreed. The agreement with Sony not only helped to establish the technology as an industrial standard but gave Philips important technical help in perfecting its error-correction algorithm. The two companies also worked out a pact that if either designed a circuit that did not work, the other would offer its own. Although the latter provision was never used, the overall cooperation with Sony resulted in a better, hybrid solution based on the expertise within both companies.

HANDLING LEFTOVER TECHNOLOGIES AND PRODUCT COMPROMISES

Regardless of how carefully the start of product development is planned, some compromises inevitably have to be made, both at the product level and in terms of how much of the enabling technology can be incorporated in it. There are basically two ways to cope with this.

One is to plan for successor models right from the beginning and to pick up incomplete technologies in subsequent models. This approach is best suited to rapidly obsolescing products, or when Taguchi's recommendation on having robust technologies available at the start of product development is especially relevant.

Among the best examples of this are found in the disk drive industry today. With hard-disk storage capacities increasing at around 60 percent a year in the 1990s—twice as fast as in previous decades—companies need to constantly apply new technologies in their products. At the same time, short product life cycles—often less than a year—leave little time to ramp up production slowly or go through an evolutionary change in manufacturing processes. The drive has to be built quickly, right the first time, and immediately produced on a commercial-scale production facility. With little room for error and long-drawn-out development programs, many companies take a conservative approach to the technologies they use in a particular model.

The other approach is to plan for some flexibility at the market level. If the initial objectives of a design are not met for one reason or another, the product itself can perhaps be repositioned to offer a somewhat different set of attributes than the one planned. The priority in such cases is to leverage whatever technological breakthrough has been achieved as quickly as possible in a precisely defined product and to then exercise marketing creativity in repositioning it for the attributes incorporated. This is essentially what Astra's Turbuhaler project team did, as discussed in Chapter 8.

SUMMARY

Demonstrating new technologies in marketable products often involves walking a fine line between what the technology itself can do at a point in time and the requirements the market has of the product or process conceived around it. The most important thing to remember is that the end result of technology demonstration is a well-designed end product or process. Phrased in these terms, this is an unexceptional statement. What it requires, however, is a complete change in mind-set and, often, a new organization for implementing it.

The attributes of a "good design" encompass several things: the paradigm of use intended, price, the core benefits or utilities to be provided, the product's completeness in use, and the time window to be met. While several tools exist for arriving at such designs, one often needs to exercise judgment in making the trade-offs these tools surface. Being able to deliver on such designs for technology-based products requires juggling not only different variables but a host of intermediate stakeholders too. The best way to do so is:

To decide what to emphasize (product or technology) right from the beginning;

To time the technology and changes in market conditions to match progress in product development;

To optimize the overlap between technology and product development;

To incorporate leftover technologies in successor models; and

To handle minor compromises made through market repositioning later.

7

MOBILIZING MARKET CONSTITUENTS

IF THERE IS ONE EXHORTATION THAT CAN BE MADE TO ANYONE LAUNCHING A new technology-based product today, it is "think systems" or, more accurately, "think systemically!" Whether the product is a stand-alone device, a new bulk material, or a minor component, one has to view its marketing as influencing a wide range of market constituents. The argument that technology commercialization is fundamentally an exercise in interest and resource mobilization applies as much to the delivery stage as it does to getting a new technology ready. The difference is that this time a more heterogeneous and wider set of stakeholders is involved. Some play a role in making available needed components of the technology; others influence its demand or help with delivering it in a cost-effective way. The key is to find out who the key influencers are and to work out a strategy for co-opting them in the delivery of the technology and the creation of its demand.

Whenever technologies required such an assembly of different downstream resources in the past, it was usually the inventor who took on all the tasks. Thomas Edison is probably the best case in point. He could have stopped at inventing the light bulb, but he went on to build the entire infrastructure needed to benefit from it: coal-fired generators, transmission lines, and street and house wirings. All this he did himself through the Edison Electric Light Co.

Fortunately, today there is no need to go through all the trouble Edison did on one's own. Nor, for that matter, is it advisable to dethrone incumbent systems heroically. A better stance is to get the many actors involved to see the world in a certain way, even without active collusion. As John Seely

Brown put it in reference to Apple's Macintosh strategy during the early 1980s,

> Steve Jobs and the designers of Macintosh understood deeply how to coproduce the "Macintosh World" with third-party developers, all independently seeing the power of the technology. They succeeded in creating cohesion among a set of autonomous working agents, all contributing to the value consumers perceived.[1]

GM Hughes's DirecTV

A recent example of effective market constituent mobilization is that of GM Hughes's launch of its DirecTV satellite service in early 1994. Conceived of in 1990 as a replacement for Hughes's failed Sky Cable TV venture, the project consisted in broadcasting digital TV signals from a high-powered satellite direct to home TV receivers equipped with just a pizza-sized dish antenna and a decoder. Despite the technical difficulties involved, including the development of a new generation of satellites as well as dishes and decoder boxes, the parameters of the design were set explicitly: $700 for the equipment consumers had to buy, since this was all they would willingly pay; $30 a month for receiving a total of 175 channels with clear images and CD-quality sound; and availability before the cable TV industry had a chance to match the technical performance of the system. With about half a dozen failures in direct-satellite TV fresh in people's memory, some skepticism was to be expected. But when the system was launched in the United States in early 1994—with all its design parameters met—it proved a phenomenal success. Within the first six months, more than 700,000 satellite dishes and decoders systems had been sold, and nearly half a million subscribers signed up to pay the fee of $30 a month. Compared to this, VCRs sold only 300,000 units in the first year of their launch, which in the early 1980s constituted a record for rapid market penetration.

Good design and development in the sense discussed in Chapter 6 were among the reasons for DirecTV's success. Equally important was the way Hughes's project team brought all of DirecTV's pieces together. A truly system technology, involving an overall investment of over $1 billion, it took several actors to bring it to market on time. To share some of the investment burden, the rights to a few channels were first presold to a couple of broadcasters for $225 million. Simultaneously, several consumer electronics firms were approached to help with the development of the decoder. Although Hughes had leading-edge technology in house, it was felt that experienced manufacturers in this field provided a better bet to achieve the $700 price target set. RCA-Thomson was the company chosen, partly for its guarantee on the price and also because its 11,000-dealer retail network would facilitate distribution later. In return for its development work, it was given exclusive rights for the first million decoders. To help with digitizing programming cost-effectively, yet another alliance was made—with Sony. Existing digital tape machines cost $100,000 and played tapes costing $130 each. Since some 320 tape machines and a 50,000-tape library were needed, this "would have broken the bank—even Hughes's bank," according to an executive. Knowing about Sony's plan to release a new generation of digital videotape players in 1996, the Hughes team offered Sony a $50 million contract to move its product introduction forward. Sony delivered a $40,000 machine (with $85 tapes) in June 1993.

Lobbying other stakeholders was also needed as part of the effort. One target was legislative bodies formulating a new cable regulation act. When this act was announced in 1992, Hughes had succeeded in introducing a clause that required programmers to offer shows to rival delivery systems, thereby avoiding preemption by the powerful cable TV industry.[2]

MARKET CONSTITUENTS FOR A NEW TECHNOLOGY

Allowing for differences in the products one is talking about, there are usually three sets of market constituents to contend with: companies that can be engaged in the delivery of the technology; advocates and/or arbitrators that play a role in its market acceptance; and, by no means least important, companies already commercializing the incumbent technology. As shown diagrammatically in Figure 7-1, all three of these seek a share of the end customer's business.

Partners in delivery can be:

Intermediate adopters (who add some value for resale);

Manufacturing partners, either as comakers (who provide parts and components on a subcontracting basis), as coproducers (who make the entire product but typically by using some critical components or technologies provided by the lead producer), or as second-source suppliers (who make the entire product to meet capacity and/or security needs of end customers);

Distributors playing some value-added and promotional role; and

Independent suppliers of complementary products and/or services needed to benefit fully from the product.

Actual or potential advocates of a technology can be various interest groups (influencing its adoption by lobbying concerned organizations); opinion leaders (whose purchase decision or simple endorsement impacts the market); or noncontestant companies which, while not disinterested in the outcome, are not contesting the technology itself. Noncontestant companies, in fact, often play a dual role; the choice they make can influence purchase decisions and, if they are powerful enough, arbitrate which technology gets adopted. The most important arbitrators for many new

FIGURE 7-1
THE MARKET CONSTITUENTS IN THE LAUNCH OF A NEW TECHNOLOGY

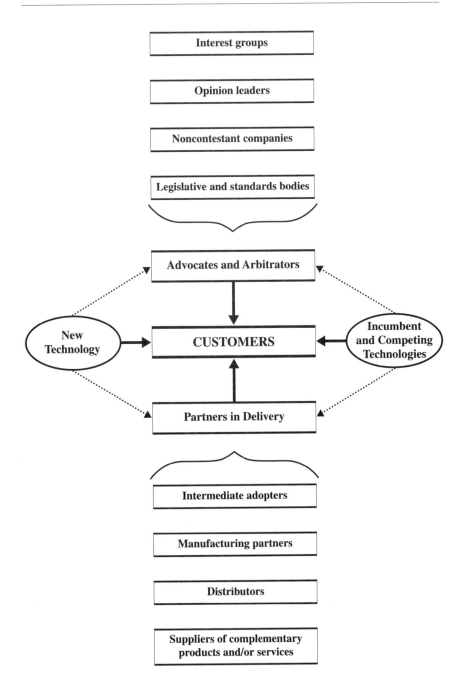

technologies are, of course, various legislative and standards bodies whose rulings can apply through fiat.

Competitors offering the incumbent technology constitute the third set of stakeholders. Threatened by the introduction of a substitute, they typically respond by improving price-performance characteristics and strengthening their bonds with the stakeholders concerned—often the same as the ones targeted by the proponent of the new technology.

A few points need to be made about these market constituents at the outset. First, their motivations can vary enormously. Most are influenced by economic considerations, but they can differ in terms of their time horizons. There are some, however, whose motivations lie outside the immediate commercial arena. Thus, in the case of automobile catalysts, the determinant stakeholders were lawmakers, introducing ever more stringent legislation that clean-burning engines (the preferred solution for most car manufacturers) could not meet.

Second, there is often a complex set of interactions among the stakeholders in each group. Competition can be as much between the value-cost relationships offered as between the power of these stakeholders to influence the outcome based on their own interests in the new technology. The relationships between them can be symbiotic, where each party gains, or it can be competitive and antagonistic. Anyone introducing a new technology that involves these stakeholders needs to understand the dynamics influencing their behavior first. Synergies need to be found at the intersection of their interests; overly relying on one group's contribution may be easier and convenient but it is seldom enough.

Finally, each new technology confronts a different power balance among stakeholders. At times, as was the case with Hughes's DirecTV, the critical stakeholders are delivery partners. Whichever system they put their weight behind is likely to succeed. In others, competitors are most important, and a good strategy requires efforts to co-opt them. Then there are cases where a new technology has little chance of being launched successfully without the indulgence and even active involvement of external advocates and arbitrators.

Strategies to cope with different stakeholders vary a great deal, too, and are often circumstantial. Sometimes it is a matter of communication alone, signalling the merits of the new technology to those concerned. In other cases, a more direct and closer relationship needs to be built with some of them.

Sulzer's HRA Technology

The importance of looking downstream in the adoption chain and examining a broad range of stakeholders can be seen from the experience of Sulzer

AG when it started to commercialize a new home refueling apparatus (HRA) for natural gas vehicles (NGV) in the late 1980s.

As a long-established manufacturer of gas compressors, the company had built a worldwide business supplying large natural gas compressors to refueling stations. The latter tended to be owned by independent operators and by companies that had converted entire fleets of trucks and vans to natural gas. With the growing interest in alternative fuels, the company had become convinced that many individuals too would want to convert their automobiles to run on natural gas. However, a dearth of public refueling stations prevented them from doing so. Why not, the company thought, offer a small compressor that people could install in their home garage? It would draw natural gas from the house mains and compress it overnight into cylinders. All the car owner had to do in the morning was to load the filled cylinder into the car and drive off.

The idea of a home refueling apparatus for NGVs was not new. Some twenty other companies had already made them to be sold to mainly "gas freaks" in certain countries. These compressors, however, were expensive and noisy, and they required frequent maintenance. Sulzer's idea consisted of designing and building a special compressor for home purposes with the following specifications:

Cost less than $2,000;

"Idiot-proof" operation;

Power consumption less than 10 amps (using ordinary domestic power outlet);

Filling speed: 100 liters at 200 bar in less than 8 hours;

Range of operating temperatures: −40°C to +40°C;

Noise 55 dB or less at 5 meters;

Maintenance intervals greater than 1,000 hours; and

Oil-free operation.

The high pressure requirement and the need for an oil-free device required repeated redesigns, the development of new types of valves, and the careful selection of materials for compressor parts and lubricants. When the first test model was ready in 1988, the company shipped 200 units to homeowners in Canada and Australia for field trials. While generally in favor of the new device, potential buyers nevertheless expressed reservations about the noise of the compressor, the space it occupied, its serviceability, slow filling rates, potential safety problems, and the cost of the compressor. This feedback created the need for further development. An improved version was then built with a noise level of 45 dB when measured at a distance of 5 meters in open field. This filled a 100 liter gas cylinder to a pressure of 200 bar at 20°C within 9 hours.

Converting homeowners' initial interest into demand for the HRA proved more difficult than solving the initial technical problems. The difficulty lay not with the HRA, but rather with the NGV system as a whole. As Jeffrey Seisler, manager of natural gas vehicle market development of the American Gas Association (AGA), put it in 1984:

> The NGV commercialization process is affected by the activities and behavior of three major groups: market demand sector [comprising] vehicle fleets and individual consumers; the industry actors who supply and distribute fuel, conversion systems, equipment and, in the long term, the manufacturers of dedicated NGVs; and the legal, regulatory, codes and standards authorities that govern the quality and safety of NGV equipment and services. Together these participants in the commercialization process form a complex, interactive web of special interests, all of whom are affected by economic and market forces operating beyond the control of any single group of actors.[3]

Figure 7-2 illustrates the main actors that were involved either as partners in delivering the HRA or as advocates and arbitrators of what customers might end up adopting.

The NGV system, however, was by no means alone in aiming to provide an environmentally superior alternative to gasoline. Electric and solar cars were being targeted to short-distance travelers but had become hampered by a lack of adequate progress in battery technology. Hydrogen, the other zero (atmospheric) polluting technology, was similarly held back by storage and safety problems whose resolution was nowhere in sight. This left alternative hydrocarbon fuels—propane (LPG) and methane—as well as new catalytic converters promising to eliminate up to 90 percent of exhaust pollutants.

The combination of economic and environmental merit of these competing systems gave no clear advantage to a particular technology. Whichever got established quickly and built its infrastructure first would capture a dominant share of the market—and make it harder for the next one in line.

Partners in Delivery

Gas utilities were naturally most likely to benefit from the HRA. With their infrastructure, they were seen quite early as candidates to play a distributor role, promoting and selling the compressor on Sulzer's behalf. After all, one vehicle converted to natural gas equaled the yearly natural gas consumption of a couple of residences. With pipes already in place, this would moreover be at no extra cost for the gas utilities.

Unfortunately, as Matthew Simmons, the project manager at Sulzer, recalled, "The reaction of these utilities was mixed. Ninety percent of them were at best good listeners; and the one or two who were really keen to help

FIGURE 7-2

MARKET CONSTITUENT ANALYSIS FOR THE INTRODUCTION OF A HOME REFUELING APPARATUS (HRA)

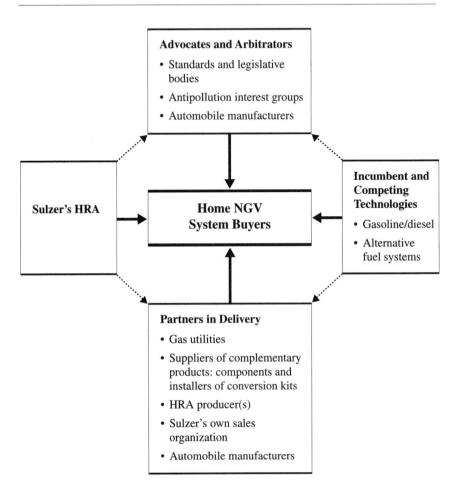

soon withdrew their support. They wanted Sulzer to go ahead with its idea but were not willing to push it, or contribute resources of their own."[4] Only gas utilities in Canada and Australia agreed to help Sulzer with its market trials in their territories, bearing some of the costs involved.

As for producing the HRA at an appropriate cost and quality level, Sulzer was fortunate in having an experienced gas compressor company already within the group—Burkhard AG. The bigger problem was with the suppliers of other components of the HRA system. Original equipment manufacturers of items such as compressed natural gas (CNG) cylinders and conversion equipment belonged to a highly fragmented industry.

Installers too were small and regionally based. This had led to a situation in which the cost of converting gasoline or diesel engines to natural gas was of the order of $2,300 in 1988 ($1,500 for the fuel metering and injection system and about $800 for a pair of gas cylinders). The fact that some people who had converted their vehicles subsequently experienced reliability and performance problems did not help either.

Advocacy Groups and Arbitrators

In addition to antipollution lobbies, the main advocates for alternatives to gasoline vehicles were national and state governments in certain countries. In order to promote alternatives to diesel and gasoline engines, many governments, such as those of Canada and New Zealand, instituted legislative and fiscal measures during the 1970s to make nontraditional fuels more attractive. While there was no positive discrimination in favor of natural gas, the latter benefited from such things as an absence of road taxes on converted vehicles, some subsidies for installing conversion equipment, and the maintenance of a significant price differential between gasoline and these alternative fuels. In the United States, the search for alternative fuels was motivated less by such fiscal incentives than by Environmental Protection Agency regulations on emission, which became progressively more stringent over time.

No government had actually expressed a will for natural gas to be *the* alternative to diesel and gasoline. Governments tended to be neutral to the outcome, preferring to wait and see how things evolved before committing themselves. Everything from propane (LPG), methanol, and ethanol to electric- and solar-powered vehicles had been advocated simultaneously. The past decade had, therefore, seen effort devoted to all of these alternatives, and all achieved varying degrees of success.

Thus, from wanting to merely develop, make, and sell a compressor whose technology it mastered—and that initial forecasts indicated would amount to a $200 million business over five years—Sulzer was caught in a web of issues over many of which it had no control.

Commercializers of the Incumbent Technology

One way to solve the conversion problem was to get large automobile companies to introduce dedicated natural gas vehicles. As Ford Motor Company found in making the first factory-built NGV in 1984 (a 2.4 liter Ranger pick-up truck), the costs associated with conversion could be reduced by half if dedicated NGVs were built in reasonable volume. The Ford Motor experience was also generally positive with regard to the feasibility of building a dedicated NGV and its performance. Unfortunately, the absence of a well-established market and the need to keep options open with regard to all alternatives to gasoline- and diesel-powered vehicles made companies like Ford reluctant to push NGVs, too.

In the absence of dedicated CNG vehicles supplied by established automobile companies, the market was essentially an independent conversion one. Although several companies had begun to supply conversion kits, the question of which conversion to choose was still in people's minds. For example, should car owners convert their vehicles entirely to natural gas (dedicated), to run on either gasoline or natural gas depending on need (bifuel), or, in the case of diesel, run on a mixture of diesel and natural gas (dual fuel)? The prevailing price differential between gasoline and natural gas did not provide a sufficient incentive to opt for more versatile but expensive kits. The vehicle range of dedicated NGVs (100 to 120 km), on the other hand, rendered dedicated vehicles less attractive.

What Sulzer Did

What the Sulzer HRA example illustrates is the complex interplay among the different stakeholders affected by the market launch of a new technology. Influencing the process to one's advantage requires a good understanding of the forces at work and aligning one's interests with those whose interests coincide most or who are most influential in determining the outcome.

While the company accepted the need for a good, economical, reliable, and safe method of vehicle conversion as a prerequisite for consumers to shift to natural gas, it did not think the resources required or the risks (in warranties and liability) justified the company's taking an active role on its own for that part of the system.

With advocates and arbitrators preferring to take a neutral stance regarding which alternatives to diesel and gasoline technologies got commercialized—provided they were nonpolluting and conserved nonrenewable energy resources—Sulzer had little choice but to align itself with one or more delivery partners. The partners chosen were those with the greatest stake in the successful introduction of the HRA: gas utilities.

In October 1989, after spending about $10 million on the project, Sulzer invited two North American utilities (British Columbia Gas of Vancouver, British Columbia, and Questar Corporation of Salt Lake City, Utah) to join as active partners for commercializing the HRA. A new company was set up, FuelMaker Corporation in Vancouver, owned one-third by Sulzer (through capitalizing its technology till then) and one-third each by the two gas companies. This new company was given an exclusive license to further develop and commercialize the compressor in home refueling applications worldwide in return for a royalty to Sulzer.

Soon after it was set up, FuelMaker Corporation received an order to supply 3,000 units of the Sulzer compressor from utilities in North

America and Australia (at $2,400 to $3,000 apiece). Instead of reselling these compressors to end-users, the utilities own them and rent them to their customers (homeowners) at a fee or with a price built into the price of the gas they supply.

Selling the HRA to the home market, however, has proved difficult for FuelMaker for the reasons cited. The latter expects this market to receive a boost when zero-emission legislation comes into effect in various states by the turn of the century. In the meantime, it is targeting small businesses and small fleet operators to keep interest in the technology alive.

The Sulzer example is in some sense an extreme illustration of the role different types of stakeholders play. But the basic message applies quite generally, whether one is speaking of a new component technology, a new material, or even a stand-alone device. What follows is a broader discussion covering these other types of technologies.

MOBILIZING PARTNERS IN DELIVERY

In many cases, the natural partner for the proponent of a new technology is the set of actors that play a role in its delivery and thus stand to gain a share of the value generated. As shown in Figure 7-1, they include intermediate adopters, manufacturing partners, distributors, and suppliers of complementary products and services. Which of these to align with most, and the approach to take, depend on the technology as well as the structure of the industry.

Influencing Intermediate Adopters

An intermediate adopter can be an original equipment manufacturer, which buys the product to incorporate into something else it is commercializing, or an application developer, which converts the product for different uses.

Motivating such intermediaries to adopt a new technology is not easy, however. After all, they bear a good part of the commercial risk; they often have to make additional investments that may render obsolete what they already have in place; the new technology, moreover, may displace a market they have developed over the years.

The way companies have chosen to deal with intermediate adopters varies greatly depending on the nature of the technology and their strategy for realizing value. In general, one can discern the following types of approaches, listed in increasing order of involvement on the part of the proponent of a new technology:

Minimum involvement on the part of the proponent;

Providing a service to facilitate adoption;

Doing the application development work for the intermediate adopter but not competing in the market; and

Engaging in joint-development and technology exchanges.

The Minimum Involvement Route

In the minimum involvement option, the technology proponent's role is typically restricted to providing technical assistance or some fact sheets on the technology. This has been the preferred mode of large companies whose main interest has been in maximizing the sale of, for example, a new material. When such companies get involved in developing and promoting specific applications, and gaining intellectual property rights over them, they either offer their downstream rights and know-how for free to all takers, or give those who helped with the particular application a lead-time advantage over others. Their preference, in fact, is not to be encumbered by downstream intellectual property rights at all so as to allow the maximum number of users to enter the market.

The minimum involvement route is especially common in situations where intermediate adopters themselves prefer to make their own contribution to the product, thereby maintaining a proprietary position in the market. It is also common where these intermediaries prefer to remain independent of *their* suppliers, guarding the freedom to switch to an alternative technology if the situation warrants.

Providing a Service to Facilitate Choice

In some situations it is necessary to assist intermediate adopters to make up their minds to adopt a new technology. The nature of this assistance can range from offering a service to help in decision making, to providing some technical assistance, all the way to help at the end-user level—i.e., the intermediate adopter's own market.

A case in point is the service some plastics manufacturers provide. Plastics are today the archetypal designer material. While choices of metals are limited to a few hundred alloys, there are over 1,000 grades of high-performance plastic material already in existence. Promoting such a variety amounts to helping potential users select what is best for them. No user can possibly be knowledgeable of all the possibilities available. In situations such as this, the onus of proposing material solutions naturally falls on manufacturers. Several companies have already responded to the challenge by establishing computer data bases with information on each of their materials. GE Plastics, for example, started by creating an engineering design data base for internal use in 1986. Properties such as tensile stress-strain, short-term creep, rheology, and fatigue/failure of each plastic were entered into the data base. Interpolative software routines were also built to provide estimates of material performance for conditions not represented in the data. Other software modules were later added to facilitate the design effort, which resulted in a plastics education and trouble-shooting system (PETS). Recently, the knowledge-based PETS was even made available to customers on an on-line basis for diagnosing and solving their molding problems with GE resins.[5]

Another type of service is that of helping customers develop products around a component or materials technology. While some companies do this application development work themselves (see next section), GE Plastics has decided to provide this service on a commercial basis and in partnership with an industrial design firm. Thus, in 1989, it formed a 50/50 partnership with Fitch Richardson Smith (Fitch RS), a design consulting firm based near Columbus, Ohio, to create Polymer Solutions, Inc. (PSI). PSI acts as a catalyst for other companies that wish to develop new products by combining Fitch RS's design know-how and GE's knowledge of thermoplastics. In coming up with recyclable plastic products, for example, PSI typically undertakes the assessment of assembly and manufacturing, the market, disassembly of the used product, and material to be used. In addition, if the client so wishes, it will even do the conceptual design and development work.[6] The choice of an industrial design firm as partner, instead of a design engineering or application development engineering firm, was motivated by the fact that such firms tend to be engaged earliest in a client's product development effort and hence have the greatest leverage when it comes to specifying the overall configuration of final products and the material to be used.

Equally consequential, from a commercialization standpoint, is the service provided to help intermediate adopters sell their end products. This is, for example, what DuPont recently did when targeting its fiber technology to the carpet industry. It surveyed consumers directly to find out what they wanted in the end product, something it had rarely done before. Finding out the need for carpets that were easy to clean, it then developed its Stainmaster carpet fiber. Then, in order to create a "pull" for the product when it was introduced in 1986, it even started to advertise the end product widely, even though it was not itself in the carpet-making business.

Doing Application Development on Behalf of Adopters

Many companies have preferred to undertake application development on their own, or to pay others to do it, because it speeds up commercialization. Thus, when Alcoa decided to promote aluminum bearings in the 1940s based on a new alloy (alloy 750), it first built some prototypes in its research laboratories. Large manufacturers of bearings were, however, reluctant to adopt them. Apart from the normal inertia associated with switching from one technology to another, these companies were discouraged by the special foundry techniques needed to make the new bearings. Alcoa, therefore, took on the task of making all initial bearing castings itself and coming up with the needed process know-how. It was only after the diesel engine companies started to show an interest in aluminum bearings that some bearing companies began taking on the commercialization burden. Only then did Alcoa settle into its material supplier role, advertising the merits of aluminum bearings and making and selling alloy 750.[7]

DuPont, too, has always played a significant role in product development in spite of seeing itself as a materials company. When introducing Kevlar in automobile tires, for example, it even set up a complete tire manufacturing line in its facilities. It did the same for mining ropes, bullet-proof vests, reinforced hoses, and racing car bodies. In fact, in all of the 50-odd applications of Kevlar, the company built complete prototypes as well as the processes needed for manufacturing them.

Such an approach is not restricted to materials companies either. Going a bit further is also what Texas Instruments Inc. did for commercializing its new digital mirror device (DMD) technology, a postage-stamp-size semiconductor covered with 400,000 mirrors that projects images far more efficiently and accurately than liquid crystals or cathode-ray tubes. Developed over five years at a cost of $200 million, DMD's main application is likely to be in high-resolution TVs.

Although mainly a component supplier, TI is taking the technology a few steps downstream on its own. It has contracted with Asian TV-screen makers to develop surfaces that exploit DMD's higher resolution. And rather than sit around hoping that TV makers will take a look, it has built prototypes of everything from portables to wall-size home theaters to grab manufacturers' attention, in effect duplicating almost everything a TV maker would do.[8]

Apart from reducing the cost and risk of adoption, doing such development work on one's own and gaining some intellectual property rights over it serve another important purpose. They permit the licensing of these application-related technologies to a select few, thereby making it more attractive for them to bear the investments and risks associated with further commercialization.

Engaging in Joint Development and Technology Exchanges

Doing the application development work for intermediate adopters can, of course, be expensive. Many companies, therefore, prefer to undertake such development in partnership with customers.

The main drawback of joint development is the potential conflict of interest it creates between the parties. Thus, in the case of new materials, a fabricator customer who does extensive technical development work has the objective of strengthening its own position in the market against existing and potential competitors. The materials producer, on the other hand, often wants to attract a large number of end-product manufacturers into the market to speed market growth and to develop outlets for the material. Occasionally this conflict of interest is manifest in the customer withholding key information from its partner, thus making long-term commercialization effort more difficult.[9]

Technology exchanges, by way of comparison, are more passive and maintain the independence of the parties involved. National Semiconductor's technology-sharing agreement with Xerox in the mid-1980s is a good example. The agreement provided Xerox with access to National's closely guarded design techniques for integrated circuits (ICs) as well as processing technologies. This enabled Xerox to use National's proprietary technology to create custom chips and then make prototype ICs for office systems it was then developing. In return, National got to produce all such chips in commercial quantities—and got to know enough about Xerox's development plans to schedule production according to Xerox's needs.

Mobilizing Manufacturing Partners

A frustration repeatedly expressed by researchers and champions of new technologies is their inability to get the resources needed to ramp up production when they should. Without adequate scale, the technology itself remains uncompetitive in many cases, which makes the creation of demand difficult.

This is where manufacturing partners can play an important role. Although contract manufacturing and original equipment manufacturing (OEM) supply arrangements tend to be associated with mature products, more and more companies are reaching out for manufacturing assistance early in technology commercialization. The agreements they sign tend to be of short duration and are often restricted to one or two early products— enough to "seed" the market quickly and accumulate the resources needed to start manufacturing on their own. Since the company assisting them takes on most of the investment risk, it naturally needs some incentive to play such a bridging role.

Kubota Corporation

An interesting case, which also illustrates the kind of incentives required, is that of the agreements Kubota Corporation of Japan made with a half-dozen start-up companies in the United States between 1985 and 1990. As a long-established manufacturer of steel pipes and farm equipment, Kubota had decided to diversify into more promising fields. One of the fields it chose was computer workstations. To assemble the technologies for this purpose, it bought a minority equity stake (around 20 percent) in companies such as

Stardent Computer, Inc., MIPS Computer Systems, Inc., Exabyte Corporation, Maxoptix Corporation, and Rasna Corporation. Each possessed one of the key enabling technologies needed.

In return for its venture capital investment, Kubota obtained exclusive rights to utilize the technology of its partner companies for a limited period (around ten years) but only in Japan and a couple of neighboring countries. This way it could build its own computer business in its home market without posing a competitive threat to the companies providing it with know-how. Since virtually all of the latter were short of capital, or inexperienced in manufacturing, Kubota also offered to become their global manufacturing partner if they so wanted. Kubota would invest in production facilities on its own and supply end products to them on an OEM basis for markets where they retained the marketing rights. As the CEO of one of the partner companies summarized the benefits of this arrangement, "The partnership with Kubota has worked out very well. They provided human resources when we needed them to support the production program. Although they invested after the product was ready, they had to do a fair amount of manufacturing engineering work, taking our process and designing a high-volume version of it."[10]

Distributors as Technology Partners

Getting access to capable and resource-rich distributors has also been a key to success in certain industries, both in launching a new technology and then in sustaining its commercialization. As more powerful international distributors emerge, this role is likely to increase and cover a broader spectrum of technologies. Unlike agents, these distributors can and do commit a significant amount of resources of their own and bear a significant share of the business risk—much like manufacturing partners.

Because of the investments they are called upon to make, it is natural that they seek an exclusive or, at least, a preferred status for a period of time. One needs to see them as full-fledged partners, rather than as a neutral (even adversary) element in a logistics chain. Some technology must be shared with them to enable them to perform their job effectively.

Different industries have different actors who play a crucial distribution role. In the computer industry, these tend to be system houses and value-added resellers (VARs). In plant and equipment technologies, such as ICI's FM-21 cell, these tend to be engineering contractors who, in addition to retailing the technology, engage in significant design and contract work of their own.

ICI and the FM-21

When ICI decided to make and sell the FM-21 membrane cell for producing chlorine and caustic soda, the company lacked experience in this type of business and had little knowledge of the markets it was seeking to enter. Furthermore, many potential customers were expected to require a range of other engineering services to enable them to install and operate cells; in some cases they might even require complete plants.

While the revenue potential offered by commercializing the FM-21 in this manner was attractive, there was, of course, the danger that much of this gain would be absorbed by building an infrastructure to promote, build, deliver, and install the cells. Since ICI was not in the equipment selling business, this meant creating a totally new organization.

Rather than do that, the route ICI took was to engage engineering contractors to help it sell the FM-21. Only two "preferred" contractors— Catalytic and Chemetics—were appointed so as to give them some incentive for prospecting for business on ICI's behalf and to develop the needed capability in a new technology. Both these contractors had experience and established contacts in the chlorine business. In addition to helping ICI promote the FM-21, they became responsible for the basic and detailed engineering needed for installing the cell within a plant as well as acting as turnkey contractors.

Promoting the Supply of Complementary or Joint Products

As with the Sulzer HRA case discussed earlier in this chapter, there are several technologies whose marketing calls for the simultaneous availability of certain complementary products. Unless the latter are available on time, the technology itself becomes a nonstarter or, at best, gets restricted to a narrow market.

Mobilizing suppliers of complementary products follows the same general logic of incentive creation and value sharing as with other delivery partners. However, since most such suppliers possess their own enabling technologies, they tend to be less dependent on whatever the initiator of a new system has to offer. What they seek is a way to commercialize *their* technology. Thus, in the case of Sulzer's HRA, conversion kit manufacturers had no special preference for CNG as a fuel. Instead, most kept their options open, developing multifuel systems so that they would be well positioned no matter which technology came to be accepted. Even if Sulzer were to develop a dedicated CNG kit for them and give it to them for nothing, it is unlikely there would have been many takers.

Getting independent suppliers of complementary products to back a new system, therefore, means selling them on the potential of the overall business first. One needs to outline an attractive vision and strategy, within which each contributor recognizes a profitable role for itself. The more this vision is supplemented by help in getting started, the easier the task.

One company that has been particularly successful in doing this recently is 3DO, Inc., of San Mateo, California. Founded in 1991 to commercialize a new interactive multiplayer for multimedia use, it not only had to confront nine other competing technologies but also a reluctance on the part of the major product and service suppliers to align themselves with a particular technology. Most of them, in fact, had invested in several start-up companies so as to be well positioned, no matter which technology eventually turned into the "industry standard."

Part of 3DO's success in mobilizing several companies to support its format was due to the vision of its founder, Trip Hawkins, and the persuasiveness with which he communicated it. Rather than presenting the company's first player as an enhanced video game apparatus—which is how some in the industry saw it—he positioned it as a platform for consumers to derive all of the benefits multimedia technology had to offer. Hooked to a conventional TV set, the 3DO interactive multiplayer would allow people to listen to CD-quality music, watch cinema-quality films, learn from education software, and eventually navigate their way through the numerous television channels being offered—all interactively. What Hawkins did, in effect, was to present 3DO's technology as an enduring basic technology, one that would evolve gradually into something much bigger, benefiting both consumers and those who supplied products for its realization.

This vision, combined with 3DO's approach to sharing its technology liberally with those who prepared to help with its realization, quickly led a large number of major companies to align themselves with the new technology, albeit not exclusively. The simple fact of their buying an option on 3DO's technology was endorsement enough for others to join in over a period of time.

The approach 3DO took consisted in prototyping all system components on its own; licensing all of these components to others better equipped to supply them; and concentrating its own resources on technology development, marketing, and participating in whichever part of the system might need an initial push.

For example, 3DO licensed one of its partners, Matsushita Electric Industrial Co., Ltd., to manufacture and sell the 3DO Interactive Multiplayer on a nonexclusive but royalty-free basis. All the company charged was a $10,000 fee for each hardware design to certify that the design met the technical standards set by 3DO for that product and was compatible with its system. In fact, to promote the adoption of the 3DO technology as an industry standard, the company even offered incentive payments based on U.S. shipments of the Multiplayer during the period 1993 to 1995. The proprietary chipset to be used in the player was also licensed to companies such as AT&T and ARM on a nonexclusive basis for a nominal royalty.

The company's approach to developers of software titles was equally generous. To assist software developers, it sold them a complete development system consisting of the hardware prototype, an operating system, and a variety of software products—all for under $10,000. It also offered them royalty-free access to its own multimedia data base, from which they could pick and choose. Unlike some other video game companies, it placed no restrictions on the number of titles they developed and produced or the content of these titles.

With so much change occurring in the delivery systems for multimedia software, the company also has an open mind regarding who its partners might be. If, for example, the dominant trend becomes delivering software through cable TV networks instead of CD-ROM, the company will be prepared to license a network version of its 3DO system as well.

The profits of 3DO are expected to come from license income, mainly from software developers. The latter will pay 3DO $3.00 for each CD-ROM they press, regardless of the retail price of their software, which can range from $50 for simple video games all the way to $1,000 for interactive encyclopedias packaged in multiple CDs. The result of this strategy was that by mid-1994, 3DO had lined up a half-dozen licensees of its interactive multiplayer, over two hundred potential providers of software as well as a number of major companies to develop and supply peripheral products and telecommunication services for its technology. Although the company was less successful in the marketplace than it hoped, this was an impressive achievement for a start-up company in a highly contested and rapidly changing industry.

ALIGNING WITH ADVOCACY GROUPS AND ARBITRATORS

In some cases, simply seeking the support of delivery partners on one's own can prove inadequate and even counterproductive. Competition among different groups, each hoping to establish its own technology, can lead to confusion among potential customers and long delays in commercialization. A more rewarding stance in such situations is to reach out to "neutral" arbitrators and advocates *before* campaigning to mobilize other companies to push one's own technology. In practice, this can mean offering the technology as a basis for an open industry standard, aligning with some noncontesting companies that can influence the outcome, or falling in line with a government initiative aimed at promoting a certain type of technology.

Industry Standards Bodies

Externally mediated standards tend to be of two main types: those having to do with public safety or the use of scarce national resources—such as for drug efficacy, environmental pollution, or the use of the radio spectrum—and those that relate to the interoperability between different elements of these systems. While the former tend to be mandatory and serve the public interest at large, the latter are usually voluntary and driven by the need for companies to put compatible (or interoperable) products on the market.

Either way, a widely agreed-on standard acts as an endorsement, facilitating both consumer acceptance and the mobilization of various market constituents. It reduces market confusion and, by virtue of being "open," ensures that basic products relating to it will be offered at competitive prices from the beginning. Only value-enhancing features that consumers can judge for themselves, and are compatible with the standards, will enjoy a premium in the market.

The question any proponent of a new system-related technology needs to answer is, of course, how open to be. Except for standards in the public interest, one has a choice between offering the technology to an entire industry or restricting it to oneself or a handful of partner companies who contribute to its realization, in the hope of eventually establishing it as a de facto standard. Which of the two paths to take in a given situation depends on the power and reputation of the company (or companies) sponsoring the technology as well as the importance consumers attach to an industry-wide open standard. A coalition among major players can indeed impose a de facto standard at an equipment level, but that does not always translate into interest on the part of consumers, especially in rapidly obsolescing technologies.

C-Cube, Inc., is one company that has leveraged its participation in industry standards bodies to become a leader in the image compression/decompression field. While Intel was working on its proprietary Digital Video Interactive (DVI) system and Philips and Sony worked jointly on their own Compact Disc Interactive (CD-I) system, C-Cube took the external standard route.

Founded in 1988, C-Cube immediately joined the two Expert Groups set up by the International Organization for Standardization (ISO) to create international standards for data compression—the Joint Photographic Expert Group (JPEG) for still image compression and the Moving Pictures Expert Group (MPEG) for video images. Certain features of its basic technology were accepted by both groups, giving C-Cube a lead-time advantage when it came to developing products. When the JPEG standard was announced in 1990, C-Cube was ready with the first single-chip processor to implement the standard. It was also the first to develop an MPEG compatible chip a couple of years later. With companies around the world rallying around the ISO standards, C-Cube's sales of processors and associated kits grew from $45 million in 1994 to $320 million in 1996. In September 1995 C-Cube also became the first chip manufacturer to win an Emmy award in recognition of its superior technology.

The point to note about contributing one's technology to an open standard is that open standards are usually framed in generic terms only. What allowed C-Cube to dominate the data compression/decompression market was partly the lead-time advantage it enjoyed as a member of the group creating the standard. Equally important was its *proprietary* chip technology and design capability for *implementing* the standard cost-effectively and the fact that it had conceived of specific *applications* of the generic technology in advance. In line with the discussion earlier in the chapter, C-Cube had also taken steps to motivate those developing applications by offering assistance and reasonably priced development kits ahead of competition.

Standards are a double-edged sword. They can help establish a technology quickly, but they can also lead to its commoditization earlier than would otherwise happen. As the C-Cube example illustrates, the best way to resort to them is to formulate one's own business strategy carefully in advance, and to make sure that one possesses some unique know-how regarding how the standard will be implemented in practice.

Noncontestants as Arbitrators

In situations where competitors have no interest in coming together on a common approach, the best option is to mobilize certain third parties to arbitrate. The most receptive people or organizations to play this role are those that desire a solution quickly but have no vested interest in the nature of the solution. The problem, in many cases, is that such noncontestants are often prepared to wait out the technology battle until a winner is decided. One needs to be imaginative in finding out and influencing those that do want a resolution quickly.

There are two types of noncontestants with the potential to influence which technology gets established based on the choice they make—resource-rich lead users and powerful delivery partners.

The combination of endorsement through investment and acting as a first lead user has played a crucial role for many small companies introducing a new technology. The experience of Qualcomm, Inc., is a case in point. Although best known for its OmniTRACs satellite communications system for monitoring long-haul truck fleets, Qualcomm has been trying since 1989 to market a new digital wireless communication technology based on code division multiple access (CDMA). Compared to analog systems, CDMA allows several calls to be sent down a single frequency channel instead of just one. The rival time division multiple access (TDMA) technology assigns time slots to callers so several can use a single channel at one time, but it does not allow as much frequency reuse as CDMA.

Although no one has disputed CDMA's theoretical superiority over analog and TDMA for cellular networks, Qualcomm had not been able to supply a single network for six years because of delays in implementing the technology. Meanwhile, it had to scale back its claims as well—from being able to carry forty times as many conversations as an analog system to twenty and then to ten. While this still gives CDMA a 3 to 1 advantage over TDMA, the latter has already found commercial use in Europe and the United States.

What has sustained Qualcomm is its close association with major U.S. telecommunication companies. AirTouch, the leading supplier of cellular services in California, not only gave the company its first commercial contract but, in June 1995, persuaded PCS PrimeCo (a consortium of Nynex Corp., Bell Atlantic Corp., U.S. West, Inc., and AirTouch) to use CDMA in its planned nationwide personal communications services network. Having given a license to large equipment suppliers such as Motorola, Inc., AT&T Corp., and Northern Telecom, Ltd., it also benefited from the lobbying the latter did vis-à-vis network operators.

In contrast with the CDMA technology, it is noncontestant delivery partners who played the key role in deciding how video-CD (known as digital video disc, or DVD) technology got established.

Ever since Sony and Philips proposed their joint system on December 16, 1994, others in the industry have riposted with competing claims as to the superiority of their own technology. Rather than pay Sony and Philips royalties by adopting their standard passively, they would prefer to establish their own standard, or at least an "open" one in which no firm gains a proprietary advantage.

The main competing technology was that of Toshiba. Compared to the Sony-Philips system based on multiple discs, each with 72 minutes of video capacity, it was able to play 270 minutes on a single disc by storing data on both sides of the disc.

The key arbitrators, in the beginning, were felt to be the software providers (Hollywood) and companies like Matsushita—the former in order to sell their products and to avoid copyright violations, and the latter as a powerful manufacturing licensee. As the owner of MCA, Inc., Matsushita, in fact, had a dual interest.

In the end, both camps decided to unify their standards, partly at the urging of yet another noncontestant group, the Technical Working Group of the computer industry, which includes companies like Microsoft, IBM, Hewlett-Packard, and Fujitsu. With an interest mainly in making entertainment and data formats compatible, the Technical Working Group did not actually endorse one standard over another. Rather, it urged the two sides to resolve their conflicts as soon as possible to avoid an all-out format war.[11]

Governments as Arbitrators and Advocates

One reason why European companies have dominated the burgeoning field of digital cellular communications since 1991 is their early start in establishing a collective standard for the technology, the Groupe Special Mobile (GSM) standard. While the United States preferred to wait until the market decided what "ought" to be the standard, the Europeans went ahead and agreed on an "early standard" under the aegis of the Conférence Européenne des Postes et Télécommunication (CEPT).

Governments, in other words, can play a dual role in the initiation of new system technologies. They can arbitrate standards as well as advocate a particular technology by influencing the time at which these standards are introduced and by providing other assistance helpful to its realization.

HDTV

A good illustration of how governments can play this dual role is found in the development of high-definition TV since the mid-1980s.

The origins of HDTV go as far back as 1964, when Japan Broadcasting Corp. (NHK) began defining a third-generation television system. The technical specifications drawn up at that time were far ahead of technological possibilities then available, but they remained substantially unchanged for more than two decades. They acted as a spur to a number of companies in Japan, which by the early 1980s could demonstrate working prototypes of the complete system, ranging from recording to broadcasting to television receivers and even videocassette recorders. Characteristically, the effort was led by NHK and other Japanese government agencies, which together invested some $400 million; private industry was given specific projects to undertake by NHK but put in more than $1 billion of its own resources in the venture.

The Japanese prepared a satellite-based multiple sub-Nyquist sample encoding (MUSE) system. As the only one ready in 1986, it was nearly adopted as a world standard by the International Radio Consultative Committee (CCIR) at its meeting in Dubrovnik, Yugoslavia, that year. The official reason for rejecting it was that it was not backward compatible, meaning that MUSE signals could not be picked up by existing sets without a special and presumably expensive adapter. Most observers, however, felt the real reason was protectionism, on the part of both Europeans, who wanted a standard of their own, and the United States, which saw HDTV as an opportunity to reenter the consumer electronics industry.

Since that time a number of forces have kept the HDTV system from being commercialized, most having to do with mobilizing the needed delivery infrastructure. As summarized in Figure 7-3, a number of different stakeholders, each with its own vision of the system and its own interests, had to be co-opted.

The main reasons for the delayed introduction of HDTV lie in the divergent interests of those who want to make and sell the sets and of suppliers of complementary products and services. While the former see nothing but opportunities in having consumers buy a new type of TV and the demand for components this will create, the latter have been concerned by the cost of conversion they will have to bear and, depending on the time horizon, the futility of the whole exercise.

According to some estimates, TV stations, the major broadcast

FIGURE 7-3

THE MARKET CONSTITUENTS FOR THE INTRODUCTION OF **HDTV** TECHNOLOGY

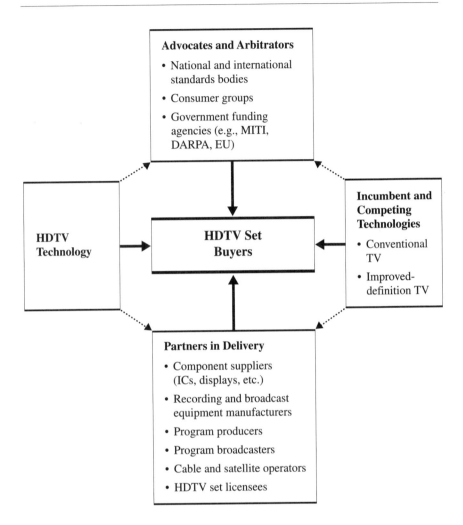

networks, cable channels, and local cable systems would have to spend $15 billion to $20 billion to achieve HDTV capability in the United States alone. While that amount is small compared with the $68 billion that consumers would have to spend to buy new sets, the estimates came at a time when many American viewers were deserting commercial network television in favor of cable channels and videocassette recorders. Consumers were apparently more interested in program quality than in technology. Addressing the latter alone would not coax viewers back to network television.[12]

Opinion was divided on whether the added expense of high definition would bring in new advertising revenues or would end up as an upgrade necessary to prevent further audience erosion. The concern of television networks was shared by broadcasters. In Europe, for example, despite a European Commission directive issued in 1986 to make the newly defined European HDTV standard mandatory for satellite broadcasts, Sky Television decided to stay with the earlier PAL (phase alternation line) standard when it began broadcasting over the Astra satellite in 1989. While the official reason given was that equipment manufacturers had not moved quickly enough to produce the technology, again the additional cost involved seemed to have been the real issue.

In the face of such disagreement between the commercial actors involved, it is natural for third parties to play a decisive role. Two roles are, in fact, sometimes needed—an *advocacy* role, which promotes the technology explicitly as desirable or funds its development, and an *arbitration* role, which facilitates the commercial parties' involved working together by, for example, imposing standards. In the case of HDTV, both roles needed to be performed.

How, and to what extent, this dual role ought to be performed has varied from one country (or region) to another based on economic ideology, with consequences for the speed with which HDTV has been established.

As in other fields in recent decades, the advocacy role of the Japanese government has been most active and consequential. Support from the Ministry of Posts and Telecommunications (through a thirty-one-member council of broadcasters, manufacturers, and customers) as well as from MITI has convinced all those involved in creating an HDTV system that the country's standard is immutable and that, even though the consumer market is still several years off, companies can start working on the various pieces of equipment needed. While the standard they worked on may not have been the most advanced, Japanese companies were the first to come up with a working HDTV system on a national level.

Next were the Europeans. Following the rejection of MUSE in 1986, the European Community had its own HDTV standard designed in 1987, called MAC (multiplexed analog components). Developed by Philips and Thomson, the MAC standard was based on 1,250 lines and the same transmission rate as the Japanese MUSE. It was also an analog system but, unlike MUSE, was designed to be backwardly compatible so that existing TV sets could receive the high-definition signals as well. In addition, to ease the transition from conventional systems, the Europeans announced an intermediate standard, called D2-MAC, based on 625 lines but with HDTV's 16-to-9 screen aspect ratio (instead of 4 to 3 as found in conventional TV sets).

To promote the development and acceptance of the MAC standard, the European Commission first spent some $500 million on R&D subsidies. Then, in 1990, it began to induce television companies and cable and satellite operators to switch to D2-MAC by drawing up a draft Memorandum of

Understanding (MOU) comprising clearly defined commitments for each of the key players (cable and satellite operators, broadcasters, producers and equipment manufacturers) to promote D2-MAC. In exchange for these commitments, the commission offered financial support of 500 million to 1 billion ECUs over five years. The aim was to incite all satellite operators to broadcast in the present standards and D2-MAC simultaneously (simulcasting) as of April 1992. New satellite TV companies launched after April 1992 were obliged to broadcast exclusively in D2-MAC, no matter the size of the market. Similarly, all TV sets with screens of more than 52 cm and all receiving equipment (aerials) placed on the market after January 1, 1993, would have to have a decoder to receive broadcasts in D2-MAC. Once true HDTV began, these D2-MAC sets would be able to receive HD-MAC as well by adding another decoder.

The Americans, in contrast, preferred to focus only on the arbitration role, with Congress refusing to fund the billions of dollars in aid U.S. companies sought to catch up with the Japanese and Europeans. About the time the Europeans defined their standards in 1987, the U.S. Federal Communications Commission (FCC) also set up an industry-funded advisory committee to rule on a U.S. standard. While aiming for backward compatibility like the Europeans, the FCC approached it through open competition among different concepts with the goal of selecting the "best available" technology for the system by the end of 1992. It was also the first to show preference for a completely digital concept, including digital transmission —with Japan's MUSE and Europe's HD-MAC ruled out in consequence.

In December 1996, the FCC finally agreed to a U.S. standard based on a technology developed by a consortium of private companies called Grand Alliance. As expected, it was mainly a framework standard, letting the market decide what display formats and products to design. In addition to being the most advanced, it is the most versatile in the sense of incorporating the needs of the computer industry as well as those of the TV industry. But the first products and services are not expected to be launched before 1998, long after the Japanese have had a taste of HDTV and the Europeans a taste of near-HDTV, based on their respective government roles.

Clearly, the role governments play in both arbitrating technical standards and advocating particular technologies can be crucial to the pace at which and the form in which a particular technology gets commercialized. The agenda governments follow can also result in unintended and unexpected endorsement of particular technologies. It is important to anticipate this agenda, often long in advance, so as to be on the right side of its rulings.

Dealing with Incumbent Technologies and Competitors

Both sets of stakeholders described so far (delivery partners and advocates) are generally sought after by competitors selling an incumbent technology as well. Confronting competitors head on, however, is neither desirable nor necessary, especially when the new technology can offer fresh market opportunities to many of them as well. Unlike the situation in mature, commodity products, where competitive battles can be zero-sum games, a new technology often creates possibilities for all to gain.

There are two ways of dealing with the obstructive role competitors play: bypassing them by going to another territory and creating a different infrastructure or co-opting some of them by offering a share of the business on favorable terms.

Bypassing Competition and the Captured Infrastructure

As pointed out in earlier chapters, many inventions require not just complementary technologies but an elaborate infrastructure before they can be fully commercialized. To the extent that the existing infrastructure can accommodate the new technology, the easier the task—provided competitors do not have a lock on it. If they do, the best option is to find ways of bypassing it.

A new technology often provides the means for bypassing an infrastructure already in place. This was, for example, the case with Sony's introduction of transistor radios in the U.S. market in the late 1950s. Since the new technology practically dispensed with the service requirements associated with vacuum tubes, Sony could sidestep existing sales channels that were controlled by the major U.S. electronics firms.

Sony has done the same with its HDTV venture more recently. Having entered the field in 1970, it quickly realized that the real constraint on the technology's commercialization was not likely to be its cost but rather the technical problems of transmission and, as discussed earlier, the reluctance of software producers and broadcasters to switch. Sony concentrated instead on the base-band part of the business, which was free from the transmission constraint and which did not depend on the cooperation of producers and broadcasters involved in commercial television. It targeted its recording and viewing HDTV technologies to applications such as home video, museums (which could display artistic work on HDTV screens along with audio commentary on what the work represented), corporate communications (video conferencing), computer-assisted design workstations, and hospitals and universities (for visualizing intricate operations, for example).

Co-opting Competitors

In some industries, the problem is not so much one of infrastructure access but customer access. With new technologies being offered to them all the time they have difficulty choosing what to buy and even whether to buy anything at all. C. H. Weijsenfeld, Program Coordination Manager at Philips Research, calls this problem market selection:

In the electronics industry today you can virtually make anything you think of by combining IC and software technology. Every big company has ten different things it thinks are marketable but only three of them can actually be accepted by the market on economic grounds. What these three are is hard to say on purely technical grounds, so the industry ends up testing all ten. The result is that we now see companies discussing among themselves in order to prevent too many products being launched that no one profits from.[13]

Co-opting comptetitors for a particular technology also has the effect of aligning other market constituents in its favor. As Weijsenfeld continues:

In flat panel displays . . . being first is sometimes better than having the best technology. But equally important is the industrial base supporting a technology. Thus, for example, the plasma display may not be the best technology in terms of intensity, efficiency, or cost, but the mere fact that a large number of Japanese companies are putting their weight behind it may turn it into an unconquerable option for someone who comes along with something better a bit later.[14]

The manner in which competitors can be mobilized around one's technology is usually circumscribed by the antitrust laws prevailing in a country. In general, such concerted action is acceptable if it is mainly at the technology level, does not hinder product-market competition later, and can be shown to benefit consumers.

These principles usually translate into broad early licensing, preferably on a nonexclusive basis. This is, for example, what Sun Microsystem, Inc., did with its RISC technology. Soon after it developed its scalable processor architecture (SPARC) with the help of computer scientists from the University of California at Berkeley, it licensed the technology to all comers, denying itself a potentially valuable lead over competition. Sun was, in fact, the first to unveil its central processing unit (CPU) architecture to the industry on a license and royalty basis. Although this meant that Sun would be only one among several SPARC vendors, it contributed to a rapid acceptance of the technology in the market. Customers liked the idea, too, since it reassured them that Sun would not be able to raise prices as the new technology gained market share; competitors, which Sun itself had created, would move in with better price and performance if that happened.

The need to mobilize competitors is especially great for radically new technologies as illustrated by Eastman Kodak's so-called smart film camera. Unlike traditional films made from cellulose triacetate requiring methylene chloride (a carcinogen), the film is made out of polyester and comes with magnetic strips that record data on when and under what conditions a photo is taken. This information is not only useful to the photographer but can be used by photofinishing equipment (compatible with the new technology) to produce clearer prints than is otherwise possible. The film, moreover, comes in a cartridge the size of an AA battery that dispenses with the need for threading. Finally, the point-and-shoot camera itself is thin enough to carry in a pocket, increasing the chances that people will use it more often than they do larger cameras.

In 1992—four years prior to the expected launch of the new system in 1996—while Kodak was still developing the technology, it recruited Fuji Photo Film, Canon, Nikon, and Minolta Camera as partners. All companies shared the patents underlying the technology, covering the camera, film, and photofinishing equipment, but would name, manufacture, and market their own products. The royalties that others adopting the system later payed were also to be shared by these initial partners.

Given the stagnant state of the conventional 35 mm camera market, Kodak really had no other choice in introducing a new system. Attracting the main camera, film, and photofinishing equipment manufacturers to promote the technology increased the chances of presenting consumers with a *single* new change. This left customers as the only, albeit the most important, stakeholders to decide whether they wanted the new technology or not, based on the added value and lower costs it offered.[15]

FINDING SYNERGY AMONG CONSTITUENTS—AT A POINT IN TIME

Mobilizing market constituents is a competitive endeavor in which several new technology proponents compete for the same set of stakeholders. With everyone promising the prospect for buying into a standard and realizing additional value, many constituents are reluctant to commit quickly and fully to one technology—unless, of course, it has large, demonstrable advantages over the others. Rather than aligning themselves proactively with a particular technology and risking their own investments, they prefer to wait until others have bought in first and the economics of the overall system becomes truly compelling.

Proponents of a new technology are sometimes better off not forcing the outcome under such circumstances. Forcing can prove expensive in terms of the incentives that need to be created. A better approach is to exercise some creativity in terms of the package being presented and to wait for the moment when one can identify greater self-interest on the part of the stakeholders themselves, thereby creating a synergy among them voluntarily.

Belland AG

This need for stakeholder synergy and timing one's approach to it is best illustrated by what Belland AG is doing with its intelligent plastics technology today. Despite an active program of interest and resource mobilization throughout the 1980s, the company could achieve only a series of test and development agreements with a number of companies. The one or two that worked out and in which the partner exercised its option to take a license on the technology were in small, niche applications, such as bottle labels. These applications mainly leveraged the technology's water solubility feature, rather than its broader environmental advantages.

It was in the environment domain, however, where the main potential of the technology lay, particularly in the packaging field. This is where the company could sell large quantities of its intelligent plastics and where it could combine its features of water solubility on demand and recyclability. But this field proved elusive for many years. Companies making packaging products found no economic advantage in switching to the Belland material, not least because it was untried and more expensive than conventional plastics. The environmental argument appealed to them intellectually, but they saw little reason to adopt Belland's material in a world where there was an inadequate infrastructure for collecting and sorting out waste packaging material and where landfills and incineration were the dominant methods of waste disposal.

The turning point for Belland occurred in Germany in 1991 when that country passed new legislation concerning packaging materials. Under this legislation, manufacturers were required to ensure that 80 percent of all packaging material got collected and that 80 percent of this amount was recycled by July 1, 1995. While the collection/recycling ratio for paper and plastic was set lower than, for example, glass and tinplate, it was nevertheless orders of magnitude higher than what the industry had become used to.

Because this was an industrywide legislation, some 600 companies got together to create a collection and recycling organization called Duales System Deutschland (DSD). The latter was financed by a fee paid by the companies concerned—which was passed on to consumers buying packaged goods marked with a green dot. While DSD solved the collection problem, it did not address the recyclability issue. A large portion of the waste it collected and sorted was either incinerated or sent overseas for disposal. The plastic that was recycled resulted in low-value products—such as construction material and park benches—making it unprofitable to recycle.

This was Belland's opportunity. Not only could its plastic be easily separated (by dissolving) but it lent itself to easy recycling back to the virgin material with little or no degradation. It was this ease of recycling and the prospects for producing higher-value recycled products that the company began to stress—in addition to the lower total energy cost of its system.

Exploiting this opportunity required Roland Belz to reconfigure his business concept and to create a new alignment among the various stakeholders concerned by the issue. Figure 7-4 summarizes what Belland is trying to achieve.

The company's strategy involves aligning the interests of three sets of

FIGURE 7-4

FINDING SYNERGY AMONG MARKET CONSTITUENTS AT A POINT IN TIME—
BELLAND'S INTELLIGENT PLASTICS

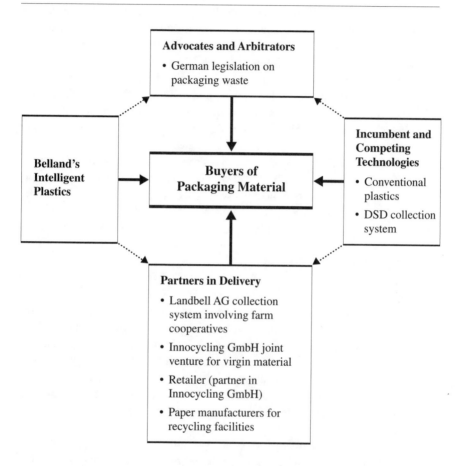

stakeholders. One relates to the collection system itself. With DSD not geared to collect and recycle Belland's material in preference to others, the company has started to create an alternative system for paper and plastic packaging mainly. A new company, Landbell AG, has been formed in partnership with farm cooperatives in Germany. Farmers, who now pay a large fee to DSD, are motivated to join this parallel collection system for two reasons: they can use their own vehicles for waste collection after delivering goods to the market, and they can earn some money from the higher-value Belland recycled material instead of just paying DSD to get rid of their waste.

In addition to neutralizing competition at the collection level, Belland has mobilized two different delivery partners. One is a large German retail organization that wants a cheaper solution to the packaging waste problem it confronts. This company has formed a joint venture with Belland to produce commercial quantities of the virgin material (Innocycling GmbH), which will supply packaging material to companies providing its retail outlets with goods.

The other pertains to the recycling system. For this, Belland teamed with a few paper companies that face the same challenge. As it happens, paper and plastic waste tend to be colocated, and both need recycling. The technology of paper recycling, moreover, lends itself well to Belland material. By taking the two together to a paper mill, the idea is to first wash away organic waste and hard objects from both materials. Following this, coarse paper fibers are filtered out in a filter press. Belland's polymer molecules, which are considerably smaller in size than paper fiber, get drained off into a follow-on tank, where they are precipitated out. Getting paper companies to use their existing recycling facilities saves Belland the time and expense of building its own dedicated facilities and at the same time brings one more partner into its collection system. For paper companies, partnering with Belland offers greater throughput in the recycling plants they need to construct with minimal changes in the way these plants are configured.

SUMMARY

Even products that are well conceived and developed sometimes have difficulty gaining market acceptance. This has more to do with the way they are launched and delivered than their intrinsic merit from an end-user standpoint. Developing a market for them involves orchestrating the contribution of several constituents—notably potential partners for delivering the technology's full benefit, competitors commercializing an incumbent technology, and various independent advocates whose role is critical for which technology gets accepted.

Mobilizing these market constituents requires an analysis of a new product's entire business system and the identification of the actors influencing it at each stage. While many inventors aspire to change the way the industry works, this is an ambition they often regret later. A less valorous but more consequential attitude is one that takes the industry structure as a given and works within it.

Aligning the interests of various market constituents is fundamentally about sharing some benefits with them. In practice, this usually means sharing some technology and part of the value created, building incentives by doing some work with them, and lobbying independent advocates who are neutral to the outcome but have their own agenda to pursue. The more radical the technology, the greater this need for mobilizing a wide range of market constituents.

8

PROMOTING ADOPTION

WHEN EMI FIRST INTRODUCED ITS CT SCANNER IN 1973, IT ANTICIPATED selling no more than ten to fifteen pieces of this $500,000 equipment a year. As it turned out, the demand was orders of magnitude larger and the adoption of the new technology among the fastest the world has ever seen. By 1976, annual sales had reached 470 scanners in the United States alone. Attracted by this potential, eight new companies had entered the business by then too.

What the CT scanner illustrates is the power of a breakthrough technology fulfilling a major need at the time it is offered. It illustrates a well-conceived and -demonstrated technology creating its own pull.

Most apparently useful new technologies are actually not as fortunate as EMI was with the CT scanner. In fact, more typical is the experience of Texas Instruments Inc. (TI) with its digital signal processor (DSP) technology. Although the DSP was developed with several potential applications in mind in the early 1980s, it took TI seven years to get the technology fully accepted by engineers who had to design products around it.

The promotion strategy involved orchestrating many things. To educate the market and influence opinion leaders, TI began by working with university professors, providing them with tools to help graduate and undergraduate engineering students understand the complex mathematics behind digital signal processing. In addition to training the next generation of design engineers, university professors were seen as a conduit for spreading use of the technology in their role as consultants. This educational effort was supplemented by an aggressive public relations campaign, announcing product applications under development and submitting case histories and how-to articles for publication. Finally, to facilitate the actual use of the technology, the company invested heavily in application development. This took various forms. It worked shoulder-to-shoulder with engineers on job sites, provided them with development tools and access to a round-the-clock technical support hot line, and it mobilized third-party support in developing new DSP-based applications to sustain enthusiasm in the technology.[1]

Regardless of how well they are conceived and demonstrated, and regardless of the market constituents mobilized around them, most technology-based products need to be "sold," often to skeptical and unenthusiastic customers. Many delays and failures are known to occur at this stage.

Marketing people have long learned to distinguish between the extent to which markets are "discovered" versus "created." Those who tend toward the "discovery" argument are constantly on the lookout for ripe opportunities for having the technology adopted. They look for niches that open up, sometimes unexpectedly, and create a pull for the technology. All the techniques described for eliciting buyer preferences in the design of products are based on this latent pull.

Those who tend toward the view that markets need to be created, not discovered, begin with a different premise altogether. For them, except in the most straightforward cases of product substitution, there is no obvious need waiting to be fulfilled. Needs have to be prompted and evoked. If there is a "fuzzy front end" to product development, having to do with linking the technology to products, there is an even fuzzier back end after the products have been developed. Customers don't necessarily perceive the same things in a product as an inventor does, and no amount of predevelopment market research can substitute for a sensitive and active orchestration of the promotion strategy *after* the product is ready.

Naturally, both the market discovery and market creation viewpoints represent extremes. A better stance is to see successful product launches as falling somewhere in between, requiring a combination of reading the market right initially followed by active steps to create demand and to reduce the resistance technology-based products encounter after launch. Such an in-between viewpoint is close to the notion of market enactment. As John Seely Brown of Xerox PARC puts it, "You don't invent or discover a market. Innovation lies as much in the head of the entrepreneur as in the real world. By enacting a market you create new competitive spaces."

The word "enacting" has the same connotation as when used in the context of a drama or play—a complex, culturally bound experience involving the playwright and actors as well as the audience. The test of great drama is how far it can take the spectators beyond their own immediate reality and to what use this imaginative release can be put. The purpose is to involve and to influence an audience, not imposing a meaning but allowing it to arise from the interaction of the audience with the actors.

Market enactment is about being empathetic to the current circumstances of buyers and adapting the promotion strategy through interactions with them. In practical terms this means adapting the "product" offered so as to stimulate demand; exercising flexibility in positioning the technology, even if it means some departure from the factors considered during the design phase; pricing for early adoption; targeting the technology to receptive segments; and building an effective communication and influence strategy to gain wide acceptance as quickly as possible.

Figure 8-1 summarizes the main components of each of these to illustrate what a technology promotion strategy encompasses.

ADAPTING THE PRODUCT

Unlike the tradition of most diffusion-of-innovation studies,[2] technology-based products should not be seen as a "given," which then have to be somehow made to be "adopted" by different categories of individuals. Rather, it is more appropriate to see the "product" itself as a variable, much as industrial marketeers do. Which facet of the technology is offered, the way it is configured, and the bundle of benefits it provides—all need to be adapted to what customers require at the time of launch and the competitive dynamics in the marketplace prevailing then.

Broadly speaking, there are three types of product adaptations sometimes needed: making the product conform to existing patterns of use; making the technology invisible when targeting a certain category of customers; and adapting the facet of the technology offered to the nature of demand at the point in time.

Conforming to Existing Patterns of Use

Buyers are seldom voluntary participants in things signifying major changes for them. Apart from any risk they may perceive in adopting a new technology, they are reluctant to change from current practices or routines. It is not that they are lazy and averse to learning. It is simply that habits constitute a psychological equilibrium between time-tested beliefs and devices already being used.[3] Breaking them requires a cognitive effort that any new device must justify first.

Habits are hard to overcome not just because of familiarity and the need to "unlearn" a tried process but also due to deeper roots—people find value in an existing mode of consumption that goes beyond the simple utility of the object. They buy newspapers in order to walk over to a newsstand. They call a stockbroker to chat about the condition of the economy.

FIGURE 8-1

THE MAIN COMPONENTS OF A STRATEGY TO PROMOTE NEW TECHNOLOGIES

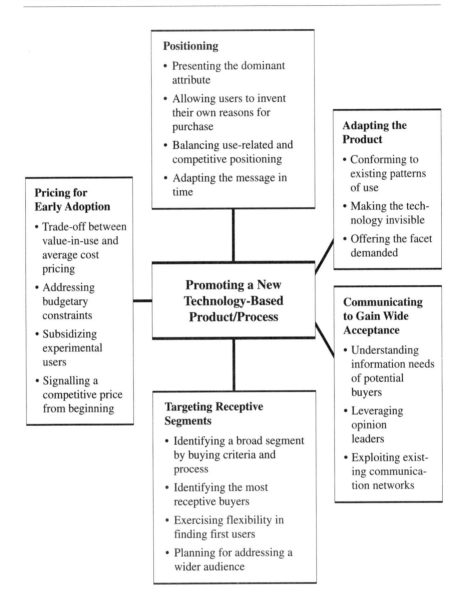

These broad symbolic needs are actually the most difficult to change. Take telemarketing or home banking as an example. Part of the initial resistance to this technology came from entrenched habits of traveling to stores and banks, which had as much to do with social contact and a recreational break from the main occupation as with convenience and cost effectiveness.

Maintaining control over the risk of transactions played a role in the early stages of introduction too.

These barriers apply as much to individuals as to organization buyers, as illustrated by the experience of Lasarray SA. Founded in 1983, this Swiss company had developed a laser-based system for quickly generating prototypes for ASICs (application-specific integrated circuits). Once a customer approved the prototype, the system prepared a chromium mask that could then be transferred to a conventional mass-production facility to produce the ASIC in volume.

Although well designed and cost-effective, Lasarray's system failed in the market. One reason was the fear that the mass-produced version would not have all the characteristics of the tested prototype since it relied on a different manufacturing process. An equally intangible reason was the habit customers had developed in procuring their ASICs. They knew who the outside suppliers were, their terms, and the service they provided, and they had established efficient procurement routines for dealing with them. Buying an ASIC fabrication equipment from Lasarray meant defining and creating a new set of internal procedures, including things like transfer pricing and priorities. Although seemingly trivial, this move from well-understood outsourcing to a captive supply unit became an important source of resistance.

The complaint by many inventors about the conservatism around them is mainly a reflection of their ignorance of cognitive psychology and the work of social psychologists over the past several decades. Human beings *are* physiologically and psychologically limited. They do have difficulty handling complexity; they tend to adapt only gradually to change, overconform to group and organizational norms, and limit their focus to repetitive activities.[4] Rather than complain about it, or excessively promote something that goes against the grain of human nature, a better course is to assess the extent of such resistance and adapt a technology's introduction accordingly.

What this means in practice is not presenting all inventions as "paradigm shifts," however much an inventor thinks such a billing is warranted. The contrary is less heroic but more rewarding. Products incorporating a new technology ought to be presented as better substitutes for what is already being used, augmenting and supporting existing products, and, where appropriate, usable with little disruption to familiar products and systems.

Promoting the Product as a Better Substitute

Although there is a tendency to use a new technology to establish products and services that do not exist or, as recommended by marketing theory, to differentiate the offering in order to avoid price competition, the easier approach is to integrate the new technology into something consumers are already familiar with. A strategy of product class dissociation, where the inventor attempts to convince customers that his or her product is in a new category by itself, rarely works.[5]

One approach consists in relating the function of a new principle to something that has been around for a long time. In other words, rather than aim for an application that has no precedents, and hence demonstrate its "newness," a safer and more reliable course is to first see it as a substitute for an existing method or an extension of what is already well known and accepted. This not only makes the application easier to understand but also easier to communicate to others who might be involved in commercializing it.

The words "substitute" and "extension" are well chosen because of the confusion surrounding how new technologies ought to be presented for rapid adoption. If they are presented as "mere substitutes," they won't sell. There has to be a good reason for buyers to choose between keeping what they already have and buying something new. One needs to offer them a "better substitute," preferably one that expands the scope of the function they want at the same time—but a substitute nevertheless.

Union Carbide's Unipol Process. This familiarity with products explains why some process technologies gain more ready acceptance than others. For example, the float glass process introduced by Pilkington plc proved such an immediate success because its main impact was at the level of cost reduction. The product, glass, was known for centuries and had both an established use and distribution infrastructure in place.

In contrast, when Union Carbide Corporation (UCC) launched its Unipol process for making polyethylene in the late 1970s, it came up against initial resistance despite its superior economics and more versatile but untried product. The technology really took off when UCC began to stress its similarity to incumbent products instead of its differences.

The Unipol process, based on a fluid-bed reactor and a new family of catalysts, had the virtue of being able to produce both low-density polyethylene (LDPE) and high-density polyethylene (HDPE) in the same plant, whereas these had been produced by different processes earlier. It also consumed less energy, polluted less, and gave an operating cost saving of about 25 percent. More than these fairly considerable production economies, the LDPE produced by Unipol also offered certain advantages over conventional LDPE. It exhibited better puncture resistance, higher elongation, and improved tensile properties so as to enable fabricators to "down-gauge" their film, allowing the same square yardage of film to be produced from less raw material.

When Unipol was first announced, many in the industry were skeptical of UCC's claims, particularly as regards product features and its acceptability by fabricators and end-users. One of the first companies to consider adopting Unipol, Northern Petrochemical Co. of Des Plaines, Illinois, hesitated mainly on these grounds. When UCC announced its process in 1977,

Northern had been thinking of building a 220-million-pound-per-year auto-
clave LDPE unit based on ICI's process technology. In deciding whether or
not to change its plans in midstream, its major concern centered around
Unipol's polymer properties. As B. J. Anderson, vice president of Northern
Petrochemical, said at that time, he had so far "not received enough material for a thorough evaluation. The company would be a reluctant licensee
because this would mean devoting one-fifth of its capacity to a process that
makes a seemingly unique product." Exxon had expressed a similar initial
reluctance. Although it too intended to learn more about the UCC process,
a company executive noted "it is not obvious that the UCC process is fundamentally unique. Also, our initial impression is that the products will be
supplements rather than wholesale substitutes for conventional LDPE
resins."[6]

The fact was that Unipol's impact at the end-product level was minor
compared to its economic benefits. It was the latter that Union Carbide
immediately began to emphasize, presenting Unipol as a better process for
conventional LDPE and HDPE. Only after users had started to adopt the
process on economic grounds did product advantages start to be used as an
additional argument.

Augmenting and Supporting Existing Products

A variant to presenting something as a substitute is to promote it as augmenting or supporting other established technologies. Thus, the computer-
based bar code reader was adopted quite readily by supermarkets even
though it was an unfamiliar technology. While it changed both manual price
marking and check-out procedures, the bar-code reader did not fundamentally affect the work flow that clerks were used to. It made their work easier and more secure without calling for a major behavioral change.

Component technologies particularly need to be seen in this manner.
Thus, when electrotransducers were first introduced, they were often
installed as redundant circuits, until users became better aware of their
superior properties.[7] More recently, companies bringing gallium arsenide
(GaAs) circuits to the market have come to the same realization.

Known derisively as a "thirty-year-old technology of the future," gallium arsenide's properties of speed, weak-signal operation, and light generation and detection caused many to think of it as a substitute for silicon
in a wide range of electronic devices—notably computers, television
receivers, and optoelectronic devices for data transmission.

Initially, gallium arsenide's technical problems held it back. It was more
difficult to manufacture and to work with, it could not be packed as densely
as silicon with transistors, and it cost up to twice as much as silicon. While
it found a market in expensive Cray supercomputers and military electronics, it was ignored by the rest of the computer industry. It was mainly used

in front-end, high-speed receivers, such as detectors in satellite dish antennas, in which fast response and low noise were needed, and in light generation in the form of laser diodes, for which there was no substitute material.[8]

The approach being taken more recently is one of coexisting with silicon, making gallium arsenide "look like, feel like and act like silicon."[9] This was forced by several factors. Silicon already had a large installed base and was considered adequate for many purposes. Gallium arsenide operated differently too, requiring users to add special interfaces for power supplies. Unlike silicon, it operated best with a negative—not a positive—voltage. To maximize its speed it also required expensive packaging.

Making gallium arsenide acceptable to an industry habituated to silicon essentially meant avoiding costly retrofitting at the expense of sacrificing some of its speed advantages. Gazelle Microcircuits of Santa Clara, California, for example, first altered the material to operate in a high-positive-voltage silicon environment without a separate power supply. By giving up some performance, Gazelle was also able to package the chips in low-cost silicon packages that could be simply plugged into a circuit board carrying other silicon chips.

The applications to which gallium arsenide chips are being targeted also illustrate the need for finding a complementary role for the technology. As new and fast microprocessors—such as Intel's i486 and Motorola's 68030—have come on the market, the problem for computer designers has become one of matching the speed of these processors with that of the peripherals surrounding them—memory chips, logic chips, disk storage, and printers, which generally run slower. This is the segment companies like Gazelle started to aim for, not the microprocessor itself. In other words, while gallium arsenide failed as an instant replacement for silicon, it started to succeed as an incremental improvement.

It is only when a new technology finds a unique niche that it should be promoted for its differences. Such is, for example, what is happening with GaAs today. Because of their inherent speed and higher signal-to-noise ratio, GaAs chips have finally found a unique use in communication equipment. The evolution in speed and capacity in the latter has been such that silicon can no longer cope in some applications, particularly in next-generation wireless phones and high-capacity phone lines. This explains the sudden surge in the demand for GaAs chips recently, causing sales to grow from around $300 million in 1991 to an expected $2 billion by 2000.[10]

Promoting Products as Usable with Little Disruption

What applies to components also applies to devices that depend on other products for their effective use. The less they disrupt the latter, the greater the likelihood of their being adopted easily, particularly when customers have recently made significant investments in the system affected.

DAT and DCC. The importance of situating a device within the context of an existing system of benefits can be seen from the recent controversy surrounding digital audio tape (DAT) players. Prior to the introduction of DAT by Sony in 1987, consumers had already been subject to three generations of audio technologies—records, tapes, and the compact disc—each requiring a special new device to be purchased. Like the compact disc, Sony's DAT represented a significant advance in that it promised sound quality to match CDs but with the additional benefit of permitting recordings to be made.

Apart from some legal problems that DAT had to confront associated with copyrights, DAT's commercialization was slowed down by several factors—the price of DAT recorders (between $850 to $950 in 1991), the price of tapes (about $13 for a blank two-hour tape), and the fact that existing tape recorders could not play these new tapes. In addition, prerecorded DAT tapes were not readily available because recording DATs cost more than ten times as much as recording CDs, and because fast duplicators were unavailable.[11]

The approach Philips is taking with its digital compact cassette (DCC) is designed to get around just the problems Sony encountered with DAT. Although encoding less information, DCC tapes sound almost as good as DATs. Their main advantage lies in the fact that the recorder on which they are expected to be used can play both existing analog tapes as well as DCC. This way, consumers can start buying digital recorders without rendering their existing cassette collection obsolete. The recorders are also expected to cost around $500, less than Sony's DAT recorders, with prerecorded DCCs priced around $12, somewhere between analog cassettes and CDs.

Making the Technology Invisible

When it is difficult to relate the new technology to existing products, the best alternative is to make the technology as invisible and user-friendly as possible, stressing only its function. This is regardless of how "advanced" the underlying technology is. The important thing is to make adoption as simple and hassle-free as possible.

The notion of invisibility is, of course, subjective. It depends on the qualifications of the user and, more importantly, how he or she intends to use the technology. Robert Chaney makes the point as follows in referring to a technology for surface analysis—electron spectroscopy for chemical analysis (ESCA)—he was involved in commercializing in the late 1970s:

> Even if you have very esoteric stuff under the hood, you don't want customers to notice it. If the information [provided by a spectroscope] is too

abstract, you reduce the number of people who can use it. In the beginning, people *want* to look at the raw spectra. These are the experts who want proof that all the algorithm embedded in the machine works. This way they are also able to protect their own know-how. If you short-circuit such people you will fall flat on your face for lack of credibility. But those who follow do not necessarily have the same needs or motivations. They want you to hide the smarts.[12]

Intel learned about this difference between specialist and mass markets the hard way with its Pentium chip. Flaws detected in these chips, according to the company, would result in miscalculations so infrequently that most users wouldn't even notice. Yet, thanks to its campaign to get more visibility for itself and evolve into a consumer technology company, these flaws sparked a great deal of anxiety—much greater than if the company had been dealing exclusively with sophisticated buyers who could either repair the flaw or assess its impact cool-headedly. The mass market is unforgiving because it does not even want to understand technological idiosyncracies. It just wants something to work as expected, perfectly and invisibly.

Adapting the Facet Offered to Demand

Like many new material technologies, Belland's intelligent plastics consisted of several elements. There was, first and foremost, the *chemistry* of water-soluble-on-demand polymers. To make this chemistry functional, there was the extruder-reactor based *process technology,* using a modified commercially available extruder and compounder. With the need to rigorously control the various stages of polymerization, a highly sophisticated computer-based *process control system* was also developed around this hardware. Finally, the above three technologies were linked by a constantly expanding *data base* containing the various chemical formulae that had been tried, the process parameters that allowed them to be produced successfully, and the properties they exhibited after being manufactured.

The strategy the company chose to commercialize the technology in 1985 consisted in keeping all of these facets in house but engaging a number of partners to find and develop end applications for the material itself—toilet seat covers, food packages, bottle labels, agricultural films, and the like. However, although most of the companies contacted were intrigued by the new material, they quickly realized the prematureness of the concept and the effort and resources that would be needed to bring applications to the market. What they found more appealing in the immediate term was Belland's process know-how and its extruder-reactor, which they saw as a valuable *research tool* for developing a variety of other plastics that interested them. Thus, one of the first major development agreements the company signed—with a large chemical company based in the United States—was for this facet of the technology.

The preference for one element or facet of a technology over others is a common feature of science-based inventions. As shown in Figure 8-2, seven different facets can be present. At the foundation of the technology may be (1) some basic concepts and algorithms including, perhaps, some experimental data. Next level down would be the embodiment of this

FIGURE 8-2

THE SEVEN FACETS OF MODERN TECHNOLOGIES

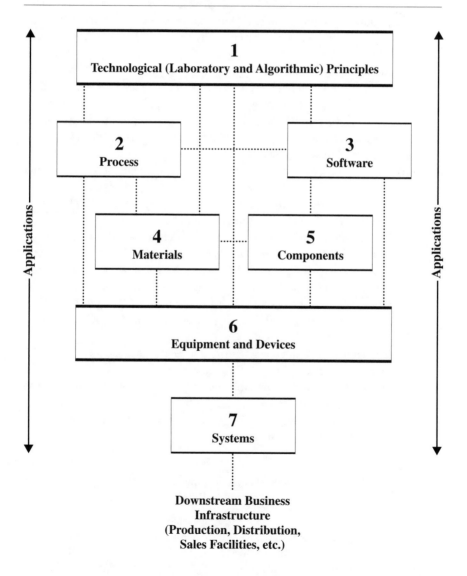

knowledge in (2) a new process technology or (3) a piece of software. These, in turn, are what most (4) materials and (5) components are based on. Finally, several of these facets, often drawn from different basic technologies, constitute (6) equipment and devices and (7) systems.

Until relatively recently, the only "market" upstream facets had were the product or system for which they were developed. They were all part of a single invention, often developed by the same person. Moreover, they often targeted a unique application that person had thought of. The reason for such vertical integration lay in the nature of these early technologies. Instead of codified, scientific principles, they relied heavily on trial-and-error experimentation, the full scope of which was only known to the person conducting the experiment. Only that person could establish the link between different facets of the technology and use the principles gleaned in other applications.

In the semiconductor industry, for example, Bell Labs first covered all the facets when inventing the transistor in 1947. It mastered and then contributed to the basic technology underlying the point contact and junction transistor; it worked out the process for producing germanium crystals of the right purity and doping them; and it made the first components at its sister company, Western Electric. Later, as the industry evolved, specialist companies emerged in each of these facets of the technology, some contributing to and commercializing process and equipment technologies, some doing additional work in the basic technology itself, and others pioneering the design and commercialization of new components and devices.

Today, while heuristic knowledge still plays an important role in distinguishing experts from novices who have merely read the concerned literature, the increasing scientific basis of technology makes it easier to borrow elements from other fields without the need for extensive rediscovery and experimentation. Inventors no longer have to do what Bell Labs did. Consequently, independent markets have emerged not only for each application but for all of the facets as well.

The ability to commercialize different facets independently allows for a better match between the way the technology is offered and its demand characteristics. Thus, it is possible either to provide the end service itself while waiting for the market for the product or equipment to develop, to offer a complete system, or to offer individual upstream facets that may fulfill a pressing need of the moment.

Providing a Service While Waiting for the Market for the Product to Develop

Buyers are typically not interested in "possessing" a technology, nor even the products incorporating it; what they really wish to pay for is the promised function and a resolution to the problems they confront. Selling them a product may be the most attractive option from a revenue standpoint, but it may not be the best way to get the technology adopted quickly. Starting with service provision is appropriate especially when:

The technology is unfamiliar to potential buyers of the equipment;

Buyers cannot justify the purchase of the equipment on economic grounds;

The technology needs to be developed further in order to become useful in particular applications;

The technology has varied uses, each representing a small and occasional niche; and

A lead user cannot be found to articulate demand or endorse the technology in order to target it to a wider market.

These reasons explain why many companies introducing a new equipment technology or exploiting a new technological principle start out by providing a service based on them.

Elektrobit Oy. One example is that of Elektrobit Oy based in Oulu, Finland. Founded in 1985, it now employs more than seventy engineers and designers, most of whom work on a principle known as spread spectrum. The latter concerns taking audio or data information in one format and communicating it in a different one, changing the signal's transmission frequency in a random sequence understood only by the receiver. In addition to making it difficult for an outsider to intercept, eavesdrop, or jam the signal, it allows many more users to operate in the same frequency allocation as opposed to conventional methods. It also requires lower power levels and thus conserves battery life on hand-held terminal equipment.

The above characteristics make the principle useful in a number of different applications ranging from secure wireless computer networks, cellular telephones, and wireless factory process control systems to military communications. Working together with the telecommunication laboratory at the University of Oulu—with one of the largest spread spectrum research groups in Europe—Elektrobit offers made-to-measure design services to a variety of users. It has built scanning supervisor equipment (which permits cellular networks to initiate handovers before voice quality audibly degrades) for Telia Mobitel (Sweden) and Tele-Mobil (Norway); it designed and manufactured the Narrow Band Normalizer for CERN's (European Laboratory for Particle Physics) Beam Orbit Measurement system in the large electron-positron (LEP) collider; and it has done work for companies such as Nokia, Valmet, and the European Space Agency.

In general, the more complex the technology in its application, the greater the need to use it internally first. This is what many writers of application software in the 1960s had to do. They wrote software as an aid to their consulting engineering business, not as a product for mass commercialization. The same is happening today in the field of combinatorial drug discovery—a computer-based approach to identifying new drug candidates based on combining various molecular structures that are known to have some useful properties. Companies such as Affymax in Palo Alto, California, and NexStar, in Boulder, Colorado, are not only conducting their own research to find leads for new drugs but are simultaneously commercializing the tools of combinatorics developed by them.[13]

Offering a Complete System

Selling a complete system in the beginning is actually an extension of service provision. It amounts to no more than offering buyers the instrument for the service in a hassle-free way. Once again, it may not be the most profitable way to exploit the technology, nor a way to gain economies of scale early, but it avoids the need to transfer a great deal of use-related know-how to buyers.

Providing a system is especially helpful in promotion when buyers cannot easily assemble the system themselves or find it uneconomical to make the investments needed to do so. The riskier and more demanding the technology is perceived to be, the more attractive they find a complete, functional package. This explains why Intel, in parallel with introducing new microprocessors, entered the motherboard business a few years ago. This strategy helped it to commercialize its Pentium chip faster since it saved PC manufacturers around the world the need to design their own circuit boards for the new chip.

Offering Individual Upstream Facets

The converse situation to providing a service or system applies in some circumstances too. Rather than wanting the complete system, or its end products and services, what buyers find more appealing is a particular element or facet of the technology.

This offering of individual facets based on demand is also consistent with research evidence that suggests that *divisible* technologies (those that can be adapted piecemeal, on an installment plan, so to speak, without major commitment and risk taking but constituting incremental extensions of things already familiar to users) tend to be transferred more easily.[14] This was, in effect, the situation confronted by Belland mentioned earlier.

Conductus Inc.'s High-Temperature Superconductors

Conductus Inc. faced a similar situation. The company was founded in 1987 to "create superconductive electronic products for the markets of computing, communications, signal processing, instrumentation and sensors." Achieving this corporate mission, however, required the company to do research on a broad front; consequently, a number of different technologies were developed, all geared to the production of superconducting ceramic thin films. Apart from general material-processing know-how, three major pieces of equipment were designed and built:

A substrate heater that is both chemically stable and capable of maintaining a constant temperature to within 5°C over a 2-inch diameter substrate;

A laser target carousel holding six separate targets; each target can be rotated individually so that successive bursts of the laser strike a different portion of the target's surface; and

Deposition systems consisting of a laser ablation system, a single-gun sputtering system, and a double-gun sputtering system.

Even though the mission of Conductus Inc. was to create, make, and sell end products exhibiting high-temperature superconductivity, it did not hesitate to commercialize these other enabling technologies, for which there was a more immediate demand.

Rather than spin off its equipment technologies into a new company, it decided to license each of them to different companies in appropriate fields. The substrate heater, for example, was licensed to US, Inc., in Campbell, California; the laser target carousel was licensed to Kurt J. Lesker Co. of Claviton, Pennsylvania; the laser ablation system was also being considered for licensing to an equipment vendor.

The point about the demand for individual facets is that it is seldom recognized, or catered to, by companies. They have a preconceived notion of what they are supposed to be bringing to market, and they see selling individual facets as a distraction or, worse, as a way of encouraging competition. In today's rapidly changing technological environment, this is not the attitude to take. Provided the facets are well protected in themselves, and a careful strategy is worked out to commercialize them independently, it is possible to use the opportunity they present to promote the overall technology better.

One company that realized this rather late was Lasarray. The Lasarray system for quickturn gate array ASICs consisted of two main components: a design unit comprising a software package with silicon compiler for the automatic generation of interconnection layers on gate arrays and a fabrication unit based on Direct Write Laser equipment. After unsuccessfully trying to sell the two together in a turnkey ASIC fabrication system, it decided to commercialize them separately starting in 1991.

The Direct Write Laser was aimed at customers who had been attracted by the possibilities of using a laser but wished to incorporate just this equipment into their standard fab lines. In such applications it could replace steppers or mask aligners for the production of prototype ICs. Compared to E-Beam technology, its main competitor, it was simpler to use, cheaper, and required no vacuum. Working as a stepper without a mask, it enabled chip designers to switch easily from prototyping to mask making for volume production using the same data. Also, as Ernest Uhlmann, the founder of Lasarray, reflected later, "We were the first company in the world to have a silicon compiler and should have formed a company just around that."

POSITIONING FOR ADOPTION

Positioning concerns what customers are finally made to see in a product, addressing expressed needs as well as the psychosocial and institutional context that influences their decision to purchase. As such, it is fundamentally about presenting the technology in a manner to elicit a favorable response in the minds of those targeted. It is, moreover, also a means of differentiating products from competitive offerings and aligning them to market characteristics at the time of launch.

ICI's FM-21 Cell

An important reason for the early success of the FM-21 cell was the way in which ICI's positioning of the technology accommodated both these use-related and competitive dimensions.

From a use standpoint, the cell was positioned to stress its environmental and energy-saving attributes. It was launched at a time when pressure had already built up to find a replacement for both diaphragm and mercury cells. Two things had happened by then. The first was environmental. Mercury and asbestos had become dirty words. Methyl mercury poisoning had caused the deaths of a number of Japanese in the notorious Minamata tragedy of the 1950s and 1960s (the process involved at Minamata was unrelated to chlorine production, however). In the diaphragm cell, the asbestos diaphragm had to be changed annually and presented a potentially hazardous handling problem. Pollution controls worldwide had become more stringent. The second factor was the escalating cost of energy. It is estimated that 60 percent of the cost of producing a ton of chlorine is the cost of power. Of all industrial processes, only aluminum smelting has a higher energy cost factor.

Both the environmental and energy attributes were naturally being stressed by other suppliers of membrane cells, too. To position its cell vis-à-vis competitors, ICI decided first to target owners of captive chlorine plants, such as major pulp and paper producers. They were the ones most likely to be attracted to the FM-21's modular design, which allowed plants of smaller capacity to be built economically. While simplicity, convenience, compactness, low weight, ease of maintenance, and low installation cost were the features being "sold," modularity turned out to be the principal advantage in the beginning. Positioning the cell based on its attributes of modularity, compactness, and ease of installation, the company did end up denying itself parts of the conversion market. As Paul Henstridge of ICI now recalls,

> We achieved our target of 20 percent in terms of new plant contracts but not in terms of tonnage. Competitors continued to sell a higher proportion of large plants. Large plant owners went for cells that appeared bigger, massive, heavy, fabricated with tons of steel because they perceived them as being more robust. FM-21 was positioned just the opposite—simple, lightweight and easy to assemble. This perception gap proved important. Now, our new FM-2000 is targeted specifically at the large-scale conversion market.[15]

More generally, positioning any new technology-based products needs to accommodate four things: presenting a dominant attribute in line with the market; allowing users to invent their own reasons for purchasing it; balancing use-related and competitive dimensions carefully; and adapting the positioning message in time should circumstances require it.

Presenting a Dominant Attribute

A common temptation in radical new technologies is to present *all* of their attributes. Apart from confusing potential buyers through information overload—precisely what effective positioning is intended to avoid—it makes evaluation of the technology difficult and reduces the scope for its adoption.

For example, not being able to settle on the dominant attribute worked against Belland in its early years. The technology had many different worthwhile attributes, but customers wanted to know what *mainly* was being proposed and how this compared with other technologies on offer. At that time there were at least three other contenders also responding to environmental concerns over plastics cluttering roadsides and overburdening landfills—recyclable, biodegradable, and photodegradable plastics. If Belland's material could do no more than these alternatives, the technology's worth would lie merely in its economics. The latter, in turn, depended on the volume Belland could capture with its material.

Table 8-1 summarizes the main attributes of these competing plastics. Compared to conventional plastics, the main advantage Belland had was its ease of recyclability and the absence of any negative environmental impacts associated with the small portion that could not be recycled. As for the two other environmentally sound plastics—biodegradable and photodegradable

TABLE 8-1

COMPARISON OF BELLAND'S INTELLIGENT PLASTICS WITH OTHER
ENVIRONMENTALLY FRIENDLY PLASTICS

	Belland	Bio-degradeable	Photo-degradeable	Recyclable
1. Recycling or Reuse System	Closed	Open	Closed	Partially closed
2. Programmability	Yes	No	No	Yes
3. Environmental Consequence of Waste	None	None	Some	Yes
4. Price	Variable	Unknown	Unknown	Known

ones—their main limitations were the uncontrolled nature of their degradation process and/or the difficulty associated with recycling and reuse.

In the beginning, Belland stressed both attributes of its plastics—their disposability in the open environment and their recyclability. Apart from making the development challenge more complex, it made the technology seem too good to be true. Faults identified in one attribute got transferred to the other, raising skepticism regarding the technology as a whole. It was only in 1991, with the passage of the "dual system" law for packaging in Germany (see Chapter 7) that specific goals for *recycling* plastic material was established. This provided the focus for Belland, causing it to settle on one attribute: recyclability.

Allowing Users to Invent Their Own Reasons for Purchase

Positioning the dominant attribute is particularly important when new functionalities have to be presented instead of straightforward price/performance comparisons. Since they offer an opportunity to create an entirely new market, which differentiation based on substitution usually cannot, they require an overarching, easily explainable concept. But the concept needs to be broad enough from a use standpoint.

The attributes thought necessary for designing a new technology-based product may not be what customers end up appreciating. Thus, when GE introduced Lexan, a high-impact-resistant polycarbonate plastic, it expected impact resistance to be its main selling proposition. As it turned out, customers actually found the plastic's dimensional stability most attractive in the beginning.[16] Customers, in other words, invent their own reasons for adopting a new technology, something that does not always show up in the market research done prior to launch.

Balancing Use-Related and Competitive Positioning

Based on the earlier discussion on minimizing resistance to the technology, the single biggest challenge in positioning technology-based products is reconciling the need to differentiate them from competing offerings and making them conform to existing use patterns. Positioning a technology as radically different from what else is on offer, including incumbent ones, runs the danger of making the promotion task that much harder.

The paradoxical need to position a new technology as different, and yet fitting existing requirements for acceptance, is greatest for technologies promising new uses. The word "differentiation" relates to competing offerings not, as some inventors think, something "new" for customers and users. One should *differentiate against competitors* but *align* the product to *existing use patterns*. Also, while the initial positioning in the demonstration phase may have been chosen mainly to differentiate the technology from competitive offerings, the way it is then promoted needs to focus on attributes that have more to do with its acceptance by a chosen category of buyers.

Adapting the Positioning Message in Time

The marketing of technology-based products is as much an exploratory exercise as research itself. Regardless of how well market studies are conducted prior to the start of development, the final product still has to be considered a variable and sold on the basis of circumstances prevailing at the time of launch.

One implication of this is the need for some flexibility in positioning a technology. The positioning information that was incorporated during the development phase is often outdated by the time the technology is ready for launch. It was mostly an inductive view of what customers might want, and a static one at that. Practically all the technologies the author encountered had to be repositioned at the time of launch, sometimes more than once.

Apple's Newton

A recent example of a technology that became hostage to its preconceived positioning is that of Apple's personal digital assistant called Newton. Although promoted as the defining technology of the digital age, its acceptance by the market has been less than enthusiastic. No one would have denied the premises on which it was developed—the blending of computer and communication technologies with entertainment and information services in a portable, easy-to-use device.

Part of the problem with Newton was its failure to use robust technologies. Although the intention was that the device could "read" handwritten notes and enable users to send and receive messages, the software turned out to be unreliable and the communications capabilities limited. As Tim Bajarin of Creative Strategies International stated, Apple's mistake was to launch the hand-held computer before the technology was reliable. "Newton came out a good 12 months before it should have." Although Apple came out later with a second version, which corrects some of the original shortcoming, "first impressions count a lot." Equally important, as stated by Pete Snell, marketing manager of MobilSoft, a software company that developed spreadsheet and calculation programs to run on Newton, "Apple's vision of Newton as a consumer product was wrong. We think that it has the potential to become a fantastic business productivity tool, but Apple seems to have missed the point from the beginning."[17]

Since all technologies experience different adoption patterns over time, it is counterproductive to get locked into a one-time positioning. Too many companies make the mistake of settling on a positioning and promotion strategy early and then not departing from it in the name of consistency. Repositioning at the time of launch is not an admission of mistakes made during the design phase. Rather, it is an intelligent response to changes that may have occurred in the meantime, the reaction of those to whom the technology was initially targeted, as well as to new opportunities that might have opened up to make the technology attractive.

Astra's Turbuhaler

An example of effective real-time positioning is that of Astra's Turbuhaler. In addition to gradually updating the design concept as development advanced, the positioning message was readapted when time came to launch the Turbuhaler in 1987. This message took into account what the technical team had achieved until then, consumer response to product trials, competitor reactions, and market opportunities that unexpectedly became available.

When Wetterlin began his work, the distinguishing trait he had in mind for the Turbuhaler was "free from additives"—no chlorofluorocarbon (CFC) gas, no lubricants, and no lactose, only pure medicine. This was the basis for the small-dose design, despite its causing some technical difficulties.

When clinical trials were done, however, patients (and their doctors) seemed to appreciate something quite different. Two-thirds preferred the Turbuhaler over MDIs and powder inhalers because "it was handy and easy to use." When the Turbuhaler was launched in 1987 (with Bricanyl, Astra's bronchodilator), it was this ease of use feature that constituted the main positioning message.

In 1988, the marketing group decided on a more direct positioning vis-à-vis MDIs—a bigger market than dry powder inhalers, which Turbuhaler was by then capable of entering. The CFC ozone layer controversy was coming to a head at that time with the pending Montreal Protocol. The Swedish government had announced that it wanted to ban CFC production by January 1, 1989. Even though medical use was to continue (unless alternatives were found), Astra decided to exploit the window of opportunity created. When it submitted its registration application for Pulmicort (Turbuhaler incorporating a corticosteroid) to Swedish authorities in the autumn of 1988, it was the "CFC free" argument that it highlighted; it got approval within three months, partly as a consequence.

The "CFC free" argument did not, however, work out elsewhere. According to Jorgen Book, Marketing Director for Turbuhaler, "Doctors were not really concerned with CFC; they had other priorities and felt that the CFC being used in MDIs was insignificant with all the refrigerators around in the world."

The next adaptation of the positioning message was caused by competitor reactions to Turbuhaler. Among the claims competitors made were that Turbuhaler was sensitive to excess humidity and was used incorrectly, causing patients to dose themselves improperly.

Astra's response was pointed. As soon as data became available that 80 percent of patients actually used the device correctly, even without instructions, the company repositioned its message to "Technology That Simplifies Technique." The fact was that the remaining 20 percent of patients used the device correctly after they were given verbal instructions. In contrast, 10 percent to 15 percent of the patients using MDIs and competing powder inhalers were unable to use these devices correctly even after they were given instructions.

A second measure used to cope with competition related to the substance incorporated in Turbuhaler and the combined positioning of this with the device. By the end of the 1980s, asthma therapy in Europe was gradually moving toward the use of corticosteroids as a first-line treatment, whereas it had traditionally been restricted to chronic cases. Rather than confront competition head-on, Astra adopted a flanking strategy, emphasizing its corticosteroid Turbuhaler combination for early and moderate symptoms of asthma and citing the new guidelines relating to asthma treatment. With competitors targeting corticosteroids for chronic treatment, this positioning opened a new, uncontested segment of the market. According to several marketing managers within Astra, this final positioning accounted for much of the early success of Turbuhaler.

PRICING FOR EARLY ADOPTION—MAKING THE TECHNOLOGY AFFORDABLE

Traditionally, in an attempt to recover development costs quickly, most companies adopted a "skimming" strategy, pricing new products high in the beginning and then lowering the price in line with manufacturing costs and the changing category of adopters. However, as pointed out in Chapter 6, the budgetary constraints of customers, and the growing competition between alternative technologies for each function, are making premium pricing more difficult today. Customers want the new functionality a technology has to offer but at a lower or, at best, the same price as incumbent products. High performance coupled with cost parity is the winning formula today.

In practice this translates into making sound trade-offs between value-in-use and average cost pricing; addressing budgetary constraints through, for example, leasing; subsidizing experimental users for promotional purposes; and signalling a competitive price from the beginning.

Trade-Off Between Value-in-Use and Average Cost Pricing

Conceptually, the "best" way to price any new product is in terms of the value it contributes to a buyer. This approach, however, is feasible only when price discrimination among uses is possible. Thus, in selling Kevlar, DuPont does try to obtain the best price each application affords; it can do so because of the way it offers the product. As A. J. Peisl, account manager for the company's European engineering fiber system division, put it:

> We never sell a product to the first stage of production and let people do with it what they want. We find the optimum way of putting the material in end products so as to meet a specific technical requirement. This allows us to understand the value of the material in the finished good which provides us with a basis for pricing it competitively.[18]

Where such price discrimination is not possible, some companies price on the basis of anticipated average costs. This method consists in projecting the long-term average total cost of the product based on anticipated volumes in the future and pricing at this level from the beginning. It is similar to the penetration pricing strategy that Japanese companies employed in a host of industries during the 1960s and 1970s.

One company that has adopted this approach is Alcoa when introducing aluminum-lithium alloys. Despite the different applications in which these alloys could be introduced, it extrapolated what the cost of the alloys would be in full production. Alcoa then communicated this anticipated cost to each potential customer as a basis for pricing. Apart from enabling the company to price competitively, this provided all potential users with an estimate of what the long-term supply conditions would be in order for them to make their own profitability estimates before going ahead.

Addressing Budgetary Constraints and Consumption Risks

High up-front costs and perceived risks in a technology often deter buyers. This partly explains the preference for buying technology-based services described earlier, rather than investing in state-of-the-art equipment. It also explains the role leasing has traditionally played in some technologies. Thus, when Xerox launched its first copier in 1959, competing copying machines sold in the $300 to $400 range. Selling the 914 profitably would have required a price as much as one hundred times higher. Hence, Xerox decided to lease rather than sell, and let the lease price fluctuate with use. Customers could try out a 914 copier for $95 a month, with the first 2,000 copies free and a charge of just four cents per copy after that. Customers made no investment in the machines, and they had the right to return them after fifteen days.

The FlowMole of UTILX Corp.

Making a technology affordable and less risky to own also explains how UTILX Corp. of Kent, Washington, introduced its FlowMole GuideDrill recently.

In 1984 this company invented a patented maneuverable fluid jet drill and reamer for drilling underground holes called the FlowMole. Instead of the traditional method of cutting and covering ditches for laying underground utilities, the FlowMole uses a remote-controlled drill that works underneath existing ground structures. Two vertical holes are dug at the beginning and end of, say, an electric cable's path. The hydraulically powered drill head is introduced in one hole and is guided underground to the second hole electromagnetically. After the drill head makes its narrow path, a reaming device then creates a tunnel of the required diameter.

In order to commercialize this trenchless technology, UTILX first tried to franchise the use of the equipment to contractors in different regions of the United States. This would have brought in much-needed capital early and speeded up the technology's introduction. Unfortunately, few contractors were interested. The company then decided to provide the service on its own, setting up sixteen contracting facilities throughout the United States. With utilities, rather than contractors, as customers, UTILX was able to get closer to end beneficiaries of the technology and make it affordable. In Europe, and later also in the United States, this direct service provision was complemented by leasing the equipment to contractors.

Subsidizing Experimental Users

Unlike the case of many consumer products, early adopters of a new technology are not always the most affluent. They are willing to try out the technology, and even add value to it to help future commercialization, but often not at commercial prices.

Thus, when ICI launched its FM-01 electrolyzer, an electrochemical synthesizer based on its FM-21 cell technology, it began by giving a few "development cells" away for free to research establishments and universities throughout the world—including Japan, where it expected the greatest competition. The result was that it was then able to sell full-sized FM-01 cells to many who took the development cells and developed their own processes around them.

Rapid market penetration based on making a new technology affordable in the beginning is what characterizes the strategy of many of today's companies writing software for the Internet, too. Netscape Communications, Inc., for example, made the first version of its Mosaic program (for browsing the World Wide Web) available for free. Following that, it started to charge for upgrades and more advanced products—a strategy that enabled it to grab over 80 percent of the market for Web browsers with its follow-on product, the Navigator 2.0.

The Importance of Signalling a Competitive Price

An important virtue of average cost pricing combined, if necessary, with financing assistance in the beginning, is the signal it gives potential buyers: that they are not in some way subsidizing those who adopt the technology later, and that the product in question *can* become available at a competitive price.

The way test samples are sometimes priced gives potential buyers the wrong signal. Enamored by the newness and proprietary nature of the technology—but also to separate genuinely interested buyers from the merely curious—these samples were priced a lot higher than what the product was expected to be available for later. The significance of this was, of course, more symbolic than economic. Yet the signal such a pricing policy sent was that the commercial version of the product would be expensive, too—perhaps not as much as the test sample, but not an order of magnitude less, either. A case in point is AlliedSignal's conducting polymers. As Gregory Smith recalls:

> AlliedSignal was selling its conducting polymers at $200 per pound from a pilot plant to converters as a means to help recover R&D costs. The equilibrium, full-scale price would probably be closer to $5 to $10 per pound. Unfortunately, it is hard to build a customer's belief in the latter if you sell it to him at $200 in the development stage.[19]

TARGETING RECEPTIVE SEGMENTS AND ENGAGING OTHERS EARLY

Practically all new technologies confront different markets as they evolve. Typically, the first market is other researchers and experimental users. They may not be the most attractive segment of the market, nor the best paying, but they are a potential market nonetheless. Next in line are companies and individuals who do not really want the burden of purchasing the technology itself but are willing to pay for the service it offers on an occasional basis. It is only much later, sometimes even never, that a full-fledged market for equipment and devices embodying the new technology emerges.

All of these markets represent different categories of buyers or segments. Today, with the need to get a new technology accepted early and widely, the marketing challenge consists in finding the most receptive segments *and* bringing in others quickly. In practice, what is needed is:

Identifying the broad segment most receptive to the technology in terms of its buying criteria and buying process;

Identifying the most receptive buyers within that segment, in order to get the technology launched successfully;

Exercising some flexibility in the actual process of identifying first users; and

Planning a strategy to address a wider audience as quickly as possible.

Segmentation by Buying Criteria and Process

This form of segmentation is familiar to most marketeers and applies equally to new products and to products that have been on the market for some time. Segments based on buyer criteria serve a dual purpose. They help match potential customers with the characteristics of the product and its delivery, and they help in positioning the product vis-à-vis competing ones, including those that the company itself may have launched earlier.

The specific criteria buyers use, and how they make their decision to purchase, depend on the nature of the product. Figure 8-3 (see page 239) illustrates one grouping that Raychem has found useful for industrial products. Based on work done by Pascal Lecordier, head of its corporate strategy group in France, this four-way classification was first applied to the company's cable accessories business. The same classification scheme is also now being employed for accessing and then progressively expanding the market for surge arresters.

While virtually all its cable accessories business was in the availability segment, the surge arrester was different. The latter fell mainly into three of the other segments, as shown below:

Surge Arrester Segment	Potential Volume (percent)	Approximate Price Range (percent)
1. Technical	10	200
2. Value	50	115
3. Price	40	100
4. Availability	0	100

The technical segment required working directly with customers, while the other two segments (value and price) called for more indirect selling. They were, moreover, characterized by standard specifications (usually minimum acceptable specifications), high-volume manufacturing, and intolerance of any variation in product. The fact that the product was produced in relatively small volumes—and was being sold mainly on its technical merits—drew the company to targeting the technical segment first. With its technical sales force, this was also the segment Raychem traditionally excelled in. The extent to which it can now successfully penetrate the much larger volume and price segments will depend on whether the company is willing to meet the different criteria used by buyers there—low product variations, conforming to standard specifications, low cost, and so on—which require a different business system to be met effectively.

Identifying Receptive Buyers Within the Segment Targeted

Among those who would be attracted to a given positioning of the technology, some respond more favorably than others. This has long been recognized by experts on the introduction of new products who have often distinguished between the so-called "early adopters" and the "late majority" in their buying decisions. Figure 8-4 (see page 240) lists one such categorization of buyers in terms of their propensity to adopt a new product in time, which is favored by industrial marketeers.

The naming of the different categories is actually not important. What is, however, is a detailed understanding of the characteristics of each category. Anyone introducing a new technology needs to come up with his own set of categories based on the product and its pattern of use. For multimedia technology as a whole, for example, 3DO recognized four types of adopter categories:

Innovators, having a history of buying new systems that offer significant technological improvements over existing alternatives. Consisting of approximately 500,000 consumers, this segment was generally insensitive to price, software availability, brand identification, breadth of distribution, and factory support.

FIGURE 8-3

RAYCHEM'S FOUR-WAY SEGMENTATION OF INDUSTRIAL MARKETS

VALUE	TECHNICAL
Buying Criteria: Highest value for lowest total life time cost	**Buying Criteria:** Technical image, technical performance for specific function and service
Premium on: Total economic value to customer (EVC)[a]	**Premium on:** Service, especially technical consulting
Buying Decision Influenced by: Team representing technical, financial, quality, environmental health and safety, and logistic functions	**Buying Decision Influenced by:** Engineer and/or installer of product
PRICE	**AVAILABILITY**
Buying Criteria: Tendered price and delivery time	**Buying Criteria:** Familiarity and immediate availability
Premium on: Low price quotation	**Premium on:** Familiarity
Buying Decision Influenced by: Nontechnical purchase manager or central buying department	**Buying Decision Influenced by:** Product installer (e.g., foreman) and/or distributor

SOURCE: Pascal Lecordier, Raychem France, 1991. Reprinted with permission.

[a]Economic value to customer (EVC) includes *all* aspects of a product that add value to it in the eyes of the customer—features, quality, supply conditions, safety, cost in use, etc. This explains the involvement of several functions in the buying process.

Early adopters, numbering in the several millions, were similar to innovators in their buying behavior and motivation but tended to consider price/performance and software availability more carefully.

Interactive system users, who currently owned at least one interactive system, such as a video game console or personal computer. Representing about 50 million households worldwide, these consumers based their purchase decision on value, software availability, and price but were otherwise receptive to the new technology.

FIGURE 8-4

BUYERS' PROPENSITY TO ADOPT A NEW PRODUCT

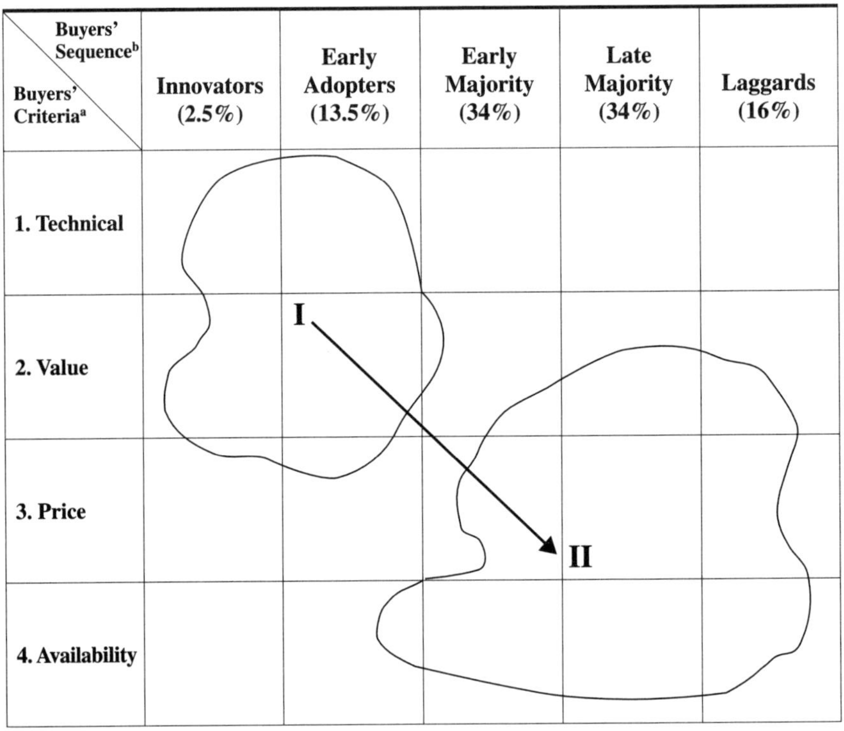

Buyers' Sequence[b] / Buyers' Criteria[a]	Innovators (2.5%)	Early Adopters (13.5%)	Early Majority (34%)	Late Majority (34%)	Laggards (16%)
1. Technical					
2. Value					
3. Price					
4. Availability					

[a]Using Raychem's classification.
[b]Using categories and percentage distribution of buyers in Frederick E. Webster, Jr., *Industrial Marketing Strategy* (New York: John Wiley & Sons, 1979), p. 118.

Mass market consumers, who had television sets but were not current users of interactive multimedia products.[20] This is the largest potential market of all but probably the least likely to buy in the beginning.

Naturally, the most important groups of adopters for anyone about to launch a new technology-based product are the innovators and early adopters. If they cannot be convinced, the technology is a nonstarter. While their nature differs from one industry to another, they tend to be those who are close to the technology and relatively familiar with its characteristics; who possess a relatively greater need for the technology to solve a pending problem; who operate in segments characterized by a history of rapid technological change and/or relatively higher profitability and growth rate; and who are organizationally avant-garde in outlook and have a sufficiently long time horizon to cope with the inevitable difficulties associated with adopting new technologies. These are all mutually reinforcing characteristics. The greater the extent to which they are present in a buyer, the more the likelihood of early adoption of the technology.

It is important to remember that finding the most receptive buyer within a particular category is largely a judgmental exercise. The key is to find out the precise time line of need within the segment targeted and to identify the organizations and people who *want* to do something with the technology. As Peter Ridley, of the University of Southern California, put it,

> It is easy to identify who the general company might be by looking at its sector of activity; the trick is to find one who has an immediate need for what you have to offer. My approach is to look especially for small companies whose time line of development offers just the gap we can fill.[21]

It has also been repeatedly shown that innovations tend to be more readily adopted when a single (entrepreneurial) individual is responsible for the decision, compared to when an organization or a group of individuals are involved. While technical people within the buying organization are often the key influencers, the need is to get to the "money brokers," those who actually approve investments.

Approaching Segmentation Flexibly

Regardless of how thoroughly the search for receptive segments is conducted, one can never capture fully the changing needs of potential buyers. Just as unforeseen uses of the technology emerge unexpectedly, new segments, more keen on the technology, constantly manifest themselves.

In the case of Seiko's focused ion beam (FIB), for example, the three functions of imaging, lithography, and processing eventually made the equipment a viable competitor vis-à-vis E-beam and lasers. However, each of these functions was perceived differently by different users. While large wafer companies bought the equipment mainly for production purposes to repair faults, smaller companies working on large-scale integrated (LSI) designs were mainly interested in using it for imaging and testing purposes. There were yet others who saw the FIB mainly as a quality control tool.

The need to keep an open mind to end-user needs is also illustrated by the ESCA technology. As Robert Chaney of Surface Science Laboratories, Inc., explained,

> One of the biggest applications for the ESCA technology in the 1970s turned out to be Winchester disk drives. A customer walked in to try out our equipment and found it worked for his need. We had not been targeting that application expressly and, in hindsight, we should have explored such opportunities more aggressively. We were all too focused on just building the instrument.[22]

Real-time market coupling is best aided by keeping lines of communication open with a broad class of customers and developing good relations with them. This is what Texas Instruments did in promoting its digital signal processing (DSP) technology too. Rather than fix on a particular application or customer group in advance, TI reached out to a broad cross-section of the market, including small customers suggesting different ways to use DSPs.

Addressing a Wide Audience Quickly

With today's premium on quick market penetration and achieving large market shares early, the challenge companies launching new technologies confront is that of approaching several segments as simultaneously as possible. It means establishing a volume business before others come in.

The need to think about the mass market at the start of the innovation process is endorsed by the history of several new product launches in the consumer goods industry. Notwithstanding the various advantages a pioneer (one who launches the product first) starts with, it is the so-called early leaders (those that enter several years later but with a different approach to the business) who usually get to dominate the industry. Thus, although it was Chicopee Mills, a unit of Johnson & Johnson, that first introduced disposable diapers in the United States in 1935, Procter & Gamble not only eventually gained the largest market share but is also associated with creating the disposable diaper business—despite entering the business in 1961.

Among the things that distinguished pioneers from early leaders who got to dominate a product category is the latter's concentration on the mass market from the beginning. They did not evolve into the mass market over time. They aimed for it right from the start, despite the enormous time and effort needed to tackle it successfully.[23]

Market segmentation for new technologies, in other words, is not just about *migrating* from one adopter category to another, but a deliberate attempt at *expanding* the market for the technology. One needs to move quickly from attracting a "lead customer," to the "first independent user," and then on to a "representative customer." Rather than the most receptive segment, it is the *biggest* segment that needs to be targeted eventually, and the company's delivery infrastructure must be configured to do so successfully.

Targeting multiple segments to get to the mass market early is akin to mass customization. As in other situations of mass customization, simultaneous targeting does not mean nondifferentiated targeting. As shown in Figure 8-4, both buyer criteria and buyer sequence need to be addressed simultaneously.

In going from segments indicated by zone I to those in zone II, the factors contributing to success can be dramatically different. Either a company's manufacturing and other capabilities must be flexible enough to meet these requirements cost-effectively, or alliances must be engaged with others who can provide the capabilities needed for different segments.

When launching its new multimedia technology system recently, 3DO aimed directly at the mass market, too. As its offering memorandum put it,

> Although some videogame consoles and personal computers have penetrated the third tier of interactive customers, no interactive multimedia system to date has gained acceptance as a mass market standard equivalent to that of the VCR and audio CD player in the consumer electronics market. To be successful in reaching the mass market, the company believes that a new interactive multimedia platform must provide a dramatic increase in audiovisual realism to appeal to innovators, attract the broad-based support of hardware system manufacturers and software developers required to reach early adopters and achieve acceptance as a standard platform, and offer sufficient value and affordability to reach current interactive system users and address the mass market. The company believes that existing interactive multimedia devices have not achieved full mass market penetration because they have not satisfied all of these criteria.[24]

LEVERAGING LEAD ADOPTERS AND ESTABLISHED COMMUNICATION NETWORKS

If enacting the market is about dialogues, then communication is the handmaiden of this dialogue. All too often, the resources devoted to communication are inadequate for the challenges to be overcome. Expenditures in advertising, personal communication, demonstration, and distribution do correlate with faster new product adoption.[25] While the statement is tautological, it is not always followed.

In the case of Lasarray's QT-GA system, for example, the prospect of other technologies becoming available made the equipment unattractive to potential buyers. New design methodologies promising more efficient ASICs and a steady stream of developments in integrated circuit technology generally caused people to adopt a wait-and-see attitude, analogous to the situation with PCs in the 1970s. "Why buy Lasarray's equipment when the industry is going for submicron technology," was an often heard argument, even though there was little substance behind the immediacy of the claim. But the fear of being stuck with an obsolescing technology acted as an important brake. Lasarray's unpreparedness to communicate the advantages of its system effectively only made matters worse.

Effective market communication needs to take into account the information needs of potential buyers, the role of opinion leaders and endorsers of the technology, and the nature of communication networks that exist or can get built.

Information Needs of Potential Buyers

According to the model of the innovation diffusion process elaborated by Everett Rogers and his colleagues the decision to adopt any new idea is preceded by two, quite separate, phases: a *knowledge* phase involving the exposure of individuals to the innovation's existence and some understanding of its functioning, and a *persuasion* phase, involving the formation of an attitude (to accept or reject) toward the innovation.[26] The channel of communication chosen vis-à-vis particular customers, therefore, depends on the extent to which one needs to merely inform, and let the decision-making process take its own course, versus persuading a decision to be made in one's interest.

Thus, one of the reasons Stanford University was so successful in licensing its Cohen-Boyer patents was its ability to both inform and persuade. Representatives from the university not only advertised extensively but visited companies throughout the United States, Europe, and Japan to explain the license, publicizing the early signing up of companies in order to keep the momentum of interest. It followed journal articles to stay abreast of new technologies in the licensed area, closely watched newly issued patents to see what companies were doing, and developed an extensive file on company portfolios and products to track potential candidates.

The Role of Opinion Leaders

In many technologies, customers wait for someone else to take the plunge before committing themselves. Demonstrating the technology in one's own facility is seldom enough. Customers want to be reassured not only that the technology works but that its superiority is demonstrated in comparative tests. This is one of the advantages of Beta tests done at a customer's premises. As reported by Christopher Voss for the software industry, purchasers place a strong reliance on the information gained from seeing a demonstration of a working system. The better the quality of a working system, the more likely a user will buy it.[27] Moreover, potential users are more likely to believe the evidence gained from a totally independent user, especially one with the status of an opinion leader.

The role of opinion leaders in the case of new technologies is generally assumed by individuals who are held in high professional regard and organizations that have an established track record of success based on innovativeness. In addition to providing much-needed feedback on the technology and helping define it better in a concrete application, such users serve a valuable demonstration effect for those who follow. This is why universities are often given new technologies to try out on concessional terms and why many start-up companies seek alliances with reputable companies.

The more novel a technology, particularly with regard to the principles on which it is based, the greater the need for endorsement by opinion leaders. This was the experience of Rasna Corporation (San Jose, California) when bringing its new finite element analysis (FEA) software called Applied Structure to market in 1989. The traditional method of FEA, pioneered by companies such as MacNeal Schwendler Corporation (Los Angeles) in the 1960s, is based on the *h-method*, the *h* standing for the size of the elements of the mesh created for computing design requirements numerically. Rasna's design software is based on an alternative approach, the *p-method*, in which these elements are represented by high-order polynomial functions. This offers two main advantages: result convergence can be obtained faster and the modeling process is simplified since relatively few elements are required.

The problem Rasna encountered when launching this new software was that most potential users already had access to FEA packages and had become accustomed to the h-method. In addition to creating awareness of the advantages offered by the new algorithm, it had to induce an important first buyer to demonstrate its value and endorse it for others. This is one reason it welcomed Kubota as an equity investor and distributor for its product in Japan (see Chapter 7). As David Pidwell, president of the company, explained:

> With the price of FEA packages today, you can't afford a direct sales force to go around demonstrating and distributing it. What you need most is credibility and an efficient distribution infrastructure. Kubota had a strong reputation in the mechanical industry, so its endorsement as a user was important. It also had a well-established distribution network in Japan through which it could channel the product.[28]

The agreement with Kubota was soon followed by an alliance with Daimler-Benz for similar reasons. Daimler-Benz took Rasna's core product and is developing its own design automation software around it, which it will use internally, within the company's various divisions, and sell to third parties in Europe as well.

Exploiting Communication Networks

In general, mass media channels are better suited to creating awareness, while persuasion requires the use of interpersonal channels. Complex innovations, moreover, is better promoted through interpersonal communication. In fact, mass media are seldom enough to prompt an adoption decision by itself. Rather, a two-step model is often at work, hypothesizing that communication messages flow from a source, via mass media channels, to opinion leaders, who in turn pass them on to followers.[29] This consideration has led to the design of communication strategies based on the nature of different adopter categories and the diffusion network that either is already established for similar innovations or can be set up efficiently for the one in question.

Completed innovations tend to diffuse through two types of networks. One consists of the communication channels already established among members of an industry. As John Czepiel found in his study on the adoption of continuous casting techniques by the U.S. steel industry, interpersonal contacts that took place between companies of similar size and type of business influenced the way individual companies adopted the new technology. In addition, early adopters of the technology were regarded as opinion leaders within this community.[30] The other kind of network is that between actors in an industry and third parties. Competitors who are reluctant to deal with one another directly tend to make inferences about each other and imitate behavior through comments they receive from third parties such as suppliers, government agencies, customers, or management consultants.

There are no hard and fast rules as to which type of network is most effective. The important recommendation is to design promotion strategies that take into account existing networks first. New networks take time to be established and can delay the adoption process. When these are necessary, an effective networking strategy consists of carefully identifying the specific links required for a particular technology and then activating these as economically as possible.[31]

SUMMARY

The ultimate arbitrator of any new concept is the end-user. While several intermediate adopters and market constituents may have earlier accepted to help promote a technology, it is end-customers buying the product or service incorporating it who rule on how valuable it is.

Promoting new technology-based products is best seen as a combination of market discovery (conceiving of products that satisfy a latent demand) and market creation (building demand where none exists). As the experience of several successful innovations indicates, one needs to exercise some flexibility in terms of what "product" is offered, as well as when and how; make the technology affordable and, if possible, conform to existing patterns of use; target segments in the order of how receptive they are, while recognizing the need to reach a wide audience quickly; and exploit communication networks already in place so as to meet the information needs of prospective buyers.

Market studies done at the start of a development program, in other words, seldom indicate how successful a product will be. The marketing done after the fact matters just as much—what some refer to today as "outbound marketing" to distinguish it from the market analysis (inbound marketing) that informed the product creation process. One needs to combine a good initial reading of the market with active promotion once a technology is ready.

9

MOBILIZING
COMPLEMENTARY ASSETS
FOR DELIVERY
AND OPTIMIZING RETURNS

AS MANY STUDENTS ATTENDING BUSINESS SCHOOLS LEARN TODAY, PILKINGTON did well to license its float glass technology, while EMI might still be in the CT scanner business today had it licensed its technology in some markets, notably the United States. Similarly, the success of Ray Dolby's noise reduction technology can be attributed as much to the business formula used to commercialize it as to its technical merits. All of these are examples of the role a business formula plays in bringing new technologies to market quickly and effectively. They relate to the contracts entered into with others for mobilizing complementary assets the inventing organization lacks.

For an inventor to make money, two things are required: the technology's value needs to become apparent quickly through rapid and broad market penetration, and a method must be found to maximize the appropriation of benefits. Maximum benefits does not, of course, mean all the benefits. That has never been possible. Reaching out to others for help inevitably means sharing some of its value. The challenge is to find a mode of commercializing the technology so as to facilitate rapid market access while, at the same time, optimizing one's own returns from the investments made.

Although knowing the formulae others have tried in particular circumstances helps, coming up with a suitable formula should be seen largely as a source of differentiation. The commonly considered choice between making and selling products versus licensing is one among many. Unfortunately, far too many inventors restrict themselves to this choice, rather than the subtle variants that are possible for optimally marketing their technologies. Some view licensing as just a means to avoid the hassles of further commercialization. Others see the make-and-sell option as the best under all circumstances, provided they can assemble the complementary assets needed in time.

THE RANGE OF BUSINESS FORMULAE TO CHOOSE FROM

One way to think about the various formulae available today is in terms of the extent to which technology is shared while keeping control over its exploitation. Figure 9-1 lays out the most commonly used instruments along these two dimensions. The spectrum covered goes all the way from keeping the technology fully proprietary (even secret), providing a service based on it, to widely publishing it and allowing all who wish to do what they want with it.

Service provision tends to be a viable alternative under rather special circumstances, and widespread publishing is commonly associated only with academic research or when a company wishes to preempt others from

FIGURE 9-1

THE INSTRUMENTS OF TECHNOLOGY COMMERCIALIZATION

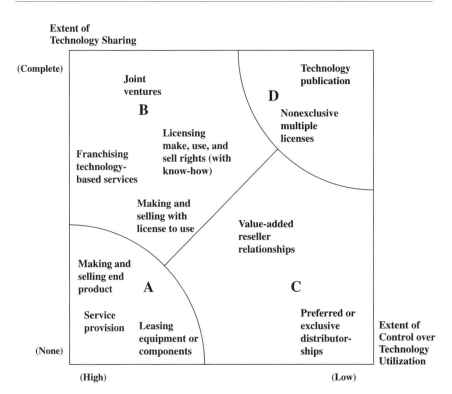

claiming protection for something and hence restricting its own future development goals. More common are the instruments shown between these extremes.

The four zones marked in Figure 9-1 represent the different ways value-added can be retained by the inventor. Thus, the formulae shown in zone A promise the maximum retention of whatever value is created. Those in zone B allow more value-added to partners throughout the business system, while zone C pertains mainly to sharing the value generated in the selling function. Zone D, finally, contains instruments that transfer virtually all the value-added to partners or whoever is interested in the technology, in the hope of creating a larger market for the technology overall.

In general, the stronger and more comprehensive the intellectual property rights established on the technology, the greater the flexibility in choosing among the instruments. A certain amount of sharing is required to get the technology widely accepted and used. Beyond a certain point, however, the profits that the owner of the technology can appropriate decline as others begin to exploit the technology independently. The challenge is to find where the optimum level lies and the type of business formula likely to achieve it.

Factors Influencing the Choice

Which formula, or combination of formulae, to use depends naturally on the circumstances of the inventing organization. Choices made earlier in the commercialization process inevitably constrain the freedom one has at this stage as well. The following, however, are the main considerations involved in making the choice:

The long-term ambition of the inventor versus the immediate economics of contracting for complementary assets;

The promotional needs of the technology itself at a point in time;

The need to mobilize certain market constituents to deliver the technology effectively and quickly;

The desire, sometimes, to focus on a high value component of the technology while, at the same time, controlling its use and enjoying the collateral benefits it offers;

The price that can be obtained for the technology itself versus the profitability of making and selling end products; and

The need to use a particular technology to support related businesses.

By looking at each of these criteria one by one, it is possible to obtain a fairly balanced set of guidelines for selecting a formula suited to any given technology and the inventor's circumstances.

LONG-TERM AMBITION VERSUS THE ECONOMICS OF CONTRACTING

Where to focus in the spectrum from making and selling the complete product and licensing it is mainly a function of the need for certain assets required in delivering the technology. Table 9-1 lists the typical assets required in making and selling most industrial products. The first two are generic assets; assets 3 and 4 relate to the product itself, both its technical elements as well as its marketing concept; assets 5 through 7 pertain to manufacturing; finally, asset 8 involves all the investments associated with market access. In many situations, an inventor starts out with either asset 3 (product) or 6 (process). To bring these to market requires assembling all the other complementary assets.

In situations where these assets can be assembled cheaply and quickly or are unique to the technology, one is usually better off making and selling end products on one's own. Thus, when in October 1985 the Korea Steel Company (KOSCO), a subsidiary of Korea's Daewoo group, found a new way to make hexaclorophene (a powerful germicide used in a variety of pharmaceutical and cosmetic applications) with no detectable dioxin content, it chose to supply the world market on its own rather than to license the process to others. With a world demand of about 100 tons per year, it was an inexpensive proposition to do so and offered the company an opportunity to enter a new business altogether. KOSCO not only decided against licensing but against patenting the process too—thereby keeping it secret and not having to enforce a patent worldwide.[1]

Yet the contracting for complementary assets is a lot more than just about affordability. As shown by the experience of companies who failed to maintain a business lead in a technology they pioneered, it is sometimes better to partner with those who already possess these assets. Thus, both EMI with its CT scanner and Bowmar with its hand-held calculator were soon overtaken by companies such as GE and Texas Instruments because the latter had developmental, manufacturing, and marketing capabilities that were needed for sustaining the commercialization effort. By licensing their technologies to them, EMI and Bowmar would have maintained a foothold in their inventions longer than they actually did.[2]

When Contracting Out Makes Short-Term Economic Sense

In general, contracting out for complementary assets makes good sense when it is not possible to appropriate the technology, when rapid market penetration in several markets is desired, when there are few transaction costs involved and the skills necessary are not specific to the technology, and when the assets already in one's possession do not offer much synergy over those one acquires.

TABLE 9-1

SUGGESTED LIST OF ASSETS REQUIRED IN THE COMMERCIALIZATION
OF A NEW TECHNOLOGY

---

1. Financial

2. Managerial and Technical Personnel

---

3. Product/Technical Know-How
   a. Patented
   b. Secret
   c. Public domain

4. Product/Market Concept
   a. Product features
   b. Function/segment relation
   c. Optimum marketing mix

---

5. Privileged Access to Raw Materials and Components

6. Equipment, Tools, and Process Know-How
   a. Patented
   b. Secret, specially designed
   c. Commercially available

7. Manufacturing Capacity for Intermediary Products, Subassemblies, and Final Products
   a. Unique, not commercially available
   b. Commercially available

---

8. Acquired Market Access
   a. Brand recognition and customer loyalty
   b. Privileged access to or control over distribution channels, transportation, and warehousing
   c. Servicing facilities and expertise
   d. Knowledge of and established relationships with market constituents and relevant institutions

---

SOURCE: Adapted from Vijay K. Jolly, "Global Competitive Strategies," in Charles C. Snow, ed., *Strategy, Organization, and Human Resource Management* (Greenwich, Conn.: JAI Press, Inc., 1989): 55–110, p. 59. Reprinted with permission.

Inability to Appropriate

Many technologies get inadequately protected by intellectual property rights, allowing others to reinvent around them easily. Such technologies are "inappropriable" to begin with and are often best commercialized through licensing. Making and selling end products will only invite competition and reduce the share of the market the inventor gains. Licensing the technology not only preempts the need on the part of potential competitors to reverse-engineer it, but co-opts them into making sure whatever rights it has are policed and protected in the licensee's market.

Rapid Market Penetration in Several Markets

Perhaps the most common reason to contract with others today is the need to introduce products rapidly over many market segments or a broad geographic area. Market access (asset 8 in Table 9-1) typically forms the basis of such agreements. Whether it is original equipment manufacturer (OEM) selling relationships, comarketing or copromotion (same brand) arrangements, or long-term preferred relationships with trading and distribution companies, the objective is to build volume quickly and gain market share while an advantage lasts.

Licensing or joint venturing with companies that already possess market access, or have the resources to build it in their own markets, serves the same purpose. If properly designed and implemented, such agreements can also help in protecting a technology and earning significant returns for its inventor.

Among the most successful strategies in this category is that which brought to market dimensionally stable anodes (DSAs), used in electrolyzer cells such as the FM-21. Invented by Henri Beer and covered by two important patents (popularly referred to as the Beer '65 and Beer '67 patents), this technology was initially commercialized by Vittorio de Nora through a holding company, Electronor SA. The strategy he adopted had two main components: accessing chlorine producers throughout the world and making it easier for them to adopt the new technology. Market access was achieved by setting up a number of joint-venture companies throughout the world, typically on a 50/50 basis with a local partner. Known as the Permelecs, these joint ventures were licensed to manufacture and commercialize DSAs in their market on an exclusive basis.

DSAs, made of titanium, cost a great deal more than traditional carbon anodes, but lasted longer and could be recoated at periodic intervals. While their overall life cycle cost was lower, chlorine producers would need to invest millions of dollars up front in order to use them—rather than paying small amounts regularly for consumable carbon anodes. To reduce this cost of possession, most Permelecs offered to lease their anodes, albeit on profitable terms, putting up their own capital to finance the lease. This strategy had some collateral benefits too. It permitted Electronor and the Permelecs to keep the entire technology in house since leasing meant retaining ownership over the electrodes in a user's plant. It also guaranteed that the Permelecs alone undertook the recoating business. Furthermore, given the way the lease contracts were written, users were under obligation to transfer any technology improvements they made to the Permelecs, which, in turn, had to turn these improvements over to Electronor.

Few Transaction Costs

As in any business alliance, the benefits a partner brings should be greater than the transaction costs associated with arranging and managing the relationship. In technology commercialization, these transaction costs tend to be a function of the specificity of the assets to be contracted. The more closely they are linked to the technology, the easier it is to manage them in house, making contracting uneconomical.

Thus, one study found that two-thirds of U.S. biotechnology companies had their own manufacturing facilities and fulfilled 80 percent of their manufacturing needs in house because of three main factors: the close technological link between lab-scale process development and scaled-up production, the preference for trade-secret protection over patents in so far as processes are concerned, and the fact that regulations require repeating stage III clinical trials each time a new source of manufacturing is planned.[3] All of these transaction costs would have made contracting externally for production difficult and uneconomical.

Transaction costs associated with assembling the right sales and distribution channels required for biopharmaceuticals also explain why some biotechnology companies integrated forward into distribution. It is the same reason, in fact, why Xerox created its own dedicated sales and maintenance organization when it launched its first copier, the Xerox 914. Because of the complexity and newness of the product, the company could not go through established distributors as other office product manufacturers did.

Lack of Synergy

The absence of synergies with the assets already in one's possession is yet another reason for contracting out certain complementary assets. While a company may possess or can easily assemble the latter on its own, they may not be the best for the business concerned.

When Hughes decided in the mid-1960s to exploit its electronic timing technology developed for the defense industry, it started to make digital watches. In fact, it was the first company making such watches and even sold them with the Hughes label, thinking that would provide an aura of excellence and technological sophistication. Even though it tried all kinds of distribution channels, including drugstores, it could not make a business out of it. But, having used its name, it could not simply withdraw. It had to keep a service operation going for two to three years even after it stopped making the watches. It would have done better to license its technology or otherwise partner with a consumer-oriented company. An aerospace company with a knowledge of sheet metal made the same error when it got into the canoe business.

The important thing, of course, is to see these synergies not on a case-by-case basis but in a long-term, strategic perspective. In the end, what one is trying to optimize is not the return on a particular technology but the returns on investments made in a business.

For example, consider the choices Astra confronted in bringing its Turbuhaler to market. The patented device could be used for asthma drugs, as well as a number of other drugs delivered through inhalation. It could, moreover, be used for Astra's own asthma drugs (Bricanyl and Pulmicort), as well as competing drugs made by other companies, including those whose patents had expired.

The choices Astra faced in deciding on which business formula to use included:

Exploiting the device immediately, and on as wide a front as possible, by licensing make, use, and sell rights to any drug company interested;

Using the advantages the device offered to increase the market share of the company's own proprietary drugs—keeping both Turbuhaler and the drugs it incorporated proprietary;

Leveraging the Turbuhaler technology to incorporate its own proprietary drugs as well as generic versions of other companies' drug; or

Leveraging the Turbuhaler technology by partnering with other drug companies, allowing them to incorporate their proprietary drugs in exchange for marketing rights to Astra.

The option finally settled on was a combination of the last two. Rather than maximize short-term returns from licensing the device itself, the company first chose to keep Turbuhaler proprietary in order to promote its own asthma drugs. Then, leveraging the superior delivery system Turbuhaler provided, it entered the generic market—which it had previously shunned—and expanded its product line.

More generally, whether to license or not depends on the control one wishes to exercise in the asset most critical to a business. Thus, if there is little to be gained by displacing existing companies that have established market access, licensing is the most reasonable strategy. If, on the other hand, the use of the technology in addressing consumer problems is critical, licensing away the technology is tantamount to transferring the access to consumers to someone else. The licensee ends up controlling the market through establishing relationships with customers, distribution channels, and the like. These relationships not only outlive the technology but turn into a larger barrier to entry than manufacturing capacity, should the inventor wish to enter the market later.

The Inventor's Long-Term Ambition

The foregoing notwithstanding, many inventors see complementary asset accumulation as a prize enabled by the success of the technology. Entrepreneurial inventors not only develop a dedicated set of complementary assets to distinguish their products but *want* to build large, complete businesses. The initial technology, in other words, is an entry ticket, a first step in the creation of an entire infrastructure that will then act as a barrier to entrants and as a platform for the commercialization of subsequent technologies. For them, the choice of business formula is a function of the risk they are willing to take in achieving a larger objective, not just a static assessment of the assets they already possess.

EMI's CT Scanner

This is, to a large extent, the reason why EMI decided to commercialize its CT scanner on its own. When EMI's CT scanner was ready for launch, the debate within the company centered around whether to license the technology to one or more medical equipment companies or to go it alone. From the moment clinical trials showed the CT scanner to be a successful diagnostic device in late 1971, several companies had contacted EMI to negotiate distribution and/or licensing rights.

The arguments in favor of licensing (advocated by the head of the central research laboratory, among others) all centered around EMI's unpreparedness to bring the device to market on its own. EMI lacked medical product experience. It had no service and logistics facilities in the United States. The manufacturing process required to produce CT scanners efficiently was different from the job-shop mode EMI was used to for its highly specialized defense products, and the company lacked a working knowledge of the North American market, where most of the demand for scanners was expected to be.

From a short-term profit standpoint, licensing the CT scanner to one or more of the large medical instrument companies made sense. But the company chose to keep the technology in house and make and sell scanners on its own, including in the North American market. Among the arguments for doing so were that the scanner needed to be seen as a basis for future diversification into the medical electronics field, justifying the building of the required infrastructure; the patents on the device provided sufficient lead time for EMI to get established; and others to whom EMI might license the technology might not push it hard enough since it would cannibalize their sales of conventional X-ray equipment and consumables.[4]

As shown by several start-ups that grew into successful businesses, long-term ambition can be an overriding reason to assemble complementary assets on one's own. Amgen, for instance, could have partnered with a large pharmaceutical company in bringing its erythropoietin and Neupogen drugs to the market in the United States, as it did with Kirin in Japan. Instead, it decided to become a fully integrated pharmaceutical company with its own clinical testing and drug approval infrastructure as well as its own sales force.

More and more biotechnology companies have gone down the route of becoming fully integrated pharmaceutical companies—the most recent being British Biotechnology in the United Kingdom. These companies are not blind to the dangers and expenses involved. Rather, they realize that technology commercialization, which involves bringing a new *capability* to market, is inherently different from the commercialization of one-off products. They see their new infrastructure partly as an insurance against failure and partly as the basis for commercializing follow-on products.

Any long-term ambition that is vague and inadequately considered is, of course, only a hope. There are three things that need to be taken into account when transcending short-term economic arguments for contracting. One is the synergy with follow-on products. If assets are to be created around the first technology, these must be made as relevant as possible to the next generation of products envisaged.

Second, a precondition for vertical integration to work is that the technology itself is unique and offers significant price and/or functional advantages. The absence of these two preconditions more recently explains why some of today's biotechnology companies do prefer to license out their discoveries to larger companies, instead of aiming to build full-fledged pharmaceutical companies.

Finally, one must decide what type of business an inventor wishes to create. As Robert Fildes of Cetus Corp. put it,

> While the technology can do much in a myriad of fields, it does not follow that a company can build a business in every area with equal success. For instance, it is a very different thing to decide you wish to enter the doctor's office market as opposed to the hospital products market. The former will require a thousand person sales force while the later will necessitate a hundred person sales force. . . . The biotechnology manager always risks being lured by the call of an exciting product opportunity into a business where he has no realistic hope of operating successfully.[5]

PROMOTIONAL NEEDS OF THE TECHNOLOGY

As important as the contracting of complementary assets in establishing a business formula is the promotional requirements to be met. It is sometimes advantageous to have different approaches in different markets rather than use a uniform global formula.

Adapting the Formula to Market Evolution

In some technbologies, the business formula chosen needs to evolve over time in line with market developments and/or progress in the technology itself.

Sulzer's LST Technology

One example of adapting the formula to the market is that of Sulzer's attempt to commercialize its laser surface treatment (LST) technology. Developed in the mid-1980s by Roger Dekumbis and his colleagues, this technology involved the use of high-powered lasers for a variety of metal-lurgical purposes—surface hardening, remelting to refine structure, and coating with special alloys and ceramics.

In 1989, after a considerable amount of theoretical and practical knowledge on the technology had been accumulated, a decision was made to start marketing the technology. Among the options considered were the following:

Sell a complete turnkey laser surface treatment system to anyone who wanted one;

Sell only certain pieces of hardware such as the laser head, powder feed system, or beam handling equipment that it had developed on its own;

License its process know-how (perhaps in combination with the above option) to users interested in the specific applications it had mastered; or

Provide a job-shop service on its own.

Figure 9-2 summarizes the components of a typical laser surface treatment facility. The laser itself and the basic mechanical handling equipment that went with it were already available from a number of companies on the open market. Sulzer's main contribution was the process know-how developed by Dekumbis and his colleagues for a variety of applications and some related hardware (components 3 and 4 in the figure). Being a machine builder with factory automation capabilities, Sulzer was also capable of assembling and installing the needed peripheral equipment if customers wanted it.

Naturally, the highest value-added and control over the technology lay in supplying turnkey systems, comprising *all* the elements shown in the figure. The greatest profit potential, on the other hand, was to be found in offering only proprietary components, accompanied perhaps by the know-how to use them successfully. The market, however, was not ready for either approach. What it wanted was an occasional service to try out the new technology first. As discussed in Chapter 8, such a demand is not uncommon when certain types of technologies are promoted for the first time.

FIGURE 9-2

COMPONENTS OF A TYPICAL LASER SURFACE TREATMENT FACILITY

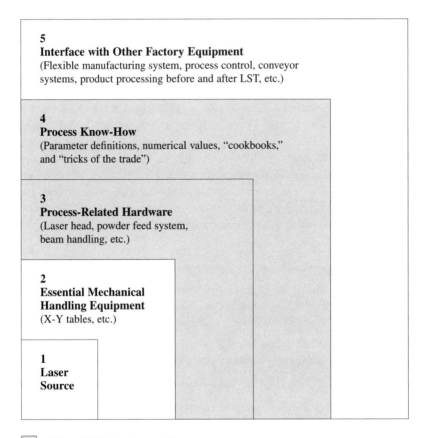

5
Interface with Other Factory Equipment
(Flexible manufacturing system, process control, conveyor
systems, product processing before and after LST, etc.)

4
Process Know-How
(Parameter definitions, numerical values, "cookbooks,"
and "tricks of the trade")

3
Process-Related Hardware
(Laser head, powder feed system,
beam handling, etc.)

2
**Essential Mechanical
Handling Equipment**
(X-Y tables, etc.)

1
**Laser
Source**

☐ = Sulzer initial development focus

The decision, in the end, consisted in starting with a job-shop service operation. This was to be followed over time by sales of proprietary hardware components to other system builders, perhaps accompanied by a royalty-bearing process license. Full-fledged system sales, based on Sulzer's excellent machine-building capabilities, would come last. Such an approach allowed introducing the technology quickly, accumulating a wider range of know-how, learning from customers about different requirements, and protecting the technology in its early phases. Component and system sales would also be postponed until sufficient demand had built up in the market. If nothing else, the service mode based on proprietary know-how would allow future collaboration options to be kept open.

Many technologists, when they start their entrepreneurial careers, begin by offering their problem-solving skills to other companies. Thus, of the 109 M.I.T.-linked technology-based firms studied by Edward Roberts, forty-one began in this way either as research contractors or consultants. What is more, among the remaining sixty-eight firms, about one-third began as job shops, making a limited number of products to special orders. Surveys done in the United Kingdom and Sweden show that this is a fairly general phenomenon there too.[6] The approach allows them to hone their skills in a commercial environment, broaden their repertoire of technologies, and benefit from customer feedback as they go about searching for products to make and sell.

Teknekron Corp. of Berkeley, California, which has been particularly successful in creating and nurturing new ventures, adopts a variant of this approach. Instead of having its ventures develop standard products for the end-user market from the outset, it encourages them to develop customized products for inclusion in other, generally larger, companies' product lines. This problem-solving orientation focusing on relatively few customers allows Teknekron-backed companies to obtain a detailed understanding of the requirements of a particular industry and of what the technology can contribute. It puts the solving of customer-defined problems ahead of the technology such that when standard products are offered they meet a well-recognized need. As a by-product, this approach also exposes venture managers to other problems and technologies that they might consider exploiting in the future.[7]

What business formula gets adopted after this initial problem-solving or service provision phase depends on the nature of the technology. Sometimes it is profitable to continue in a service mode for a long time, as Air Products, Inc., did with oxygen. Founded by Leonard Pool immediately after World War II, Air Products's concept was to design a reliable oxygen plant that could be operated with semiskilled labor. This plant would be located at the site of major consumers of industrial oxygen and would supply them by pipeline directly rather than with high-pressure cylinders as was then the case. While the company could easily have sold its first commercial oxygen plants to steel mills, it chose to keep the technology in house and sell the gas instead—a more expensive proposition involving a greater commitment of financial resources. This strategy, which Pool referred to as "keeping the cows and selling the milk," allowed the company to maintain a technological lead for several years.[8]

In other cases, the path from providing a service on one's own to selling a product takes the following sequence: (1) own service (job shop), to (2) franchising service, to (3) making and selling products or licensing others to do so. The intermediate stage of franchising helps expand the market for the service and allows the sale of certain proprietary components while waiting for the market for the end product to develop.

Franchising technology-based services is a natural extension of providing them oneself. As a commercial instrument, franchising has traditionally been associated with trade names and business formats. They range from simple product distribution agreements, in which franchises are closely identified with a particular manufacturer, all the way to fully integrated relationships involving trademarks, products (or ingredients), service, operating manuals and standards, and marketing methods. In the former category fall the ubiquitous gasoline stations, automobile dealers, and soft drink bottlers. In the latter, which has become a growth industry in its own right, are fast-food chains, real estate agencies, hotels, and a broad range of personal and business services. The important feature of all these traditional franchises is that they are principally a marketing tool. By transferring the right to use a trademark and business format to others, franchisors are able to access a larger consumer base, albeit indirectly, than they would be able to do on their own.

Franchising has not traditionally been used in the commercialization of a new technology or in situations where a complex science-based technology is involved. This is for several reasons. First, franchising involves the widespread retailing of a concept, whereas technology has tended to be licensed to relatively few companies in a field. Second, franchising, by its very nature, involves the transfer of know-how to a number of individuals, which makes it impossible to maintain trade secrets for any length of time—even though confidentiality agreements are often used. The fact that most national and state franchise laws require adequate disclosures to be made by a franchisor (to protect franchisees) makes this all the more problematic. Third, licensing a technology offers the possibility to break up its commercialization by field of use, which franchising usually cannot. Finally, franchise agreements generally last two to five years (renewable) and hence contain the danger that a franchisee would appropriate the know-how and then not renew the agreement.

Even so, franchising can be suited to certain equipment technologies that lend themselves naturally to job-shopping or the provision of a know-how-based service. Such was the case of American Leak Detection, Inc. Founded in 1974 by Richard Rennick, the company's technology consists in using a combination of radio, sound, and sonar to pinpoint the exact location of a water or gas leak—under concrete or inside walls. The system involves injecting compressed air or an inert gas into a closed piping system and electronically "listening" for the otherwise imperceptible sound of the air or gas escaping from the leak. In order to expand the availability of this leak detection service, Rennick chose business format franchising as the commercialization mode. In addition to a $40,000 one-time fee, covering training and a proprietary equipment package, franchisees pay him between 8 percent and 10 percent royalty on the sales they generate.

Separating the Formula by Market and/or Business Segment

Technologies whose markets are separable, either geographically or in terms of field of use, lend themselves to a mix of formulae too. Thus, one can license the technology in some markets, while making and selling end products elsewhere.

One approach consists in using some markets as test or reference markets. By licensing big, established companies in one market, it is possible to gain knowledge and experience in advance of making and selling the product in other markets that the technology owner has reserved for himself. Such an approach also helps establish credibility for successfully exploiting these other markets. EMI, for example, might have considered this option—licensing rights to the CT scanner in the United States, where the technology was most needed in the beginning and where the strongest medical electronics companies were located, and then making and selling the scanner itself in Europe.

MOBILIZING MARKET CONSTITUENTS TO DELIVER THE TECHNOLOGY EFFECTIVELY

As discussed in Chapter 7, certain technologies require a concerted effort on the part of many actors in order to be fully accepted. Many of the well-known examples of successful formulae have, in fact, been designed mainly with a view to mobilizing these actors. In practice, three types of situations tend to present themselves: mobilizing intermediate adopters of a technology, co-opting competitors for delivering a technology on a worldwide basis, and licensing of second-source suppliers in certain industries. Each of these situations involves the sharing of technology regardless of whether the inventing organization possesses the needed complementary assets or can accumulate them on its own over a period of time.

Mobilizing Intermediate Adopters

A key actor in bringing new technologies to market in many industries is an intermediate adopter. These adopters must be convinced about the merits of the technology and motivated enough to incorporate it into the products they sell. Sharing the technology, even on attractive terms, is a sine qua non for commercialization to start.

Dolby's Noise Reduction Circuits

Perhaps the most famous case of mobilizing intermediate adopters to help commercialize a new technology is Dolby's noise reduction circuits. The underlying principle, thought of by Ray Dolby in the early 1960s, consists in distinguishing sounds of different pitch and loudness. In the process of recording music, for example, low-level sounds that might otherwise be smothered by hissing tape noise are first selectively amplified. Then, during playback, the volume is automatically reduced in just those places where it was increased during recording. This second step restores the amplified signals to their original form while suppressing tape noise in places where it would have interfered.

When Ray Dolby incorporated his company, Dolby Laboratories, Ltd., in London in 1965, his initial plan was to commercialize the principle itself—getting others to build and sell circuits based on his design. Finding no ready takers, he was, however, soon obliged to manufacture these circuits himself. Since the professional segment was easiest to access and most receptive to the new technology, this was where he started. A complete "box" incorporating the so-called Dolby-A (for professional) circuits was supplied to recording studios, which hooked them between the microphones and the tape recorder. Another box was supplied to broadcasting stations, for decoding the specially recorded tapes.

For the consumer segment, a simplified circuit based on the same principle was developed in partnership with K. L. H. Research and Development Corporation of Cambridge, Massachusetts, in 1968. With the large number of actors involved in this segment, licensing was chosen as the obvious business formula to pursue. Compared to relatively few manufacturers of audio equipment in the professional segment, there were literally hundreds of manufacturers making different types of devices for the consumer segment all around the world. Other constituents in the market—recording companies, tape manufacturers, and component suppliers—had to be mobilized too. Recording companies were sold a special Dolby-B encoder at a reasonable price and given a royalty-free license to the technology. A royalty-free, nonexclusive license was also given to manufacturers of integrated circuits. The only actors that paid royalties were manufacturers of tape recorders, amplifiers, and receivers.

The success of Dolby's licensing strategy can be measured today by the fact that more than 209 licensees in forty-three countries have produced 350,000,000 consumer products incorporating Dolby technologies. Licensees have access to thirty-nine different Dolby-B-type integrated circuits today. More than 90 percent of music cassettes made in the United States, and 75 percent of those being made worldwide, are made incorporating the Dolby technology.[9]

Co-opting Competitors for Delivery

Although motivated differently than intermediate adopters, competitors are often as important in mobilizing a new technology. Guarding a technology jealously from them can lead to compromising its marketability; in the face of unfulfilled demand, it can invite imitators sooner and more aggressively than would otherwise happen.

Eli Whitney was one inventor who learned this lesson long ago. Obsessed with keeping full control over the commercialization of his cotton gin, which he patented in 1794, he refused to license his invention to others despite rising unmet demand. Imitators entered the market nevertheless, contesting his patents. The result was that the money he could have made with this valuable invention was squandered in litigation instead.

Pilkington's Float Glass Technology

The most famous case of a company that benefited by sharing its technology with competitors is that of Pilkington plc.

Pilkington's float glass technology was licensed on the basis of the following main considerations:

> The product to which the process applied, flat glass, had a large market already being served by major, well-established companies;

> Despite its enormous savings, each float glass plant required some $30 million in investments, and being a private company, Pilkington was in no position to serve the market on its own;

> The technology was well protected, with some fifty patents covering different aspects of the process; yet

> In view of the significance of this technology to the industry, it was unlikely that competitors, many of which were larger than Pilkington, would stand by idly and not develop a competing process that got around the patents on float glass somehow or would fail to come up with an equally good alternative process.

Partly because of the last point, the choice Pilkington made was to license the technology quite early—almost at the same time that it began to produce glass using the new process. Also, although the announced goal was to license on a "first come" basis, it was mainly existing, large competitors in markets not served by Pilkington at that time that became the first licensees.

Co-opting competitors into its strategy early not only prevented alternative technologies to float glass from being developed but, in fact, helped Pilkington advance its own technology and stay at the forefront of glass technology for many years. Saint-Gobain, its competitor in France, for example, had been working on an improved method for polishing plate glass using hydrofluoric acid instead of brushes when float glass was invented. As soon as it obtained a license from Pilkington in 1963—only a year after the first license had been given to Pittsburgh Plate Glass (PPG) in the United States—it terminated this development work.

What allowed Pilkington to stay at the forefront of flat glass technology was the nature of the license agreements it entered into. The company had a grant-back provision whereby all unpatented improvements made by licensees had to be made available to Pilkington, with a right of the latter to transfer these to all other licensees free of charge. As for patented improvements, Pilkington had a right to a royalty-free, nonexclusive license on these too. The licensee that made such improvements, however, reserved the right to making these available to other float glass licensees on its own terms. For its part, Pilkington offered to make all its own improvements to float glass available to licensees without further charges.[10]

More generally, sharing a technology with competitors after it is ready makes good sense when antimonopoly legislation would come in the way of exploiting the technology exclusively on one's own (something that played a role in Pilkington's decision too), when human welfare arguments call for a large number of companies to contribute to a certain technology (as is the case with the human genome project today), and when the technology presents such an advance over current practice that competitors are bound to challenge patent validity or design around issued patents. Also, as pointed out in Chapter 7, sharing a technology with competitors is sometimes needed for establishing it as a standard, but this usually occurs *before* products or processes are ready. When such sharing takes place *after* products or processes have been fully developed, the hope is to create a de facto standard by engaging the most powerful companies. For this to be successful, one needs a technology that truly represents a quantum improvement—as Pilkington's float glass did.

Licensing Second-Source Suppliers

Certain technologies require multiple sources of supply for security reasons. Second-source licensing began in the United States with military procurement, but its major impetus came with the semiconductor industry. At first, it was a defensive move against potential antitrust actions and the vulnerability of patents. The 1956 antitrust consent decree between Western Electric (AT&T) and the U.S. Department of Justice had compelled the former to license its basic patents widely, a precedent that was followed voluntarily by other pioneers in the industry such as Texas Instruments and Fairchild Camera. Later, the principal buyers of semiconductor devices started to insist on second-source suppliers. Apart from the problem of dependence, part of the reason for this was the manufacturing problems traditionally associated with semiconductors.

The difficulties associated with developing high- and stable-yield manufacturing processes meant that buyers wanted alternatives just in case the developer ran into production problems and "lost" the process—that is, encountered a change in the process that the engineers could not figure out. The other reasons all had to do with the OEM relationships that characterized the industry. Customers wanted to make sure the developer of the chip stayed in business long enough or, in case of bankruptcy, had licensed its design to others.[11]

Typically, these second-source licensees were competitors of a chip developer or, in the case of companies like IBM, a major buyer. Preference was given to competitors that would not only manufacture and promote the component, but be able to return the favor by offering their designs too on a second-source basis. As for large buyers like IBM, the license mainly served a comfort need in that IBM could make the chip if, for whatever reason, it could not obtain a regular supply from other vendors.

As the semiconductor industry has matured, such second-source agreements have become less necessary today. To the extent that the practice continues, it is now more to establish a particular chip as an industry standard—thereby gaining acceptance and attracting system and software designers to build products around them—than to reassure buyers.

PERMITTING FOCUS ON HIGH-VALUE COMPONENTS WHILE ENJOYING COLLATERAL BENEFITS

Many companies fail with their technologies because they try to do too much with them. The business one can build on the strength of a new technology can be seen along three dimensions: the scope (or the number of facets) of the technology controlled; the building of productive capacity to deliver them; and the investments made in accessing markets for them. Rather than make and sell a complete device or system, because one's technology scope extends to all its facets, a more rewarding stance sometimes is to concentrate on the most important facet and contract for the rest of the business with partners—the caveat regarding ambition mentioned earlier notwithstanding.

In practice, such contracting can take any of three forms: making and selling the facet that leverages the technology most, combining the licensing of some facet with the making and selling of another facet, or making and selling (or leasing) one set of facets tied to the provision of services and components covering the others.

Making and Selling Components That Leverage the Technology Most

Focusing on making and selling just the component and allowing others to commercialize a complete device has always been a common strategy on the part of those wishing to extract high returns from their investment in

R&D. They commercialize those facets where the technology's leverage is greatest, without wanting to mobilize the complementary assets that would be required for the product(s) in which these get incorporated.

Canon's Laser Printer Mechanism

This is essentially the approach Canon took in launching its LBP-CX laser printing mechanism. When introduced in 1984, the laser printers available at that time cost between $50,000 and $400,000. These printers had been developed as an alternative to daisy-wheel systems (which offered good text quality but no graphics capability) and dot-matrix systems (which could print graphics but had low resolution).

Canon's LBP-CX laser printer engine consisted of an inexpensive imaging system with a disposable xerographic printing cartridge. This disposability was a key advantage in Canon's design. Instead of having to rely on constant servicing, users having problems with their photoconductor drum could simply replace it with another cartridge. Although not as fast or high-resolution as top-of-the-line laser printers, the Canon engine was offered at $1,000 apiece in OEM quantities, allowing laser printers costing $5,000 to $10,000 to be offered for the first time.

Rather than actually make and sell such low-cost printers on its own, Canon supplied only the laser imaging mechanism, the xerographic printer, and a case on an OEM basis to companies such as Hewlett-Packard, Imagen, and Quality Micro Systems. The latter designed their own printer-driver portion—the electronics that takes the information from the host computer and turns it into a modulated signal for the laser imager. As Koichi Kadakura, a product planning manager at Canon, put it, "We're at a disadvantage in the end-user market because we don't have the distribution channels set up to reach customers. We'll leave that market to the companies who are best equipped to address it—the personal computer and printer suppliers."[12]

The important thing to note about focusing on a particular facet is that its value changes over time. Some of this is due to the technology's own evolution but it is also caused by changes in the marketplace. In the early years of the semiconductor industry, for example, many companies making semiconductors and integrated circuits moved into end products, partly in order to gain extra value-added. Texas Instrument integrated forward into hand-held calculators and microcomputers, and Fairchild did the same. Today, with growing sophistication and a better articulation of customers' needs, such package solutions have become less valuable. In fact, profit goes to those who contribute the best technology for individual components of the system, such as Intel in microprocessors and Microsoft in software. The traditional system builders such as IBM, DEC, and Bull are seeing their competitiveness and profit margins erode.

Combining Licensing with the Sale of Components

This is a variant on the making and selling of key components and is usually feasible only in the presence of certain intellectual property rights. Since one cannot sell and license the same object, it involves possessing rights that extend beyond the component to be sold. To show what is involved, Figure 9-3 summarizes the scope of ICI's FM-21 technology.

Among the components, cathodes were commercially available, although ICI possessed its own superior version; membranes were proprietary to a handful of companies, notably DuPont and Asahi, but were sold openly on the market; the only restricted component technology was the dimensionally stable anode (DSA), for which ICI had special permission

FIGURE 9-3
FACETS OF THE FM-21 TECHNOLOGY

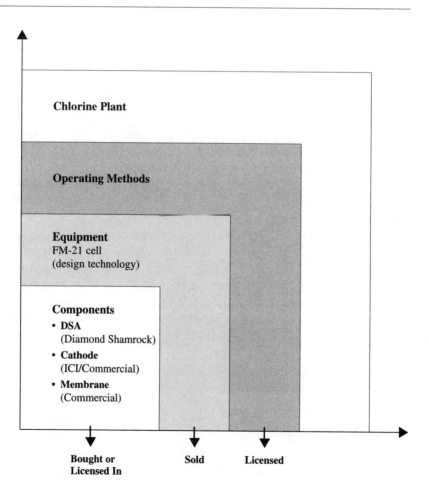

to supply with the FM-21; ICI's own technology, which it had patented, related to the design of the cell. Moreover, it had accumulated significant experience and know-how in the installation and operation of these cells (shown in dark shade) that was both unique and valuable in its own right.

The way ICI chose to commercialize the FM-21 consisted in making and selling complete cells along with a license on the operating methods. This offered three main advantages: It extended ICI's control over the technology, provided a fairly attractive royalty income (of the order of £1 per ton of chlorine produced), and gave ICI a priority in the supply and recoating of anodes. Since a "tie-in" of the anode or other component (such as cathodes) business could not be legally justified, this priority meant that ICI had the first right to bid. If its terms were competitive, an FM-21 licensee was expected to turn to it for this part of the business.

Sulzer-Escher Wyss's NIPCO Rollers

A more elaborate case of combining sales with licensing is that of Escher Wyss's NIPCO roller technology, where an entirely different facet of the technology from the one sold constitutes the object of the license. A company long engaged in heavy machinery, Escher Wyss (part of Switzerland's Sulzer Group) had at one point experimented with replacing roller bearings by hydrostatic bearings in the turntable of one of its large-diameter horizontal lathes. Then, in the early 1970s, in response to some problems being encountered in its paper machinery department, it tried out the same approach on the roller presses this department was building.

In the manufacture of paper, the sheet of material is passed through wide presses that squeeze out the water still in the paper. In this application, two, sometimes more, rolls are pressed against each other with pressing forces applied through bearings at each end of the roll. As the industry moved to ever-wider rolls with smaller clearances at the contact surface, these forces began to create undesirable deflections in the rolls. This, in turn, resulted in unequal distribution of the roll nip forces over the strip width, causing serious problems in the rolling process and adversely affecting product quality.

Escher Wyss's approach to tackling this problem consisted in counteracting the forces acting on the rolls by placing hydrostatic bearings on the inner side of the roll. The NIPCO press, as it came to be called, comprised three mechanical elements: (1) a fixed beam, (2) the rotating roll sleeve, and (3) the hydrostatic bearings mounted on top of hydraulic cylinders. Further development work resulted in a mechanism for the quick exchange of rollers, a closed-loop computerized control system for regulating process parameters automatically, and a redesign of the mill stand. A number of patents covering the device and its operation were granted to the company.

It was soon realized that the NIPCO roller had applications in a wide range of other industries using rollers applying large forces. Internal brainstorming sessions were conducted to search out and prioritize these other applications and to assess what would be needed for Escher Wyss to exploit them. Among the industries identified were rotogravure printing, paper calendering, steel rolling, aluminum foil rolling, plastic calendering, and textile calendering. Each of these applications, however, involved fitting NIPCO rollers into a piece of equipment differently.

The option offering maximum value-added as well as control over commercialization was that of using the new technology to build complete equipment for the paper, steel, and other industries identified by the company. The company, however, decided against such forward integration. Each application of NIPCO rollers would need considerable further development work to adapt the component in particular configurations. Sulzer was intimately familiar with only some of these applications, and building complete assemblies would mean competing against well-established and specialized firms with a service infrastructure already in place. Most of the user industries, moreover, were going through a period of slow growth, making entry all the more difficult.

Selling NIPCO rollers to these companies, on the other hand, would mean parting with valuable know-how and becoming dependent on their specifications and requirements. It would turn Escher Wyss into a component supplier under an OEM contract in which the buyer not only had a strong bargaining position but also a dominant role in the innovations taking place in his industry. The alternative, that of licensing rights to make and sell its rollers to plant builders outside the paper machine application, had the same weakness. Although a common strategy under these circumstances, it too would have meant parting with technology in return for a royalty.

After considerable discussion, something in between these options was settled upon—that of becoming a supplier of NIPCO rollers to existing plant builders but under a license agreement that would put Escher Wyss in a commanding role vis-à-vis the technology. Since the company was not entitled to sell and license the NIPCO roller at the same time, the license was not on the rolls but on the equipment surrounding it, whose design depended on the use of the new roll. To make the latter licensable, Escher Wyss had to go beyond its core NIPCO roll technology, do further development work for each intended application, and develop some proprietary position in areas where it had no intention to compete.[13]

Collateral Benefits Through Tie-Ins

Apart from the value that can be extracted for patents and know-how related to a new technology, the use of instruments such as licensing, franchising, and leasing allow the realization of certain collateral benefits as well. These include the obtaining of preferential rights for the supply of intermediate products; the revenue that comes from maintenance and service, including replacement parts; and control over the diffusion and utilization of the technology.

The extent to which such tie-ins and control over licensees are feasible, however, is limited by antimonopoly legislations. Formal tie-ins are generally illegal under the laws of most countries unless they can be justified for guaranteeing performance or do not otherwise constitute an abuse of legitimate intellectual property rights.

This said, some companies intentionally leave it up to buyers of their equipment to decide where they wish to purchase their consumables. Others, notably in the scientific instruments and high-technology equipment fields, see such consumables as a legitimate means of gaining additional value from their technology. In the process industry, for example, catalysts are often the "component" whose sale accompanies a license. ICI, which has traditionally licensed several of its process technologies, has done so partly to profit from its strength in catalyst development and manufacture. In some processes, in fact, the amount earned from catalyst sales has actually equaled that earned as royalties on the process.

Tetra Pak's Aseptic Packaging System

Tie-in sales are conceptually similar to providing a system of benefits. This is the argument Tetra Pak used in justifying its business formula vis-à-vis potential customers and regulatory authorities.

In developing its Tetra Brik system for ultra high temperature (UHT) long-life milk in the 1960s, Tetra Pak worked on and patented three key facets of the technology—the machines for filling and packaging; the cartons used in the machines; and various aspects of the overall process, including the method of folding the carton. To retain full control over the technology and optimize the returns on the investment it made, the company chose the following business formula:

(i) *Machines:* These could be either sold with a license to use Tetra Pak's technology or leased. In either case, a number of restrictive conditions applied, with some variations across countries. Tetra Pak:

Retained the exclusive right to inspect, maintain, and repair equipment;

In lease contracts, had the right to control the equipment's configuration, prohibiting the lessee from adding accessories, modifying the equipment, or moving it;

Limited the rights of the purchaser to resell or transfer the equipment to third parties;

Had the exclusive right to supply spare parts; and

Especially in lease contracts, required the user to inform it of any improvements or modifications to the equipment and to grant it ownership of any resulting intellectual property rights.

(ii) *Cartons:* In all countries, Tetra Pak retained the exclusive right of control over the end product by requiring the purchaser or lessee of its equipment to use only Tetra Pak cartons from it or a designated supplier.

All of the above conditions applied for so long as purchasers remained in possession of the machines (for sales contracts) or for the term of the lease, which ranged from three to nine years depending on the country.

In effect, the company sold or leased its equipment at a low price but obliged buyers to source their packaging material from it at much higher profit.

When confronted by the European Commission's antitrust body recently, Tetra Pak justified these restrictive clauses on the following grounds:

That its packaging systems are complete and indivisible systems, comprising the machine, the packaging material, training, and after-sales service;

That the marketing of complete packaging systems was objectively justified by the concern to protect public health (cartons are much more sophisticated containers than traditional containers such as bottles and thus add a significant risk of technical errors likely to cause serious problems in vulnerable sectors of the population); and

That all manufacturers of carton-packaging systems within the European Community supplied complete systems too.

Were it not for Tetra Pak's dominant position in the industry (90 percent market share in the case of aseptic [UHT] machines), this commercial strategy would probably have gone unnoticed. The *combination* of a dominant position and a restrictive business formula, however, caused the European Commission to administer an ECU 75 million fine on the company.

Collateral Benefits with Leasing

As the Tetra Pak example illustrates, leasing offers similar benefits to licensing for controlling the utilization of a technology. Although the main objective served by leasing may be to reduce the financial burden on buyers, it allows the lessor to obtain a variety of collateral benefits, especially if the object concerned is covered by strong intellectual property rights.

Unlike sales transactions, leasing implies the retention of ownership in the hands of the lessor. This allows the lessor to charge a rental for the use of the equipment while controlling how it is used in practice, including issues such as operation, maintenance, and the use of spare parts and components.

UTILX's FlowMole

The example of UTILX given in the previous chapter illustrates the tie-in possibilities associated with equipment leasing too. While the main reason for leasing was to help promote the technology, it offered several advantages to UTILX. It lowered the risk and cost of possession to contractors that provided underground trenching services but, at the same time, it enabled UTILX to:

Separate the territories in which different contractors operated, hence making it more attractive for them;

Sell nonproprietary spares on a privileged basis;

Earn income from providing certain services to the lessee, such as training of personnel;

Prevent lessees from modifying the equipment;

Have the lessee use, operate, maintain, support, repair, and advertise the equipment only in accordance with manuals and other instructions furnished by UTILX; and

Lease proprietary spare parts on a sole and exclusive basis in return for a fixed rental. These parts were (i) subject to UTILX's patents or patent applications within the territory, (ii) required for a technically satisfactory exploitation of such patents, and (iii) parts for which manufacture was made possible through use of the company's proprietary know-how or trade secrets.

Apart from directly protecting its technology, the lease mode made contractors partners of the company. The establishment of rental charges with a base rent and an additional rent linked to the lessee's monthly gross equipment revenue reinforced this spirit of partnership.

Although title to or ownership of what is being leased does not get transferred to a lessee, the latter can be made to take appropriate steps to protect the intellectual property rights involved, too. In addition to providing reasonable assistance in prosecuting infringers in their territory, lessees can be made to retain labels and other notices on the leased object identifying the ownership of these rights, maintain trade secrets, and even grant back rights to inventions they make relating to the leased technology.

The Razor Blade Strategy

A variant of formal tie-ins is the so-called razor blade strategy, practiced by companies selling consumables for their devices. The traditional version of this strategy consists of selling the razor cheap and making money on the blades it uses. This is, for example, the approach taken by companies that entered the market for video games, such as Nintendo and Sega—selling their players cheap but making their money on the software. Nintendo, for example, gets roughly half its sales from software in the form of game cartridges and half from game consoles, which is the "hardware." In order to capture a wide market, it sells the consoles close to cost, leaving software to produce the profits.

The tie-in is justified by Nintendo on quality grounds. Blaming the computer game debacle of the early 1980s on poor software, Nintendo controls all the software written for its machines. Since it owns the patents on the cartridges that go into its consoles, it supplies its cartridges only to approved software houses under license. Under the terms of this license, it has the right to modify the games written and even refuse publication. It also controls the number of cartridges produced in order to avoid flooding the market and forbids software companies to publish their games for use on other computers for at least two years.[14]

The precondition for such a strategy to work is that the "razor" itself must be unique and competitive. This is, for example, what 3DO found out when commercializing its interactive multimedia system. Rather than come up with its own business formula, it decided to take the same approach as Nintendo and Sega—selling hardware cheap and making its money on royalties charged to software developers.

As with any me-too approach, the consequence was price erosion and a limited freedom of action. Thus, in the beginning, 3DO charged a $3 royalty to software developers compared to the $9 to $12 Nintendo and Sega were charging. As for the machine itself, 3DO had planned to sell it at near the cost of manufacture by licensees. The problem was that the first model of 3DO's game machine itself turned out to be uncompetitive. Lowering the royalty charged to software developers didn't help because their main objective was to maximize revenue. If the machine sold poorly, so would their software.

THE PRICE THAT CAN BE CHARGED FOR THE TECHNOLOGY ITSELF

The commonly held belief that licensing is a second-best choice compared to making and selling end products is based on two main assumptions: first, that licensing involves the creation of potential competitors, and second, that the profits that can be realized from licensing are lower than what could be gained by assembling and deploying the needed complementary assets on one's own.

The price one can charge for a technology is ultimately a function of the value it creates for the buyer. However, the market for a technology is usually imperfect. The seller and buyer seldom have equal information on what the technology can do. Each buyer's circumstances are different. Buyers may also have different judgments regarding the alternatives available to them, including licensing in some other technology, the cost of developing the same technology themselves without infringing the licensor's rights, and competitive pressures. Conversely, the licensor may have an opinion regarding the opportunity loss associated with licensing.

Methods for Determining the Price of Technology

In the absence of acceptable market prices and standard (objective) criteria, actual pricing decisions are generally based on weighing different factors and on rules of thumb that experienced negotiators have found useful. Table 9-2 summarizes the most common factors taken into account, along with the manner in which payments are affected.

Given the wide range of factors that need to be borne in mind, the actual process of arriving at a price for technology is often one of negotiation—especially for the first transaction, which may then set a precedent for others. Typically, one of the four factors listed in Table 9-2 is used to come up with some benchmark value, followed by negotiations bringing out the special circumstances of the parties involved. The greater the comfort with the benchmark on all sides, the less adversarial these negotiations tend to be, and the greater the likelihood of achieving a standard fee that can be applied to a wide range of licensees—something that is often desirable for commercial reasons.

Norms

Norms are often the most popular starting point for any licensing negotiation in industries that are already well established. Although individual cases might differ, most licensing professionals know more or less what the appropriate level of remuneration tends to be; for example, in the metallurgical industry (2 percent to 3 percent royalty), electronics (5 percent to 8 percent), or pharmaceuticals (10 percent to 20 percent).

There is nothing objective about these norms, except that over time they have come to reflect the contribution of technology to profit potential in that particular industry. Naturally, the more competitive the industry, and the greater the price pressures it is subject to, the lower the norm tends to be. This explains the low (1 percent to 5 percent) royalty rates that were practiced in the personal computer industry in recent years and why the steel and cement industries have traditionally had low (1 percent to 2 percent) royalty rates.

Norms also tend to reflect the R&D intensity of an industry. The rough

TABLE 9-2

Methods for Determining and Accounting for Licensing Income

Estimating the Amount	Method of Accounting for Payment
1. Norms	1. Paid-up licenses

2. Amortizing costs
  • R&D investments
  • Transfer costs
  • Protection costs
    (patents, trademarks, etc.)
	2. Installments

	3. Running royalties based on
	  • Capacity
	  • Output (quantity)
	  • Sales (net)

3. Impact on licensee's business
  • Share in profits (10%–40%)
  • Share cost savings
  • Time savings
	• Time
	  • Use of something
	    (e.g., a circuit or component)

4. Restrictive conditions and the
   licensee's contribution
	4. Down payments combined with
	   running royalties

correspondence between royalty rates and the percentage of sales devoted to R&D basically captures the cost a licensee will need to incur to develop the technology itself—inclusive of the cost of failed attempts. In industries such as pharmaceuticals, it is even possible to arrive at approximate ranges for drugs in different stages of development. Since roughly 40 percent of the R&D is spent up to the stage of preclinical trials, a licensee buying in a new drug at this stage pays about 60 percent less than it would pay for an approved drug—adjusting, of course, for decreasing risks as trials progress. A similar calculation by stage can be done for other industries, although generalizations are harder to find.

Amortizing Costs

Amortizing the cost of R&D is also a common starting point. Like norms, it is easily quantifiable and can be added to the other costs incurred in licensing a technology, such as protecting intellectual property rights in the market being licensed and the cost of actually transferring the technology to the licensee. However, like norms, the approach has several deficiencies when applied to individual cases. What a company has spent in developing something may not seem relevant to a licensee that considers its own R&D more efficient. The approach, moreover, does not take into account the market potential of the technology, nor the competitive situation in which it will be deployed.

Impact on Licensee's Business

The third approach, that of sharing in the value the technology creates for a potential licensee, is the most objective and fair. As such, it is the preferred approach in most cases. Aiming for a share of the profits that the technology generates, or the cost and time it saves a licensee, is also easy to justify—provided all these can be estimated objectively enough. Compared to norms and cost amortization, it has the virtue of being based on the individual merits of a particular technology and the true benefits provided to the licensee.

As a rule of thumb, the royalty charged tends to be between 10 percent and 40 percent of the licensee's profit, depending on the technology's contribution to overall business success and the licensee's share of the risk. Tthe approach used by Union Carbide when licensing its Unipol process was based on this notion of value sharing. Royalty rates were established to price the new product at parity with existing products so that downgauging benefits accrued to the fabricator and/or its customer. Within these overall objectives, the royalty was set so as to provide licensees with a good rate of return on their investment, yet yielding a fair return to Union Carbide. In addition, the license package was tailored so as to give each licensee the same overall benefit as the others.

Although the pricing of the Unipol technology was on a case-by-case basis, the magnitudes involved were in the following range: $100,000 in disclosure fees after the signing of a secrecy agreement, between $18 million and $25 million up-front fees for the process license, and royalty of between 2 percent and 4 percent of net sales over a ten- to fifteen-year period.[15]

Restrictive Conditions and the Licensee's Contribution

The duration of the contract, its exclusivity, and the nature of guarantees given to the licensee all have an impact on the price. Contracts that provide exclusive rights for a long period of time tend to earn higher royalties than shorter ones. Similarly, if a licensor guarantees the technology and its patent validity, a licensee is willing to pay more. The offer of continuing improvements is yet another factor making the technology more valuable to a licensee.

Offsetting this is the nature of the grant-back clause and any obligations (explicit or implied) placed on the licensee. The more licensees are expected to exchange their patent rights, contribute to the licensor's technology through grant-backs, or give priority to buying certain products and services from the licensor, the less they are naturally willing to pay. The same applies to field of use and territorial restrictions imposed on the licensee, which have the effect of reducing the attractiveness of what is being licensed.

Whether explicitly included in the contract or agreed to separately, the collateral advantages that a licensor is expected to enjoy influence the price a licensee is willing to pay. Thus, if the licensor obtains the status of a "privileged supplier" (or has a first right of refusal) for intermediate components and certain services, the understanding is that he will be making part of his profit from these. What one is really negotiating in such cases is the *total* profits a licensor is expected to make, rather than just the royalty rate.

Judging the Profitability of Technology Sales

Judging the adequacy of the price one comes up with using these methods is, of course, the hard part. Simple comparison of royalty rates with the sales margin an inventor can earn in making and selling end products almost invariably favors the latter. But motives such as setting of standards, promoting the widespread utilization of a technology, or co-opting competitors in one's strategy all tend to result in lower royalties than one would expect from the methods described above.

An appreciation of the role these strategic factors play can be obtained from the way Pilkington priced its float glass technology. Although the new process saved roughly 35 percent of the total cost of making plate glass, the royalty rate charged by Pilkington was nowhere near the 10 percent to 15 percent rate that a straightforward value-sharing formula would have indicated. Had Pilkington kept the technology to itself, it could probably have achieved a profit margin of the order of 20 percent to 25 percent of sales over the life of its patent—and in an industry used to profit margins of around 3 percent.

With large competitors being the main licensees in the beginning, taking all the investment risk, and helping Pilkington advance its own technology to boot, it was only natural that a royalty rate closer to the "norm" got charged eventually. As the overall technology improved—with the help of the early licensees—the royalty rate charged to other licensees grew over time. Then, sometime in the early 1970s, this royalty rate started to fall again, this time because of the expiry of Pilkington's core patents and the fact that the price of flat glass itself had started to drop as earlier licensees began sharing some of the cost savings induced by the technology with consumers.

The generic trends such royalty agreements take are illustrated in Figure 9-4. Path I corresponds to the situation when business conditions and the technology's worth do not change over time, calling for an equal treatment of all licensees regardless of when they sign their agreements. Everyone is a "most-favored" customer, so to speak. Path II represents cases where the most attractive markets get licensed first; licensees that come in later not only tend to be in smaller markets—and hence can pay less—but also come in at a time when the price of the end product itself may have

FIGURE 9-4
THE TIME PATH OF ROYALTY RATES

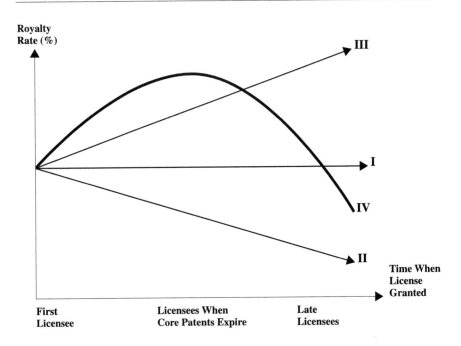

fallen. The opposite case is that illustrated by path III, in which higher royalties can be charged to later licensees because they get a more secure and improved technology than those who came in first.

In the case of Pilkington, all of the above-mentioned factors played a role in determining how much licensees paid by way of royalties depending on when they signed their contract. The actual path observed was path IV, combining the arguments for path III in the early stages and those of path II.

What the Pilkington example illustrates is that simple comparisons between the different modes shown in Figure 9-1 for commercializing a new technology are usually inappropriate. The choice is a lot more than which mode offers the greatest short-term return on investment. Rather, it is about meeting a variety of strategic criteria and doing so in a manner that the business formula chosen itself contributes to getting a new technology on the market most effectively.

SUMMARY

Profiting from certain technological innovations depends on the type of business formula adopted for delivering them. In some cases, this depends on the decisions made earlier in mobilizing resources for demonstration or co-opting various market constituents. But, even in situations where the technology and its end products are fully owned by an inventing organization, a choice needs to be made between making and selling end products worldwide on one's own versus engaging the cooperation of others.

The fundamental basis of this choice is to have the technology commercialized as quickly and widely as possible while, at the same time, allowing the technology owner to appropriate a fair share of the profits earned. It is not an easy choice, especially when long-term business considerations and entrepreneurial ambitions are taken into account. Just as with all the other subprocesses in technology commercialization, the choice of business formula should be seen as a competitive tool and as a way of differentiating the technology offered. Unfortunately, many inventors give insufficient thought to this.

This chapter offers a list of the instruments generally used in establishing a business formula and the factors that need to be taken into account in choosing among them. The most important factors are the inventor's long-term business ambition; the promotional needs of the technology, both in time and in terms of the market targeted; the role market constituents are expected to play in delivering the technology; the extent to which one wishes to sell just the element derived from the new technology versus a complete system; and the price that can be charged for the technology itself.

10

SUSTAINING COMMERCIALIZATION AND REALIZING LONG-TERM VALUE

ALL THE ACTIVITIES DESCRIBED UNTIL NOW HAD TO DO WITH GETTING A NEW technology developed and launched. While some money may have been made along the way, the real payoff comes *after* the launch of the technology in products or processes. The size of this payoff depends both on how attractive the latter are and on some deliberate actions taken to ensure that they have a long enough presence on the market.

The importance of considering the postlaunch stage as an integral part of technology commercialization is highlighted by the inclusion of product support in the definition of the innovation process of many companies today (see Table 1-1). The activities product support covers—solving customer problems, upgrading the product, developing line extensions, and keeping an eye on market trends—all contribute to the profitability of products after launch. Sustaining technology commercialization, however, is a wider notion. It covers many facets of the technology (not just end products) and includes interactions with a number of market constituents (not just consumers).

Three sets of activities are involved in extending the life of any enabling (or core) technology after its first launch and earning profits over a period of time: entrenching the product or process incorporating it in the market, thereby creating the conditions for the technology itself to have a long life; expanding the use of the technology by migrating it to new segments of the market or to new applications; and dominating critical facets of the technology to secure long-term profits for the inventor. The purpose of this chapter is to discuss the issues each of them raises in practice and the things anyone launching a new technology should watch for. It concludes with some comments on how long a technology ought to be sustained, given that competing ones will inevitably emerge.

ENTRENCHING APPLICATIONS OF THE TECHNOLOGY

Sustaining a technology's commercialization is, first and foremost, about making sure that the product or process it gets incorporated in has a long run in the marketplace. This involves attention to three main activities: making rapid progress in key facets of the technology, sustaining the interest of delivery partners, and creating dependence on the part of users.

Making Rapid Progress in Key Facets of the Technology

All technologies are subject to a constant threat of substitution. With new technologies with better value-cost relationships on offer all the time, the surest way to entrench a technology is by making quick progress in it. This progress, moreover, has to be in multiple facets, covering both its underlying principles and processes as well as its applications (see Figure 8-2).

However these improvements get made, it is progress in its value-cost relationship that establishes a technology and expands its use over time. A good case in point is that of aluminum and how it got to substitute for other metals in a wide range of uses.

Prior to the invention of the Hall-Héroult process for refining aluminum in 1886 by electrolytic reduction, aluminum was considered a precious metal. Although comprising 8 percent of the earth's crust, it was difficult to refine in large quantities and cost $500 per pound as recently as the middle of the last century—more than twice, in fact, the value of gold or platinum. Copper, by way of comparison, cost $0.60 per pound. Naturally, the main use of aluminum then was in finely crafted eating utensils and jewelry.[1] The Hall-Héroult process had a dramatic impact on the cost of aluminum. A couple of years after the process was installed at what is now Alcoa, the price dropped to $8 per pound. A year later, it fell to $2 per pound in 1890 and continued to decline to $0.36 per pound by 1897.[2]

The process for manufacturing aluminum today is essentially the same as it was a century ago. Improvements in the process and the scale of operations, have, however, made it a great deal more efficient. Thus, by the late 1940s, the largest Hall-Héroult smelting cell at Alcoa was rated at 50,000 amperes and required 9 kilowatt-hours for each pound of metal produced. Today, Alcoa's most advanced Hall-Héroult smelting cells operate at up to 285,000 amperes and produce aluminum at less than 6.5 kilowatt-hours per pound. Alternatives to the Hall-Héroult process, such as aluminum chloride electrolysis, are also being experimented with; these promise to be even more efficient and, incidentally, environmentally sound.[3]

In parallel with this development in the process, several alloys of aluminum have been introduced over the years, expanding the uses to which the metal can be put. Starting with Alfred Wilm's patented Duralumin (the first light and strong alloy comprising aluminum, copper, and magnesium) in 1908 until today's aluminum—lithium alloys and laminates of various kinds, the main driver behind the widespread use of the metal has been the improvements in its properties. Although the underlying technology was drawn from progress in material science, it involved a great deal of experimentation on how different alloys would behave when processed. Studies had to be done on not only the microstructure of each alloy but also on how it would react when cast, forged, heat-treated, or age-hardened.

Finally, incorporating these alloys in particular end products required its own research. Appropriate fabrication processes needed to be developed for producing components cost-effectively and tests done to evaluate each alloy's design requirements for each envisaged application. The widespread use of aluminum beverage cans during the past couple of decades, for example, was brought about through a host of developments—improved alloys for aluminum rigid container sheet (RCS), advanced container designs, lubricants, high-speed electrocutting technologies, and ingot casting and rolling technology. Compared to the use of 43.5 pounds of alloys for producing 1,000 can bodies in 1975, a company like Alcoa can now produce the same number of cans with 25 pounds of metal. Lightweighting and superior coating have not only improved the appeal of aluminum as a food container material but improved its economics as well.

Which facet of a technology to emphasize most depends on the requirements of the application(s) targeted. Thus, when nuclear magnetic resonance (NMR) technology was first introduced in the early 1950s, it was for spectrometers. To make the technology useful for medical diagnostics, a much larger application, progress had to be made on different fronts simultaneously. Apart from new magnets and computation methods, a number of application-related questions had to be answered before the technology could establish itself as a viable competitor to conventional X rays and CT scanners in medical imaging: What type of magnet would deliver the best results at the lowest cost? What are the optimal instrument settings, for example, of magnetic field strengths for NMR imaging? For which types of diseases will NMR be most helpful? Which elements in the body best lend themselves to NMR imaging, and what information do they carry? And to what extent could the size and cost of the equipment be reduced?[4]

Even the technological principle underlying NMR was at that time still being debated. While most agreed that the principle was capable of identifying variations in body water on account of the magnetic properties of hydrogen nuclei, there were questions relating to the source of the NMR signal. Some researchers were arguing that it arose from free-moving water in body tissues; others argued that it was generated by relatively stationary molecules. Far from being of mere academic interest, resolving this question was necessary for gaining insight into the biology of cancer and other diseases and for helping physicians determine instrument settings for optimal image contrast.

Sustaining the Interest of Delivery Partners

The progress that needs to be made in various facets does not have to be the sole responsibility of the inventor. Unfortunately, while many inventors eagerly search out a number of delivery partners for the launch of a technology, they fail to show the same eagerness in motivating them to build a long-term commitment to it. The reason for this is often to preserve some flexibility with regard to their own strategic options. Depending on how successful the technology becomes, they would like to take on the roles others played at launch, hoping thereby to increase their share of the profits. This is a shortsighted attitude. Many technologies get superseded by competing ones because delivery partners themselves switch allegiances in the absence of mechanisms to sustain their interest over a period of time.

An example of a technology that lasted a long time because of what its inventor did vis-à-vis partners is that of Escher Wyss's NIPCO rollers mentioned in Chapter 9. While its strategy consisted in making and selling the rollers to original equipment manufacturers (OEMs), who then incorporated them in the machines they built, its ongoing R&D and licensing approach made sure that these OEMs remained constantly interested in the technology.

Figure 10-1 summarizes the relationship established between Sulzer-Escher Wyss and its various licensees. The company's own R&D covered both the rollers and their applications, which were the object of the license agreements. Both the roller technology and these applications were, furthermore, placed in a pool, to which licensees contributed their improvements too. This growing pool of know-how was available to all licensees for building a new generation of machines. Such an approach offered the following main advantages: not competing with partners helped incorporate them in the company's own strategy; the patent pool, coupled with a widely applied identical trademark, assured cash flow over a long period; and supplying licensees with a variety of improvements assured renewal of license agreements.

In Dolby's case, licensees were seen as part of a permanent network geared to advancing the technology, too. As Gary Holt, managing director of Dolby Laboratories (UK), Ltd., put it,

> Ours was a true partnership agreement with licensees, not a one-off patent license; we organized a patent pool and made sure licensees were visited on

FIGURE 10-1

THE TECHNOLOGY POOL FOR NIPCO ROLLERS

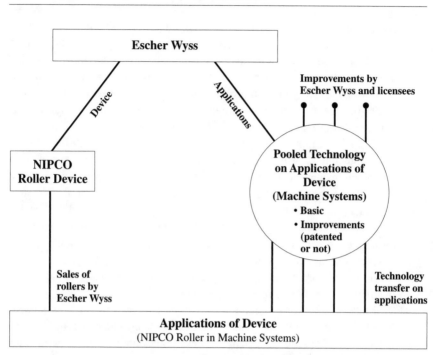

SOURCE: Valentin Heuss and Vijay K. Jolly, "Commercializing Multifaceted Technologies Through Partnerships," *International Journal of Technology Management* 6, nos. 1/2 (1991): 73.

a regular basis. We continue to review their designs, tell them how to make the circuits and obtain their prototypes for testing within our facilities. We see the relationship as a life-time alliance. Although licensees are not obliged to use the Dolby trademark, most do. This acts as a further source of identity, a cement for the relationship and a motive for Dolby Laboratories to remain closely involved with its licensees.[5]

As these examples show, sustaining the interest of delivery partners requires a certain amount of long-term consistency in the strategy adopted and an effort to keep partners interested in the technology. The proponent's own R&D, furthermore, needs to focus explicitly on the needs of these partners.

Creating Dependence on the Part of Users

In the end, a technology-based application becomes entrenched because its users see value in it over a long period of time. One way this value comes about is through what economists term positive consumption externalities. The greater the number of customers a technology attracts, the more valuable it is thought to be by those who are still contemplating adopting it. In addition to the purely psychological bandwagon effect and the role of market share as a signal of product quality, these externalities can arise from a number of causes: from physical links as in telephones and fax machines, where the utility a consumer derives from purchasing a set depends on how many other people already subscribe to the network; from joint-products such as computer hardware and software, where the amount of software written tends to be associated with the number of hardware units sold; and from the availability of postpurchase services as in the case of automobiles, where the scope of the service network is proportional to the number of automobiles of a particular kind already on the market.[6]

Such consumption or network externalities mainly contribute to the horizontal spread of a technology—attracting new buyers and preempting competing technologies from serving their needs. What truly entrenches a particular technology's use is when buyers start to depend on the technology, adapting their consumption pattern and work habits around it. This, for example, explains the success bar-code scanners have enjoyed ever since they first got adopted by supermarket chains and factories. Starting with simple front-end control at check-out counters, the use of the technology quickly expanded to sales activity analysis and inventory management, making the entire organization dependent on them.[7]

Making sure that a technology's use deepens over time requires keeping close contact with customers and users to determine which product (or process) features are important to them and adapting the latter to their evolving needs. It also requires expanding the context in which the application is used and communicating new use opportunities to those who have already adopted the technology for a more restrictive purpose. Furthermore, by co-opting other suppliers to offer the product concerned, such as through licensing, one can increase the chances of its being established as a "dominant design" in the industry, making it harder to dislodge.[8]

Synergy Among Factors

The important point about these three sets of factors is that they all tend to act in a mutually reinforcing manner. Technologies that get to benefit from the resulting virtuous circle become entrenched sooner and more securely.

Automobile Engine Technology

An old but nevertheless illustrative example of the synergy among factors that entrench a technology in a particular application is offered by the history of automobile engine technology. At the beginning of the twentieth century, three types of technologies competed for automobile applications—steam (invented in 1769 and considerably improved in the years that followed), electric (first launched in 1881), and internal combustion (IC) engines (first introduced in 1885, based on Nicolaus Otto's four-stroke engine). The even nature of the contest between them was evident from their respective shares of the automobile market. In the United States, 40 percent of the vehicles ran on steam, 38 percent were electric, and 22 percent gasoline-powered.[9] Of the cars built in 1900 in the United States, 1,681 were powered by steam, 1,575 were electrics, and 936 used spark-ignition engines.[10] The fact that a steamer had set the speed record of 127 miles per hour in 1906 made any prediction regarding which of the three would win in the end all the more difficult.

By the end of the 1920s, however, automobiles based on IC engine technology had virtually displaced all others. The first to be eliminated were the steamers, for technical reasons. They had become far too complicated and expensive, their use required constant stops for water and fuel, and they took time to build adequate steam pressure to perform as well as the competing technologies. Their production stopped altogether in 1926.

Odd as it may seem today, electric cars were seen as the most natural successor to steamers. Despite drawbacks of battery weight, relatively low torque, and short range between charges, they offered several advantages over IC engines. They were silent, needed minimal maintenance, and started immediately. These advantages did not last long, however. As it turned out, IC engines offered a better platform for technical improvements. With the introduction of electric starters in 1912, and then exhaust mufflers a few years later, IC engines quickly caught up with electric cars in the areas of instant starting and lowered noise. As demand for them grew, based on their inherently greater driving range, more companies contributed other technical improvements that greatly increased their performance in the 1920s and 1930s.

Certain market constituents joined in to entrench IC engines as the dominant technology. One problem that had proved particularly difficult in the beginning was that of combustion knocking. But as the automobile population multiplied, more and more effort was devoted to solving this problem by both automobile manufacturers and the burgeoning oil industry that developed in the wake of the gasoline engine. Starting in the late 1920s, the Cooperative Fuel Research (CFR) Committee, grouping automobile manufacturers and gasoline producers, also established formal procedures for ranking the knock resistance of various hydrocarbon fuels and developed a variable-compression engine for rating gasolines and additives. Thus emerged the octane rating scale. While the automotive industry pushed ahead with higher compression ratios, the oil industry responded with increased-octane fuel, setting the stage for a symbiotic relationship that made gasoline-powered cars the dominant technology worldwide by the 1920s. Once the technology was established, the cost benefits of the overall industry created a formidable barrier to the introduction of a competing technology, which has lasted until today. Large-volume production, typified by the Ford Model T, gave rise to economies of scale that drove down unit costs for what was actually a complex, multicomponent technology; these economies were extended to the supply of fuel by the oil industry and the development of a widespread and qualified distribution and service network for gasoline automobiles.

As the automobile example illustrates, while the forces determining which technology gets entrenched act synergistically, they are seldom predictable or controllable. What is needed is to act on several fronts simultaneously—improving different facets of the technology in a planned fashion, mobilizing the relevant market constituents to contribute to it, and, perhaps most important, making sure that the product incorporating the technology offers superior value so that buyers start to depend on it.

EXPANDING USE

Entrenching a technology in a market that shrinks or becomes unattractive for one reason or another is of little use in practice. What is needed in such cases is to change the features of the products that incorporate it or to seek altogether new applications. While the former allows access to new segments of the market, the latter opens up new uses for the technology.

New Features and Segments

Figure 10-2 summarizes a common evolution in product characteristics for devices and equipment technologies. The first three steps—improving functionality, making the product compatible with existing patterns of use, and making it easy to use—are associated with the early adoption of the technology. The next three steps—instituting a low, standardized price, establishing multifunctionality, and adding new functionality—relate to accessing a wider market (mass market, for instance) and segments that are amenable to a somewhat different set of functions than the one initially offered. As costs get reduced, as the technology becomes easier to use, and as the scope of functions offered expands, the number of potential buyers increases over time. The challenge for an inventing organization is to be able to drive this product evolution proactively and to adapt the business infrastructure in accordance with it.

The stages up to the creation of a standardized, low-price version of the product to access a wide market are the best understood. They correspond to what Dolby did in moving from professional equipment, where the new function of noise reduction mattered more than price, to consumer electronic products that required standardized, low-cost circuits.

Not all technologies, of course, are appropriate for targeting to a mass market, nor are they amenable to a purely price-based strategy. What they

FIGURE 10-2

THE EVOLUTION OF TECHNOLOGY-BASED PRODUCTS

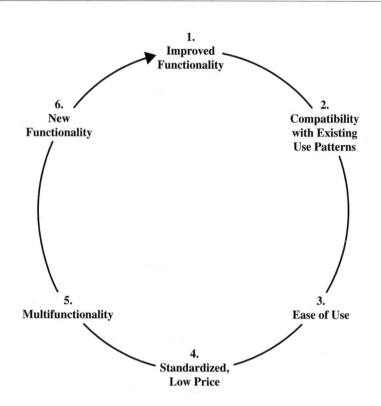

respond to instead is a strategy consisting of *adding* to the function they began with. The author has observed in practice that new functions are often added after reaching a mass market; companies first try to access a mass market with the function that derives from their enabling (core) technology, and only when this doesn't work do they contemplate adding other, usually nonproprietary functions to their product to access a wider segment.

Offering multiple functions is like a strategy of bundling. As such, it needs to take into account the standard economic arguments for and against supplying systems versus components.[11] Where technology-based products differ, however, is their ability to supply synergies of use beyond just putting functions together. As such, multifunction products tend to be associated with later stages of a technology's life cycle, while bundling typically occurs in the beginning.

Packard Bell Electronics succeeded in the PC field during the late 1980s and early 1990s by offering a combination of functions in a simple package. Although a recent entrant in a highly competitive industry, it quickly rose to fourth place (by sales) worldwide—after Compaq, Apple, and

IBM—by 1994. It did so by concentrating on home buyers through mass retailers and providing a fully-loaded PC that is easy to use. It was the first company to sell PCs with hard disk, preloaded software, and a built-in CD-ROM drive. Its latest family of systems are even called "home appliances." Packaged in a single cabinet is a multimedia PC that doubles as a compact disc player, a stereo system, a TV and video player, a telephone-answering system, and a facsimile machine, complete with modem for attachment to the telephone network—all for the price of a medium-range PC made by other companies.[12]

Japanese telecommunications equipment makers are doing something similar today in an attempt to gain a bigger share of the digital cellular market. Having lost out to Groupe Special Mobile (GSM) suppliers, whose standard now dominates much of the world market, they are promoting a hybrid solution—combining their own personal handyphone system (PHS) with GSM in the same handset. This way customers can enjoy both the low cost of PHS and the greater coverage and mobility offered by GSM.[13]

Seiko's FIB

Adding new functions and then, later, offering a new function to expand the market segment targeted is also what Seiko Instruments did in sustaining its focused ion beam (FIB). As mentioned in Chapter 2, the first FIB model Seiko launched in 1985 was an imaging-cum-microfabrication tool. Although well received, the real success of the FIB came from the rapid progress made in it subsequently.

Compared to an imaging resolution of 100 nm in 1986, the resolution has been brought down to 5 nm in 1996. At the same time, the ion beam density has been increased tenfold, allowing for greater precision in the process. To make the FIB into a more versatile tool, the company has also added a scanning electron microscope (SEM) to the instrument in the model introduced in 1995. This added feature allows for both less destructive testing (since ion beams sputter away the material being tested) and easier characterization of the impurities detected. As of this writing, this combined instrument is undergoing Beta tests at an IBM facility in the United States.

Seiko's FIB is now also being migrated into new segments of the semiconductor industry. While the company has maintained a one-third share of the market and generates over $30 million in sales, the present use of the instrument is mainly for off-line monitoring of semiconductor manufacturing. The initially narrow focus on one application within a single industry served the company well in the past and provided a focus for the marketing and application development work needed to establish the technology. Now, with the growing versatility of the technology and the experience gained in using it, the company plans to extend the use of the FIB in other fields.

One new use is likely to be in semiconductor manufacturing itself. However, instead of targeting the FIB as an off-line process monitoring tool, with an occasional repair function for defective chips, the idea is to develop it into an on-line monitoring device. As circuit dimensions become smaller, the traditional approach using optical microscopes will need to be replaced by either electron microscopes or ion beam microscopes. Seiko Instruments, with a capability now in both technologies, would like to be in a position to provide the substitute technology. Whereas, at present, semiconductor factories use one or two FIBs for off-line checks, the potential market for on-line systems is ten times larger.

Other future applications of the FIB draw upon its milling properties—in fact, the property used in the first application, that of repairing photomasks. With the growing market for micromachining, the company is already looking into the "machining" of small magnetic recording heads for disk drives, atomic force microscope (AFM) tips, and superconducting quantum interference devices (SQUIDs). Seiko is, in effect, trying to position the FIB as a new production tool—a far cry from the monitoring device it first commercialized.

In the pharmaceutical industry, these product-level changes take the form of line extensions, which often involve new segments or medical indications for the same function. One example of line extensions is what Astra has done with its local anesthetic Xylocaine. Unlike Merck, which has sometimes tended to introduce a new chemical entity in a particular form and then stay with it, Astra has adapted the product for different indications, changes in dosage, and changes in delivery form (including a cream). Each new indication calls for product development and clinical studies. As shown in Figure 10-3, the company has been able to constantly grow its local anesthesia business based on a fifty-year-old invention.

New Applications

The emphasis to put on migrating a technology to new segments depends on the long-term market potential of the product incorporating it. Where this potential is limited or where the product is likely to be taken over by a competing technology, the applications themselves need to be reconsidered and expanded.

The Stirling engine example given in Chapter 1 is illustrative in this regard. The interest in Stirling engines never really disappeared, even though the technology was conceived of as long ago as 1816. It was mostly a low-level interest with relatively few resources being put behind it. Every now and then, however, one saw a resurgence in interest as problems with other technologies arose or when new applications started to be considered. In recent years, for example, work on Stirling engines has been targeted toward nitrogen liquefiers (used in military sensors and supercomputers),

FIGURE 10-3

ASTRA AB—XYLOCAINE'S LINE EXTENSIONS (1972–1994)

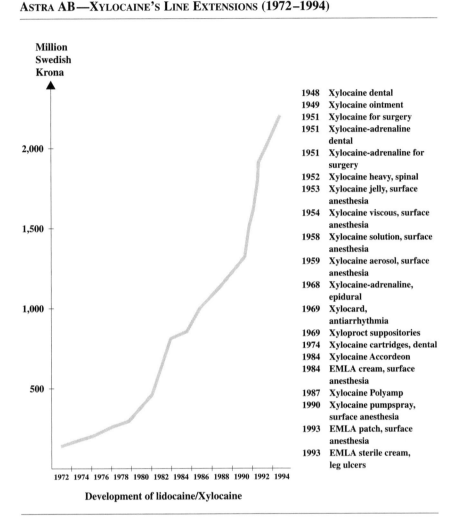

1948	Xylocaine dental
1949	Xylocaine ointment
1951	Xylocaine for surgery
1951	Xylocaine-adrenaline dental
1951	Xylocaine-adrenaline for surgery
1952	Xylocaine heavy, spinal
1953	Xylocaine jelly, surface anesthesia
1954	Xylocaine viscous, surface anesthesia
1958	Xylocaine solution, surface anesthesia
1959	Xylocaine aerosol, surface anesthesia
1968	Xylocaine-adrenaline, epidural
1969	Xylocard, antiarrhythmia
1969	Xyloproct suppositories
1974	Xylocaine cartridges, dental
1984	Xylocaine Accordeon
1984	EMLA cream, surface anesthesia
1987	Xylocaine Polyamp
1990	Xylocaine pumpspray, surface anesthesia
1993	EMLA patch, surface anesthesia
1993	EMLA sterile cream, leg ulcers

Development of lidocaine/Xylocaine

SOURCE: Astra AB. Reprinted with permission.

remote power on earth and in space (where cost is less important than the engine's ability to use heat sources such as solar energy or radioisotopes), and quiet, low-polluting heat pumps. The latter application is being driven mainly by the concern over the use of chlorofluorocarbons (CFCs) in conventional refrigerators and the difficulty of finding adequate substitutes for them.

The basic argument is that even if a particular product fails in the market, the technology itself is not lost. It can be combined into new devices or extended into new application areas. GE is one company that consciously searches for new applications in house if particular technologies fail in an application for which they were initially developed. This is, for example, what recently happened with its jet-engine technology. When its aircraft engines unit lost out in the competition for the next generation of fighter planes—to Pratt & Whitney—despite having spent nearly a decade and $1 billion developing the needed technologies—it quickly diverted the technologies to other uses in the aeroengine field. Innovations in composite materials and ceramics, electronic controls, engine combustion, and variable cycle technology (in which air flow valves allow maximum engine efficiency to be achieved at both supersonic and subsonic speed) are now being deployed in a variety of military and civil projects.[14]

The migration of technologies from one use to another can best be seen in new materials. Just as some applications become uneconomical after they have been pursued for a time, new applications continually appear as technology advances. Depending on which facet of the technology progresses most, these new applications can result from an improvement in the material's properties, a reduction in its cost of manufacture, or some developments in downstream technologies relating to the processing of the material. They can also result from unexpected developments in the macroeconomic environment or in the conditions users are subject to.

Thus, when Kevlar was first introduced in 1971 as Kevlar-29, its properties mainly suited applications where some reinforcement was called for. As a result, DuPont settled on automobile radial tires as its first major application. Tire companies were just beginning to move from bias to radial technology, and Kevlar was offered as an alternative to steel belts. Not only was it five times stronger than steel for the same weight, but tire companies were more used to handling fibers than steel.

The automobile tire application for Kevlar in 1970 was large but subject to price competition. When the oil price increased in 1973, the relatively small advantage offered by Kevlar was immediately eroded as steel companies dropped their prices and the cost of Kevlar itself rose. However, as it turned out, the oil price increase also put pressure on aircraft manufacturers at the same time to reduce the weight of aircraft in order to improve fuel consumption. In a 1975 study, Boeing had estimated that each kilogram in reduced weight resulted in a $300 saving over the life of aircraft with the new oil price—a much more significant albeit smaller opportunity for Kevlar from a value-in-use standpoint. Aircraft, therefore, became the next target for Kevlar.

This was followed by a flame-resistant material, Nomex III, a meta-aramid, and several Kevlar derivates such as Kevlar-49 (with high modules of elasticity), Kevlar "HT" (high tensile strength), Kevlar "Ha" (greater adhesion), and so on. Other applications grew out of changes within user industries. In the case of the automobile industry, for example, a recent application for Kevlar has come from a trend among manufacturers to improve on the efficiency of internal combustion engines. Of the many options being explored, one is to raise the temperature at which the engine runs. Hot-running cars, however, call for new materials that can withstand high temperatures over a long period of time in things like radiator hoses. Conventional rubbers cannot, but Kevlar can; it retains all its properties even when continuously subject to 200°C temperatures.

Occasionally, user industries become receptive to a new material that they had previously turned down. This is what happened with Kevlar in the tire industry. Although the latter preferred steel for passenger cars, it came around back to Kevlar when, more recently, it introduced "High Speed Rated Tires." The tire application, in other words, never really died. One just had to wait for it to come back at the right time and for a better use.

This retargeting of a technology to sustain its commercialization applies to all industries today. As one might expect, the greater the rate of change in the industry, particularly at the user level, the quicker a technology's proponent needs to retarget it. Not being able to do so, in fact, explains partly why General Magic's Telescript and MagicCap products fared badly since they were launched. While Telescript was targeted to "intelligent" telecommunication networks built around computers, the Internet started to provide many of the functions these networks promised. Before General Magic could redirect its product to the latter, Sun Microsystem Inc. had already launched its highly successful Java program.

From Product to Technology Commercialization Road Maps

Many companies today systematically prepare product road maps after the launch of the first product. These help guide R&D strategy and, when communicated to users, sustain interest in the technology. Typically, these road maps get defined in technical (or functional) terms, indicating the facets of the technology to be worked on in order to achieve some planned performance characteristic in the future. An illustration of this is shown by DEC's Alpha Chip road map in Table 10-1.

Such road maps are useful primarily when price/performance characteristics are a good surrogate for both value and cost and when these characteristics translate into just a handful of variables that can be projected on the basis of historical trends—for example, technology type, wafer size, number of transistors, speed, and line width, as in the case of DEC's Alpha Chip.

In many other technologies, such simple road maps are harder to construct. Sustaining their commercialization requires advancing on many fronts—on different facets of the technology as well as on the application and use level. This is what Seiko is doing with its FIB. Road maps need to encompass both the value the technology can create in alternative applications and the cost with which its function is delivered. While most inventors understand the drivers of cost—mainly scale, learning effects,

TABLE 10-1

DEC's ALPHA CHIP ROAD MAP

Year[a]	Technology	Wafer Size	Transistors (Millions)	MHz[b]	Line Width (Microns)
1992	CMOS-4	6-inch	1.68	150–200	0.75
1993	CMOS-5	6-inch	4	225–275	0.5
1996	CMOS-6	8-inch	10	325–375	0.35
1999	CMOS-7	8-inch	30	450–525	0.25
2002	CMOS-8	8-inch	100	675–750	0.18

SOURCE: DEC, as quoted in *Electronic Business,* March 30, 1992, p. 16.

[a]Year of manufacturing capability, not availability of computer systems.
[b]Estimates based on industry average gain of 30 percent a year.

process improvements supported by product redesigns, and location—value enhancement tends to be more difficult to plan for. It requires constant assessment of market needs, across a wider range of customers than that for which the technology was initially targeted.

DOMINATING CRITICAL FACETS TO SECURE LONG-TERM PROFITS

Making sure that a particular technology has a long run in the market is, of course, no guarantee that its inventor will benefit. For this to happen, the latter needs to dominate the most critical facets of the technology over a period of time. This is what results in a sustainable and, where it counts, a proprietary lead for the inventor.

The history of electromagnetic casting (EMC) technology illustrates some of the issues involved here. Compared to the continuous casting of metal ingots using mechanical molds, EMC is based on confining the molten metal in an electromagnetic field. With the latter serving as a "contactless" mold, the ingot is solidified exclusively by cooling with water. The technique results in ingots with uniform metallurgical characteristics as well as smooth surfaces, thereby reducing or eliminating the need to trim edges or scalp the surface prior to subsequent working.

The EMC process was first developed in the Soviet Union in the late 1960s and described in a patent granted to Z. N. Getselev et al.[15] The aluminum samples the Soviets produced, however, were not of sufficiently good quality. The process was instead licensed to all the major aluminum companies for a $2 million down payment and a small royalty.

Alusuisse of Switzerland was one of the companies to take this license in 1973, and it began developing its own EMC technology. With an expenditure of approximately $15 million over a five-year period, it came up with a completely automated process with controlled cooling and solidification, a patented adjustable EMC mold with movable end walls to increase the flexibility in ingot dimensions, and noncontacting metal level sensors for accurate positioning. These improvements soon made Alusuisse's EMC technology the leader in the field. Obtaining the rights to sublicense the Russian patents along with its own patents and know-how, the company started to commercialize EMC technology throughout the world along with the proprietary components it had developed. Within five years it had captured 15 percent of the available world market.

The marketing strategy consisted in selling either retrofits or complete turnkey plants as customers wanted. In addition to the cost of the equipment, customers typically paid a significant down payment and running royalties for the technology. Most, moreover, agreed to grant any non-patented improvements they made back to Alusuisse, thus keeping the latter constantly ahead in EMC developments worldwide. Today, when one thinks about EMC technology, it is the Alusuisse version, not the Russian one that got it started.

Principles-Process/Component Link

Which facets of a technology to emphasize after launch depends on the basis on which the product (or process) competes. Sometimes, preserving technological leadership calls for dominating the basic research underlying end products. The willingness to do this explains the success many specialist companies have enjoyed over decades, despite their relatively small size. One such company is Saes Getters SPA, based in Italy. The technology it was founded on in 1950 was that of getters: gas-absorbing metals that "get" residual molecules after a vacuum has been created by some other means, thereby improving or maintaining the vacuum over an extended period of time.

Saes Getters started with what are known as evaporable getters, based on highly stabilized barium alloys. Their main application was in television tubes, where the silver mirror in these early tubes was the barium from the getter. The success of this product was so great that at the beginning of the 1960s the company was producing 3 million getters a day, with all the major manufacturers of electron tubes as customers worldwide. However, as stated by P. della Porta, who joined the company as its research director in 1950,

> With the success of this product in the market, I realized the need of a
> better understanding of what I was doing. In close cooperation with a

Professor from Turin University, we started basic research on the behaviour of gases with the barium films. We started publishing the results at conferences and in specialized journals. This basic research was of fundamental importance, first, because we had to develop instrumentation and equipment for the experiments which were not available on the market and which became very important for the applied research in the following years. Second, because we were able to develop techniques to access the quality of our products before their actual use by the customers. Third, we gained prestige in the market, creating a good way for our introduction to the customers. Fourth, we began to be accepted in the scientific world.[16]

Thus, after Saes Getters successfully launched its first family of evaporable getters in the early 1950s, it started research on nonevaporable getters a few years later based on chemically active metal alloys. After testing hundreds of alloys, Saes Getters invented its zirconium-aluminum nonevaporable getter in the early 1960s, which is still the most acceptable getter in its category today. From television tubes, the company started selling its technology to a much broader set of applications, including nuclear fusion experimental reactors and the large electron-positron (LEP) collider at the European Laboratory for Particle Physics (CERN) near Geneva.

Process/Component–Device Link

The most common link in many fabricated devices and equipment is between the two and the process or component technologies on which they are based. In such cases, one needs to look out constantly for all the process and component technologies that go into making it competitive—covering, if necessary, disciplines and technologies that the inventor may not have initially thought of.

DNA Synthesizers

An example is offered by what happened to automated DNA synthesizing machines, or "gene machines" as they were called. Before their invention, DNA synthesis was a laborious manual process restricted to highly trained chemists.

The first automated DNA synthesizer was introduced in 1980 by a Canadian company, Bio Logicals, of Toronto. Based on the principle of building DNA chains one nucleoside (comprising a base and sugar molecule) at a time by linking the building blocks together chemically, this synthesizer was quickly overtaken as soon as a better process was discovered. The "second generation" machine, developed by Marvin Caruthers and Serge Beaucage of the University of Colorado at Boulder in 1982, was based on a family of activatable nucleoside derivatives called phosphoramidites. This new process offered substantial improvements in speed, efficiency, and reliability. Unable to cope, Bio Logicals was forced to write off its gene-synthesis machine program.[17]

GCA Steppers

At times, component technologies play the same role as new processes. Staying ahead with a device or type of equipment requires progressing simultaneously in the design of the former as well as in the relevant component technology.

Take semiconductor steppers as an example. These are machines that project circuit patterns onto a silicon wafer. Light passes through material similar to a photographic negative and then onto a wafer coated with photosensitive chemicals. The result is a circuit pattern etched on the wafer.

Steppers were invented in 1977 by GCA Corp., an equipment manufacturer based in Andover, Massachusetts, which had been the undisputed world leader until the mid-1980s. However, it lost this lead to Japanese camera makers Nikon and Canon. Nikon, which introduced its first model in 1980, today controls around 60 percent of the market.

One reason why GCA lost its lead was its dependence on outside suppliers for lenses—which were a critical component. Another was its failure to improve the stability of its products. For example, the performance of early steppers made by GCA was highly vulnerable to changes in external conditions. When the weather was fair and atmospheric pressure high, they tended to create a larger image than desired, while bad weather resulted in smaller images. Nikon resolved the problem with a computerized correction mechanism.

What these examples illustrate is that, while a certain component technology may make a new device possible, the link between the two is an ephemeral one. Most devices, once established, outlive the components and processes on which they were initially based. Who gets to derive most benefits from the device depends on who dominates the appropriate enabling technologies over time.

This link between components and devices is becoming increasingly hard to manage because of the wide scope of research it implies. On the one hand, companies want to avoid excessive product changes in order to reduce design costs and keep products on the market longer to amortize investments. On the other hand, component suppliers are creating pressures of their own. Faced with shorter technological life cycles, they are increasingly selling their components to whoever will buy them to get volume early, thereby intensifying competition at the device level.

One company that has been able to strike a balance between these opposing forces is Sony. As a study of the company's Walkman product line between 1980 and 1991 found, it not only launched a *variety* of different models to capture new niches, but ensured the *longevity* of these models through innovative designs and the speedy incorporation of technological improvements.[18] What has enabled the company to do this is its own technological strength at the component level. While it does sell these components on the open market, it does so six to twelve months after they have been used internally first. This enables Sony to refresh both its product platforms and the derivative products, rather than target product proliferation for its own sake.

Device-Infrastructure Link

Finally, just as a system already in place can act as a barrier to the introduction of a new technology, the express creation of a new system becomes a means to sustaining the technology around which it is built. This bringing together of a complete system has often been invoked for explaining the dramatic success of personal computers. When this device was first introduced, the main buyers were technically sophisticated "computer freaks" and hobbyists. It was not a particular functionality that interested them— they themselves wanted to decide what its eventual use should be. Some simply played with it, programming it in machine language to do interesting things. Others even reconfigured the hardware itself.

Had personal computers remained this way, it is unlikely that mass commercialization on the scale we see today would have occurred. This started to come about when several things happened—the development of application software (notably spreadsheets such as Visicalc), the setting of peripheral standards, and the publication of books on the subject. An entirely new infrastructure of sales, service, supplies, and education and training also had to be mobilized as part of the system.[19]

The company that gets to dominate these "collateral assets," by extension, also stands a better chance of having its design established as the dominant one.[20] When IBM launched its PC in 1981, it was not necessarily the best personal computer. But IBM's size, image, and marketing strength caused buyers to flock to it, thinking it would be easier to service and that most application software would be written around an IBM standard, as had been the case in the past.

Multifaceted Links

While the foregoing discussion has centered around the main links that need to be managed in sustaining a technology's commercialization, a frequent requirement is to manage many of them in parallel. Thus, as shown in Table 10-2, the success of Sony's TR-55 camcorder referred to in Chapter 2 can be attributed not just to the technologies developed for its initial launch (the period 1985 to 1989), but to the progress made subsequently in

TABLE 10-2

Key Enabling Technologies Developed for Sony's TR-55 and TRV 90 Camcorders (1985–1995)

Key Technology Areas	Description of Achievement	
	(1985–1989)	(1990–1995)
1. Printed Circuit Board (PCB)	• Four-layer PCB • Pattern rule 250 μm • Board thickness 0.8 mm	• Six-layer PCB • Pattern rule 100 μm (partly) • Board thickness 0.6 mm • Blind via hole
2. Soldering Material	• Heat-proof preflux • Uniform soldering powder • Low-melting-point solder (Sn 46%, Pb 46%, B 8%)	• Metal mask by additive method • Uniform soldering powder • Low-melting-point solder (Sn 46%, Pb 46%, B 8%)
3. Components	• Miniaturization of standard components—size reduction from 2.0 × 1.25 mm to 1.6 × 0.8 mm • IC pin pitch 0.8 mm very quad flat package with 26% area reduction and 58% thickness reduction	• Miniaturization of standard components—1.0 × 0.5 mm (partly) • IC pin pitch 0.5 mm
4. Devices	• Sendus metal in gap (MIG) recording head, instead of ferrite • 1/2" charge-coupled device with power zoom, combining camera lens with camera circuitry	• Sendus metal in gap (MIG) recording head • 1/4" charge-coupled device with power zoom, combining camera lens with camera circuitry
5. Production Equipment and Processes	• High-precision screen printer for soldering • Three times air reflow furnace • Chip mount placer with positioning accuracy ±0.15 mm • Automatic straightening of cassettes • Feed-forward (not feed-back) quality improvement system	• High-precision screen printer for soldering • Two times air reflow furnace • Chip mount placer with positioning accuracy ±0.05 mm • Automatic straightening of cassettes • Optical chip place checker

SOURCE: Interviews at Sony Corporation, 1991, 1996.

multiple areas—components and materials, the device itself, and production equipment and processes used in manufacturing it.

The more versatile the technology, the greater the need for such a multifaceted research effort, including going back to the principles underlying it. As Paul Becker of Raychem explained regarding sustaining the Poly-Switch technology,

> We have ongoing efforts directed at both reducing cost and expanding the performance of PolySwitch technology. On the cost side, we have to do more than just compete against other resettable fuse technologies [bi-metal and PTC ceramic]; to continue to grow, we must also lower costs to where PolySwitch devices can be priced competitively with standard *non-resettable* fuses. Part of our strategy involves taking a step back to see if we can design our system in an entirely new manner. We are exploring novel and potentially low cost manufacturing processes that could replace conventional melt compounding and extrusion. In order to expand performance, we have to gain a better scientific understanding of the factors which limit polymeric PTC technology. PolySwitch devices today are suited to telecommunications applications [high voltage, low current] and battery/electronics applications [low voltage/high current]. There is a large segment, namely conventional mains power applications [120/220 volts and 20/10 amps], that falls outside our present product rating. PolySwitch business could achieve dramatic growth with the development of polymeric PTC materials suited to this environment. Our longer term R&D effort is focused on addressing this opportunity.[21]

SUSTAINING A TECHNOLOGY VERSUS THE BUSINESS CREATED

The important point to remember about sustaining commercialization is that it is about realizing long-term value from investments made in bringing a technology to market, *not* about perpetuating the technology itself. All technologies, sooner or later, get overtaken by better ones; persevering with them for too long can be wasteful and counterproductive.

The basic argument is as follows: If the objective is to maximize returns on *all* the investments made in bringing a new technology to market, one needs to sustain both the technology and the complementary assets created to deliver it. Thus, if the technological principle on which the first set of products were built becomes obsolete, one needs to move on to a different set of principles to keep the products themselves competitive. Similarly, if a product design become uncompetitive, one needs to go on to another design concept—based on a different set of component technologies perhaps—in order to maintain the profitability of the infrastructure that was created to bring it to market.

Unless the original inventor also comes up with the superior substituting technology, a rare occurrence in itself, the approach needed is one of *alternating the emphasis*—investing in the technology and its derived products for a period of time, then in the infrastructure to commercialize it (e.g., plants, distribution systems, and market access), and then in an alternative technology to sustain the viability of the latter.

This is essentially what virtually all the major pharmaceutical companies that missed out on the biotechnology revolution did—Roche buying Genentech, Inc., Ciba-Geigy buying Chiron, Inc., and so on. While the biotechnology industry was evolving, these companies were busy exploiting discoveries they had made earlier based on traditional pharmaceutical methods. Some of the cash flow they earned from the latter was then ploughed into biotechnology—which they saw as a promising new technology for future products. The same is happening with telecommunication equipment companies worldwide when confronted with new component and wireless communication technologies. Many of them are reaching out to smaller companies with technologies that are more promising than their own, so as to preserve the investments they made earlier in commercializing equipment and devices based on an earlier technology.

How to manage this alternation between technology and the business created around it depends on two main things: the prospects for further progress in key facets of the technology and the vulnerability of standards and dominant designs to substitution.

Prospects for Further Progress

Recent research on how technologies evolve and mature provides a number of indicators for judging when a particular technology should be abandoned. One such set of indicators is provided by Richard Foster, who studied several industries to illustrate how technologies reach maturity and get overtaken by new ones. Each one's performance rises steadily at first in proportion to the investments made, accelerating for a while, and then flattening out in S-curve fashion. He lists ten questions to help identify when this flattening out starts to occur:

1. Is there increasing discomfort among top management about R&D output?

2. Have development costs and delays started increasing instead of falling?

3. Are you doing more process R&D, less product R&D?

4. Is creativity waning?

5. Is there disharmony and discouragement in the labs?

6. Is market segmentation becoming the key to sales increases?

7. Are there wide differences in R&D spending among competitors with no apparent market effects?

8. Have there been frequent changes in R&D management with no impact?

9. Are some leaders losing share to smaller competitors in market niches?

10. Are supposedly weaker competitors succeeding with radical approaches that everyone else says cannot work?[22]

Michael Rappa's work on the duration of contribution spans of researchers in a particular field offers yet another index of approaching maturity. He found that if researchers judge that a technology has reached its limits, they tend to cease work in the field and turn their attention and energies to more promising areas where they can make a contribution. Researchers working on EPDM (a synthetic rubber) catalysts, for example, started contributing to the field soon after the discovery of the Ziegler-Natta catalyst process in the 1950s. However, they abandoned the field some fifteen years ago because no new breakthroughs seemed to be forthcoming. Those working on catalysts for polypropylene, on the other hand, continued their effort over a longer period. Four major breakthroughs in this field had resulted in three well-defined generations of catalysts.[23]

The phenomenon of diminishing returns applies mainly to the upstream facets of the technology—the principles and processes used and, to some extent, component technologies. Devices and systems comprising several different technologies are less affected. Progress in various components and enabling technologies at different points in time can result in a regular increase in their overall performance over a length of time. In some cases, they can replace one enabling technology with a totally new one that is more promising—electronic fuel injection instead of mechanical carburetors in automobiles, for example.

When one encounters diminishing returns, sticking obstinately to the initial technology is not the best way to optimize returns on the investments made in it. Attention needs to shift to preserving the value of the infrastructure that was built to commercialize it.

Vulnerability of Standards and Dominant Designs

Product standards and dominant designs do indeed help entrench the technologies beyond the point when diminishing returns set in. The question in practice is to decide between how much to rely on standards to sustain the technology's commercialization (even standards that might have been vital in having the technology accepted in the first place) versus intentionally branching out to a new functionality. As the example of RCA versus Sony's Trinitron technology illustrates, staying too long in a standard in the face of rapid technological advances by others can prove self-defeating, no matter who is involved in adopting the initial standard. Dramatic step-changes in technology, which occur frequently today, may not obviate the need for standards, but they do make the latter more vulnerable to obsolescence.

Taking active steps to establish a particular technology as a standard makes sense especially when there are significant positive feedback effects envisaged and the technology itself is relatively stable. In such instances, the more people adopt the technology, the greater the likelihood of gaining scale economies, having the delivery infrastructure expand quickly, and having potential customers recognize its value. For the technology's owner, the prospects of side payments (in the form of license fees) and suggestions for incremental improvements from others makes it all the more attractive. This is the case shown by line AC in Figure 10-4.

In contrast, as shown by line AB, technologies that go through rapid evolution and promise relatively minor positive feedback effects are best exploited independently. Not only do they tend to offer unattractive side payments because of the constant threat of substitution, but they also tend to gain little from sheer market expansion. Allowing others who have not borne the cost of developing the technology to enter free amounts to a subsidy and can result in rapidly transforming the technology into a commodity. A case in point is the many "open standards" in the electronics industry today.

The tricky situation is the one illustrated by line AD in the figure, where both positive feedback effects are important and where the technology itself changes rapidly. Today's multimedia technologies are good examples of this. Here is where careful trade-offs need to be made.

As a general rule, the more a standard serves as a tool to attract customers, the greater its justification in such cases. If its purpose is mainly to prolong a technology's life cycle and gain market share for its proponent, it is unlikely to last long. Disclosures made in getting to it can also result in diminished profits for a technology owner, unless compensated by side payments in the form of royalties. There are far too many opportunities for others, especially those excluded from the standard, to enter with a superior technology.

SUMMARY

The value of a new technology is not realized at launch, nor even when it penetrates the market. It is realized in the process of sustaining its commercialization. Warding off competition, entrenching the use of the technology, and appropriating its benefits for the inventor are partly technical processes, requiring progress in different facets of the technology. They are

FIGURE 10-4

**PROMOTING A TECHNOLOGY AS A STANDARD VERSUS
EXPLOITING IT INDEPENDENTLY**

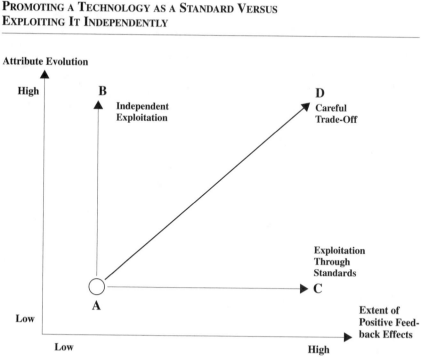

also sociopolitical processes, involving the mobilization of various actors around the technology over a period of time.

Sustaining a technology's commercialization is entrenching its use in the marketplace vis-à-vis competing technologies. Just staying competitive is not enough. What one needs to do is to establish it as a dominant design where relevant, cause it to benefit from a variety of network externalities that enhance its attractiveness as more people adopt it, and deepen its use in particular applications, thereby creating dependence.

The caveat to bear in mind is that no technology should be held onto longer than is optimum. This is self-defeating. Sometimes one needs to alternate the investment emphasis between improving the technology first commercialized and the infrastructure created around it—buying in other technologies to do the latter, if necessary.

Finally, entrenching the use of a technology by itself is not enough. Its proponent needs to be able to appropriate a fair share of its benefits over a period of time, too. This requires paying attention to the relationship among the different facets of the technology and staying ahead in those that matter. The more others can be co-opted in this process and made to contribute to it, the longer the technology can be sustained and profits realized from it.

11

CLOSING THE CIRCLE

Speed, Timing,
and Effectiveness

LOOKING AT TECHNOLOGY COMMERCIALIZATION AS A SERIES OF DISTINCT, value-adding subprocesses naturally evokes the question of how these link together in time. Speed and time-to-market thinking now pervade just about everything managers do today. Does the same apply to technology commercialization? To the extent that the time dimension is important, how does it contribute to value, and what needs to be done to manage it effectively?

These are the questions posed for this penultimate chapter. Its basic message is that, while speed has indeed become more important for technology commercialization than in the past, there are some nuances to consider.

THE TIME DIMENSION IN TECHNOLOGY COMMERCIALIZATION

The now ubiquitous smart card was thought up by a Frenchman, Roland Moreno, in 1974 while pacing his Paris apartment one night. He had figured out not only what such a credit-card-sized device would do, but how it might be built using integrated circuits. But, despite having licensed the patents rights to companies in a position to build the card—notably Bull and Schlumberger—the first consumer trials were not conducted until twelve years later.

Part of the reason for the delay was a lack of adequate funding in the beginning, a common roadblock for independent inventors. Equally important, however, were the difficulties associated with assembling the right technologies and persuading French banks to codefine and invest in the system. It was not that no one was interested. Rather, a whole range of issues such as technical performance and reliability, security, and expected patterns of use had to be explored and addressed one by one.[1]

The time taken notwithstanding, Moreno's smart card did turn into a commercial success. Although the inventor started to earn significant royalties only in the early 1990s—just a few years before his patent expired—the technology itself has experienced rapid growth and use in a large number of applications.

The smart card illustrates the long time many technology-based innovations take to reach the market and the multiple reasons for this delay. It also illustrates that delays are not always fatal, though they might reduce the value the inventor appropriates in the end.

The overall time that innovations take to reach the market varies enormously and depends on how one identifies the starting and ending points. Even so, ten years has been a good average from the time a product idea based on a new technology is conceived to its first market launch. This was, for example, the time taken by transistors—first conceived in 1940 and introduced in 1950. Magnetic ferrites, the videotape recorder, the oral contraceptive pill, the electron microscope, and matrix isolation—technologies examined by the first Technology in Retrospect and Critical Events in Science (TRACES) study in 1968—averaged nine years.[2] Similarly, eight to ten years from invention to a net return of royalties was also the average for projects financed more recently by the British Technology Group.[3] High-temperature superconductors have taken ten years since their discovery in 1986 to become available in commercial products, too.

Like most averages, this ten-year duration does not reveal much. More interesting is the experience of individual technologies and the fact that delays can occur at any stage of the commercialization process. Some technologies, like Moreno's smart card, get invented in a few hours, but then take years to be demonstrated in end products. There are others that do just the opposite—a painstakingly long and thorough discovery process followed by almost immediate demonstration. Many science-based technologies fall into this category, where the bulk of the time is spent on elucidating principles, trying them out, and linking them to specific applications. Finally, we all know of inventions that got invented and demonstrated quickly, only to spend years gaining market acceptance—they were simply too early for the market. Some of these delays are influenced by forces beyond an inventor's control. There are, however, certain delays that can be traced to particular actions taken by an inventor.

Whether anything should be done to speed up the overall process, or particular elements of it, depends on how this affects value creation. Rushing certain technologies to completion can sometimes amount to rushing their failure. In a recent study involving fourteen new ventures started by a large aluminum company, Utterback et al., too, came to the conclusion that all ventures should not be equally speeded up. Ventures based on a new technology whose products are to be launched in unfamiliar or new markets are particularly vulnerable to the dangers of haste. Telescoping the commercialization process can result in compromising the technical development of products, misreading of the market, and ignoring some key activities necessary for ensuring new product success.[4]

Speeding a technology to market never makes sense if it results in a poor-quality product that the market won't accept. This aside, it is also unequivocally beneficial only when the function, the product, or the process incorporating the technology is well established in the market; when customers are eager to adopt anything that promises a better price-performance characteristic for competitive or other reasons; when competitors are actively working on similar technologies and products; and when delaying the introduction of the technology offers few prospects for a proprietary, step-change improvement in the product being offered.

The most dramatic illustrations of the value of speed under these circumstances today are offered by the semiconductor and pharmaceutical industries. Although science-based, they both serve well-established markets in which it is hard for anyone to maintain a unique, high-value position for long until a better substitute comes along. Getting to market a few months earlier in the semiconductor industry can produce over \$1 billion in additional revenues for an innovative company. In the pharmaceutical industry, each day of delay in getting a drug to market can cost as much as \$1 million.

Failure to be first in such situations usually also means missing the product opportunity altogether. Thus, when Searle terminated its TPA program (a drug to dissolve blood clots in heart attack victims) in the early 1990s, it did so because competitors were too far ahead in their development work. There are, however, many instances where being first to the market is not want counts most. What matters more is the nature of the end product and the timing of certain stages in the commercialization process. These tend to be associated with cases where the final window of opportunity is neither imminent nor clearly defined; where slight delays that contribute to major enhancements at the product level can yield a larger market overall or a significant competitive advantage that compensates for lost revenues; and where there are good reasons for performing certain tasks at a point in time and then intentionally delaying the undertaking of subsequent stages of the process.

Thus there are two, quite distinct types of situations: those where the overall process benefits unequivocally from speed, and those where the value of the outcome depends on time in a more subtle way. The important thing is to decide in advance which category a particular invention belongs to and then manage it accordingly. The two sections that follow treat each category in turn, elaborating on their characteristics and suggesting how they ought to be managed. The last two sections then discuss issues that concern both categories—that of bridging stages in the commercialization process and how external resource providers, notably government agencies, can help in bringing new technologies to market on time.

MANAGING FOR OVERALL SPEED

As the examples of the semiconductor and pharmaceutical industries pointed out, there are certain cases where being first to market is almost always desirable. One needs to come up with a good techno-market insight and then quickly accomplish all the stages leading to the launch of end products.

Such a situation exists today for anyone working on blue lasers for compact disc recording. The market is big, well established, and constantly on the lookout for technologies that offer higher recording densities. Anyone who comes up with a working blue laser diode for reading information on CDs first—which promises a threefold increase in recording density over the current near-infrared lasers—will immediately capture a highly valuable market. This explains the multitude of organizations around the world working on the technology and the eagerness with which news of progress in the area gets followed.

The appropriate way to manage such technologies is to see their commercialization process as one continuum from start to finish. Each stage in the process needs to be managed for greatest efficiency, since value resides only in the final outcome itself—when products get launched. In practice, this means assembling as many resources and as much information on downstream stages up front as possible, defining the scope of one's own R&D precisely for the objective being achieved and being consequential in going from one stage to the next.

Assembling Resources and Information Up Front

As Roland Moreno put it, reflecting on why Apple Computer Inc. got off to a good start while his smart card invention treaded water for twelve years, Apple "went the industrial route by [itself]. The two Steves [Jobs and Wozniak] had the backing to put their idea into production."[5] Moreno was referring to the two things most responsible for delays in technology commercialization—the unavailability of adequate funding and resources at the start, and the multiple partners and organizations involved.

Projects that are well funded and supported from the beginning do get completed sooner. Countries with an active and entrepreneurial venture capital community, such as the United States, have a natural advantage over others in this regard. Even so, are the several things inventors can do to influence their chances for assembling resources up front—defining their technology in an attractive manner, taking steps to mobilize interest and resources from the beginning, and so on. The greater the potential created and the more credible the plan for implementing the downstream stages of commercialization, the greater the resources that can be attracted up front.

Early information regarding what needs to be done is another important contributor to speed. As recent studies on the subject have demonstrated, the earlier and closer the integration of R&D with other functions (especially marketing), the better the outcome. This is as true in the United States[6] as it is in Japan.[7] Close cooperation between R&D and marketing during the early stages of product design is also associated with reduced cycle time and the timeliness with which projects get executed.[8]

While the need for marketing involvement early is generally well accepted, that of manufacturing remains controversial. Yet a case can be made for the integration of manufacturing as early as possible too.[9] Apart from the obvious contribution toward design for manufacturability, getting manufacturing involved in the front end of new product development as a full partner in decision making helps in:

Forging networks and strong links among all the functions concerned so as to create companywide ownership of the project;

Bringing value and cost considerations early and together into the development phase, which is especially important since 60 percent to 80 percent of the cost of a product tends to become fixed at the design stage;

Initiating choice of process, test, and assembly strategies early so as to be ready with production processes in time or to flag what can or cannot be done. In some cases this can also have a major influence on the marketing strategy, such as the nature and size of segments that should be targeted, and pricing;

Exposing manufacturing to potential customers early so as to benefit from the feedback provided; and

Enriching and adding realism to formal design techniques such as QFD.

Today's recommendations about creating multifunctional teams early in the commercialization process follow from this. In addition to bringing as much relevant information up front as possible, they help in facilitating technology transfer later as well. When marketing and production are involved from the beginning, they tend to have a greater sense of ownership and familiarity over the technology, making them more willing recipients when they need to take over.

Defining the Scope of One's Own R&D Precisely

Given the nature of laboratory research, it is often difficult to speed up technology development itself. What one can do, however, is to avoid some self-imposed causes of delay. One area is the scope and depth of the research done.

The amount spent on R&D has to be seen not so much as preserving an in-house research capability but in relation to the needs of specific projects. If a project requires a bulk of the resources to go into searching for and acquiring technologies outside or doing subcontract research, this is no reflection on in-house competence. How deeply to research an area on one's own has to be constantly traded off against the scope of technologies to be accessed to meet a commercial objective.

With the interpenetration of different disciplines and technologies, the breadth of what constitutes a "core technology" has also expanded enormously in recent years. A company engaged in making semiconductors, for example, today requires expertise in everything from solid-state physics, material science, and chemistry (physical, surface, inorganic, and organic), all the way to optics and various process technologies. The consequence is that companies need to define ever more core technologies, not fewer. Thus, while NEC came up with a list of twenty-seven core technologies in 1975, the number had grown to thirty-four by 1990.[10] Also, focusing on one core technology at the expense of another can result in poor products.[11]

With such proliferation one inevitably needs to make choices. Does, for example, a company have to cover all the upstream facets of each technology it considers its core? Are some technologies more "core" than others? Is there a trade-off between covering multiple technologies superficially versus a few in depth? Which is the better approach to follow?

Vertical integration in a technology sense is a double-edged weapon. It can result in an impregnable position at the product level, but it can also lead to compromises in product conception to suit proprietary component technologies; it can blindside vis-à-vis technologies developed by others that may be superior and reduce time to market. In general, the approach needed today is to expand access to a range of technologies while concentrating one's own efforts on researching deeply one or two areas to form the basis for a proprietary position. As Praveen Chaudhari of IBM puts it,

> The organization, reward system, and, most importantly, the attitude of R&D personnel in corporate research laboratories in the United States has to change from just research to both research and search. This search may be in the U.S. or in other parts of the world where expertise resides. This is nontrivial, for it requires researchers to be willing to embrace solutions other than their own to problems on which they may have already invested their time. Alternatively, it may require an increasing number of them to

spend more time on search and acquisition [S&A] than just research and development [R&D].[12]

Evidence of such an attitude is already to be found in a growing resort to outside help in bringing new technologies to market through the purchase of complementary technologies and performing contract or joint R&D. As Roy Rothwell and his colleagues at the Science Policy Research Unit (SPRU) found for the United Kingdom, small British firms obtained on average 7 percent of their external ideas from other companies (excluding universities and research institutes) during the period from 1945 to 1969; in the following period from 1970 to 1979 this had increased to 25 percent. A survey covering the period from 1983 to 1986 found that 47.5 percent of small firms had some form of technical link with other firms, and 39 percent of the firms in this survey contracted out R&D. Significantly enough, in 34 percent of the cases, the main motive was to gain access to technology new to the firm, but, in 50 percent of the cases, the motive was to shorten lead times.[13]

Sandoz is one company that has tried to offset the dangers of a narrow research focus by establishing a worldwide network of partnerships with fledgling biotechnology firms. Paul Herrling, corporate research director who heads basic-science discovery activities for Sandoz, sees such alliances as a way to defend the firm's traditional strengths such as transplantation, as well as to move rapidly into new therapeutic areas such as cancer, where the company historically was weak.[14]

Nokia's GSM Codec

The importance of tailoring ones own research effort and searching for partners to meet the time window in technology demonstration is illustrated by Nokia's recent success with its speech codec for Groupe Special Mobile (GSM) and other digital cellular networks.

When first deployed in 1991, GSM networks incorporated a so-called full-rate speech codec (coder/decoder system). While this codec provided good communications-quality speech, it was noticeably inferior to that available on fixed telephone networks. Recognizing the need for a better codec, Nokia launched a project to develop an enhanced full-rate (EFR) speech codec for GSM in 1993.

There had been substantial theoretical advances in speech-coding technology since the development of the GSM full-rate codec. The pressure to develop the new codec rapidly came mainly from the United States. Personal communication services (PCS) operators adopting GSM-based technology wanted to maximize the competitiveness of their choice and were looking for an enhanced codec. The relevant standards body in Europe, European Telecommunications Standards Institute (ETSI), had also started its own study for an improved GSM codec. Nokia had to propose its own solution quickly if it wanted to have any opportunity to influence the standard. Faced with these time pressures, Nokia's research center opted for a collaboration strategy. Like many others in the industry, it knew that a technology known as Algebraic Code Excited Linear Prediction (ACELP) was suitable for this purpose and was familiar with its principles. Nokia approached the University of Sherbrooke in Canada, which had developed it initially and had a new version suitable for implementation and standard specification almost ready. Licensing the core technology from the university, Nokia entered into a research collaboration agreement with it in late 1994.

The collaboration allowed the Nokia EFR codec to be selected as the PCS 1900 standard in the United States in April 1995 in the face of several competing proposals. The various proposals were evaluated and the ACELP choice was unanimously supported by all major manufacturers. This then influenced the Europeans, who accepted it as a GSM standard, too, a choice supported by the majority of operators and manufacturers. The choice was motivated both by the technical performance of the PCS 1900 EFR codec and by the synergy and implementation advantages of using the same codec as in the PCS 1900 system. The European selection was finalized in late 1995, and the specifications for GSM were completed in January 1996.

The success of the Nokia proposal in the PCS 1900 and GSM systems was quickly followed by similar success in all the other major PCS digital cellular systems in the United States. The digital Advanced Mobile Phone System (AMPS) (IS-136 standard) has adopted the Nokia proposal based on ACELP technology, and the new code-division multiple access (CDMA) system will use a joint proposal of Nokia and AT&T as an enhanced codec, too.

Nokia has benefited from all of this in two ways: it has enhanced both its reputation as a technical leader in mobile communications and its patent portfolio through rights for exclusive licensing. As Petri Haavisto of Nokia Research Center reflects:

> We could have developed a candidate codec on our own, but it would have taken six to nine months longer. But that was not the only advantage we gained from the collaboration with the University of Sherbrooke. Their past reputation in the field gave us greater credibility in having our technology accepted as a standard.[15]

Searching for technologies outside must, however, be combined with good patent analyses early and a well-thought-out strategy for assembling the technologies required. Just as a great deal of duplicative research gets done because no one took the trouble to look at patents and patent disclosures, a number of research projects get stalled or constantly modified because of the possible infringement of the patents of others. To avoid these delays, some companies have entire departments devoted to search for patents continuously. Hitachi, for example, now employs 150 people for this purpose.

Another approach is to seek out partners for cross-licensing and the creation of patent pools to jointly exploit a technology. A recent example is the agreement entered into between Fujitsu and Samsung. In an effort to improve their respective positions in the fast-growing liquid crystal display (LCD) business by coming up with better products quickly, Fujitsu of Japan and Samsung of Korea cross-licensed their patents so that Fujitsu will provide Samsung with its wide-angle viewing technology, which overcomes the problem of clearly viewing LCD screens from different angles. In return, Samsung agreed to provide Fujitsu with high aperture ratio efficiency coating technology, which enables the LCD panel to remain bright even at low power consumption. As technological fields converge, such cross-licensing and patent pooling arrangements are likely to increase in several industries in the future.

Making Consequential Transitions from One Stage to the Next

The mystery surrounding technological innovation has often led managers to reduce it to a game of probabilities. A consequence is that many companies do not select the technologies they want to win with on time. A lot of simmering goes on, but nothing boils.

An illustration of what happens is provided by AlliedSignal's experience with conducting polymers. After twelve years of effort and some fifty patents to its credit, including a dominating one in electroluminescence, the company and its people are beginning to lose interest. Typically, the first applications worked on in the early 1980s were related to automobile batteries because there was a battery company within the group. Then, in 1985 to 1986, when the battery company was sold, the number of people working in the field got reduced. Those remaining redirected their efforts to a different technology—polyaniline as a blending additive instead of polyacetylene. The class of applications they had in mind by 1988 was electromagnetic shielding and antistatic coatings.

But rather than go all the way downstream to specific product applications, the approach taken was to produce powder only. An agreement was signed with Zipplin, Inc., whereby the latter would use AlliedSignal's dispersion technology to sell formulations to end-users. This, the company now recognizes, was too low-level an effort to get into the market in a significant way. Rather than a policy of benign neglect on the part of senior management, what is needed instead is an active involvement in selecting the technologies to back and making sure they get taken to the end consequentially.

Terminating projects on time serves not only the corporation but individuals too. As stated by Lowell Steele, the former head of technology planning at GE,

> The human cost of dragging on research projects can be horrendous. Some people do end up devoting an entire research career to projects that lead to nothing. Companies should be more consequential in their choices and encourage only those projects they are really serious about.[16]

To some extent, stage-gate processes (where a project must successfully complete each stage in order to pass through the "gate" into the next) help companies arrive more quickly at fewer, better-resourced projects. An example of such a process covering the various stages in technology commercialization described here is that of the one now used at DuPont's Lycra division (see Figure 11-1).

Each stage involves concurrent activities across several functions and anticipates some of what is required for implementing stages downstream in the process. For example, once an idea makes it to the scouting stage, lab scale tests are conducted to explore the process options, a small pilot plant demonstration is conducted, and some end-use evaluations are made to determine the product value and fit into the product portfolio. Also, the market potential, raw material availability, and product safety are confirmed. Prior to evolving to a new stage, the program is reviewed and management decides to continue funding the program or stop it.

Roughly 80 percent of projects going through the process get culled during the idea stage itself. Of those that remain, a majority then get eliminated in the scouting stage, with most of the rest being taken through to market launch. In other words, once a project enters into development, it gets whatever is required by way of resources and commitment to make it succeed. As Norman D'Allura, technical manager of the Lycra division's European operation, puts it:

> Reviews after the scouting stage are mainly to ensure that the defined set of objectives have been achieved and to discuss what needs to be done in time for the following review. The role of management is not just to approve or disapprove, but to act as an enabler, helping out with problems as they arise.[17]

MANAGING FOR TIMING

Technologies for which there is no imminent demand require a different approach to time. Instead of taking an idea through to product development and launch as quickly as possible, one needs to make sure that the product itself is truly market worthy. Apart from design features, the latter means *finding* the appropriate time to launch it. To profit fully from such technologies, one also sometimes needs to meet certain intermediate

FIGURE 11-1
DuPont Lycra Fishbone Project Management Model

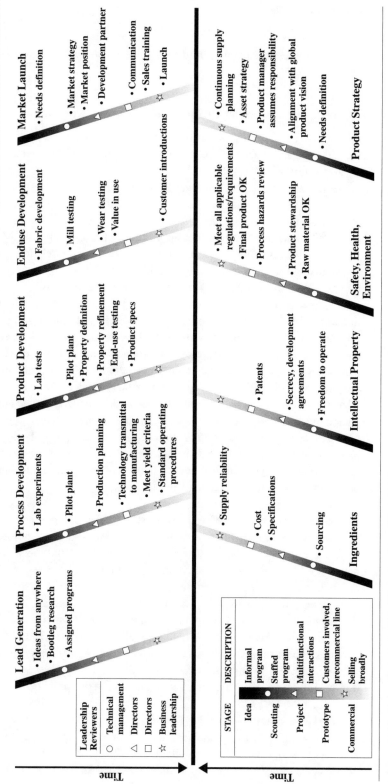

SOURCE: DuPont Lycra Technical, 1995, © H. L. Snyder and N. J. D'Allura.

time windows, corresponding to different stages of the commercialization process.

The Different Time Windows in Technology Commercialization

Figure 11-2 summarizes the various time windows one typically sees leading up to the acceptance of end products by the market. This figure will be discussed further later in this chapter.

At the start of technology commercialization, the issue of timing relates to being first with an idea and staking a proprietary claim over the uses it represents. Thus, Moreno did eventually earn royalties on the smart card because he was the first to come up with the idea and patent it. Making inventions and obtaining patent grants need to be timed in relation to competing discoveries and inventions, even if their subsequent commercialization may be some years away for technical or market reasons.

Perhaps the best illustration of the reward of being first with an invention and patenting it ahead of others is that of Jerome Lemelson. A prolific inventor based in Incline, Nevada, Lemelson patented several inventions back in the 1950s and 1960s, covering products such as bar-code readers, machine vision, fax machines, and even camcorders. Although he himself did not come up with working models of these devices, he was granted what some consider unfairly broad claims on their underlying technology, something most early patentees enjoy.[18] His patent on bar-code reading systems alone has earned him $500 million in royalties, partly because the patent took so long to be granted. Although filed in 1954, the basic patent on bar codes was granted to him only in 1992—long after the technology became well established and valuable.[19]

This said, inventions that are made too much in advance of a commercial opportunity, or long before relevant stakeholders are prepared to support it, don't do much for an inventor. Both Dennis Gabor's holography patents filed in the 1950s (see Chapter 4) and Sir Frank Whittle's jet engine patent filed in 1930 earned their inventors little because they expired long before commercial products got launched on the market.

The need to time the *start* of an activity applies particularly to product development. Unlike the case of invention patents, being first is not always rewarding. One needs to wait sometimes until the market is ready and then undertake the process as efficiently as possible. Apart from permitting the incorporation of the latest enabling and complementary technologies, this benefits from the latest market requirements the product must have to succeed.

Market readiness, as Chapter 7 pointed out, is more than just consumer willingness to buy. It also includes the readiness of several market constituents to adopt the technology. Some may have just invested in a competing technology and are simply not interested in anything else for a

FIGURE 11-2
TIME WINDOWS AND GAPS IN THE TECHNOLOGY COMMERCIALIZATION PROCESS

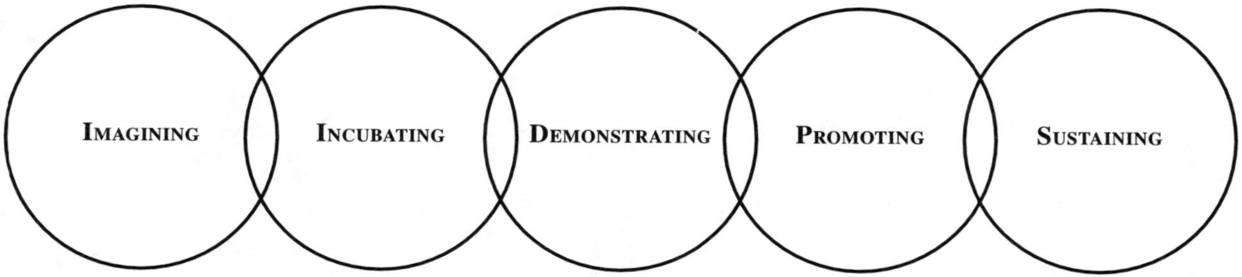

	IMAGINING	INCUBATING	DEMONSTRATING	PROMOTING	SUSTAINING
WINDOW OF OPPORTUNITY AND TIMING REQUIREMENTS	Competing discoveries in the field, including patenting by others, readiness of peers to endorse discovery	Application-specific time windows, time line of intermediate adopters, selection by resource providers, filing patents to consolidate position	Availability of competing products or processes for the function targeted, availability of complementary technologies	Readiness of market constituents to support commercialization and of end-users to adopt the product or process	Launch of more cost-effective products or processes by competitors
TRANSFER GAPS	INTEREST GAP	TECHNOLOGY TRANSFER GAP	MARKET TRANSFER GAP	DIFFUSION GAP	

period of time. Others may have committed themselves to a technology that seems more promising, which they are willing to wait for.

The importance of getting market timing right is illustrated by the experience of several telecommunications equipment manufacturers who started work on multimedia products in the late 1980s. Finding that service providers (their customers) had just finished investing heavily in more basic services and were unprepared to take on anything new, many of them scaled back their efforts in the mid-1990s, after incurring considerable expenditures. They are now waiting for demand to materialize before restarting their development programs.

Misreading the market is particularly costly in highly competitive industries, as illustrated by what happened with LCDs. A large number of companies entered the market simultaneously, hoping to establish an early position. But the demand for their products turned out to be far less than they expected, resulting in excess capacity and price competition. With world demand of just 3 million active-matrix screens for notebook computers in 1995, the Japanese and Koreans had created a total capacity for 14 million units.[20]

For the stages that follow product launch, the need for timing is associated with the segments targeted and the introduction of competing technologies. While reaching for a mass market can be delayed in some cases, it needs to be approached sooner in others. Similarly, deciding which facet of the technology to work on first to sustain its commercialization depends on where one expects competition to arise. Sometimes it is better to work on the process first, so as to establish the technology's cost competitiveness. In other cases, where the introduction of an alternative, better process does not seem imminent, it may be wiser to concentrate on application development first.

Difficult as timing these time windows can be, one nevertheless has to try. In practice it helps to manage each stage for its own competitive logic, vary the investment and effort in line with opportunities as they emerge, find more proximate time windows where possible, and be open to partners that may have thought of opportunities of their own.

Managing Each Stage for Its Own Logic

The best way to meet the window of opportunity at each stage of the commercialization process is to manage each stage for its own logic. As pointed out in Chapter 1, competition in technology-based innovation is increasingly manifest by stage, too. One needs to understand the nature of this competition and adapt one's approach to time accordingly.

At the imagining stage, there is growing need to be quick with a discovery both because of competition from other researchers and because of the way science and technology are progressing. Thus, for the technologies covered in the original TRACES study—magnetic ferrites, videotape recorders, the oral contraceptive pill, the electron microscope, and matrix isolation—approximately 90 percent of the nonmission research pertaining to them had been accomplished ten years prior to the invention. This left a relatively wide time period within which to assemble the accumulating body of knowledge and apply it to a concrete use.[21] Today, the situation is different in many industries. As Jürgen Drews, the head of research of Hoffman-La Roche Inc., put it in reference to the pharmaceutical industry:

> The scientific discoveries on which the development of calcium channel blockers, beta-blockers, H_2 blockers, [and] ACE inhibitors was based preceded the initiation of drug development by at least a decade. At present, we are witnessing a drastic change of these lead times. Very often scientific discoveries such as the identification of a new cytokine, the cloning and sequencing of a new receptor or the description of a new signalling path way are immediately followed by the formulation of therapeutic concepts. As a new scientific theory emerges so do ideas for its medical exploitation.[22]

Product development requires a greater emphasis on its own logic too. A frequent reason why product development activities become ill-timed is that they are seen as an immediate sequel to some piece of enabling research rather than being driven by an imminent demand and the availability of adequate complementary technologies. The same applies to all of the other subprocesses.

Completing each stage for its own requirements also ensures that it does not become a stumbling block for the ones further downstream in the commercialization process. Instead of cycling back and forth *between* stages in the hope of gaining time, it is often better to cycle a little *within* each stage, waiting to tackle the next at the appropriate moment.

One of the reasons why Roland Belz experienced delays in getting his intelligent plastics demonstrated in marketable end products was the way the earlier stage got handled. While he was able to create an attractive vision for his technology in terms of its potential, he failed to define applications that would bring it to market expeditiously. The initial market analysis done by AD Little was comprehensive and pointed to several near-term opportunities for water-soluble-on-demand plastics. However, not enough was done to explore these applications in depth on an individual basis, which is what an incubation phase is meant to do. Essentially, they were not taken far enough to interest potential partners, both in terms of establishing technical feasibility and understanding the real demand (instead of need) that existed for them.

An important implication of managing certain technologies stage by stage is the way information needs to be assembled up front and how each stage is managed. Compared to the situation where a final window of opportunity is clearly defined and is the only one that matters, these technologies require meeting different intermediate outcomes. If this means working within a different context than, for example, what the marketing department thinks is desirable, so be it. Force-fitting an end-consumer or a product/market context right from the beginning can be counterproductive. As concluded by a working group of the European Industrial Research Management Association investigating the interface between R&D and marketing, successful innovations require not an equal but a properly balanced involvement of the two functions. Thus, long-term exploratory R&D requires a rather loose coupling with its counterpart in marketing, that is, strategic marketing. Both, moreover, need to be driven by an overriding strategic mission and an understanding of each other's perspective. Later, when R&D and marketing have mutually decided on freezing the specifications, a closer, more formal cooperation with well-defined rules is needed to speed up the development process. The interfacing, in other words, needs to be a function of both time and content.[23]

In a similar vein, early top management involvement, a highly influential product champion, and a project manager with broad authority are generally correlated with success, but *not* under conditions of high technical uncertainty—that is, when the technological phenomenon is not well known to the developer, there is little information to draw on for guidance, and the development involves complex trial and error methods. Lengthy and uncertain technology demonstrations are better handled through occasional contacts among research personnel, marketing, and production, than by permanent teams.[24]

Varying the Investment and Effort

It is a well-known fact that many breakthrough technologies turn out to be unprofitable on a discounted cash flow basis because of the time they take. But this does not have to be the case. By varying the investment and effort at each stage of the process in line with its proximity to the final revenue opportunity, it is still possible to come up with an acceptable net present value (NPV). This requires putting certain technologies on the "back burner" for a while, maintaining only a regular but small investment in them, rather than always choosing a crash program to get them to market quickly.

An example is that of IBM's recent approach to Josephson junction and gallium arsenide technologies. Having invented Josephson junctions, the company first moved the technology to one of its development groups to build a complete system. However, in the process of solving all the nitty-gritty engineering details involved, it found the advantages of this technology slipping vis-à-vis silicon. With rapid progress occurring in silicon, what was initially a 100-fold advantage dropped to tenfold or so. By the time Josephson junctions actually came to the market, this difference was expected to narrow even further. As one IBM researcher recalls, "So, the question came up, would anybody buy a brand new, unknown technology instead of something that was already tried and tested which, moreover, was making excellent progress? And the answer was no. It was not that the technology was bad or that we couldn't do it. It was simply a practical recognition of the odds against Josephson junctions."

IBM did not altogether get out of this technology. Rather, it scaled down the size of its effort, continuing to monitor the technology. "You never know when a breakthrough will occur, and this way we can get back in quickly," says the researcher. IBM has done the same with gallium arsenide.

Many companies have entered what seemed promising technologies—such as photovoltaics, biotechnology, and new materials—only to abandon the effort when the payoffs looked too far out in the future. Conversely, one sometimes sees companies sustaining large R&D efforts in a technology just in case something comes out of them. While the former can result in a cavalier attitude toward exploring new technologies, the latter has been found to be unprofitable in practice. Rather than accelerating behind-schedule projects by flooding them with funds, it is often advisable to fund them leanly for a while, waiting for the right moment to push them forward.[25]

The same logic applies between the demonstration and delivery stages. Slowing down to meet the market window of opportunity is sometimes better than pushing ahead and intensifying efforts. This, more than anything else, explains the success many companies have enjoyed by being "fast followers." By competently developing a me-too product that is somewhat superior to the one launched prematurely by a pioneer, they benefit from all the work the latter has done in building primary demand.

Things need to be done quickly to meet windows of opportunity as they open at each stage, but simultaneous preparations can be costly. There have been many instances where a sales force has been hired and deployed even before the company had a product. Such was, for instance, the case with Raychem's Taliq venture. The origins of this go back to 1984 when Raychem's founder, Paul Cook, bought a license for encapsulated liquid crystals to enter the LCD market. Unlike its earlier practice of keeping such new technologies within its central R&D unit, Cook wanted to try out a new model this time, hoping it would speed things up. The LCD venture was immediately set up as an independent company with Raychem owning 80 percent of the stock. As an executive associated with this venture recalls,

> Because it was set up as a separate business unit, managers felt a pressure to generate some revenues quickly. They went after "oddball" applications

without thinking the whole thing through. The marketing people did just what they are expected to—bring the technology to market. But they went with half-developed products and an insufficient understanding of the material. Naturally, customers started to return products. In the end, overheads killed the project.[26]

The problem with a variable approach to R&D is, of course, the assignment of individual researchers. Moving people with specific skills and disciplinary knowledge from one project to another is neither easy nor desirable. The only way to do it is by resorting more to outside contract research and by making a conscious effort to get researchers to take on new challenges. Judging from the scores of researchers the author talked to, this is not altogether impossible. Researchers see such challenges as a refreshing break from whatever else they are struggling with. Deep down, they want the time to think through their individual problem, the one they want to tackle as the crowning achievement of their own career. Low levels of effort don't upset them. They welcome it. What they fear most is an abrupt cancellation—an embargo on something on which they have staked their career aspirations.

Finding Proximate Time Windows

Varying the investment effort to match commercialization opportunities does not mean settling on a particular use and then waiting passively for it to mature. Many technologies get developed painstakingly with a valid need in mind, only to be scuttled by unforeseeable events. The impact of this is particularly discouraging when products are just about to be launched, but it can occur at any stage. The best way to cope with such exogenous causes of delays and failures is to find more proximate windows of opportunity that one is sure about. This does not mean giving up on the main purpose one had in the beginning. It only means lessening one's dependence on the original need and finding more immediate uses while waiting for it to mature.

Time windows can, to a large extent, be influenced by the way applications get defined. Thus, when Kyocera had trouble recently making crystals big enough to use in specialized chips, Inamori redirected the effort into the production of synthetic jewelry, now a $100-million-a-year business.[27]

In speaking of multimedia, today's hot new technology, Robert Kerwin of AT&T captures the argument well:

> The twenty-year time horizon is still there, but a whole variety of intermediate solutions are being brought to market along the way. Many inventors in the computer industry talked about multi-media during the 1960s. We are not there yet but the industry itself grew enormously in the meantime with other applications.[28]

The history of LCDs over the past twenty years has also been one of matching further progress in the technology with new products in an alternating, irregular manner—starting with hand calculators that used segment displays (display of all numbers based on segments of the character 8) in the early 1970s, to small toys and calculators based on dot-type displays (expansion of displayable items to characters and graphics), and then on to color displays and expansion of screen size. At first, the latter were used primarily in Japanese-language word processors and color notebook personal computers. Today, with improved resolution and wider viewing angles, LCD displays are starting to be used in portable TVs too.

In practice, finding proximate time windows is aided by maintaining close customer contacts in a broad range of industries and anticipating what their needs might be. Janet Hammill, technical specialist at Alcoa's research center, expressed the need for anticipation in the materials industry as follows:

> Instead of supplying materials, we have to build a complete technology. Presently, we produce materials and put their properties into a book. But a material supplier has other options that are not in the book. If we talk to users about their structures directly, we might be able to come up with other options. In any case, we should imagine and anticipate uses so as to get into a customer's program of development early.[29]

To achieve this, Alcoa holds continuing "what if" discussions with potential customers, asking what they would do if, for example, it offered a new material that resulted in a 20 percent weight reduction on a part. It tries to understand a customer's design priorities and technology. It engages in a constant dialogue so as to comprehend what the customer's business is all about.

The other way to find proximate time windows is to respond flexibly to opportunities when they arise. This is what permitted Roland Belz to reconfigure his strategy as soon as the German government announced its stringent new environmental legislation concerning the recycling of packaging material in 1991 (see Chapter 7). The same opportunism has served Conductus Inc. well, too. Thus, while following Linda Capuano's "food chain" approach (see Chapter 4) of taking technically easy applications first, it remained open to applications where money for demonstrating high temperature superconductivity was more forthcoming. One such attractive area it found was cellular telecommunications. With its rapid growth and competitive pressure to experiment with new enabling technologies to save on cost and limited channel space, this suddenly became an attractive area to target in the early 1990s. In partnership with AT&T, CTI-Cryogenics, IBM, and MIT Lincoln Laboratory, Conductus began a program to develop cellular base stations in 1989. Because of its potential application in the defense industry, this effort obtained ARPA support as well.

Being Open to Partners

The more one is open to partners from the beginning, the greater the chances of influencing the early adoption of the technology securely. As Robert Kerwin put it,

> Holding a technology proprietary [nondivulged] results in slowing down its development. When AT&T licensed out its semiconductor technology in the early 1950s, applications mushroomed quickly. There were many minds and many laboratories who applied themselves. While one's own share of the profits may be smaller, the final market is invariably bigger when one does this.[30]

Promoting externally and widely is especially important when decisions to support a new technology are tightly constrained by the strategy and preoccupation of existing business. Those outside may have different reasons for seeing value in a technology. This was, for instance, the experience with IBM's magneto-optic technology. While IBM saw the technology as potentially, but not immediately, suited to data storage, many Japanese companies latched onto it sooner for audio compact discs.

Many researchers within large companies have found it easier to make the bridge to downstream stages externally. As a research manager at AlliedSignal explains,

> The key challenge for R&D organizations such as ours today is strengthening the pull for new technologies on the part of divisions. The internal pull by divisions is uncreative and weak. They don't think beyond existing products, even simply how to make it distinctive vis-à-vis competition. The business structure often tries to force-fit applications. If it is conductive polymers, for example, should you put it in the polymer business unit? But they actually make molds.[31]

The short-term performance criteria to which business units are subject provides them with little incentive to incorporate new technologies readily. While competitive forces eventually force them to do so, the signals emanating from the market are weak. As stated by a colleague of the research manager quoted above, "The competitive situation is not truly visible until it is almost a cataclysmic finish." This partly explains the preference for corporate spin-offs that are an attempt to get the best of both worlds—the freedom of independent inventors to transact with the most suitable and interested partners, those who share an inventor's vision of what the technology can achieve, combined with the resources a large company can bring.

Outside partners can provide much-needed information on trends and opportunities, and they can help speed up the process when these opportunities need to be finely timed. As Paul Henstridge of ICI put it in referring to the FM-21 commercialization:

Don't do it all yourself; you will only scratch the surface, others will come in and do many of the things you should have been doing. If you have patent protection you will simply stop the development. The fact that you have good technology today does not mean that someone will not develop something twice as good tomorrow. So exploit it as quickly as possible by looking for the right type of partners to work with.

Such openness does not have to mean losing control over the technology, either. As Henstridge continues:

You have to create an environment right from the start where you are prepared to allow the technology to flow freely between different people such as in the "hub-and-spoke" arrangement in many license agreements. By staying at the hub and controlling the flow you avoid a total free-for-all which diminishes the confidence and incentive of those involved to make the necessary effort and investment. You have to convince all the people down the spokes that what they are likely to gain from others in the system is worth more than what they are likely to lose by contributing their developments to the hub.[32]

The same spirit of cooperation needs to exist in the demonstration phase, this time with potential customers. Buyers of a new material, for example, need to be co-opted early to provide information on their requirements; conversely, product designers need to work closely with materials engineers to modify existing designs to ensure that they capture the advantages of the new material. The latter is especially important since most codes and standards for the use of materials in products have been established for incumbent materials and take a long time to change to accommodate new ones.[33]

MANAGING THE FOUR BRIDGES

Regardless of which of the two categories a new technology belongs to, timing relates not only to demand and competitive forces but also to capturing the interest of stakeholders and resource providers. If stakeholder interest gets delayed, for whatever reason, progress at the level of the technology itself counts for little.

Closing the circle of commercialization, therefore, is as much about managing the bridges between stages as it is about effective management of the stages themselves. What often makes this challenging is the long time horizons involved, the episodic nature of progress, and the sheer number of different actors to deal with.

As illustrated earlier in Figure 11-2, closing the circle of commercialization involves the bridging of four distinct gaps: an *interest* gap between the conception of an idea and having it explored and incubated; the traditional *technology transfer* gap, which requires moving a half-developed technology to the stage of product development; a *market transfer* gap, associated with the launch of products; and, finally, a *diffusion* gap, involving the spread of the technology from its initial market to wider use by a larger number of customers.

Many individuals are involved in taking a technology to market, and all these gaps are symptoms of what happens when these individuals change. People are the hysteresis in the commercialization process: Their impact is manifest between a research institute and an organization wishing to commercialize its results; among various departments of an organization; and, in some cases, between the organization and market constituents, whether they be converters and value-added resellers or end-users. It is no mark of great cynicism to state that, with human beings at its core, the technology transfer problem will never be fully overcome. The best one can do is to mitigate it by heeding some basic recommendations that research on the subject highlights. These include defining the technology for the receivers' context so that they can see its benefits clearly; communicating effectively, including the two-way interaction all good communications require; making sure that both the giver and the receiver have an incentive to effect the transfer; providing support to the recipients and meeting them halfway; and orchestrating the overall process actively.

Defining the Technology for the Receiver's Context

The mistake many company researchers make is to see the output of R&D as a body of concepts and data, supplemented perhaps by a working prototype. Those that succeed in commercialization, however, are not content with producing something that is just useful. They try to make this "interesting" too.

While a good presentation on the economic opportunities offered by the technology helps, this is seldom enough to motivate adoption. Recipients of a technology are fundamentally interested in a business opportunity, not just the technology. This means defining the technology so as to convince them of its economic benefits, the ease with which they can absorb it, and the effort the giver will make to ensure that the benefits are realized. One needs to couple this with aid in identifying concrete opportunities and bringing the technology close to the context of the recipient, modifying the package of capabilities and benefits if required.

Communicating Effectively

Bridging any context gap is first and foremost a matter of communication. As a recent study on technology transfer from universities and government-funded research laboratories to industry in the United States concluded,

"awareness of research" and "communication" were rated twice as important as the "lack of willingness of organizations to absorb a technology
from another organization."[34]

What is important in technology transfer is to whom communication is
targeted and the way in which it is affected. Within organizations, four roles
have been identified as important to successful technology transfer.[35]
Boundary spanners range freely throughout an organization and link
resources across several departments. They tend to derive their power infor-
mally, as a result of their alliances and informal power bases. The author
has often found planning and business development staff performing this
role, but it could include virtually anyone—an executive assistant to the
president, for instance. *Gatekeepers,* without controlling any resources,
channel information to those having the power to act on it. *Champions,* as
the term implies, take on the task as a personal mission and find whatever
way possible to advance it through organizational obstacles; Souder and
colleagues refer to them as "guerilla-warfare agents." Finally, *angels* are
high-level executives who protect start-up projects until they have demonstrated their merit unequivocally. In all successful cases of technology
transfer, the transfer organizations carefully sought out these various players within the *user* organizations, cultivated them, and used them as a team
to aid in the successful transfer. Problems arise when researchers talk
mainly to "researchers" in the recipient company. The NIH (not invented
here) syndrome aside, the latter tended to be distant from the actual "users"
of the technology within their companies—those with reasons for developing products around it.

The challenge, of course, is to mobilize interest in and facilitate the
transfer of something whose potential and attributes are evolving and ill
understood. It is perhaps because of this fluidity that most researchers on
the subject of technology transfer have come around to seeing the process
as a people-to-people interaction—a dialogue—rather than as a transmission of instructions from one party to another. A dialogue, after all, has the
virtue of allowing not only feedback and clarifications to be sought, but also
of widening the understanding of context. As John Seely Brown of Xerox
PARC puts it:

> Technology transfer is an oxymoron; you don't transfer technology, you
> design the context in which you have conversations. Technology gets devel-
> oped through a set of conversations and a true dialogue between two par-
> ties; you coinvent an idea, make it robust, and then make it real.[36]

The need for personalized communication has been found true in studies done both in the United States and in Japan.[37] In fact, one of the reasons
why technology transfer poses less of a problem in Japan is the presence of
intense horizontal communications and the fact that people tend to move
with a project.[38]

The need for face-to-face interactions also explains the personal training and transfer program instituted by General Motors Research Laboratories (GMR) in 1982. Seeing technology more as a *capability* than a product, this program consists of hiring a certain number of recently graduated engineers each year with the understanding that they will receive on-the-job training at GMR and then transfer to an operating division. During the twelve to eighteen months that these recruits spend within GMR, they are first exposed to a variety of new technologies being worked on; then, during the last four to six months, they work on a "transition" project that, in addition to providing practical experience, serves as a bridge between GMR and the operating division they will be assigned to along with the project. Both the recruits themselves and the "transition" project are coselected by GMR and the concerned operating division, thereby making the transfer easier.[39]

Providing Incentives for the Giver and Receiver

While good definition of the technology and effective communication help break down many barriers to technology transfer, they are seldom enough. In many cases, the individuals involved in giving the technology don't see why they should take the trouble; recipients, in their turn, are not particularly motivated either.

In Dorf and Worthington's study alluded to earlier,[40] "lack of incentives for the laboratory and the laboratory personnel" was the second most important barrier mentioned after "lack of awareness and communication between laboratory and industry." The most important incentive laboratory personnel considered helpful in facilitating technology transfer was, unsurprisingly, a monetary one—"returns on royalties" for themselves and their colleagues.

Many companies are now evolving schemes to provide their researchers with such incentives. An intriguing method of creating incentives is Bell Atlantic's Champion program. Under this, any employee with a good idea gets to leave his or her job for a while at full pay and benefits; in addition to training, such employees receive some money and can invest 10 percent of their salary in the project, and can give up their bonus in return for 5 percent of the revenues (subject to a certain cap) if the product gets to market.[41]

The U.S. Federal Technology Transfer Act of 1986 and a subsequent executive order in 1987 also provided explicit incentives (such as cash awards) to federal employees to encourage the commercialization of federal technology. Universities, similarly, have initiated royalty distribution policies where some provide as much as 50 percent of the net licensing income received to the inventor. Others provide between 15 percent and 50 percent.

There are also signs that recipient organizations are becoming more motivated to absorb new technologies than in the past. In the case of private companies, this motivation comes from competitive pressures and the drive for higher profits. Internal processes within companies aimed at continuous improvement and total quality management (TQM) are acting as a pull for new technologies too. As stated by Warren Grobman, program director of the advanced technology modeling laboratory in IBM's corporate laboratory,

> The measurement of performance and the setting of ever more demanding milestones for improvement has made operating divisions eager to reach out for new process and product technologies like never before. In the semiconductor field this now covers all the steps from design, circuit simulation to manufacture. Increasing process yields, diminishing impurities and defects has begun to challenge capabilities, causing operating divisions to make more frequent calls on the corporate research laboratory.[42]

If there is a need for incentives in recipient organizations, it is at the level of the individuals affected. One reason for them to be reluctant is the perceived status of the giver compared to the receiver. Glory and fame tend to go to those who invent, not to those who take the idea and then do something with it. No matter how much effort is put into obtaining a successful outcome by the receiver, it will always be the inventor's idea in the minds of peers and colleagues.

Creating a sense of ownership on the part of receivers is best achieved by involving them in the invention itself, to the extent this is possible. Thus, government-funded projects in which private companies participated in the demonstration phase—even when not bearing the cost and risk in the same proportion as the government—tended to be realized more quickly once the demonstration proved a success than those where the government took full responsibility and only subsequently disseminated the information on the results obtained.[43] This also explains the preference for multicompany research projects on the part of government funding agencies today, as discussed in Chapter 5.

Providing Support and Meeting Halfway

The fact that technology transfer is easiest between people of comparable ability speaks to the difficulty many recipients have in absorbing new technologies. This can lead to frustration and rejection or, what is even more common, sheer inertia. Basically, what is involved is the replication of capability rather than simply the right to use something.

The need for active involvement and why it is sometimes difficult to put in practice is illustrated by IBM Zürich Laboratory's invention and commercialization of Trellis Code Modulation (TCM). The invention was based on a theoretical discovery made in 1972 by one of the laboratory researchers, Gottfried Ungerboeck, relating to the transmission speed of modems. While existing modems at that time had a maximum speed of 9.6 kbit/second, it was known that the theoretical capacity was of the order of 20 to 30 kbit/second. Ungerboeck's discovery of TCM opened the door to transmission speeds above 9.6 kbit/second, for example, 14.4 kbit/second, 19.2 kbit/second, and so forth. As Karl Kümmerle, the director of the laboratory, recounted:

> The development of modems within IBM was the responsibility of the La Gaude laboratory near Nice. Ungerboeck went down to see them in 1973 to get their interest. However, it takes more than theory to convince product developers about a new direction.
>
> Since Zürich had the necessary know-how, it was decided to build a prototype there. This involved overcoming several technical hurdles. Not least among these was the fact that implementation of the TCM algorithms required more MIPS than what the most powerful mainframe could deliver then. So, we had to develop the architecture of a specialized processor, nowadays called a digital signal processor, tailored to the specific signal-processing operations needed in modems. A prototype of this processor based on vendor components was built, and we implemented the TCM algorithms on it. This convinced the product development organization. Subsequently, La Gaude, Essonnes, and Zürich designed, implemented, and produced a DSP chip that was used in IBM's first product, a 14.4 kbit/second modem, and in subsequent products.
>
> The follow-on product, taking the modem from 14.4 to 19.2 kbit/second, was handled differently. Having learnt our lesson, we negotiated a joint project with La Gaude from the beginning. Although the prototype was built in Zürich, people from La Gaude spent time in Zürich, working together and understanding everything in detail. This allowed them to prepare the product in parallel and move the production to La Gaude much quicker.[44]

Today, such transfer teams are used commonly at IBM, where groups of scientists from corporate labs take a technology themselves to divisions and teach the recipient how to use it for the best result.

The best means of motivating the use of a technology by partners is to do some of the work for them. The proponents of the technology are usually the most suited to understand its potential as well as its risks. The more they are able to reduce the latter and give comfort in the technology, the readier others are to join in.

Many companies have established special bridging organizations whose mission is to work more on an idea and to fit it directly to a user's needs. At Ford Motor Co., for example, the bridge between basic or long-term research and product development is now being established by a formal skunkworks program. Ford research laboratories deal with technologies that *could* find application in the marketplace in ten to twenty years. Advanced engineering groups in the operating divisions, on the other hand, deal with technologies that *should* be deliverable as vehicle applications in three to five years. Skunkworks cover the gap between the two and are seen as a means to accelerate the introduction of new technologies in the company's products.

Two such intermediate organizations were established in 1991 and 1992 consisting of cross-functional teams located in rented quarters physically separated from other parts of the company and free from bureaucratic controls. Their mission was to relate technologies directly to new car features and "sell" these to carline program managers for incorporation in forthcoming models. Their role was not constrained by any starting technology Ford Research had invented. They were encouraged to hunt for technologies outside when necessary and to monitor trends in various technological areas relevant to their work. They could equally come up with their own ideas for technologies needed and encourage others to work on them—whether it be Ford's scientific research laboratories, division laboratories, or outside suppliers.[45]

Orchestrating the Overall Process

In general, the greater the value demonstrated in one stage of the commercialization process, the easier it is to build a bridge to the next one. Unfortunately, because intermediate values are mainly based on expectations, they tend to be subjective. Prices, the chief crutch of economists, are seldom available at each stage to guide resource allocation for those involved. Even if available, they are not the main source of information required in judging how to proceed, not least because of future uncertainties.

This is what ultimately makes bridging mainly a political act. Human nature and psychology are as much parts of the calculus as objectively derived costs and benefits. Bridging involves taking the interests and the understandably different criteria of those whose help is sought into account while being evangelical. And it involves actively orchestrating the entire process by intervening across all the issues that matter—just as good politicians do all the time.

If there is a single inventor who exemplifies successful tackling of each of the stages and establishing bridges between them, it would be Elihu Thomson, one of the founders of GE. A contemporary of Thomas Edison, he is best known for the pioneering work he did during the 1880s and 1890s in electricity generation and lighting technology.

Although seeing his primary mission as that of a scientific researcher, he engaged himself in all the processes of commercialization with balanced enthusiasm. Teaching himself the intricacies of the patent system, he defined his inventions both in relation to applications in the electric lighting industry as they evolved and in relation to what others were doing. Despite 696 patents to his credit, he constantly made presentations to scientific bodies and published widely to establish his credibility. When combined with his obsession for demonstrating inventions safely and effectively, this won him the respect of peers and business partners alike.

Unlike his mentor and partner, Edwin J. Houston, Thomson was a business entrepreneur too. Constantly open to working with others, he was able to mobilize the enormous financial resources needed for launching new systems. This ability to attract the cooperation of others was not restricted to capital, either; it extended to his role as a research manager within an organizational setting. Thomson was at equal ease in motivating fellow researchers, as in dealing with senior management colleagues—often getting his own way in the end. Moreover, if one set of backers did not work out, he was not averse to reaching out to others. Thus, when his first partnership in Philadelphia failed to meet his sales expectations for an electric arc lighting system, he did not hesitate to find new backers in New Britain, Connecticut. When the American Electric Co. he founded there in 1880 did not pursue his marketing strategy aggressively enough, he moved on to Lynn, Massachusetts, to form the Thomson-Houston Co. two years later. His overriding passion was to see his inventions succeed in the marketplace. If some of his backers preferred to cash in early, exploiting the speculative potential the new industry offered, he simply moved on to find others more committed to the technology.

To see his inventions succeed in the marketplace, Thomson directed his attention to how customers could be "invented" too. The first approach considered by his Philadelphia partners consisted in selling his dynamos and the accompanying lighting system as captive units to industrial and railway companies. The limitations of this approach lay in the high costs each customer had to bear in relation to the competing technology of gas lighting and the relatively few customers available. A better approach seemed that of central utility companies providing a service to a wide range of customers. To implement this approach required stakeholder mobilization of a different kind—that of downstream market constituents. This is the approach the Thomson-Houston Co. took starting in 1882 with great success. Its marketing department not only identified potential business partners interested in establishing central-station utilities but helped arrange the needed finance and realized the project on their behalf as well. The patents were used too, licensing exclusively to make it more attractive to these central-station investors.[46]

For many inventors, unfortunately, getting a product or process developed marks an important watershed. This is when they have proven themselves; if lucky, this is also when they start cashing in, hoping perhaps to do other things. The fact of the matter, however, is that everything until this point was really an investment—whether theirs or that of all the resource providers who backed them. The real payoff comes *after* these products are launched. They need to learn how to orchestrate that part of the process too.

How Resource Providers and Government Agencies Can Help

Seasoned venture capitalists have often intervened across a wide range of issues beyond the provision of capital to projects they support—performing part of the orchestration role in the place of inventors. Business "champions" within large companies do much the same. What is new today is the fact that government agencies also now wish to be more consequential when funding new technologies. While they have sometimes been both the cause and the victim of many of the issues highlighted in this chapter, they are more determined to see a better payoff from the investments they make. Given the levers at their command, they can actually do this well, too.

Figure 11-3 summarizes the various things governments can do to generate and commercialize new technologies. These cover signalling the importance of the technology and thereby mobilizing private individuals and companies to work on them, encouraging demand for end products and processes, encouraging the supply of the technology, and facilitating various transactions involved in moving the technology from one group and/or stage to another.

Since most people agree on the circumstances under which government support of R&D is justified from an economic standpoint, the question is not *whether* governments should support commercially oriented research but rather *which instruments* outlined in Figure 11-3 to use and *how much* to intervene in taking ideas to market. Since market failures accompany technologies through all stages of the commercialization process, though perhaps more so in the early stages, the extent of government involvement is the real issue. By overdoing it they run the danger of picking the wrong technologies to back and orchestrating their commercialization inefficiently—substituting "government failure" in lieu of market failure, in other words. Not doing enough, on the other hand, can make government support inconsequential.

Working toward a balance means several things: taking steps to alleviate market failures where they are most pronounced, supporting technologies with as little discrimination as possible, and co-opting private companies and helping to bridge stages for those who need this. The full panoply of instruments listed in Figure 11-3 should be used only in exceptional cases.

Since market failures are most pronounced in the early stages, the greatest leverage comes from creating better markets for early-stage

FIGURE 11-3

Instruments Governments Can Use to Promote Technology Commercialization

---

Signalling Importance

- Announcing needs and government priorities
- Formulating challenging projects at the national level
- Recognizing achievements in the targeted field (e.g., prizes)
- Signalling impending regulations (e.g., environmental)

Facilitating Transactions

- Improving the market for technologies (e.g., patents)
- Generating and disseminating information (e.g., market studies)
- Fostering network building among market constituents

Encouraging Demand

- Arranging trials and demonstrations for endorsing the technology
- Financial support to buyers (e.g., tax incentives and subsidies)
- Directing government procurement toward the new technology to seed its market
- Establishing standards to give confidence and, where relevant, ensure interoperability
- Setting challenging regulations

Encouraging Supply

- Supplementing private R&D
- Providing opportunities for contract research in the target area
- Making government labs available to outside researchers
- Promoting the development of appropriate skills and infrastructure
- Encouraging cooperative R&D (e.g., through modifying antitrust legislation)

---

technologies. To some extent, this is already beginning to happen. Efforts being made to strengthen the patent system and to accelerate the review of patents will enable lone inventors and small companies to raise capital sooner. In January 1995, the U.S. Patent and Trademark Office (PTO) announced, for example, that biotechnology patent applications will no longer need to be supported by clinical data showing efficacy of their products in humans. Less expensive animal tests or in vitro data that demonstrate "potential" efficacy in humans would suffice for the granting of patents—leaving the evaluation of clinical data to the FDA later. The hope is that this will make it easier for biotechnology companies to raise venture capital earlier, including for the clinical trials themselves. The U.K. Patent Office's new fast-track service for small businesses and individual inventors is similarly motivated. To the extent possible, it would like to rule on patent applications submitted by them within a year of their filing, thereby helping them mobilize funds sooner.

Developing good markets for early-stage technologies is actually better than forcing a commercial orientation on them through, for example, insisting on private participation. Thus, while some commercial backing of university research appears to improve academic productivity and the value of the research, an excessive amount doesn't.[47]

Instead of targeting a particular technology right from the beginning, it is usually also better to concentrate on the mission or function to be achieved. Government support should be *function-specific* but *technology-neutral,* allowing different technologies to prove themselves for particular applications, as companies do during the incubation phase. Apart from minimizing the risk of error, such a hands-off approach permits the flexibility each technology requires to link up to its best application. Governments, for example, ought to support new energy technologies without too much discrimination, and then let particular technologies find the most appropriate use (and partners) for them.

When technologies are sufficiently advanced to be demonstrated in concrete products, a more interventionist approach is, however, sometimes needed. The best governments can do to facilitate the process of linking new technologies to concrete product opportunities is to encourage the different parties concerned to come together—those working on the technology and those possessing the industry-specific knowledge that will make the application a success. This can be done either by insisting on shared funding or by actively orchestrating the contacts needed, preferably both together.

One government agency that does both is Australia's Energy Research and Development Corporation (ERDC). Like many funding agencies today, it complements private investments through cost sharing. If anything, it sees the increased ratio of industry money to ERDC money invested in projects as one of the key indicators of its achievement. In fact, this ratio has been raised from 0.7 in 1990 to 2.0 in 1994, demonstrating the confidence on the part of those who receive funds that commercial results will be forthcoming.

Realizing that such private industry participation does not come automatically, ERDC plays an active role in assisting research groups in the projects it supports. As Bruce Godfrey, ERDC's managing director, explains:

> ERDC of Australia shepherds its projects right through all the stages of commercialization. It helps those with ideas define them into a fundable proposal, it checks on their progress, and then assists in establishing the contacts for marketing and any of the other problem-solving requirements the technology proponent might have.[48]

All of the above-mentioned things government agencies can do help in getting new technologies to the stage of end products only. A more controversial issue is whether government support for a particular technology should go beyond, intervening in its market acceptance. How this issue should be resolved is really a matter of economic ideology. What we know is that governments are not best suited to sift through all the competing technologies on offer and find winners to back. Yet because of the panoply of instruments at their command (see Figure 11-3), governments can influence the fate of individual technologies in the marketplace, as is best illustrated by the effectiveness with which Japan's MITI has been able to promote certain technologies in recent years.[49]

The most reasonable stance is to recommend such downstream intervention in exceptional cases only—those in which a particular technology is clearly deemed important for national reasons. Once having made the choice, the costs of intervening at the demand level (including the costs associated with error) enter the domain of political will rather than economic efficiency per se.

Photovoltaic Technology

One such case of government-sponsored technology demonstration encompassing downstream commercialization is that of the U.S. effort in photovoltaic energy. It began with the Solar Photovoltaic Research, Development and Demonstration Act of 1978 (Public Law 95-590—November 4, 1978). Motivated by pending shortages of conventional (hydrocarbon) fuels as well as the need to consolidate the lead of U.S. industry in photovoltaics, this act charged the Department of Energy (DOE) to promote the technology across a wide front. A total of $1.5 billion was to be committed by the federal government for this purpose over a ten-year period.

The effort was exemplary in several respects. It set out clear targets to be achieved *both* for the technology and for its commercialization. It included funding for research, the development of specific products, and for incentives to be eventually given for adopting the technology. Finally, it was to be orchestrated by a federal agency (the U.S. DOE) with the active support of industry and academia, as well as at least two federal laboratories (Sandia National Laboratories and a newly created National Renewable Energy Laboratory).

The specific goals established in the 1978 act were:

1. To double the production of solar photovoltaic energy systems each year during the decade starting with fiscal year 1979, measured by the peak generating capacity of the systems produced, so as to reach a total annual U.S. production of solar photovoltaic energy systems of approximately 2 million peak kilowatts, and a total cumulative production of such systems of approximately 4 million peak kilowatts by fiscal year 1988;

2. To reduce the average cost of installed solar photovoltaic energy systems to $1 per peak watt by fiscal year 1988; and

3. To stimulate the purchase by private buyers of at least 90 percent of all solar photovoltaic energy systems produced in the United States during fiscal year 1988. (Public Law 95-590—November 4, 1978, 42 USC 5581, 92 STAT 2515).

Virtually no constraints were placed on what type of research to support and how much of a project's cost the federal government was to bear. If no industrial partner was willing or able to fund a particular project, the DOE could bear the entire cost itself, including having the project performed in one or more federal laboratories. As for incentives for adopting photovoltaic systems, the federal government was ready to fund up to 75 percent of the purchase cost.

As often happens in such cases, the targets were not achieved. Instead of 4 million kilowatts of cumulative installed capacity by 1988, the actual number was only about 100,000 kilowatts. By 1994 the total had grown to just 250,000 kilowatts. Similarly, instead of the $1 per peak watt of installation cost projected for 1988, the actual figure achieved was of the order of $5—still a considerable improvement over the $500 per watt cost in 1972! By 1994, the cost had dropped further to between $4.00 and $4.50 per peak watt.

Even so, many would argue that the 1978 act served its purpose by accelerating the demonstration of an otherwise difficult technology. In view of the enormous cost disadvantage and uncertainties the technology started out with relative to conventional power sources, it is unlikely that private industry would have made the necessary investments on its own. By 1994, photovoltaic systems still cost five or six times as much as fossil-fuel-powered plants and continued to be relegated to small niche applications.

Despite considerable reductions in funding during the Reagan administration, the U.S. photovoltaic program has been sustained until today. By 1993, some $1 billion had been spent by the federal government alone (instead of the $1.5 billion initially budgeted up to 1988) and another $2 billion by U.S. industry (which was not fully estimated in 1978). The spirit of the 1978 act, moreover, has been retained. Assistance continues to be given for R&D, for demonstration purposes at various sites, and to provide an incentive for private entities to adopt photovoltaic systems. Thus, the 1991 to 1995 program plan included conducting basic and applied research on promising new materials, processes, devices, and encapsulation schemes, including the supporting measurements and modeling capabilities; manufacturing technology development for cost-effective photovoltaic modules; and systems and market development assistance.

The DOE's support, in effect, covers both the supply of the technology and its demand. By promoting the two in tandem, the U.S. government hoped that the commercialization of photovoltaics would occur sooner than if left entirely to market forces. If nothing else, it has signalled that photovoltaics is important and has succeeded in mobilizing a vast range of potential suppliers to contribute to the effort while simultaneously preparing buyers as well.

The DOE's photovoltaic program is a good illustration of how governments *can* get certain technologies commercialized sooner than would otherwise happen. But the process can be an expensive one. Having chosen a technology area, governments should be willing to encourage a variety of approaches and then intervene across both demand and supply issues to ensure follow-through. The latter, however, often requires coordination among several government departments, which very few funding agencies have been able to do.

SUMMARY

Although the need for speed pervades many business activities today, its role in technology commercialization is a subtle one. Some technology-based ideas should indeed be taken from the imagining to the promoting stage as quickly as possible. Others, however, do not confront an imminent market opportunity. For them, it is better to time intermediate stages of the commercialization process for their own window of opportunity, varying the effort if necessary.

The age-old challenge of bridging stages and overcoming technology transfer problems applies no matter which category an idea belongs to. Fortunately, research done on the subject over the past few decades suggests a number of ways to alleviate the problem. Inventors can play a role in making these bridges by actively orchestrating the entire process. Government agencies supporting commercially oriented research are increasingly helping, too, by creating better markets for technology and intervening selectively through the different stages of the commercialization process.

12

IMPLICATIONS FOR MANAGING TECHNOLOGICAL INNOVATION WITHIN COMPANIES

THE PROCESS OF GETTING "FROM MIND TO MARKET" DESCRIBED IN THIS BOOK has implications for several actors—lone inventors and researchers hoping to strike it rich, government agencies wanting to have a greater impact when they support science and technology, and large companies wanting to improve the return on their R&D investments. This book was written mainly with lone inventors and university researchers in mind. They experience all the process's nuances in practice, including exposure to the various stakeholders mentioned (external peers, resource providers, and commercialization partners). Because of this focus, the role of government agencies was treated in some depth here, too. Governments' policies, and the range of support they extend, can be crucial to the success of the technologies lone inventors and university researchers work on.

The purpose of this concluding chapter is to extend the discussion to the management of technological innovation within companies. While several examples from them were used throughout the book, these were mainly to illustrate particular aspects of the process. The attention here is on how an understanding of the overall process of technology commercialization informs some of the major issues *they* are struggling with today—their role in the research landscape, how they organize their R&D, and how they can get more out of the investments they make in research. Confronted with a number of new business pressures, many companies are changing their approach to R&D today. Some of these changes, it is argued, may be appropriate for faster product development but can be counterproductive when it comes to major innovations that rely on new technologies.

The Emerging Paradigm of R&D Management

Disappointed by their experience with the linear model of research and the segmentation of R&D into specialized units it implied, many companies now prefer virtually the opposite model. This has three main attributes: less emphasis on basic research, integration of different types of R&D, and closer integration between R&D and the business.

Less Emphasis on Basic Research

Most of the disenchantment today is with basic, curiosity-driven research. Xerox PARC was pilloried in the 1980s, RCA's David Sarnoff Research Center was given away in 1986, and, more recently, Bellcore was put up for sale—and these are only the most conspicuous illustrations. Private company R&D budgets devoted to basic research peaked around 1990, and virtually all the large central laboratories have seen their budgets and staffing decline since then. Japanese companies, which had been increasing their basic research outlays during this period, have not been spared either.

Instead the emphasis is on near-term research goals, even if that means letting the occasional breakthrough slip away. Companies are rearranging their R&D to speed new products to customers, allowing business units to improve production processes already in place, finding customer-related solutions quickly, and making modifications at the end-product level.

All of this translates into a new paradigm for looking at research within companies. In its extreme version it consists in letting universities, research institutes, and small companies do basic and preliminary applied research, while large companies concentrate on product development and technical support. Possessing the means to conduct product development efficiently, large companies want to buy in basic technologies when needed, rather than incur the cost and risk of generating them themselves.

Since the pharmaceutical industry is the best illustration of science-based, stage-by-stage research today, it is here where the degree of specialization is most noticeable. Thus, of the roughly 3,000 candidate drugs being examined worldwide, some 1,000 are being researched by the twenty largest multinational drug companies; the remaining 2,000 are being researched by some 400 small, speciality companies without the resources needed to fund clinical trials. Most are likely to license their drugs to larger companies should their research prove successful.

Integration Within R&D

The traditional organization of the R&D function followed differences in the work, skills, and time horizons required for various types of research. Thus, corporate laboratories conducted long-term, exploratory research, with the mission of generating new generic capabilities. Development laboratories, as their name implies, tended to be charged with applied research and the development of products. Depending on the size of a company, engineering work—and all that is associated with building commercial products and their accompanying manufacturing processes—was further specialized to an operating-unit level.

A number of companies now question whether having such specialized units makes sense. In many cases it has apparently not worked. Business groups found the work of corporate R&D irrelevant to their needs; corporate R&D, in turn, bemoaned the fact that there were few takers for their work and complained of the short-term, fire-fighting orientation of the labs attached to business groups. In essence, there was no synergy among these various labs and no bridges to link long-term exploratory research to commercial opportunities.

The alternatives being pursued are quite radical. Some companies have started to eliminate their intermediate laboratories. In addition to slowing innovation, this acted as a barrier to technology transfer between basic research and the laboratories within divisions. Others, such as DuPont (medical products and imaging systems divisions), Corning Glass, and Kodak Copy Products Divisions, have concentrated research, development, and manufacturing engineering under one organization. This integration is buttressed by the creation of product-oriented teams composed of people from research and development, engineering, and marketing. In the case of DuPont, some symbolic changes reinforce this integration further, such as blurring the distinction between applied research and development, and removing the distinction in level of skills between R&D staff and manufacturing engineers (calling them all members of the same "technical community.")

Integration of R&D with the Business

The bringing together of different types of research has been mainly at a divisional or business unit level. A parallel trend, however, involves integrating *all* R&D, including that conducted in central laboratories, closer with the business. By letting business groups drive the overall research agenda, companies hope to make the technologies worked on more relevant and to speed their commercialization through the organization. The most dramatic form this takes is the elimination of a "corporate" research function altogether—as AlliedSignal did in early 1996. Equally effective ways include changes in funding policies and integration at the planning level.

Until the early 1960s, many companies funded their basic and applied research 100 percent from corporate sources—the chairperson's pocket, so to speak. Product development and engineering, on the other hand, were paid for by business divisions, regardless of where this work took place. From the mid-1960s onward, a larger and larger share of early-stage research performed in central (corporate) laboratories started to be funded jointly. General Electric, for example, moved from 100 percent corporate funding to 65 percent corporate and 35 percent business division around this time. In the early 1980s, the proportion funded by business groups at GE was raised further to 85 percent. IBM moved in the same direction in the early 1990s, with 80 percent of the budget of its corporate research laboratories provided by business units. Philips of Holland followed the trend too. Until relatively recently, its central research organization, consisting of five laboratories around the world and representing one-seventh of the company's total expenditure on R&D, received 100 percent of its funds directly from headquarters. Starting in 1990, the latter's share was reduced to one-third, with the remainder coming from contracts between the central research organization and business groups.

Integration through planning is another way of getting business units to drive the research agenda. Among western companies, Philips is perhaps placing the greatest emphasis on using the planning process as a means for integrating technology with the business—particularly to its product strategy. Since research and product development were not well coordinated in the past, a number of technologies went unexploited; conversely, some products were planned without adequate attention being paid to the technologies they would need. The company had, for instance, invested heavily in its digital compact cassette (DCC) before considering the feasibility of a crucial component, the magnetic head for reading both digital and analog tapes. The head cost far more to develop than expected, complicating Philip's battle against Sony's MiniDisc. Philips now has a road-map process throughout the organization, forcing divisions to coordinate five-year plans with the labs and factories.[1]

The coordination of this road map is the responsibility of the international research coordination group within Philips's central research organization. It regularly analyzes the business strategies submitted by each of the company's thirty-eight business groups and maps them along two dimensions—a capability dimension relating to the people and skills that will be needed to fulfill the plan, and an application dimension that captures the generic technologies needed for specific R&D projects.

Drawbacks of the Paradigm

Whether these trends constitute a robust new paradigm, or simply reactions to some excesses of the past, depends on what role companies see R&D playing in their business. For those committed to harnessing R&D for differentiating their products and creating new growth opportunities, there are some important warnings to consider.

One concerns the growing cost of bought-in technologies. In recent years there has been a growing number of universities and research institutes willing to step in with technologies for sale. However, as more companies adopt the same attitude of relying on outside technologies, the price of technology is bound to rise. With the strengthening of intellectual property rights, a more competitive market for new technologies is already beginning to emerge.

People want more not only for completed technologies but for early-stage ones as well. Anecdotal evidence on the escalating price of early-stage technologies abounds. Rockefeller University recently received $20 million in up-front payment from Amgen Inc. for rights to its *ob* gene—despite the fact that it is still unclear whether it causes obesity in humans. The average up-front payment to universities until then was only $30,000. In addition to the $20 million, Rockefeller University expects to collect milestone payments several times that amount, as well as royalties once products reach the market.[2]

Companies are earning more for their patents too, even in situations where this was not the norm. The best illustration of this today is in the semiconductor industry. Until about a decade ago, the prevailing dogma in this industry was that intellectual property rights served no purpose other than a defensive one; when companies did end up possessing an extensive portfolio of these rights, they often licensed them liberally for modest fees or exchanged them with others. Priority was given to the freedom to develop, make, and sell the circuits themselves, and to winning the price/performance game. In the early 1980s, however, more and more companies realized the profit erosion this strategy was causing and returned to their technology base, not only as a means of differentiating their end products, but as a valuable source of revenues in its own right. Thus, IBM alone reportedly earned $500 million in royalties and fees in 1993, twice what it did a couple of years ago.[3] Texas Instruments Inc. collected over $1.2 billion in royalties between 1987 and 1992.

Cost and difficulty of acquiring technologies aside, there is also evidence to suggest that companies that generate their own technologies tend to have shorter technology cycle times (as measured, for example, by the median age of the patents cited in the firms' own patents) than companies that rely primarily on external sources of technology. While external technology plays a critical role in the success of innovations, in other words, it is *not* a substitute for internal learning.[4] The accelerating pace of technology is putting a premium on doing one's own research too. While, previously, it was possible to wait for someone else to make a discovery and then incorporate it into one's own products later, this is becoming less viable in some industries. The role of generic research is not just to enable products, but to increase a firm's ability to effectively scan and absorb new technologies. As several studies on the subject have shown, the greater the prior knowledge a company possesses in an area, the greater its ability to evaluate and utilize external technologies when these become identified.[5]

Integrating different types of research has drawbacks too. Pioneering research follows a different logic from development-oriented work. The former is associated with individual creativity, not tacit knowledge shared by members of an organization. It is typically done by individuals who have devoted a lifetime of effort in a narrow discipline, which they alone have mastered. They are also the ones who recoil at the suggestion, "invent me this by June next year." To harness their creativity, it is vital to give them some space. Some of their ideas may not be pursued, but it is important to let them explore beyond the interest of business groups, bringing a business context in later. Development-oriented research, on the other hand, follows a more focused logic whose purpose is set out fully in advance.

One company that recently endorsed this difference is Sandoz AG of Switzerland. Traditionally, pharmaceutical research and development were part of the same organization, reporting to a single individual. In December 1993, to increase the depth of its know-how in biotechnology and to search for new substances and mechanisms of action, Sandoz split the R&D organization into two units—each with independent managers. As Urs Baerlocher, CEO of Sandoz Pharma explained, "Research and development have different laws. Research is creative. Development can be run as an efficient product center. . . . The new organization will allow the development department to concentrate on the quality of product development and time to market."[6]

As for the final trend of integrating R&D with the business, the problem is more of form than of substance. Some researchers support mixed funding (corporate and business unit) because of the dialogue it forces between researchers and business unit managers. Others decry the selling and negotiations associated with mixed funding as a time waster. Given the choice, they would much rather have corporate research divided up and fully owned by business groups—as AlliedSignal has done.

While making all research a part of business groups does help in getting a context early, some doubt whether it is always the right context. Also, as Joseph G. Wirth, chief technical officer of Raychem, puts it,

> I feel uneasy about this solution not just because of the short-term orientation it creates but the possibility of silos emerging. People working within one division are unlikely to see any reason to get involved in another division's issues. Yet, it's probably a better solution than mixed funding.[7]

A major problem with integrating R&D tightly to business needs is that time horizons don't always match. As Ambros Speiser, the former head of Brown Boveri Research, states, "Technologists have to look ten to fifteen years out; businesses often cannot, or do not want to do that." The other, more serious, problem is that the mapping of business strategies onto technology requirements seldom leads to an obvious recommendation as to what R&D should do. Virtually all companies that integrate business and company plans today, either qualitatively or through portfolio-based approaches (such as positioning technology according to its risk, maturity, or role in business competitiveness, and positioning businesses according to growth and present competitiveness), admit to the ambiguous and overly general signals these provide. What they endorse instead is the dialogue between R&D and business units the process engenders.

Whatever the method used, aligning R&D projects primarily to the strategic needs of the business in a planned fashion runs the danger that innovative suggestions of younger staff and creative, new ideas do not get the hearing they deserve. In the words of Marvin Johnson, an accomplished researcher at Philips Petroleum, "We believe that failure to respond effectively to such suggestions will reduce the number to near zero, and unless it is possible to nurture and support the new innovation, the need for research could end."[8]

As indicated by several companies' experience, research that is primarily driven by business units tends to sustain the status quo. While necessary in its own right, it compromises the generation of *new* business ideas and growth platforms for the future—something that increasingly interests companies.

Some companies are already modifying their funding schemes to accommodate the need for long-term, capability-building research. Philips, for example, introduced a new twist to its divisional contract system in 1994. Roughly half of the two-thirds budget of the central research organization controlled by business groups is now devoted to immediate product development projects; the remaining half has to be for longer-term capability development in certain technology clusters, such as signal processing for TVs. Typically, this part is funded by more than one business group as well.

WHAT A VALUE-BASED COMMERCIALIZATION FRAMEWORK REQUIRES

The fact that there is room for opposing viewpoints on how R&D should be managed indicates that today's paradigm is still tentative. To the extent that the framework adopted in this book helps in taking a second look at this function, it is through reframing the role of R&D. By seeing each type of R&D as creating commercial value unique to the activities it performs, one can put more (though not all) of the burden of proof on R&D itself. For this to happen, and to get the most out of the investments made in research, one needs to rethink how R&D is organized and evaluated. One also needs to reconsider the link between R&D and business-level strategies, making the two more equal partners.

The Different Roles a Research Organization Plays

A major reason why the debate on R&D management has proved hard to resolve is that the subject is not always clear. All research organizations have multiple roles to perform; a policy prescription relevant to one role may not be appropriate for others.

Figure 12-1 summarizes the main roles R&D organizations are typically required to play. The vertical axis denotes the three strategic dimensions of these roles: maintaining a good research *infrastructure,* one that is aligned to both the company's current needs and its ability to innovate; a *defensive* role, implying maintaining the business against competition; and an *offensive* role, contributing to expansion and change. The horizontal axis, in turn, captures the two broad segments in technology commercialization: *innovating* something (the first four subprocesses of imagining, incubating, demonstrating, and promoting) and *sustaining* what was brought to market earlier (the fifth subprocess with the same name).

Several things need to be noted about this six-way classification of roles. First, while the conventional debate on the type of R&D to perform considers things like basic versus applied research, or the time horizon of research, such a classification is built around outcomes—things that have to get done. As discussed in Chapter 10, basic research is not done only at the start of technology commercialization. It occurs throughout the process and can even play a key role in sustaining products launched earlier. Also, while the time horizon of research may have corresponded well with research types—basic, applied, experimental development, and so on—its relevance as an organizing principle is much less today.

Different types of research, with different time horizons, can be associated with all six roles. And many technologies, especially in the information field, do not even go through the traditional stages from basic to applied to development research. In software, for example, the basic research is often the product itself—the rest being mostly a matter of debugging and production.

Second, each of these roles has a different organizational logic. Some, such as the defensive ones, need a focused, cross-disciplinary single team to be performed well. Others in the innovation category need a more segmented organization, as described later in this section. The infrastructure role, in turn, requires a different organization and managerial orientation to fully help solve others' technical problems, act as a back-up for marketing, or prepare new competencies for the future.

The third point, which touches on the issue of relevance and integration with business strategies, concerns the clarity (and confidence) with which a business strategy can be translated into meaningful directions for R&D. For defensive roles and for sustaining technologies commercialized in the past, the translation from strategy to R&D can be quite rigorous. What is more difficult is the offensive/innovation role of R&D highlighted in the figure.

FIGURE 12-1

THE DIFFERENT ROLES AN **R&D** ORGANIZATION PERFORMS

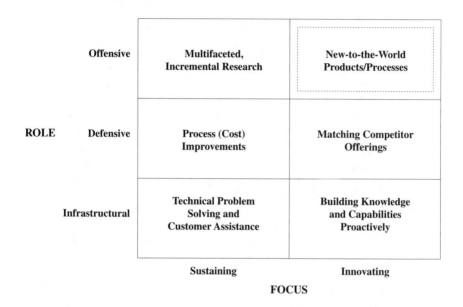

Since this book has been about the commercialization of new-to-the-world products and processes, most of what follows is devoted to this last role. By isolating it from all the other things a research organization does, one can grapple in a more focused manner with the issues it raises.

Segmenting the Research Process by Commercial Mission

The traditional basis for dividing R&D into basic research, applied research, experimental development, and technical support was mainly to accommodate differences in skills, time horizons, and the nature of research itself. The problem with this is that it took too much of a functional view, emphasizing inputs rather than outcomes. From a commercialization standpoint, companies really need units that imagine technology-based ideas, incubate them to define their commercializability better, demonstrate them in marketable products, and then help promote and sustain them after launch.

When entrusted with such missions, independent research units offer several advantages. They help widen the context and opportunities at each stage, thereby offering greater scope for utilizing the output of research. They allow real-time response to changing events, including better timing. They optimize decisions about whether to make, buy, or sell. And finally, they allow intermediate values to be judged, if no more than in option terms.

One company that has chosen to preserve a segmented R&D organization is Sony, as illustrated by its R&D organization in Figure 12-2. On the surface, the organizational units look like those of any other company: the corporate research center is devoted to basic research and some applied research; the corporate research laboratories work mainly on applied research and some development; defining new products and demonstrating the technology for them is the responsibility of various development groups; finally, the actual design and building of products are done within R&D units attached to each of the business groups.

The reason why Sony is able to get value from these units, whereas many other companies found them unworkable, is the commercial orientation that pervades all of them. As Hans-Georg Junginger, head of Sony's European R&D, explains,

> When work began on CCDs at the research center in the mid-1960s, they were already thinking in terms of a camcorder—which appeared fifteen years later! Unlike in some other companies, basic research at Sony is not for learning new things. If the initial product idea doesn't work, we simply change it. Research is application-driven throughout. This has been reinforced in the recent reorganization of R&D. Whereas the research center used to be organized by discipline, a large part of it is now based on a project organization too.[9]

It is also at the imagining stage that Sony management sees the greatest leverage in setting the future direction of the company. This explains why Nobuyuki Idei, when he took over as president of Sony in 1995, actually *strengthened* corporate-level research. In a reorganization introduced in April 1996, the number of people in the research center and the various technology-specific corporate research laboratories grew from 600 to over 800 through reassignments from development laboratories and some business groups.

The mission of central research laboratories is not just to come up with interesting new breakthroughs or advance knowledge, but to create generic technologies that can be leveraged across a range of applications and products. This can involve basic research, some applied research (in a preliminary application), as well as a fair amount of market input—whatever, in fact, is needed to convince people about its potential.

The role of the development groups is interesting, too. They perform an incubation role and act as the link between the corporate laboratories and the business groups, working on three- to five-year projects that will benefit several business groups. As shown in Figure 12-2, for display technologies, they ensure a smooth flow from long-term research to development and on to commercialization. Thus, the company can work on multimedia

FIGURE 12-2
SONY'S R&D ORGANIZATION WITH DETAILS FOR THE DISPLAY BUSINESS

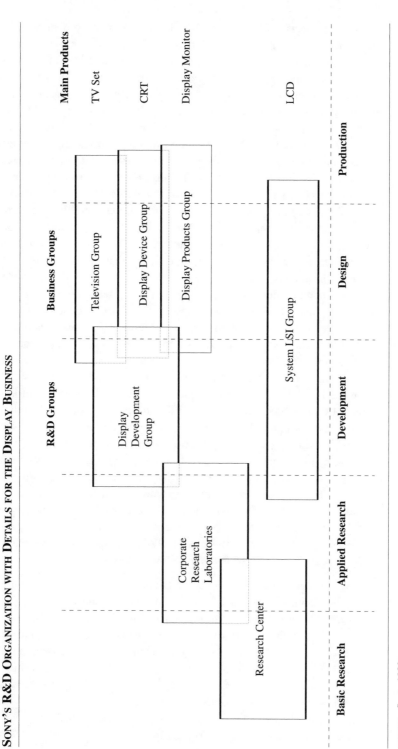

SOURCE: Sony, 1992.

research projects without knowing what the ultimate products will be, while at the same time permitting individual business groups to set product goals and reach back to development labs for the needed technologies.

All innovation-minded corporations actually need such intermediate development groups to explore new technologies and applications unfettered by the dictates of existing businesses. It is the stage that Microsoft cofounder Paul Allen's Interval Research Corp. (Palo Alto, California) has been formed to occupy. Rather than do exploratory research, it focuses on finding new uses of what is already available; to the extent basic research is done, it is of a directed kind aimed at going below some of the application-specific development needs that have been identified. Unlike Xerox PARC, which inspired it, the company does not wish to be restricted to a particular product/market domain dictated by a corporation. It wants to explore every use of the ideas it comes up with, incubating these to the point when it can license or joint-venture with third parties that can take them further.

Even in situations where there is no need for broad-based market exploration or finding alternative uses to exploit a new technology's full potential, a segmented organization helps leverage new technologies better. Xerox's technical organization, shown in Figure 12-3, illustrates one version of this. The company divides its R&D into four main components: pioneering research, technology platforms, product platforms, and products. Pioneering research, which corresponds roughly to the imagining stage, is conducted within three main centers—PARC (Palo Alto, California), XRCC (Mississauga, Ontario), and XERC (Grenoble, France). Its mission is to create discontinuities in the technology component of the business. The insights and technologies it develops next get grouped into a set of technology platforms, which could be things like the digital subsystem of a copier, a video pass system, a marking engine, or a novel paper-handling system. These, in turn, get all grouped into a product platform (strategic architecture), such as a printer. The printer platform is finally the basis on which a number of different products can be conceived, usually by more than one division. John Seely Brown of PARC explains the advantages of such an organization of R&D in the following terms:

> What we are looking for in our R&D is a scalable architecture that cuts across multiple divisions. It is only if you are able to step back and go to the root of the technology (the mission of pioneering research) that you can achieve such an architecture, allowing you to use a technology in multiple products. This way you also create an implicit synergy between the divisions and bring about a coherence between products without superimposition by the CEO. You get a "plug and play" feature and a similar "look and feel" in a whole line of Xerox products that would otherwise be missing. Since our sales force is organized geographically selling multiple products, it makes their job easier, too. You get more bang for the buck, in effect.[10]

FIGURE 12-3

THE ORGANIZATION OF R&D WITHIN XEROX

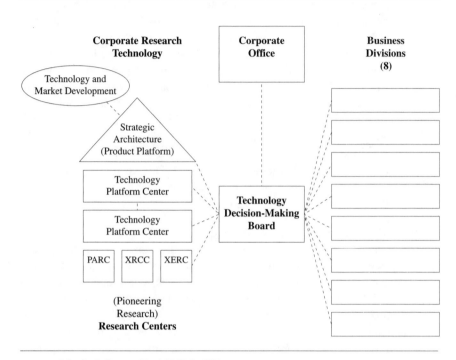

SOURCE: John Seely Brown, Xerox PARC, 1995.

The independent space given to incubation also explains the success of many companies that are able to turn apparent failures in research projects into commercial successes. If one application does not work, they can redirect the technology to something else. But to be able to do so requires an organizational mechanism, whether this be a formal incubation group or time given to individual researchers for the purpose. Thus, while the catalyst developed by Steven Kuznicki of Engelhard Corp. (Iselin, New Jersey) failed in its targeted application in the petroleum industry, it recently found a lucrative new home as a desiccant in the air-conditioning industry because of the company's policy of encouraging researchers to spend up to 20 percent of their time on projects outside their assigned responsibilities.[11] This new application is expected to generate $80 million in revenues in 1997.

Finally, a dedicated group is often needed for promoting and sustaining the technology's commercialization. It may also require basic research capabilities just like the initial group of researchers. As Paul Becker, head of conductive polymer R&D at Raychem put it,

When PolySwitch technology was first commercialized in the early 80s, the R&D effort dropped off rapidly. Some of the technologists took up assignments in the PolySwitch venture; others had their efforts redirected to new projects. As a result, there was no one left to continue developing the basic technology, and our knowledge base for this technology dispersed. In the late 80s, when PolySwitch sales reached significant proportions with signs of continued growth, we were no longer in a position to provide immediate R&D support. The PolySwitch technical group was busy ramping up production and didn't have the time to focus on improving the performance of their basic polymer materials. By this time, also, a few competitors had emerged and our initial patents were due to expire in several years. In order to defend the technology, we realized we needed to reestablish a strong technical program in central R&D. Thus, in 1989, a new group was formed with the aim of developing improved proprietary materials and shunting these into the division over the next three to five years.[12]

There are three things worth noting about such specialization in the research process. First, breaking up functions into smaller and more focused entities, oddly enough, actually breaks down barriers to the management of the commercialization process. It is large units with broad missions that pose a problem; the more all-encompassing their missions, the greater the distance they take from other units. This was the contrasting experience of Fairchild and Intel. Fairchild's Palo Alto R&D center was intentionally created as a stand-alone and complete R&D unit. Its mission was to develop new technologies to the stage of production scale-up and market launch, and it did just that with metal-oxide semiconductors (MOS). Despite the seminal nature of its work, it was unable to transfer the new technology to its production operation in Mountain View, a few miles down the road. As a result, it never competed effectively in the MOS integrated circuit business.

Intel's founders, who came out of Fairchild, learned something from this experience. Instead of a two-stage (R&D to production) structure, they adopted a three-step "waterfall"—one in which each successive organization within Intel faced progressively larger-scale production goals. This allowed people to talk on the same level with personnel in adjacent organizations, as well as allowing a more frequent transfer of people from one organization to another.[13]

Second, the fact that people staffing a unit have more precise missions means that they become less dependent on a particular technology. Those in business incubators, for example, know that their task is to come up with a plan to take the technology forward—or recommend stopping it. They don't need to keep pushing things along, hoping not to do themselves out of a job.

Third, such a segmentation of R&D does not presuppose different organizations or locations. Some of Xerox's technology platforms are actually located within its research centers, while others are within divisions. The group concerned with a particular technology platform may even be dispersed in several locations, coordinated by one unit. The same applies to product platforms, although these tend to be housed within particular divisions with a mission to coordinate their activities across the company. The links among pioneering research, technology platforms, and product platforms involve a fair amount of joint work among the groups concerned. Thus, each product platform actually has two champions—one in the technology platform and the other within the concerned business division.

R&D organizations, in other words, are best seen as organizations in time. While the supporting infrastructure and laboratory facilities may be relatively permanent, the grouping of tasks and individuals changes constantly. The more these groupings can be made to conform to the stages of commercialization, the better the follow-through and greater the ultimate value created. Thus, at Sony, the nature of "labs" within the central research organization changes every three or four years depending on the area the company would like to explore. The same goes for development labs and groups. As people complete incubating a particular technology and identifying products opportunities to pursue, they move on to the relevant product divisions with the technology; new development labs get created then to take on the next technology.

Allowing for a Broad, Dynamic Link Between Technology and Strategy

A precondition for these different research units to create the value asked of them is to treat them as equal partners in the strategy process itself. While most managers admit the need to establish a better link between a company's strategy and what R&D does, they hesitate to make this link too constraining—and rightly so. Technology and strategy are not fully dependent variables. Moreover, just about as many external forces affect the course of strategy, not least what a competitor might do the next day, as they affect innovation itself. The two variables often also have altogether different time frames; by force-fitting them one does justice to neither.

What is needed instead is a loose coupling between strategies and technology. Depending on the nature of the strategy this can take any of three forms: fixing the product/market domain (or competitive space) and exploring a wide range of technologies around it; fixing the technology domain (or core technologies) and being flexible regarding the products and markets to compete in; and encouraging an evolutionary, iterative relationship between technologies and products.

Fixed Product/Market Domain with Broad Technological Exploration

This approach is taken by many companies that anchor themselves in known problems of a familiar customer base. They explore a number of different technologies while focusing on a narrow product/market domain. Thus, while Saes Getters has focused exclusively on vacuum enhancement products throughout its history, it researches widely the technologies related to surface phenomena, particularly the reaction of gases with metals and the metallurgy of sophisticated alloys. All of the company's products, whether evaporable or nonevaporable getters, draw from a broad technology base in which it is a world leader and to which it consistently devotes between 7 percent and 10 percent of sales turnover for R&D.

Preserving a lead in a narrowly defined product/market domain often means expanding, not restricting, the range of technologies covered. Companies in this category tend to have a broad range of technologies at their command, often with considerable depth in each. With rapid shifts occurring in the kind of technology needed for the function they provide to a targeted customer group, they constantly add new core technologies.

Focusing on product/market combinations does not mean short-term research either. Reconfiguring existing product platforms and periodically introducing new generations of products can involve extensive and deep research. Hitachi does this in its advance research lab in Tokyo: exploring light-sensitive proteins, information carried in the genetic material of living cells, and atomic-scale phenomena, among others, which may one day result in dramatically new forms of computers.

Fixed Technological Domain with Flexible Product/Market Scope

The mission of these companies can be best described as leveraging a hard-won technological position across a wide range of businesses and markets. Technology fit, for such companies, is as important as customer fit in the allocation of R&D resources. Whether it is Hewlett-Packard leveraging its measurement know-how into a wide range of products and markets, or AlliedSignal leveraging its nylon technology from its fundamental position in caprolactam, the long-term commitment is to a technology field. The basic idea is to achieve depth and, preferably, a proprietary position in certain technological areas. This leaves room for some opportunism when it comes to the products to be commercialized.

The need to build and stay close to certain core technologies is vindicated by empirical findings too. According to recent research on computer-related companies in New England, "The building of an internal critical mass of engineering talent in a focused technological area, yielding a distinctive core technology that becomes the foundation of the company's product development, offers the best opportunity for rapid growth of a young firm."[14] Such an approach has been shown to be more successful than working on multiple and perhaps unrelated technologies, especially for young companies. Major enhancements to this core technology, furthermore, result in superior growth and financial performance than a less aggressive stance consisting of minor improvements.

One company that has recently adopted this framework is Kodak. Having once established a consumer franchise in the photographic film market on the strength of its silver halide emulsion technology, it recently announced the mission of its main business to be that of being a world leader in "pictorial imaging," which can include photography, electrophotography, and electronics. The technical core competencies needed to cover this strategic domain with sufficient scope in the future include, in addition to silver halide imaging materials, other imaging materials, precision thin film coatings and finishing, optomechatronics, imaging electronics, and imaging science.

Evolutionary and Iterative Coupling

The previous approaches are, of course, snapshots of what one observes companies doing in the medium term. Over an extended period of time, say ten or twenty years, all companies widen both their strategic context and the scope of their R&D. But some do so more intentionally and regularly than others. Such companies see existing business competencies as vestiges of a past strategy while the purpose of R&D is to provide a platform for entering new businesses and redefining strategies. Rather than force-fitting technology generation to currently conceived product/market strategies, they recognize the idiosyncrasies of both and, therefore, tolerate a somewhat looser coupling between them.

The need for doing so, moreover, increases every day. While it took more than half a century for voice-based, fixed-receiver telephony to get established, the last decade alone has seen the emergence of mobile phones, videophones, wireless switches, and even personal communication networks. Each of these businesses represents not just a new set of technologies but redefined markets as well.

Asahi Chemical Ltd. is one company that has been successful in both creating the seeds for new technologies and combining them synergistically in coming up with distinctive products. At times, attempts at improving existing businesses gave rise to a new technology. At others, new technologies emerged out of simply exploring and extending a technological base that had been established before. Once a seed had been planted, moreover, the company sometimes encouraged researchers to pursue particular projects they had an interest in so as to stake out new proprietary domains for the company.

Starting with monosodium glutamate and chlorine production, the company first built expertise in fermentation and electrochemistry, the technologies related to these products. Later, when it entered synthetic fiber production, a third base consisting of polymerization technology was created. Additions to and major extensions of these technologies then led the company into the fields of inorganic chemistry, photosensitive resins, membranes, and separation technology. These, in turn, expanded the company's product base and provided stimulus for the creation of new technologies.

Unlike some other companies, Asahi avoided defining its business scope too narrowly so as not to constrain the course its technologies took. By 1992 the company's business domain was considered to fall within four sectors—life sciences, electronics and information processing, high-performance materials, and energy. Apart from being a far cry from how the company defined its mission just a decade back, the breadth of these areas offers ample scope for its researchers to continue exploring new ideas.

The process of linking technologies to products is a relatively flexible one. However, the company constantly strives to find synergies among its expanding repertoire of technology and targets applications where it can obtain a dominant, proprietary position—regardless of whether it has to deal with a new market or not.

The electronics and information processing sector illustrates how the process works (see Figure 12-4). In 1980 a researcher in one of Asahi's laboratories became interested in sensor technology, particularly highly sensitive sensors based on indium antimonite (InSb). InSb was known to have high electron mobility characteristics (as a narrow band-gap semiconductor), but no one had been able to make the thin films needed. The research, therefore, involved entering a new technological field for Asahi—metal vapor deposition (MVD). Once the company had succeeded in mastering the new process, the next issue was to find applications for the sensor. Instead of finding the most familiar and least demanding applications such as motors, floppy disk drives, and printers, the company gambled on the emerging videotape recorder (VTR) market where these Hall-effect detectors could be used for controlling the speed and position of the rotating drum. By putting the needed resources to improve the process and come up with a suitable device, Asahi was able to obtain 70 percent of the world market in VTR drum sensors. It is today extending this lead to CD-ROM drives.

The mastery over MVD technology did not, however, become restricted to these sensors alone. Nor did the experience with the motor business stop at VTR drums. By combining MVD with its resin and precision injection molding technologies, the company has begun producing a range of optical disks. Ultra-thin, fine-pattern coils based on MVD are also now being produced for miniature motors, actuators, and other electrical components.

The same kind of interaction between products and technologies, building on each other to create new technologies and businesses for Asahi, can be seen in its high-performance materials sector. Here the starting technological base was the company's expertise in photosensitive polymers. This

FIGURE 12-4

THE EMERGENCE OF TECHNOLOGY-BASED BUSINESSES AT ASAHI
CHEMICAL (1982–1995)

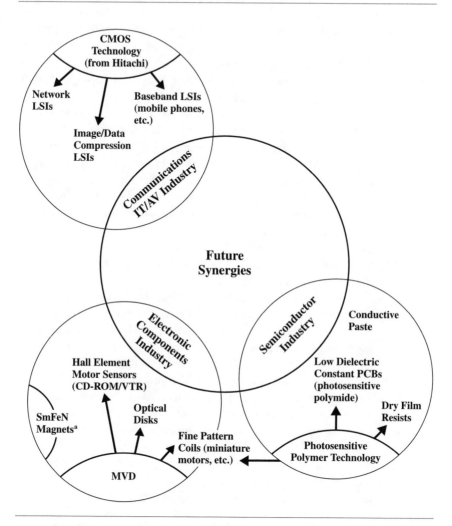

SOURCE: Interviews at Asahi Chemical Ltd., 1993, 1996.

aStill in development.

provided an entree into the semiconductor industry with products such as photo resins (APR) and dry film resists (Sunfort). Building on this, the company is now positioning itself as a supplier to the industry for other products as well, such as low dielectric constant printed circuit boards (PCBs), new pastes, and epoxy resin chip seals.

In parallel with these sales to the semiconductor industry, the company set up a wholly owned subsidiary, Asahi Kasei Microsystems Co. Ltd, to design and fabricate chips itself. Acquiring the needed complementary metal oxide semiconductor (CMOS) technology from Hitachi, it began focusing on application-specific integrated circuits (ASICs), especially those featuring mixed analog-digital circuits used in mobile telephones, among other things. In fact, the company now has a 70 percent market share in baseband large-scale integrated circuits (LSIs). Just as with the electronic components and materials sectors, this platform is being expanded both in terms of technologies and products.

As shown by Figure 12-4, the company has already managed to create three new business areas—electronic components, materials for the semiconductor industry, and products for the audiovisual (AV) and information technology (IT) industry. Today these represent a combined turnover in excess of $300 million; in fact, since 1991, these areas are among the fastest-growing and profitable in the company's portfolio. More important, all the technologies put together are being constantly combined to come up with new products for the future.

Three implications follow from this iterative link between technology and product/market strategies. One is the need to take a flexible, long-term view of a technology's potential.

Many large companies today have set minimum market size thresholds for technologies to be of interest. Some want to be among the first couple of players in the world, or get out of the business. Others would like to create a new "pillar" technology for the future, but one with a potential turnover of, say, $1 billion a year. The problem with such an approach is that many "niche" technologies get ignored or prematurely spun off. Except in commodity businesses, the dynamics of technology-based innovations is such that market position is seldom permanent or definable in advance. The market size for any new technology is ultimately a function of the applications it gets targeted to and the degree of vertical integration contemplated. Seemingly small niche technologies *can* form the basis for a large business if the end products are defined broadly enough.

The second implication pertains to how one thinks of core technologies and competencies. Rather than identifying these in advance and then leveraging them to exploit new opportunities more confidently, one needs to see synergies and competencies as an *outcome* of the process of exploration. The important thing is to do this gradually. Thus, Asahi Chemical did not just jump from chemicals into electronics, of which it knew little. It proceeded through functional extensions—selling chemistry-based products to the electronics industry, learning more about the products the latter makes, mastering the business system and operations of that industry, and only then introducing electronic products of its own.

The third implication is the need to define strategy as much in technology as in product/market terms. Swedish pharmaceutical company Astra

AB does that successfully. As Håkan Mogren, the president of the company, puts it,

> While we have well-defined therapeutic areas [respiratory, cardiovascular, gastrointestinal, and pain control] centered around Product Companies, we prefer to think in terms of competence areas when it comes to research. The main question we pose is whether we have a *unique approach* in some field and whether that approach can be targeted to some medical need. The research can cut across therapeutic areas, or give rise to a new area to build on.[15]

The point is that choosing one strategic path too rigidly can result not only in missed opportunities but in pushing a strategy that may have been flawed to begin with.

GETTING THE MOST OUT OF INVESTMENTS IN RESEARCH

Judging from the experience of companies and past research on the subject, none of the approaches described above is always preferable. More important is the conscious manner in which the choice is made and how the organization is geared to cope with its requirements. In the end, what companies get out of investments in R&D depends on how they manage different stages of the research process itself, and how they get *other* parts of the organization to contribute to the innovation process. Among the main policies relating to this are the attitude to diversification and the role of other functions; the ability to coordinate technologies effectively on a real-time basis, providing some freedom to transact to different R&D units; and the design of monitoring and control systems adapted to the logic of commercialization.

The Attitude to Diversification and the Role of Other Functions

Each of the three ways of coupling technology to business strategy described above involves diversification of one kind or another. In one case it is at the technology level, in another at the market level, and in the third a gradual diversification into both new technologies and markets.

The literature on the merits of diversification is actually quite equivocal. What we know is that the highest profitability is to be expected from products belonging to the same nexus (essentially a single product line) sold to one business market (characterized by distinct customer needs, competitors, and channels of distribution). While industry maturity and competitive pressures—the reason why most firms diversify in the first place—might make this counterintuitive, the result derives from several factors: that one is mainly considering incremental investments on an amortized asset base, familiarity with existing competitive requirements, and a better utilization of resources and capacity already in place. What happens next is not fully clear. While some authors have found related diversification (into related products/technologies or markets) resulting in superior performance,[16] others have come to the opposite conclusion[17] or, at least, found that there is no significant difference.[18]

Equally unclear is whether product (or technology) diversification gives better results than market diversification. Nathanson and Cassano, who looked at this for 206 major U.S. corporations, found a consistent decline in return on capital employed as product diversity increases while diversification into new markets had fewer ill effects. This is in contrast to several clinical field studies of diversification that find both product and market diversification to have a negative impact on success. For a large sample of high-technology firms, Ed Roberts, in fact, found market diversity to pose a somewhat larger problem than technological diversification—while confirming the superiority of focus on both measures.[19] A survey by Booz, Allen & Hamilton Inc. of diversification by large European companies hints at a similar ordering. Between 1980 and 1985 these companies had diversified somewhat more technologically than in their markets and were more successful with technological diversification.[20]

Raychem's experience with its new ventures launched since the late 1960s is in line with this, too. Figure 12-5 summarizes venture performance when mapped on market and technology lines. As can be seen, ventures in familiar markets and technologies outperformed those that were new on both counts. Newness of market, moreover, had a somewhat greater adverse impact on performance than new technologies. Ken Frederick, who worked on this study, has one explanation for this difference between technology and market diversification:

> Playing in R&D and writing a few patents is cheap; building a sales force is expensive. If you know particular customers, sell them any technology you can lay your hands on. Take Boeing as an example. We could walk into Boeing and call on the electrical connector group, because we had been dealing with them for years. When we started to sell pipe couplings we didn't know anyone in the hydraulics world. It was a totally new business as far as we were concerned.[21]

Whatever the pitfalls in diversification, the fact remains that straining to avoid it can mean missing valuable opportunities. As Robert Cooper concludes on the basis of his own empirical evidence, "Sometimes it is necessary to venture into new and unfamiliar markets, technologies or manufacturing processes. Do so with caution, and be aware that success rates will suffer; but note that the odds of disaster are not so high as to justify not making the move altogether."[22] Successful commercializers of new technologies

FIGURE 12-5

HISTORICAL PERFORMANCE OF RAYCHEM'S NEW VENTURES

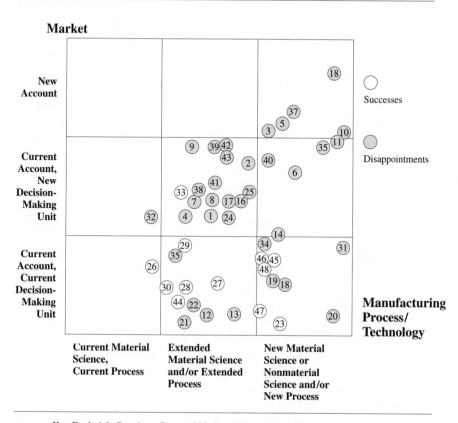

SOURCE: Ken Frederick, Raychem Corp., 1993. Reprinted with permission.

not only introduce more products incorporating a greater breadth of technologies but do so across a wider range of markets.[23] Also, getting leverage at the imagining stage means targeting effort to where the potential for discoveries lie, not the area circumscribed by the product/market domain.

Most authors agree that some companies are better at handling diversification than others. This can be on account of their organization structure and administrative systems,[24] their management profile and capabilities, their ability to transfer key skills and resources for realizing synergies,[25] and the commitment they make to new ventures.[26] The challenge of coping with all three paths and the diversification they imply, therefore, is ultimately a managerial one. To gain from the possibilities new technologies offer is not to constrain their development, but rather to get the rest of the organization to learn new skills too.

Understanding new customers, distribution channels, and promotion techniques appears to be more difficult than mastering new technologies; this means that marketing people share an even greater responsibility for learning. However, while companies have been perfectly willing to invest 5 percent to 10 percent of their turnover in technological research, they have shied away from spending even a fraction of that on market research. Delays caused by poor definition of product requirements is only one consequence. Equally important are the mistakes and blind alleys encountered in the process of going to market itself. What applies to marketing applies to other functions as well. Instead of bringing a "routine paradigm" when contributing to discussions on new technologies, they too need to take a developmental, exploratory approach.

Real-Time Coordination

No matter how elaborate the systems for planning R&D, technology commercialization is ultimately driven by people themselves—individuals reaching out for support, picking up new initiatives, and solving problems together. Recognizing this, many companies have started to promote broad-based information exchanges on technology. GEC of the United Kingdom started to emphasize this in the mid-1980s. Concerted efforts were made for people from its 100-odd operating divisions to talk to one another. Regular meetings on subjects such as factory automation, new materials, and emerging technologies of interest to the group started to be held. Intracompany newsletters and the distribution of short videos were used to give a wide cross-section of employees a taste of the research programs going on in other parts of the company.

Broad-based communication is, of course, seldom a sure-fire way to promote linkages, even when there is a sense of technology sharing. Many companies have, therefore, supplemented this by formal liaison roles, committees, and special planning departments. At AT&T Bell Laboratories, the traditional approach consisted in disseminating research results without any coupling as such. This was done mostly through internal seminars and memoranda, the hope being that businesses exposed to the information would take the initiative from that point on. Today, research managers have been appointed, each looking out for the interests of a particular business unit. Based within Bell Labs, they act as a permanent link between the work done there and the various businesses.

To get a better overview and senior management commitment, many companies have established high-level steering committees usually composed of heads of business divisions, the head of R&D, and usually the CEO. Thus, key to the working of Xerox's decentralized structure is also the company's technology decision-making board shown in Figure 12-3. The eight business division presidents, the heads of the technology platform centers, and the heads of research all sit on this board. The chairman is the head of research and technology, who is also a member of the corporate office. The board meets once a month and acts as the principal bridge between the technology and the business side of the company.

Many Japanese companies supplement such committees by well-staffed planning departments. Thus, it is the task of Asahi Chemical's strategic planning department (in particular, the corporate R&D administration department within it) to coordinate the company's technology-based diversification process described earlier. Sony's planning department plays a coordination role too. The department houses a technology planning department, which is aware of all the technologies being worked on and the priorities business groups have expressed. In orchestrating the approval of R&D programs submitted by each division, it intervenes in the establishment of broad priorities as well as day-to-day coordination needs.

The interesting feature of such planning departments is their operational orientation. As Koichi Tagawa of Sony puts it,

> Our role is to somehow grab what is going on in the world, what is going on in R&D and what is going on in business, and by coordinating through people who would be involved in this, establish a mutually agreeable strategy and program to follow. There is no formal, written process for linking technology to business strategy. The Sony culture is to be open and encourage anyone with a good idea to sell it internally to whomever he thinks will be most receptive. Our role is to orchestrate the process.[27]

Where this orchestration is most common is when an idea doesn't fit any existing business need. The R&D strategy department then takes on the main burden of assembling the resources and arranging for funding.

Providing Some Freedom to Transact at Each Stage

Allowing different types of research groups to achieve their mission necessarily means providing them with a certain amount of organizational autonomy as well. The opportunities and challenges early-stage technologies pose often go beyond the concerns and capabilities of existing businesses. Treating them as "ill fitting" is a convention marked by business strategy, circumscribing what is legitimate to pursue and what is not. This is particularly constraining when business units are themselves rigidly restricted to narrow product/market domains.

The way to handle misfitting projects has been through licensing and spin-offs. Unfortunately, spinning off usually means spinning away, losing all the long-term potential the technology offers as well as the human talent associated with it. The bigger problem is the organizational context in which it tends to occur and the suboptimization this causes. Technologies that don't fit are treated as orphans early and tend to limp along with no major resource commitment to make them sellable, and no freedom to commercialize, until senior management or business groups finally agree to get rid of them. Delays encountered in vain attempts to sell them internally only compound the problem.

If businesses themselves cannot create the conditions for pulling technologies out to the market, the R&D organization itself needs to reach out. But this requires redefining its mission somewhat and a greater freedom to transact internally and externally. Thus, had Xerox PARC, the archetypal imagining and incubating lab, been organized differently with a commercial mission, it might have had considerably greater success than it did. Being entirely dependent on a hypothetical pull from Xerox Corp. and business groups with narrow missions, it had neither the motivation nor the mandate to take its discoveries in the personal computer field far enough to capture interest in the late 1970s.

Many companies have now started to give their early-stage research units greater freedom to push their discoveries and take them further on their own. IBM, at its central research laboratories, is experimenting with this approach. A first research spin-off from its Watson Research Laboratory in Hawthorne, New York, was a sixty-engineer team working on an advanced visualization system—the power visualization system (PVS). It was the first time the company's central research personnel got involved directly marketing technology, avoiding the need to interest operating divisions as a sine qua non for pursuing a business. Also, whereas such projects were previously judged in terms of their direct contribution to higher revenues or lower costs, the value of PVS is being seen more broadly to include new markets and new businesses.[28] The technology is being targeted to a whole range of users—Hollywood studios, car designers, and even financial institutions—with the special marketing and technical support each requires, rather than being limited to an existing customer base or sales infrastructure.

Philips in Holland is yet another company that has recognized the need for its research units to have some freedom in "pushing" their discoveries to market while, perhaps, waiting for a "pull" from business units. Since 1990 it has set up some ten "business enterprises" within Corporate Research as self-funding ventures. Together, they already account for $65 million in turnover and are generally profitable.

Designing Monitoring Systems Adapted to the Stages of Technology Commercialization

Inherent to managing any activity is the control system designed to monitor its progress and the taking of timely corrective action. Such systems have proved particularly elusive, however, when it comes to technology. In its most recent annual poll of members, the U.S. Industrial Research

Institute (IRI) also found "measuring and improving R&D productivity/effectiveness" as the most serious problem facing technology leaders today.[29] The way technological innovation has been described here makes the need for good measurement systems even greater. The more flexible and exploratory a process, the more precise and multidimensional its control measures need to be.

Popular measures, such as the percentage of sales (or profits) accounted for by products introduced, say, over the last three years, have always been known to be too retrospective. They also do not distinguish the role R&D played from the contribution made by other functions. What most people have been searching for instead are measures that evaluate R&D performance while it is being done.

The tools of total quality management provide one way to achieve this. For example, the Westinghouse Science and Technology Center (WSTC) gets its "customers" (the business groups) to regularly rate WSTC's performance on a number of preidentified processes grouped into three main categories—planning and preparation, responsiveness, and technical performance.[30] This feedback then becomes the basis for improvement programs undertaken by WSTC management.

Recognizing that the mission of R&D is to go beyond serving the *existing* needs of business groups, Philips has come up with a more complete set of measures. The latter are based on Szakonyi's research on processes more generally associated with effective research management.[31] Table 12-1 lists Philips's version of these processes as adapted to its own needs and the metrics by which they are evaluated. While an improvement over retrospective measures of the past, these customer-driven process measures do not adequately differentiate between the different types of activities an R&D organization performs (see Figure 12-1) and the different stages of the commercialization process.

Stage-by-stage measures are particularly important for lengthy development programs—for selecting projects to back and for culling those that offer little prospect for success. Using a value-based framework of the type discussed in this book allows these decisions to be made on a real-time basis, instead of on the basis of milestones set in advance, which may no longer be relevant. It also provides a basis for judging the amount and timing of resource commitments for individual projects as they advance.

Naturally, the best situation is one where the intermediate value created at each stage can be "priced," thereby permitting meaningful comparisons between units responsible for them. Apart from creating the conditions for self-assessment, this would highlight the subsidy (or penalty) that one stage or unit provides to those further downstream. However, while intermediate prices for certain types of technologies are gradually emerging, they are far too inaccurate to be of much use. Other, more judgmental measures are still needed.

TABLE 12-1

PHILIPS—PROCESSES EVALUATED IN JUDGING R&D PERFORMANCE

Process	Evaluation[a] A (Worst)	B	C	D	E	F (Best)
1. Linking R&D to business planning						
2. Coordinating R&D and marketing						
3. Managing R&D capabilities						
4. Generating new ideas						
5. Selecting R&D projects						
6. Planning and managing projects						
7. Establishing cross-disciplinary teams						
8. Designing and executing experiments						
9. Generating patents						
10. Transferring technology to Product Groups						

SOURCE: Philips, NV, 1995. Reprinted with permission.

[a]Measures of evaluation are defined as follows:

A. (Worst.) Nobody in the organization is aware or convinced of the need for quality. When the work does not bring the right results, the *problems are solved on an ad hoc basis.* No evidence of control on own work.

B. *Rudimentary improvement efforts* are initiated by a limited number of people. These are based *only on personal motivation.* It is more that they believe something should be done than that they know what and how to do it.

C. *Mastering key processes* becomes applied more and more broadly in the organization. *This is seen as a good step to improvement* but is often *executed only in terms of corrective actions.*

D. *The process approach is accepted* as the basis for delivering good quality. Other concepts/tools have been used in a systematic and appropriate way. *Improvement activities are executed more and more in a planned way.*

E. The organization and all activities of the process are transparent for all relevant persons. *Evaluation and corrective actions are routine.* The greater part of the organization has *explicit control over its work.*

F. (Best.) All processes are totally mastered and reach the *valid norm of excellence. People challenge themselves to perform at a world-class level,* even if customers do not ask for it. Striving for *quality is totally incorporated* in all business processes.

Table 12-2 lists a generic set of measures one could use in practice, combining measurable outcomes expected at each stage with the processes needed to achieve that outcome. At the imagining stage, the purpose is to come up with valuable new ideas to pursue. The more proprietary these are, and the greater the value of the patents they represent, the better. A measure related to this is what Philips calls "virtual income," the amount that would have to be spent in buying in the technology from others.

Some companies are now attempting to rank their patents by the commercial value they represent—both in terms of the revenue they help generate and their value in cross-licensing deals. Starting in the early 1990s, IBM, for example, began paying special bonuses to the top 25 percent of the patents issued, with a somewhat larger sum paid to the top 5 percent. The committee making these rankings used criteria similar to those in judging whether to file for patents (see Chapter 4), obtaining the opinion of the patent attorney who had done the search, the business group that would benefit most, and the technology person in that group who understood what the patent represented form a technical standpoint.

The work done in challenging the status quo, and keeping the business aware of threats, is as important as the commercial value of what is generated at this stage. The mere act of imagining a new techno-market insight is to question the assumptions on which the business is based. The greater the range of these insights—whether they get pursued or not—the more robust the test that one is on the right track or capable of confronting whatever scenario might come about. As Brown of Xerox PARC puts it, "The underlying metaphor to capture this is to think in terms of providing the genetic variance in a species. If you do that, you can use some mathematics from population ecology to show how increasing the genetic variance helps you adapt in a more rapidly changing landscape."[32]

As for the processes used, one relates to the search for ideas themselves. Ideas should not originate only in R&D labs. Mechanisms need to be in place to search for them both within the organization and from the outside. Measures taken to ensure the quality of science done and obtaining peer endorsement early are a second important process, whose value in technology commercialization was discussed in Chapter 3. Finally, idea generation is never enough. Crucial to the imagining stage are the practices put in place to generate excitement and to mobilize resources to take them further.

The metrics for measuring the performance of the incubating stage are equally multidimensional. At the outcome level, they include the value added after the initial idea gets formulated. With a better feel for the technology's characteristics and its market potential, this value can be judged by the projected sales and profits of the chosen applications portfolio. From this stage one expects to determine the number of high-value options created for new businesses—whether these get bought (or some other way appreciated) internally or sold to others. Thus, in the case of Xerox's technology platform centers (see Figure 12-3), performance is being gauged by the number of technology platforms created and how many of these get shared across business divisions. As for the measures of process effectiveness, these mirror the outcomes expected and are derived from the discussion on the subject in Chapter 4.

TABLE 12-2

MANAGING R&D FOR VALUE CREATION

Stage and Mission	Value-Based Outcomes	Process Effectiveness Indices
1. Imagining Exciting, preferably unique technology-based idea linked to a market need	• Valuable know-how and/or key patent(s) obtained as measured by citation rates • Value if sold, licensed, or used in an initial public offering (IPO) • Virtual income generated (avoiding the need to buy in a required technology) • Challenging the assumptions on which the business is currently based—value of negative surprises avoided	• Research process—grounding, depth, and arrangements for establishing context early (see Chapter 2) • Quality of science and obtaining peer endorsement • Selling of idea internally and externally to mobilize interest
2. Incubating Definition of idea's technical feasibility and commercial potential, and plan for taking it further	• Value addition after imagining the idea (see above) as measured by customer-perceived value of prototype and the options created for profitable new businesses, including new technology platforms • Patent portfolio • Resources (capital, context, and capability) mobilized to proceed further	• Scope and efficiency of application search or platform definition • Tools and criteria to get to an optimum portfolio of applications based on realistic need and demand assessment • Quality and objectiveness of product validation and business plans
3. Demonstrating Incorporating the technology in attractive, market-ready products and/or processes	• Performance against design goals (see Chapter 6) • Incorporation of proprietary technology in products as measured by patent or valuable secret know-how coverage of end product/process	• Following good practice in development protocols (see Figure 6-1) • Timing product/process development to match technology availability (see Chapter 6)

TABLE 12-2

continued

Stage and Mission	Value-Based Outcomes	Process Effectiveness Indices
4. Promoting Getting products or processes rapidly accepted by various market constituents	• Revenue growth rate and/or time to achieve market potential • Collateral (e.g., licensing) income generated	• Knowledge of market dynamics on the part of researchers and quality of assistance provided to marketing and sales • Supervising product to make sure it is accepted in the marketplace
5. Sustaining Generating long-term value by entrenching and expanding use of the technology and retaining a lead in it	• Duration of peak market share • Duration of price premium • Duration of technological lead • New applications/line extensions introduced	• Ongoing competitive assessment and problem analysis of launched products/processes • Process for defining and implementing research programs on relevant facets of the technology
6. Overall R&D's overall contribution to business success	• Business impact—percentage of sales (and/or profits) accounted for by products introduced during last 3 years • R&D productivity = Income from new products this year ÷ R&D expenditure lagged 3–5 years • Percentage of sales covered by patents/secret know-how	• "Customer" satisfaction indices measured, for example, by business units requiring R&D support (see Philips and Westinghouse examples in text) • Total technology cycle time from imagining to peak market share

The demonstration stage, associated with product and process development, is perhaps the easiest to evaluate because of the planned nature of its activities. Not only are concrete objectives against which to assess performance settable in advance, but the process protocols are well known too. The only qualifications needed for technology-based development relate to the extent to which a proprietary technology gets to be incorporated in the product(s) developed and the process used to ensure that this occurs.

More difficult and controversial is the judgment of R&D's contribution to the promotion stage. As the discussion in Chapter 9 implied, this contribution can sometimes be critical. R&D people not only need to interact with customers to explain things, they also need to contribute their own knowledge of the market to help marketing do its job effectively. Whether this is tracked by the amount of time they spend on such activities or how satisfied marketing is with their performance depends on a company's notion of the role their researchers should play.

The final stage, that of sustaining technology commercialization, has the same set of issues as promotion. We know what is important by way of outcome—the maintenance of market share and price premiums. The question is one of defining R&D's role in making sure that these get realized. Following from the discussion in Chapter 10, the areas where R&D can help are in assessing the points of diminishing returns; defining and implementing research programs on the various technology facets that matter most competitively; and in extending the technology's use by migrating it to other, new applications.

The outcome and process measures summarized in Table 12-2 should be seen as indicative only. The actual measures a company designs depends on its industry, the factors contributing to competitive success, and the role it wishes to assign to R&D.

MOBILIZING RESEARCHERS FOR A COMMERCIAL MISSION

In the end, commercial orientation within R&D really depends on the attitude and motivation of researchers themselves. The schizophrenia R&D personnel experience today is understandable. Hired to explore at the frontiers of new technologies, they increasingly find themselves involved in product-related and commercial issues. Trained to aspire to scientific recognition and peer endorsement, often outside the confines of a particular organization, they rightfully question their role.

Yet, during the scores of interviews the author conducted with technologists, one thing clearly stood out: R&D people are increasingly interested in commercialization possibilities and even excited by it. They want to see their laboratory creations incorporated in successful products and processes that contribute to the success of their companies. Companies can get more out of the talent and energy of their researchers by defining their roles better and motivating and rewarding them for achieving innovation-linked goals.

Redefining Roles and Expectations

In any large research laboratory today, one is likely to find three types of individuals:

Scientific researchers who are skilled in a particular set of disciplines and can efficiently tackle technical problems presented to them;

Inventors who imagine the problems to be solved and who are constantly searching for ways to apply science to concrete products or processes; and

Technical entrepreneurs who have a good grounding in science but are really motivated by a desire to create new business ventures. They tend to have a broad understanding of several fields, including business-related ones, and have a high tolerance for risk.

With the many different roles R&D organizations play, there is room for all three types. Some prefer to be engaged in infrastructure-related tasks, helping out and solving problems. Others seek more nebulous and long-term challenges and are good at inventing. Finally, technical entrepreneurs are those for whom research is really a springboard to do business. They are the potential venture managers, seeking ever broader challenges and comfortable with team roles required to launch a business.

The first obvious thing, therefore, is to find out the preferences of researchers themselves and fit them in roles to which they are best suited. This said, there is nothing immutable about the category to which a researcher belongs. Many either want to "graduate" into being inventors or technical entrepreneurs or, at least, want to understand what the other roles are about. To help them accomplish this requires guiding their efforts differently.

As Praveen Chaudhari of IBM puts it,

Large organizations have not come to grips with how to optimize inventions. A lot can be achieved by changing the way researchers are managed. You need to feed them with information on what the company needs; they seek this stimulus; it will remain in the back of their minds and challenge them. Their role, moreover, should not stop after the patent has been filed. You need to give inventors the incentive to involve themselves in the subsequent commercialization.[33]

Management's role is to translate strategy into specific problems that researchers can understand and relate to—something that has apparently not been handled too well in many companies. If necessity is the mother of invention, researchers want to know what the necessity of their work is. The reason for some of the disparaging comments about curiosity-driven research is that it is seen as empty (just-for-the-fun-of-it) curiosity, or a totally idiosyncratic curiosity of the researcher. This does not have to be the curiosity driver. Curiosity-driven research is actually the most creative type of research because it is fundamentally problem-based. The more intractable the problem, the more one is curious about it. Researchers want to know the precise problem they are supposed to solve because using knowledge and creativity to solve concrete problems is what they were trained for and what they are challenged by. Not appreciating all that goes into the formulation of strategy, they have difficulty in translating general statements of strategy in research terms themselves. They simply want someone to tell them whether the problem they are being assigned is a significant or trivial one for the company and how much the company would appreciate their applying their minds to it—not necessarily how much revenue or profit will be directly generated, but simply how much management values their contribution.

Very often, unfortunately, problems are not expressed in these terms. Senior management and research managers either have no clear idea of the value of a problem—mainly because they have not taken the trouble to break down their strategies in such terms—or they simply wish to keep encouraging their researchers to do what they seem apt at doing. Very few have the courage or certainty to say that a particular problem is trivial for the company.

Similarly, if marketing and customer orientation are to be truly instilled, it means fostering an organization-wide culture of opportunity seeking. So long as the commercial and entrepreneurial role is reserved to marketing people, traditional behavioral patterns will only remain entrenched. Similarly, dragging R&D people along to visit customers will always be resisted if, as the author has experienced, the main purpose is to win the clients rather than wanting to benefit from the feedback received.

Motivation and Reward

Commercial orientation naturally translates into an expectation for commercial rewards. More and more researchers in large organizations see their counterparts in start-up companies being handsomely rewarded for their ideas, and they aspire to something similar for themselves. The rewards need not be as generous, but they should recognize those whose ideas have made major contributions to the company's business.

In the past, most companies evaluated and rewarded their researchers using measures such as papers published, the giving of invited talks, helping in fire-fighting roles, and patents granted. A nominal bonus was also typically paid for patents, with little effort made to distinguish their value.

Just as with the evaluation of research, the fact that so many functions and individuals contribute to innovation (both to its success and its failure) makes it hard to distinguish what role a researcher's own idea plays. This is compounded by the fact that the actual value created may be several years down the road. Bringing monetary rewards closer in line with the contribution researchers make by, for example, recognizing the value of the stage they work on, is probably better than forcing them to be involved in the entire commercialization process. Companies that have offered their researchers an equity stake in a venture, such as Bell Atlantic's Champion program, referred to in Chapter 11, have sometimes had little response because all researchers are unwilling to risk their savings in a venture they cannot fully control.

Monetary rewards directly attributable to a researcher's own contribution are important but not all. Researchers gain enormous joy from simply being kept informed of what happens to their brainchild. Instead of being sidelined once they have invented something, they welcome being approached to solve problems relating to it. They want to make themselves available when difficulties arise, and they want to be somehow recognized for the idea they conceived—regardless of the form it ultimately takes.

SUMMARY

All large companies today want to increase the return on their R&D investments and link the research they do more closely to business needs. While this objective is laudable, some of the approaches being considered may turn out to be counterproductive in the long run.

Understanding the "mind to market" process gives certain pointers as to how research can be managed to contribute to profitable growth. One important, though somewhat contrarian, conclusion is that research needs to be organized by specialized units, rather than collapsed into a single organization. These specialized units, moreover, conform to the five stages in the technology commercialization process—each with its own mission and research emphasis. The difference from earlier research specializations—which apparently have not worked—is that, rather than being functional, they have a commercial orientation from the beginning.

To fully benefit from such specialized units, however, several things are needed: giving them some freedom to transact internally and even externally, if necessary; interpreting the link between technology and strategy in a flexible manner, in order to allow R&D to make its full contribution; exposing *all* types of R&D to the rest of the organization; evaluating *all* types of R&D by value-based outcomes; and instilling a commercial orientation among researchers, who seem to welcome it.

Notes

INTRODUCTION

1. Fumio Kodama, "Technology Fusion and the New R&D," *Harvard Business Review* (July–August 1992): 70–78.

2. H. P. Hertzfeld, *Measuring the Economic Impact of Federal Research and Development in Civilian Space Activities* (Washington, D.C.: National Academy of Science Workshop on the Federal Role in R&D, November 22, 1985).

3. In particular, see Robert G. Cooper, *Winning at New Products* (Reading, Mass.: Addison-Wesley Publishing Co., 1986); Preston G. Smith and Donald G. Reinertsen, *Developing Products in Half the Time* (New York: Van Nostrand Reinhold, 1991); and Steven C. Wheelwright and Kim B. Clark, *Revolutionizing Product Development: Quantum Leaps in Speed, Efficiency, and Quality* (New York: The Free Press, 1992).

4. See William L. Shanklin and John K. Ryans, Jr., *Marketing High Technology* (Lexington, Mass.: Lexington Books, 1984); and William H. Davidow, *Marketing High Technology: An Insider's View* (New York: The Free Press, 1986).

5. Michiyo Nakamoto, "A Merchant Takes Stock," *Financial Times,* March 5, 1993, p. 12.

6. "Japan Keeps Its Shirts in Shape," *Financial Times,* October 21, 1993, p. 12.

7. T. Michael Nevens, Gregory L. Summe, and Bro Uttal, "Commercializing Technology: What the Best Companies Do," *Harvard Business Review* (May–June 1990): 154–163.

8. Philip H. Abelson, "Atomic, Molecular, and Optical Science," *Science* 265 (August 5, 1995): 719.

9. *Webster's Third New International Dictionary* (Chicago: Encyclopedia Brittanica, 1986), p. 457.

10. Edward B. Roberts, "Managing Invention and Innovation," *Research-Technology Management* (January–February 1988): 11–29.

11. William E. Souder, *Managing New Product Innovations* (Lexington, Mass.: Lexington Books, 1987), p. 3.

12. Ralph Gomory, "From the 'Ladder of Science' to the Product Development Cycle," *Harvard Business Review* (November–December 1989): 99–105.

13. Souder, *Managing New Product Innovations,* p. 75.

14. David P. Hamilton, "Industry Steps to Fill in the Gap in Basic Research," *Science* 258 (October 23, 1992): 570.

CHAPTER 1

1. Gleason Archer, *The History of Radio to 1926* (New York: American Historical Society, 1938), p. 94.

2. Gordon Graf, "Food Irradiation Comes Down to Earth," *High Technology* (March 1984): 21–23.

3. Povl A. Hansen, "Publicly Produced Knowledge for Business: When Is It Effective?" *Technovation* 15, no. 6 (August 1995): 387–397.

4. Mel Mandell, "Smart Fluids: Wavelet of the Future," *High Technology Business* (July–August 1989): 20–23.

5. Technical Insights Inc., *Smart Fluids: New Route to Advanced Hydraulic Systems/Devices* (Fort Lee, New Jersey, 1989). Quoted in Gina Goldstein, "Electrorheological Fluids: Applications Begin to Gel," *Mechanical Engineering* (October 1990): 48–51.

6. Summer Myers and Eldon E. Sweezy, "Why Innovations Fail," *Technology Review* (March–April 1978): 41–46.

7. *Science* 260 (May 21, 1993): 1168.

8. William J. Abernathy and Kim B. Clark, "Innovation: Mapping the Winds of Creative Destruction," *Research Policy* 14 (1985): 3–22.

9. Andrew H. Van de Ven and Raghu Garud, "A Framework for Understanding the Emergence of New Industries," in Richard S. Rosenbloom and R. Burgelman, eds., *Research on Technological Innovation, Management and Policy* 4 (Greenwich, CT.: JAI Press, 1989): 195–225.

10. E. Raymond Corey, *The Development of Markets for New Materials* (Boston: Division of Research, Graduate School of Business Administration, Harvard University, 1956).

11. "Bright Ideas Play a Game of Chance," *Financial Times,* April 16, 1992, p. 12.

12. David H. Austin, "An Event-Study Approach to Measuring Innovative Output: The Case of Biotechnology," *American Economic Review* 83, no. 2 (May 1993): 253–258.

13. Kathryn M. Kelm, V. K. Narayanan, and George E. Pinches, "The Response of Capital Markets to the R&D Process," *Technological Forecasting and Social Change* 49, no. 1 (May 1995): 75–88.

14. Personal interview with a director of R&D (anonymity preferred), February 1996.

15. For a detailed discussion, see Avinash K. Dixit and Robert S. Pindyck, *Investment Under Uncertainty* (Princeton, N.J.: Princeton University Press, 1994); Terrence W. Faulkner, "Applying 'Options Thinking' to R&D Valuation," *Research-Technology Management* 39, no. 3 (May–June 1996): 50–56.

16. Thomas W. Eagar, "Bringing New Materials to Market," *Technology Review* (February–March 1995): 42–49.

17. Souder, *Managing New Product Innovations,* pp. 57–58.

18. Personal interview, May 1996, New York, New York.

CHAPTER 2

1. "Gold Is Cast in a Different Mould," *Financial Times,* July 25, 1995, p. 8.

2. John F. Heanue, Mathew C. Bashaw, and Lambertus Hesselink, "Volume Holographic Storage and Retrieval of Digital Data," *Science* 265 (August 5, 1994): 749–752.

3. James Glanz, "Will Holograms Tame the Data Glut?," *Science* 265 (August 5, 1994): 736–737.

4. Philip E. Ross, "The Hologram Remembers," *Forbes*, September 26, 1994, pp. 170–174.

5. SONY, *The Case of the Walkman* (Tokyo: SONY's Innovation in Management Series 1, June 1988), p. 7.

6. Vijay K. Jolly, *FM-21 Membrane Cell* (Geneva, Switzerland: IMI Case Study, 1982).

7. Povl A. Hansen, "Publicly Produced Knowledge for Business: When Is It Effective?" *Technovation* 15, no. 6 (August 1995): 388.

8. *IEEE Spectrum* (December 1989): 44.

9. Akio Morita, *Made in Japan* (Glasgow, Scotland: William Collins Sons & Co. Ltd., 1986), pp. 247–248.

10. Jolly, *FM-21 Membrane Cell.*

11. J. Donald LaZerte, "3M's Scotchgard Brand Fabric Protector," *Research-Technology Management* (March–April 1989): 25–27.

12. Kjell Lindqvist and Sven Sundling, *Xylocaine: A Discovery—A Drama—An Industry* (Södertälje: Astra AB, 1993), pp. 21–27.

13. See David Mowery and Nathan Rosenberg, "The Influence of Market Demand upon Innovation: A Critical Review of Some Recent Empirical Studies," *Research Policy* 8 (1979): 102–153 for a full discussion.

14. David N. Perkins, "The Topography of Invention," in Robert J. Weber and David N. Perkins, eds., *Inventive Minds: Creativity in Technology* (New York: Oxford University Press, 1992): 239–245.

15. John Teresko, "Reinventing the Future," *Industry Week,* April 17, 1995, p. 34.

16. Personal interview, December 1992, Tokyo, Japan.

17. Ibid.

18. Personal interview, January 1993, Yorktown Heights, New York.

19. James Brian Quinn, "Innovation and Corporate Strategy: Managed Chaos," *Technology in Society* 7 (1985): 263–279, p. 271.

20. David A. Hounshell, "Invention in the Industrial Research Laboratory: Individual Act or Collective Process?" in Robert J. Weber and David N. Perkins, *Inventive Minds: Creativity in Technology* (New York: Oxford University Press, 1992), pp. 275–282.

21. Personal interview, June 1992, Warren, New Jersey.

22. Personal interview, September 1993, Palo Alto, California.

23. *Science* 273 (August 2, 1996): 572.

24. Robert H. Becker, Lantz S. Crawley, and Robert J. Little, Jr., "Have You Looked into Your Pool of Unexploited Technology Lately?" *Research-Technology Management* (May–June 1989): 33–35.

25. *Wall Street Journal Europe,* October 17, 1995.

26. Personal interview, June 1992, Warren, New Jersey.

27. Personal interview, January 1993, Yorktown Heights, New York.

28. Eric von Hippel, *The Sources of Innovation* (New York: Oxford University Press, 1988), Table 4-1, p. 44.

29. Personal interview, July 1996, Hamamatsu, Japan.

CHAPTER 3

1. Marilyn A. Brown, T. Randall Curlee, and Steven R. Elliott, "Evaluating Technology Innovation Programs: The Use of Comparison Groups to Identify Impacts," *Research Policy* 24, no. 5 (September 1995): 669–684.

2. Norman Haber, "Chemoelectronic Mobilization of Chemical Species in Low Conductivity Fluids: New Electrokinetic Effect," *Proceedings of the National Academy of Sciences USA* 79, no. 2 (January 1982): 272–276.

3. Haber, Inc., Company Brochure, "The Haber Technology," 1991.

4. Ibid.

5. Personal interview, March 1992, Towaco, New Jersey.

6. Gary Taubes, *Bad Science: The Short Life and Bad Times of Cold Fusion* (New York: Random House, 1993), p. 342.

7. Ibid., p. 343.

8. Ibid., p. 344.

9. George Wise, "Ring Master," *Invention & Technology* (Spring/Summer 1991): 58–63.

10. Personal interview, December 1995, Zürich, Switzerland

11. Francis Narin and Anthony Breitzman, "Inventive Productivity," *Research Policy* 24, no. 4 (July 1995): 507–519.

12. *Science* 264 (May 13, 1994): 1001.

13. Andrew Lawler, "Earthly Politics Boosts Space Probe," *Science* 267 (March 24, 1995): 1756.

14. Personal interview, October 1995, Lausanne, Switzerland.

15. F. C. H. D. van den Beemt and C. le Pair, "Grading the Grain: Consistent Evaluation of Research Proposals," *Research Evaluation* 1, no. 1 (April 1991): 3–10.

16. STW, *Profiteren van Kennis* [Profit by Knowledge] (Utrecht, Netherlands: Stichting voor de Technische Wetenschappen, 1993).

17. D. Crane, *Invisible College: Diffusion of Knowledge in Scientific Communities* (Chicago: University of Chicago Press, 1972).

18. See Thomas J. Allen, *Managing the Flow of Technology* (Cambridge, Mass.: MIT Press, 1977), pp. 90–110 for a fuller treatment of this point.

19. Yar M. Ebadi and James M. Utterback, "The Effects of Communication on Technological Innovation," *Management Science* 30, no. 5 (1984): 572–585.

20. "Emphasis on Information Flow," *Financial Times,* October 30, 1986, p. v.

21. *Science* 267 (January 27, 1995): 435.

22. Michael A. Rappa, "Assessing the Emergence of New Technologies: The Case of Compound Semiconductors," in Andrew H. Van de Ven et al., *Research on the Management of Innovation: The Minnesota Studies* (New York: Harper & Row, 1989).

23. John Seely Brown, "Research that Reinvents the Corporation," *Harvard Business Review* (January–February 1991): 102–111, p. 110.

24. Stuart S. Blume, *Insight and Industry: On the Dynamics of Technological Change in Medicine* (Cambridge, Mass.: The MIT Press, 1992).

25. Gregory C. Kunkle, "Technology in the Seamless Web; 'Success' and 'Failure' in the History of the Electron Microscope," *Technology and Culture* 36, no. 1 (January 1995): 80–103.

26. Arielle Emmett, "Karmarkar's Algorithm: A Threat to Simplex?" *IEEE Spectrum* (December 1985): 55.

27. *European Wall Street Journal,* February 9, 1993, p. 1

28. Personal interview, February 1992, Palo Alto, California.

29. *Scientific American* (June 1992): 106–107.

CHAPTER 4

1. *Industry Week,* June 3, 1996, p. 22.

2. Personal interview, November 1995, Geneva, Switzerland.

3. Personal interview, June 1992, Warren, New Jersey.

4. Personal interview, September 1993, Menlo Park, California.

5. Valentin Heuss and Vijay K. Jolly, "Commercializing Multifaced Technologies Through Partnerships," *International Journal of Technology Management* 6, nos. 1/2 (1991): 59–74, p. 66.

6. John A. S. Green, John Brupbacher, and David Goldheim, "Strategic Partnering Aids Technology Transfer," *Research-Technology Management* 34, no. 4 (July–August 1991): 26–31.

7. Joan Lisa Bromberg "Engineering Knowledge in the Laser Field," *Technology and Culture* 27, no. 4 (1986): 798–818.

8. John R. Whinnery, "Interactions Between the Science and Technology of Lasers," in John R. Whinnery, et. al., eds., *Lasers: Invention to Application* (Washington, D.C.: National Academy Press, 1987): 123–130.

9. *Financial Times,* September 19, 1996, p. xxi.

10. Daniel E. Koshland, Jr., "The Crystal Ball and the Trumpet Call," *Science* 267 (March 17, 1995): 1575.

11. Carl Gosline, "Doing Something With Really New Ideas," *Les Nouvelles* 5 (November 1970): 231–240.

12. Steven P. Schnaars, *Megamistakes: Forecasting and the Myth of Rapid Technological Change* (New York: The Free Press, 1989).

13. Ibid., pp. 72–73.

14. *International Herald Tribune,* January 3, 1991, p. 6.

15. Robert G. Cooper, "Debunking the Myths of New Product Development," *Research-Technology Management* 37, no. 4. (July–August 1994): 40–50.

16. Personal interview, June 1996, telephone.

17. Souder, *Managing New Product Innovations,* p. 68.

18. Vijay K. Jolly and Haruhisa Kayama, "Venture Management in Japanese Companies," *Journal of Business Venturing* 5, no. 4 (July 1990): 249–269.

19. Robert E. Burkart, "Reducing R&D Cycle Time," *Research-Technology Management* 37, no. 3 (May–June 1994): 27–32, p. 30.

20. John E. Ettlie, "The Commercialization of Federally Sponsored Technological Innovations," *Research Policy* 11, no. 3 (June 1982): 173–192.

21. U.S. Congress, Office of Technology Assessment, *Commercial Biotechnology: An International Analysis* (Washington, D.C.: OTA-B-218, January 1984), p. 5.

22. Personal interview, June 1991, Sunnyvale, California.

23. James Glanz, "Will Holograms Tame the Data Glut?" *Science,* 265 (August 5, 1994): 736–737.

24. *Wired* (March 1996), p. 54.

25. *Journal of Japanese Trade & Industry,* no. 4 (1994): 14.

26. Personal interview, August 1993, Morristown, New Jersey.

27. Personal interview with Brian Cronin, November 1995, Lausanne, Switzerland.

28. For example see Stanley G. Winter, "Knowledge and Competence as Strategic Assets," in David J. Teece, ed., *The Competitive Challenge: Strategies for Industrial Innovation and Renewal* (Cambridge, Mass.: Ballinger Publishing Co., 1987): 159–184.

29. Personal interview, December 1995, Zürich, Switzerland.

30. Personal interview, February 1996, Morristown, New Jersey.

31. CSII, *On the Shelf: A Survey of Industrial R&D Projects Abandoned for Non-Technical Reasons* (London: Center for the Study of Industrial Innovation, July 1971).

32. *Business Week,* June 6, 1983, p. 94.

CHAPTER 5

1. Quoted in Pat Janowski, "Waxahachie Blues," *The Sciences* (January–February 1994): 8.

2. Speech text.

3. Edward B. Roberts and Oscar Hauptman, "The Financing Threshold Effect on Success and Failure of Biomedical and Pharmaceutical Start-Ups," *Management Science* 33, no. 3 (March 1987): 381–394.

4. Vivien Walsh, Jorge Niosi, and Philippe Mustar, "Small-Firm Formation in Biotechnology: A Comparison of France, Britain and Canada," *Technovation* 15, no. 5 (June 1995): 303–328.

5. Personal interview, June 1995, telephone.

6. National Science Board, *Science & Engineering Indicators 1996* (Washington, D.C.: U.S. Government Printing Office, 1996, NSB 96-21), pp. 3–4.

7. For details see Organization for Economic Cooperation and Development, *Science and Technology Policy: Review and Outlook 1994* (Paris: OECD, 1994), pp. 111–116.

8. "How Not to Catch Up," *The Economist,* January 9, 1993, pp. 21–22.

9. Personal interview, May 1996, Morristown, New Jersey.

10. Howard E. Aldrich and Toshihiro Sasaki, "Governance Structure and Technology Transfer Management in R&D Consortia in the United States and Japan," in Jeffrey K. Liker, John E. Ettlie, and John C. Campbell, eds., *Engineered in Japan: Japanese Technology Management Practices* (New York: Oxford University Press, 1995).

11. "2-for-1 Time for Europe's Startups," *Business Week,* July 15, 1996, p. 19.

12. C. Paul Robinson, "National Laboratories' Collaboration with Industry," in *AAAS Science and Technology Policy Yearbook 1994* (Washington, D.C., American Association for the Advancement of Science, 1994), pp. 346–348.

13. "Collaboration at the Fraunhofer," *Financial Times,* February 21, 1995, p. 11.

14. David Swinbanks, "Extended Life of Japanese Bioresearch Institute," *Research-Technology Management* 38, no. 4 (July–August 1995): 4–5.

15. "France Plots Course to Tap Gene Research for Commercial Ends," *Wall Street Journal Europe,* June 13, 1995, pp. 1 and 8.

16. Walsh, Niosi, and Mustar, "Small-Firm Formation."

17. *Electronic Business* 17, no. 10 (May 20, 1991): 94.

18. *Mechanical Engineering* (February 1992): 17–18.

19. *Financial Times,* December 14, 1994, p. 8.

20. "Israeli Firm's New Battery Turns On Europe Car Makers," *Wall Street Journal Europe,* May 29, 1995, p. 7.

21. "A Label That Sticks," *Financial Times,* July 13, 1995, p. 8.

22. Personal interview, March 1992, Lausanne, Switzerland.

23. Bernard Cole, "DOE Labs: Models for Tech Transfer," *IEEE Spectrum* (December 1992): 53–57.

24. B. Sheldon Sprague, "An Industrial Innovation That Was Nearly Shelved," *Research-Technology Management* (May–June 1986): 26–29.

25. Personal interview, September 1993, Menlo Park, California.
26. Personal interview, November 1995, Grandson, Switzerland.

CHAPTER 6

1. C. Gordon Bell, *High-Tech Ventures: The Guide for Entrepreneurial Success* (Reading, Mass.: Addison-Wesley Publishing Co., Inc., 1991), p. 129.
2. Robert F. Hartley, *Marketing Mistakes,* 3rd ed. (New York: John Wiley & Sons, 1986), pp. 204–214.
3. Robert G. Cooper and Elko J. Kleinschmidt, "Screening New Products for Potential Winners," *Long Range Planning* 26, no. 6 (December 1993): 74–81.
4. Donald A. Norman, *The Psychology of Everyday Things* (New York: Basic Books, Inc., 1988), p. 151.
5. "AT&T Studies Interactive TV's Future," *Wall Street Journal Europe,* July 29, 1993, p. 4.
6. "Comfort Is Sought from New Inventions," *Asian Wall Street Journal,* September 25, 1989, p. 24.
7. Vijay K. Jolly, *FM-21 Membrane Cell* (Geneva, Switzerland: IMI Case Study, 1982).
8. William H. Davidow, *Marketing High Technology: An Insider's View* (New York: The Free Press, 1986), p. 27.
9. Glenn Bacon, Sara Beckman, David Mowery, and Edith Wilson, "Managing Product Definition in High-Technology Industries: A Pilot Study," *California Management Review* 36, no. 3 (Spring 1994): 32–56, p. 43.
10. *Microprocessor Report* 7, no. 4 (March 29, 1993): 4.
11. *Wall Street Journal Europe,* September 15–16, 1995, p. 4.
12. Sylvia D. Fries, "2001 to 1994: Political Environment and the Design of NASA's Space Station System," *Technology and Culture* 29, no. 3 (July 1988): 568–593.
13. W. Brian Arthur, "Positive Feedbacks in the Economy," *Scientific American* (February 1990): 92–99, p. 99.
14. For details see George Basala, *The Evolution of Technology* (Cambridge: Cambridge University Press, 1988), pp. 161–181.
15. Vijay Mahajan and Jerry Wind, "New Product Models: Practice, Shortcomings and Desired Improvements," *Journal of Product Innovation Management* 9, no. 2 (June 1992): 128–139.
16. See Robert J. Dolan, *Managing The New Product Development Process: Cases and Notes* (Reading, Mass.: Addison-Wesley Publishing Company, 1993); and Richard H. Evans, "Analyzing the Potential of a New Market," *Industrial Marketing Management* 22, no. 1 (February 1993): 35–39.
17. See John R. Hauser and Don Clausing, "The House of Quality," *Harvard Business Review* (May–June 1988): 63–73.
18. For details see H. Kent Bowen, Kim B. Clark, Charles A. Holloway, and Steven C. Wheelwright, eds., *The Perpetual Enterprise Machine* (New York: Oxford University Press, 1994), Chapter 7.
19. For a discussion see Dorothy Leonard-Barton, Edith Wilson, and John Doyle, "Commercializing Technology: Imaginative Understanding of User Needs," Case 9-694-102, Rev. 21 September 1994 (Boston: Harvard Business School, 1994).
20. See Joseph L. Bower and Clayton M. Christensen, "Disruptive Technology: Catching the Wave," *Harvard Business Review* (January–February 1995): 43–53.

21. Personal interview, July 1996, Tokyo, Japan.

22. For examples from the materials industry, see John Busch, "Cost Modelling as a Technical Management Tool," *Research-Technology Management* (November–December 1994): 50–56.

23. Margaret B. W. Graham, *RCA and the VideoDisc: The Business of Research* (Cambridge: Cambridge University Press, 1986).

24. Bernard N. Slade, *Compressing the Product Development Cycle from Research to Marketplace* (New York: AMACOM Books, 1993).

25. Bacon et al., "Managing Product Definition," pp. 48–49.

26. Genichi Taguchi, *Taguchi on Robust Technology Development: Bringing Quality Engineering Upstream* (New York: ASME Press, 1993), pp. 87–88.

27. Steven E. Prokesch, "Mastering Chaos at the High-Tech Frontier: An Interview with Silicon Graphics's Ed McCracken," *Harvard Business Review* (November–December 1993): 135–143, p. 137.

28. Personal interview, March 1993, telephone.

29. *Electronics Business Today* (April 1996): 76.

30. Robert G. Cooper, "Debunking the Myths of New Product Development," *Research-Technology Management* 37, no. 4. (July–August 1994): 44.

31. Speech at The First Global Forum on The Business Implications of Technology, Boston, June 22–23, 1992, organized by Management Center Europe.

32. E. Jurgen Duhm and Armand Wielockx, "From Research to Volume Production," *International Journal of Technology Management* 6, no. 2 (1991): 123–130.

CHAPTER 7

1. Personal interview, September 1993, Palo Alto, California.

2. *Business Week,* March 13, 1995, pp. 45–47.

3. Jeffrey M. Seisler, *Toward Commercialization of Natural Gas Vehicles* (Arlington, Virginia, American Gas Association, Background paper. March 1984), p. 1.

4. Personal interview, June 1988, Winterthur, Switzerland.

5. Bill Evans, "Finding New Parts for Plastics," *Mechanical Engineering* (August 1989): 52–56.

6. Karen Bronikowski, "Speeding New Products to Market," *The Journal of Business Strategy* (September–October 1990): 34–37.

7. E. Raymond Corey, *The Development of Markets for New Materials* (Boston: Division of Research, Graduate School of Business Administration, Harvard University, 1956), pp. 82–95.

8. *Business Week,* May 15, 1995, p. 58.

9. Corey, *Development of Markets,* p. 53.

10. Personal interview, June 1991, San Jose, California.

11. "Electronic Firms, Studios Seek Videodisk Standard," *Wall Street Journal Europe,* August 28, 1995, p. 5.

12. "High Definition TV Has Networks, Stations in the U.S. Worried," *Wall Street Journal Europe,* November 16, 1992, p. 1.

13. Personal interview, January 1996, Eindhoven, Netherlands.

14. Ibid.

15. "Companies Try Refocusing Photography," *Wall Street Journal Europe,* July 25, 1994, p. 5.

CHAPTER 8

1. Rich Templeton, "How to Market a Better Mousetrap," *Asian Wall Street Journal,* July 23, 1996.

2. See Everett M. Rogers, *Diffusion of Innovations,* 3rd ed. (New York: The Free Press, 1983).

3. S. Ram, "Successful Innovation Using Strategies to Reduce Consumer Resistance: An Empirical Test," *Journal of Product Innovation Management* 6 (1989): 20–34.

4. Andrew H. Van den Ven, "Central Problems in the Management of Innovation," *Management Science* 32 (1986): 590–607.

5. Chee Meng Yap and William E. Souder, "Factors Influencing New Product Success and Failures in Small Entrepreneurial High-Technology Electronics Firms," *Journal of Product Innovation Management* 11, no. 5 (November 1994): 418–432, p. 429.

6. *Chemical Engineering* (January 2, 1978): 26–27.

7. William E. Souder, "Improving Productivity Through Technology Push," *Research-Technology Management* (March–April 1989): p. 20.

8. Marc H. Brodsky, "Progress in Gallium Arsenide Semiconductors," *Scientific American* (February 1990): 68–75.

9. Kathleen K. Wiegner, "Living with Silicon," *Forbes,* January 22, 1990, pp. 112–113.

10. *Business Week,* August 19, 1996, pp. 38–39.

11. Andrew Kupfer, "The Next Wave in Cassette Tapes," *Fortune,* June 3, 1991, pp. 153–158.

12. Personal interview, September 1993, Palo Alto, California.

13. Aris Persidis, "Building Molecular Value," *Journal of Business Strategy* 17, no. 2 (March–April 1996): 18–20, p. 19.

14. W. E. Souder, A. S. Nashar, and V. Padmanabhan, "A Guide to the Best Practice in Technology Transfer," *The Journal of Technology Transfer* 15, no. 1 (Spring 1990): 5–16, p. 11.

15. Personal interview, May 1993, Runcorn, U.K.

16. Lowell Steele, "Managers' Misconceptions About Technology," *Harvard Business Review* (November–December 1983): 133–140, p. 137.

17. *Financial Times,* April 23–24, 1994, p. 9.

18. Personal interview, November 1991, Geneva, Switzerland.

19. Personal interview, August 1993, Morristown, New Jersey.

20. Morgan Stanley Co. and Alex Brown & Sons, *The 3DO Company,* Offering Memorandum, May 3, 1993, p. 27.

21. Personal interview, June 1989, Los Angeles, California.

22. Personal interview, September 1993, Palo Alto, California.

23. Gerard J. Tellis and Peter N. Golder, "First to Market, First to Fail? Real Causes of Enduring Market Leadership," *Sloan Management Review* (Winter 1996): 65–76.

24. Morgan Stanley, *The 3DO Company,* p. 27.

25. Hubert Gatignon and Thomas S. Robertson, "A Propositional Inventory for New Diffusion Research," *Journal of Consumer Research* 11 (1985): 849–867, p. 860.

26. Rogers, *Diffusion of Innovations,* pp. 20–22.

27. Christopher A. Voss, "Determinants of Success in the Development of Applications Software," *Journal of Product Innovation Management* 2 (1985): 122–129.

28. Personal interview, June 1991, San Jose, California.

29. Rogers, *Diffusion of Innovations,* pp. 272–273.

30. John A. Czepiel, "Patterns of Interorganizational Communications and the Diffusion of a Major Technological Innovation in a Competitive Industrial Community," *Academy of Management Journal* 8, no. 1 (1975): 6–24.

31. David F. Midgley, Pamela D. Morrison, and John H. Roberts, "The Effect of Network Structure in Industrial Diffusion Processes," *Research Policy* 21, no. 6. (December 1992): 532–552.

CHAPTER 9

1. "Abandoned Chemical's Comeback," *Financial Times,* August 21, 1986.

2. David J. Teece, "Profiting from Technological Innovation: Implications for Integration, Collaboration, Licensing and Public Policy," in David J. Teece, ed., *The Competitive Challenge: Strategies for Industrial Innovation and Renewal* (Cambridge, Mass.: Ballinger Publishing Co., 1987): 185–220.

3. Gary P. Pisano, "The Governance of Innovation: Vertical Integration and Collaborative Arrangements in the Biotechnology Industry," *Research Policy* 20 (1991): 237–249.

4. C. A. Bartlett, "EMI and the CT Scanner (A)," Case 9-383-194 (Boston: Harvard Business School, 1983).

5. Robert A. Fildes, "Strategic Challenges in Commercializing Biotechnology," *California Management Review* 32, no. 3 (Spring 1990): 63–72, p. 67.

6. Edward B. Roberts, *Entrepreneurs in High Technology: Lessons from MIT and Beyond* (New York: Oxford University Press, 1991), p. 166.

7. Harvey E. Wagner, "The Open Corporation," *California Management Review* (Summer 1991): 46–60, p. 51.

8. Dexter F. Baker, "Role of Innovation in Air Product's Growth," *Research-Technology Management* (November–December 1986): 18–21.

9. Company visit, January 1992, London.

10. James Brian Quinn, *Pilkington Brothers, Ltd.,* Case Study (Geneva: Centre d'Etudes Industrielles, 1977), pp. 12–14.

11. Alan H. MacPherson, "Licensing and Semiconductor Industry," *Les Nouvelles* (September 1982): 10–13.

12. Cary Lu, "Laser Printers Zap the Price Barrier," *High Technology* (September 1984): 52–57.

13. Valentin Heuss and Vijay K. Jolly, "Commercializing Multifaced Technologies Through Partnerships," *International Journal of Technology Management* 6, nos. 1/2 (1991): 59–74, pp. 70–71.

14. *The Economist,* February 24, 1990, p. 73.

15. U.S. Congress, Office of Technology Assessment, *Technology Transfer in the Middle East* (Washington, D.C.: OTA-ISC-173, September 1984), p. 148.

CHAPTER 10

1. George D. Smith, *From Monopoly to Competition: The Transformation of Alcoa, 1888–1986* (Cambridge: Cambridge University Press, 1988), p. 2.

2. Ibid., p. 34.

3. Alcoa, *The Material Difference* (Pittsburgh: Alcoa Laboratories, 1987).

4. Franklin H. Portugal, "NMR: Promises to Keep," *High Technology* (August 1984): 66–74.

5. Personal interview, January 1992, London.

6. Michael L. Katz and Carl Shapiro, "Technology Adoption in the Presence of Network Externalities," *Journal of Political Economy* 94, no. 4 (1986): 822–841.

7. See Robert W. Zmud and L. Eugene Apple, "Measuring Technology Incorporation/Infusion," *Journal of Product Innovation Management* 9, no. 2 (June 1992): 148–155.

8. For a comprehensive discussion on the notion of a dominant design and how it comes about, see James M. Utterback, *Mastering the Dynamics of Innovation* (Boston: Harvard Business School Press, 1994), pp. 23–29.

9. *Encyclopedia Brittanica*, p. 775.

10. Charles A. Amann, "Power to Burn: A History of the Spark-Ignition Engine," *Mechanical Engineering* (April 1990): 46–54, p. 46.

11. For example, see Dorothy Paun, "When to Bundle or Unbundle Products," *Industrial Marketing Management* 22, no. 1 (February 1993): 29–34.

12. *Financial Times,* October 31, 1994, p. 11.

13. "Japan Eyes Market for Cheap Mobile Phones," *Financial Times,* February 5, 1995, p. 5

14. *Wall Street Journal Europe,* April 30, 1991.

15. U.S. Patent no. 3 467 166, *Method of Continuous and Semicontinuous Casting of Metals and a Plant for Same, 1969.*

16. P. della Porta, "Creating the Structure to Maximize R&D Contribution," in EIRMA, *Integrating R&D into the Company* (Paris: European Industrial Research Management Association, Conference Paper 33, 1986): 14–21, p. 15.

17. Jonathan B. Tucker, "Gene Machines: The Second Wave," *High Technology* (March 1984): 50–59.

18. Susan Sanderson and Mustafa Uzumeri, "Managing Product Families: The Case of the SONY Walkman," *Research Policy* 24, no. 5 (September 1995): 761–782.

19. William H. Davidow, *Marketing High Technology: An Insider's View* (New York: The Free Press, 1986), p. 31.

20. Utterback, *Mastering the Dynamics,* pp. 27–28.

21. Personal interview, September 1993, Menlo Park, California.

22. Richard N. Foster, *Innovation: The Attacker's Advantage* (New York: Summit Books, 1986), pp. 214–217.

23. Michael A. Rappa, Koenraad Debackere, and Raghu Garud, "Technological Progress and the Duration of Contribution Spans," *Technological Forecasting and Social Change* 42, no. 2 (September 1992): 133–145.

CHAPTER 11

1. *International Herald Tribune,* February 4, 1986, p. 5.

2. Robert Kostoff, "Methods for Research Impact Assessment," *Technology Forecasting and Social Change* 44, no. 3 (1993): 231–244.

3. Robert D. Hanscombe, "New Challenges to Academic Research," in U. Täger and A. von Witzleben, eds., *Patinova '90: Strategies for the Protection of Innovation* (Dordrecht: Kluwer Academic Publishers, 1991), p. 168.

4. James Utterback, Mark Meyer, Timothy Tuff, and Lisa Richardson, "When Speeding Concepts to Market Can Be a Mistake" (Cambridge, Mass.: Sloan School of Management, WP 45-91, 1991).

5. *International Herald Tribune,* February 4, 1986, p. 6.

6. Ashok K. Gupta, S. P. Raj, and David Wilemon, "Managing the R&D-Marketing Interface," *Research Management* (March–April 1987): 38–43.

7. X. Michael Song and Mark E. Parry, "How the Japanese Manage the R&D-Marketing Interface," *Research-Technology Management* 36, no. 4 (July–August 1993): 32–38.

8. Robert G. Cooper and Elko J. Kleinschmidt, "Determinants of Timeliness in Product Development," *Journal of Product Innovation Management* 11, no. 5 (November 1994): 381–396.

9. Donald Gerwin, "Integrating Manufacturing into the Strategic Phases of New Product Development," *California Management Review* (Summer 1993): 123–136.

10. Fumio Kodama, "Technology Fusion and the New R&D," *Harvard Business Review* (July–August 1992): 70–78, p. 75.

11. Marc H. Meyer and Luis Lopez, "Technology Strategy in a Software Products Company," *Journal of Product Innovation Management* 12, no. 4 (September 1995): 294–306.

12. Personal interview, January 1993, Yorktown Heights, New York.

13. Roy Rothwell, "External Networking and Innovation in Small and Medium-Sized Manufacturing Firms in Europe," *Technovation* 11 (1991): 93–112.

14. *Wall Street Journal Europe,* 18 May 1995, p. 4.

15. Personal interview, August 1996, telephone.

16. Personal interview, May 1996, New York, New York.

17. Personal interview, September 1996, telephone.

18. *Wall Street Journal Europe,* August 2, 1994, p. 4.

19. *Business Week,* April 3, 1995, p. 53.

20. *International Herald Tribune,* May 30, 1995, p. 15.

21. Kostoff 1993, op. cit.

22. Jürgen Drews, *Science and Technology as the Prime Movers of the Pharmaceutical Industry* (Boston, The First Global Forum on the Business Implications of Technology, June 22–23, 1992).

23. EIRMA, *New Aspects of the Interface Between R&D and Marketing* (Paris: European Industrial Research Management Association, Report 42, 1991).

24. Chee Meng Yap and William E. Souder, "Factors Influencing New Product Success and Failures in Small Entrepreneurial High-Technology Electronics Firms," *Journal of Product Innovation Management* 11, no. 5 (November 1994): 418–432, p. 424.

25. William E. Souder, *Managing New Product Innovations* (Lexington, Mass.: Lexington Books, 1987), pp. 49–65 and 72.

26. Personal interview, September 1993, Menlo Park, California.

27. *Fortune,* January 1, 1990, p. 53.

28. Personal interview, September 1993, Warren, New Jersey.

29. Personal interview, March 1992, Pittsburgh, Pennsylvania.

30. Personal interview, September 1993, Warren, New Jersey.

31. Personal interview, August 1993, Morristown, New Jersey.

32. Personal interview, May 1993, Runcorn, England.

33. Thomas W. Eagar, "Bringing New Materials to Market," *Technology Review* (February–March 1995): 42–49.

34. Richard C. Dorf and Kirby K. F. Worthington, "Technology Transfer from Universities and Research Laboratories," *Technology Forecasting and Social Change* 37, no. 3 (May 1990): 251–266.

35. W. E. Souder, A. S. Nashar, and V. Padmanabhan, "A Guide to the Best Practice in Technology Transfer," *The Journal of Technology Transfer* 15, no. 1 (Spring 1990): 5–16, p. 10.

36. Personal interview, September 1993, Palo Alto, California.

37. Robert S. Cutler, "A Comparison of Japanese and U.S. High-Technology Transfer Practices," *IEEE Transactions on Engineering Management* 36, no. 1 (February 1989): 17–24.

38. Vijay K. Jolly and Haruhisa Kayama, "Venture Management in Japanese Companies," *Journal of Business Venturing* 5, no. 4 (July 1990): 249–269.

39. Hazem A. Ezzat, Larry J. Howell, and Mounir M. Kamal, "Transferring Technology at General Motors," *Research-Technology Management* 32, no. 2 (March–April 1989): 32–35.

40. Dorf and Worthington, "Technology Transfer."

41. *Fortune,* December 2, 1991, p. 76.

42. Personal interview, January 1993, Yorktown Heights, New York.

43. Walter S. Baer, Leland L. Johnson, and Edward W. Merrow, "Government-Supported Demonstration of New Technologies," *Science* 196 (May 27, 1977): 950–957.

44. Personal interview, March 1993, Zürich, Switzerland.

45. Arthur W. Single and William M. Spurgeon, "Creating and Commercializing Innovation Inside a Skunk Works," *Research-Technology Management* 39, no. 1 (January–February 1996): 38–41.

46. W. Bernard Carlson, *Innovation as a Social Process: Elihu Thomson and the Rise of General Electric, 1870–1900* (Cambridge: Cambridge University Press, 1991).

47. "Commercial Backing Could Improve Academic Influence," *Nature* 384 (December 12, 1996): 501.

48. Personal interview, November 1995, Lausanne, Switzerland.

49. Daniel I. Okimoto, *Between MITI and the Market: Japanese Industrial Policy for High Technology* (Stanford, California: Stanford University Press, 1989).

CHAPTER 12

1. *Business Week,* September 6, 1993, pp. 82–84.

2. *Science* 268 (May 5, 1995): 631.

3. *Financial Times,* March 28, 1994, p. 14.

4. Paul Bierly and Alok Chakrabarti, "Determinants of Technology Cycle Time in the U.S. Pharmaceutical Industry," *R&D Management* 26, no. 2 (April 1996): 115–126.

5. For example, see W. M. Cohen and D. A. Levinthal, "A New Perspective on Learning and Innovation," *Administrative Science Quarterly* 35 (1990): 128–152.

6. *Wall Street Journal Europe,* December 10–11, 1993, p. 4.

7. Personal interview, May 1996, Menlo Park, California.

8. Marvin M. Johnson, "Refocusing the Innovation Process at Philips Petroleum," *Research-Technology Management* 37, no. 5 (September–October 1994): 46–49.

9. Personal interview, April 1996, Stuttgart, Germany.

10. Personal interview, May 1996, Palo Alto, California.

11. *Industry Week* (June 3, 1996): 17.

12. Personal interview, May 1996, Menlo Park, California.

13. William G. Howard, Jr., and Bruce R. Guile, eds., *Profiting from Innovation* (New York: The Free Press, 1992), pp. 115–116.

14. Marc H. Meyer and Edward B. Roberts, "Focusing Product Technology for Corporate Growth," *Sloan Management Review* (Summer 1988): 7–16.

15. Lecture to Astra executives, March 1996, IMD Lausanne, Switzerland.

16. See Richard P. Rumelt, "Diversification Strategy and Profitability," *Strategic Management Journal* 3 (December 1982): 359–369; Richard A. Bettis and William K. Hall, "Diversification Strategy, Accounting Determined Risk and Accounting Determined Return," *Academy of Management Journal* 25 (June 1982): 254–264; and Kenneth M. Sundas and Peter R. Richardson, "Implementing the Unrelated Product Strategy," *Strategic Management Journal* 3 (1982): 287–301.

17. For example, see Allen Michel and Israel Shaked, "Does Business Diversification Affect Performance?" *Financial Management* (Winter 1984): 18–25.

18. H. Kurt Christensen and Cynthia A. Montgomery, "Corporate Economic Performance: Diversification Strategy Versus Market Structure," *Strategic Management Journal* 2, (October–December 1981): 327–343; and Bettis and Hall 1982, op. cit.

19. Edward B. Roberts, *Entrepreneurs in High Technology: Lessons from MIT and Beyond* (New York: Oxford University Press, 1991), pp. 282–308.

20. Booz, Allen & Hamilton Inc., *Diversification: A Survey of European Chief Executives* (New York: Booz, Allen & Hamilton, 1985).

21. Personal interview, September 1993, Menlo Park, California.

22. Robert G. Cooper, "Debunking the Myths of New Product Development," *Research-Technology Management* 37, no. 4. (July–August 1994): 40–50, p. 47.

23. T. Michael Nevens, Gregory L. Summe, and Bro Uttal, "Commercializing Technology: What the Best Companies Do," *Harvard Business Review* (May–June 1990): 154–163.

24. Sundas and Richardson, "Implementing the Unrelated Strategy."

25. Michael A. Hitt and R. Duane Ireland, "Relationships Among Corporate Level Distinctive Competences, Diversification Strategy, Corporate Structure and Performance," *Journal of Management Studies* 23, no. 4 (July 1986): 401–416.

26. Ralph Biggadike, "The Risky Business of Diversification," *Harvard Business Review* (May–June 1979): 103–111.

27. Personal interview, July 1996, Tokyo, Japan.

28. *Financial Times,* April 27, 1993.

29. National Science Board, *Science & Engineering Indicators—1996* (Washington, D.C.: U.S. Government Printing Office, 1996, NSB 96-21), pp. 4–13.

30. Ted M. Foster, "Making R&D More Effective at Westinghouse," *Research-Technology Management* 39, no. 1 (January–February 1996): 31–37.

31. Robert Szakonyi, "Measuring R&D Effectiveness—I," *Research-Technology Management* 37, no. 2 (March–April 1994): 27–32, and "Measuring R&D Effectiveness—II, *Research-Technology Management* 37, no. 3 (May–June 1994): 44–55.

32. Personal interview, May 1996, Palo Alto, California.

33. Personal interview, May 1996, Yorktown Heights, New York.

Index

About the Author

VIJAY JOLLY IS A PROFESSOR OF STRATEGY AND TECHNOLOGY MANAGEMENT AT the International Institute for Management Development in Lausanne, Switzerland. He graduated in mechanical engineering from the Indian Institute of Technology, New Delhi, and gained a Ph.D. in business economics from Harvard University. His areas of special interest are strategic management, international strategy formulation, new business creation, and the commercialization of technology.

Jolly also taught at the International Management Institute in Geneva, where he initiated and directed several programs and seminars and served as faculty chairman for three years. Prior to joining academia, he worked for several years in banking, holding positions at Citibank and the World Bank. He is a member of the Licensing Executive Society and the author or co-author of numerous articles and case studies.